WOMEN AND ISLAMIC LAW IN A NON-MUSLIM STATE

A STUDY BASED ON DECISIONS OF THE *SHARĪʿA* COURTS IN ISRAEL

Aharon Layish

A HALSTED PRESS BOOK

JOHN WILEY & SONS
New York · Toronto

ISRAEL UNIVERSITIES PRESS
Jerusalem

ISRAEL UNIVERSITIES PRESS
is a publishing division of
KETER PUBLISHING HOUSE JERUSALEM LTD.
P.O.Box 7145, Jerusalem, Israel

Published in the Western Hemisphere by
HALSTED PRESS, a division of
JOHN WILEY & SONS, INC., NEW YORK

Library of Congress Cataloging in Publication Data

Layish, Aharon, 1933–
Women and Islamic law in a non-Muslim state.

"A Halsted Press book."
1. Women—Legal status, laws, etc. (Islamic law)
2. Women—Legal status, laws, etc.—Israel. I. Title.
Law 340.5′9 75–1280
ISBN 0–470–51925–8

Distributors for Japan, Southeast Asia and India
TOPPAN COMPANY, LTD., TOKYO AND SINGAPORE

Distributed in the rest of the world by
KETER PUBLISHING HOUSE JERUSALEM LTD.
IUP Cat. No. 25101 9
ISBN 0 7065 1410 6

Set, printed and bound by Keterpress Enterprises, Jerusalem
PRINTED IN ISRAEL

To the Memory of
my Mother

CONTENTS

LIST OF TABLES

FOREWORD

This book is methodologically unique in scholarly literature on Muslim society. Its originality lies in the fact that the rich material offered by the *sharīʿa* courts is here subjected to a thorough analysis with a view to drawing conclusions as to present-day phenomena in Arab society and processes which that society has been undergoing during the past generation. It is based on close acquaintance with Islamic legal literature, but its most significant contribution is to social history. I know of no work on any Muslim country following the same method.

The author examines every aspect of the social status of Muslim women that finds expression in the *sharīʿa* courts: the age of marriage, stipulations inserted in the marriage contract, dower, polygamy, maintenance and obedience, divorce, the custody of children, guardianship and succession. In respect of each of these subjects, he at first deals with the legal background, i.e., Islamic law, legislation in this country prior to the establishment of the State of Israel, and then with Israeli legislation; he then analyses cases recorded by the *sharīʿa* courts and problems arising in day-to-day life; and lastly, he studies the attitude and approach of the *qāḍī*s. The questions he raises and attempts to answer involve the relationship between Israeli legislation and the *sharīʿa*; whether the *sharīʿa* courts have regard to the provisions of Israeli law; the relationship between the *sharīʿa* and social custom, and which of them is decisive in respect of Israeli Muslim women; to what extent Israeli legislation actually affects Israeli Muslim women; the attitude of the *qāḍīs* toward provisions of the *sharīʿa* inconsistent with the social development of modern Muslim women in general; and the attitude of the *qāḍī*s toward Israeli legislation.

To answer these questions, the author studied thousands of cases contained in the records of Israeli *sharīʿa* courts, inspected the registers of marriage contracts from the establishment of the State until 1970, compared these records and registers with those of earlier periods, attended court hearings, interviewed *qāḍī*s and other persons concerned, and analyzed the proceedings of *qāḍī*s' conferences and articles published by *qāḍī*s in the bulletin of the Ministry of Religious Affairs. All this vast material is woven into a lucid and revealing account.

Dr. Layish's work joins a steadily growing series of researches on the culture and history of the modern Middle East published in recent years by young Israeli scholars. He himself has given us a number of instructive articles on legal and social problems of different communities in Israel which appeared in *Hamizraḥ Heḥadash* (The New East) and *Asian and African Studies*, the publications of the Israel Oriental Society.

The Shiloah Center of Tel Aviv University is to be congratulated for its contribution to the appearance of this important and original study.

October 1974

Gabriel Baer
The Institute of Asian and African Studies,
The Hebrew University of Jerusalem

PREFACE

In recent times much effort has gone into analyzing Israel's relations with the Muslim Arab states which surround it. It is pertinent within the contexts of Israel-Arab relations and of the treatment of minorities within the Middle East to examine what effects Israel has had on those Muslim Arabs within its borders: such, within the specific field of the personal status of Muslim woman, is the aim of this study; should it also widen the perspective of current debate on female emancipation, so much the better.

Muslim women in Israel find themselves half-way between a religious norm, suited to a patrilineal and patriarchal society, and a secular-legal norm based on the principle of woman's equality to man. This study uncovers the reactions of different strata of Muslim society to the radical reforms introduced by the Israeli legislator in matrimonial matters—the very core of the *sharīʿa* (Islamic law); it shows the extent to which women enjoy their legal rights as laid down for their protection by both religious and secular law. Special attention is given to the age of marriage, to the stipulations inserted in the marriage contract, to dower, polygamy, maintenance and obedience, divorce, the custody of the children, guardianship and succession. Some subjects, such as marriage guardianship (*wilāyat al-nikāḥ*) and equality between the spouses (*kafāʾa*), have not been included because the *sijill*s (records of the *sharīʿa* courts) do not contain sufficient data on them.

The status of women is not only a subject of study in itself but a means to evaluate the position of the *sharīʿa* in modern Muslim society. The traditional equilibrium between the *sharīʿa* and Muslim society has been irrevocably upset, not by change from within, but as the result of direct contact with a modern Western society. This study attempts to demonstrate, through the medium of the *sharīʿa* courts, how the *sharīʿa* has reacted to the challenges thrust on it in an alien environment. The *sharīʿa* court—perhaps the last stronghold of the Muslim establishment in our day—is the most significant meeting point between the *sharīʿa* and social custom on the one hand, and non-Muslim secular legislation on the other.

The role of the *qāḍī*s (Muslim judges) is crucial in the continuing process of Islamization of social custom, both traditional (among the Beduin) and modern (in the cities). The reader is shown how the *qāḍī*s, entrusted with the application of the *sharīʿa*, react to social change and the modernization of the law: to what extent they exercise their powers—in the absence of *muftī*s (Muslim specialists in religious law)—as interpreters of the law, to adapt the *sharīʿa* to the needs of present-day society, and apply secular legislation in accordance with the intention of the Knesset (Israel's parliament); light is shed on their motives and ideological attitudes and on their approach to social customs and the conflict between religious and secular legal norms.

Each chapter opens with a short legal introduction based on all the sources of law applying in *sharīʿa* courts. The introductions are not to be regarded as fully comprehensive of all the legal aspects of the relevant subjects but simply serve as aids to the social analyses which follow; these analyses stress especially the changes in the traditional status of Israeli Muslim women, and attempt to assess their causes. The analysis of the changes is generally qualitative, but an attempt has also been made to assess them, as far as possible, in quantitative terms.

Important research on the position of women and the family has been conducted, of course, by anthropologists and sociologists, and their findings were available to the author. But the present study claims attention on the grounds of the unusual nature of its sources, and of the method of approach toward them, for although the sources are almost wholly legal, the mode of analysis has been that of the social historian. The study is based on judgments and orders of the *sharīʿa* courts, on attendance of the author at court hearings, on registers of marriage contracts, minutes of *qāḍī*s' conferences, interviews with Muslim religious functionaries and public figures, on the Official Gazette, statistical data, newspapers and periodicals, and on other relevant literature. The documentary material is, as stated, mostly legal but it also embodies valuable information on the social position of women in regard to matrimonial matters. The *sharīʿa* courts are sufficiently informal in their atmosphere to encourage the disclosure of intimate matters without embellishment, and their findings are recorded without any of the inhibitions usually attendant on the collection of data of this kind.

This study is intended for the Orientalist, the Muslim lawyer, the student of comparative law, the sociologist, and those concerned with problems of modernization, particularly with regard to the legislature.

The period reviewed extends from the establishment of the *sharīʿa* courts in Israel (following the collapse of the legal structure during the 1948 War) to the end of the 1960s. The position of the *sharīʿa* and the Muslims in Israel constitutes a chapter in itself because of the quality and intensity of the transformations accompanying the change of regime, following a legal and social heritage of continuity dating back to the late Ottoman period. In order to elucidate to what extent various phenomena are to be attributed specifically to processes which occurred in Israel, *sijill*s of the Ottoman and Mandate periods are referred to for comparison. However, the years of reference have been chosen at random, and the findings should not be regarded as representative samples. East Jerusalem, which since 1967 has been under the authority of the *Sharīʿa* Court of Jaffa (but whose Muslims use a local *sharīʿa* court not recognized by the authorities), is not included in the present study except insofar as pertinent matters are reflected in the Jaffa *sijill*s.

The notes give only abbreviated titles of the sources quoted. A list of the full titles of the archival sources, and another of the full titles of the books and articles, in the alphabetical order of the names of the authors, appear at the back of the book.

Arabic technical and legal terms are given in exact scientific transliteration in order to facilitate their location in dictionaries and professional literature. They are explained on their first occurrence in the relevant chapters. Reference is also made in this connection to the Index and Glossary of Arabic Technical Terms at the back of the book. For the sake of simplicity some concessions have been made with regard to the transliteration of Hebrew titles of books and periodicals. Nevertheless, in order to make it easier for the reader to locate them their exact English translation has also been included in parentheses. Names of persons, newspapers and periodicals in Hebrew have been given the transliteration which they use themselves even where these deviate from the rules of transliteration.

This study is based on a doctoral thesis by the author, written under the supervision of Professor G. Baer of the Institute of Asian and African Studies, at the Hebrew University of Jerusalem, and submitted to that University. The author's sincere thanks are offered to Professor Baer for his solicitous guidance and valuable advice during the various stages of the work. The author is also indebted to Professor N. J. Coulson, Head of the Department of Islamic Law, School of Oriental and African Studies, at the University of London, and to Dr. Doreen Hinchcliffe, of the same School, both of whom conscientiously steered him through the intricacies of Islamic law, especially the law of succession. Professor Coulson, moreover, read parts of the book and made valuable observations. Any remaining errors are entirely the author's.

The work could not have been carried out had not Their Honors, the *sharʿī Qāḍī*s, Shaykh Tawfīq Maḥmūd ʿAsaliyya, Shaykh Ḥasan Amīn al-Ḥabash, the late Shaykh Ṭāhir Ḥamād, Shaykh Muḥammad Ḥubayshī, the late Shaykh Amīn Qāsim Mudlij and Shaykh Ḥusnī al-Zuʿbī, and Mr. S. Nawi, Director of the Muslim Division in the Ministry of Religious Affairs, allowed the author free access to the archives of the *sharīʿa* courts and given him much of their time and energy; his profound gratitude is hereby expressed to them.

Between 1966 and 1968 the author was Visiting Research Associate at the Shiloah Center for Middle Eastern and African Studies at Tel Aviv University for the purpose of concluding this study. The author's sincere thanks are expressed to the staff of this Center, and particularly to its former head, Professor Shimon Shamir, for their help and encouragement during the various stages of the study, its translation into English and publication.

Tribute is further due to Mr. S. Toledano, Adviser on Arab Affairs to the Prime Minister, for enabling the author to devote his time to the work; thanks are due also to Mr. R. Twite, Representative of the British Council in Israel for assisting the author in pursuing advanced studies in Islamic law at the University of London; and to Mrs. Nuzhat Katsab, Member of the Knesset, who helped him in her capacity as Director of the Arab Women's Section of the Executive of the General Labor Federation. The work was supported by the Fund for the Encouragement of Research and Advanced Study of the Executive of the Labor Federation and won the Mifʿal ha-Payis Award. In addition to all these, the author heartily thanks Professor H. Rosenfeld, Professor Y. Ben-Porath, Professor U. Yadin, Dr. Y. Meron, Mr. J. Yehoshua, the dozens of interviewees (a list of whom appears at the end of the book) and many others who helped with advice and guidance and in other ways.

Thanks are especially due to Dr. M. Eichelberg, who painstakingly translated the book into English and made useful suggestions for the reformulation of many passages. Sincere thanks are due also to the staff of Israel Universities Press and particularly to Mr. Robert Amoils and to Mr. Raymond J. M. Dennerstein for their help and advice in editing the book and seeing it through all stages of publication.

Lastly, the author has the pleasant duty of thanking his wife, Bilha, who typed a first draft from the manuscript and encouraged him to persist in the endeavor.

Jerusalem
October 1974

Aharon Layish

INTRODUCTION

The *Sharīʿa* Court and Knesset Legislation

With the end of the British Mandate and the outbreak of the 1948 War, the communal organization of Muslims in Israel collapsed completely. The members of the Supreme Muslim Council and the *sharʿī* élite (*muftī*s, *qāḍī*s and *ʿulamāʾ*—religious scholars of Islam) left the country; the religious judicial system, the *waqf* (religious endowment) administration and communal educational and welfare institutions crumbled and ceased to exist. The Israel Government set about rehabilitating the organization of the Muslim community[1]: the judicial system was reconstituted; the management of endowment for public purposes (*waqf khayrī*), consisting of holy places (mosques and cemeteries) with their secular appurtenances, was in part entrusted to Muslim boards of trustees, while at the same time far-reaching reforms in the institution of the *waqf* itself were introduced by the Knesset (Israeli Parliament): most of the restrictions on the transfer of property and the use of its income were lifted with regard to *waqf khayrī*, and the family *waqf* was abolished altogether with a view to handing over the property to the beneficiaries as full owners.[2]

The Government administered Muslim religious services, paid the salaries of the religious functionaries—*imām*s (prayer leaders), *khaṭīb*s (preachers at Friday prayer in the mosque), etc.—and assisted in the establishment of mosques and communal educational, welfare and health institutions. At the same time, the Muslims had no autonomous communal organization or religious-political leadership such as they had enjoyed in Mandate days.

Thus, the *sharʿī* judicial system was integrated into the general judicial system of Israel.[3] The *qāḍī*s were appointed by the President of the State and had to pledge allegiance to the State and dispense justice in accordance with its laws. There were four *sharīʿa* courts of first instance in the State; in Nazareth (since 1948; area of jurisdiction: Nazareth and Eastern and Upper Galilee); in Acre (since 1948; area of jurisdiction: Acre, Haifa and Western Galilee); in Jaffa (since 1950; area of jurisdiction: Lod, Ramla, Jerusalem and its countryside, the Southern Region and the Negev); and in Ṭayyiba (since 1950; area of jurisdiction: the Little Triangle—Hadera, Sharon and Petah Tikva subdistricts). A *sharīʿa* court of the first instance consisted of a single *qāḍī*. In 1953 a *Sharīʿa* Court of Appeal was established with a bench of two or three *qāḍī*s, its permanent seat being Jerusalem. The Appeal Court was formed by *qāḍī*s of the courts of first instance, excluding the one whose judgment was appealed against. Seven *qāḍī*s served in the *sharīʿa* courts in the period under review. Shaykh Ṭāhir al-Ṭabarī served in Nazareth and as President of the Court of Appeal. He died in 1959 and was succeeded in Nazareth in 1963 by Shaykh Ḥusnī al-Zuʿbī. Shaykh Mūsā al-Ṭabarī served in Acre until his death in 1962, and his successor, after 1963, was Shaykh Amīn Qāsim Mudlij. Shaykh Ṭāhir Ḥamād served in Jaffa, and as President of the Court of Appeal in succession to Shaykh Ṭāhir al-Ṭabarī; he retired on pension in 1963 and was succeeded in Jaffa in 1965 by Shaykh Tawfīq Maḥmūd ʿAsaliyya. Shaykh Ḥasan Amīn al-Ḥabash has served in Ṭayyiba since the establishment of the local *sharīʿa* court and was the successor of Shaykh Ṭāhir Ḥamād as President of the Court of Appeal. Most of the *qāḍī*s received a *sharʿī* training at Cairo's al-Azhar, the central institution of higher religious learning in the Muslim Middle East. Shaykh Ḥusnī al-Zuʿbī was a *sharʿī* advocate by profession.

Despite the *sharīʿa* court's integration into Israel's legal system, the Muslim religious community enjoyed the widest judicial autonomy of any religious community in the country. Article 51 of the Palestine Order in Council, the principal enactment defining the powers of the *sharīʿa* courts, granted them exclusive jurisdiction in all matters of personal status and *waqf* of Muslims, both nationals and foreigners, the latter on condition that under their own national law they were amenable to the jurisdiction of Muslim religious courts. In Israel, the competence of the *sharīʿa* court was restricted in some matters. The Age of Marriage Law, 5710–1950, empowered the district court to permit under certain circumstances—but not to perform—the marriage of a girl under 17, and a welfare officer was empowered to request the dissolution of such a marriage—but the power to dissolve it remained with the religious court.[4] The Succession Law, 5725–1965, downgraded the jurisdiction of the *sharīʿa* court in matters of succession and wills from exclusive to concurrent, i.e., jurisdiction in these matters was transferred to the district court except where all the parties had consented in writing to the jurisdiction of the religious court.[5] In Israel, the Beduin, too, were amenable to the *sharīʿa* court in matters of personal status.

The legal status of women is a function of the various sources of material law and of the judicial authority interpreting it, in this case the *sharʿī qāḍī*. The material law applicable to personal status in *sharīʿa* courts in Israel is a mixture of religious and secular sources. Its basis is the theoretically immutable *sharīʿa*, which reflects the structure of the pre-Islamic Arab family with all its typical features, with variations resulting from Muḥammad's reforms. The religious norms imposed on the family on its absorption into Islam did not essentially alter the concept underlying patrilineal and patriarchal society of the superiority of men to women and precedence of agnatic (*ʿaṣabāt*) over cognatic relatives.[6] The Ottoman legal heritage in the country includes important legal reforms concerning marriage, divorce and succession. The Family Rights Law of 1917 did not disrupt the *sharʿī* legal system; reforms were mainly carried out by means of the *talfīq* principle, i.e., by combining various elements of different schools of religious law. The Succession Law of 1913, framed on the basis of a European source, maintains complete equality of the sexes.[7] Israeli *qāḍī*s frequently relied in their decisions on the well-known collection of laws of personal status and succession by an Egyptian, Qadrī Pasha, which has no statutory standing locally; they sometimes even gave it preference over provisions of the Ottoman Family Rights Law not based on the Ḥanafī school.[8] The Ḥanafī school is dominant in the *sharīʿa* courts although most of the population, especially in the villages, belongs to the Shāfiʿī school and even some followers of the Ḥanbalī school can be found in the villages of the Little Triangle. This, too, is a legacy of Ottoman rule.[9] The Mandatory legislator gave effect to the recent Ottoman reforms and scrupulously preserved the status quo as to the material law relating to Muslims; when introducing reforms by means of criminal legislation, such as the ban on the marriage of minor girls and on polygamy, he provided a good defense to Muslims and exempted them from penal sanctions.[10]

The Knesset intervened in many matters of personal status, going extremely far in some. The purpose of its legislation was to improve the legal status of women in Israel and to adapt it to present-day conditions.

It abolished some of the provisions of religious law discriminating against women and granted them social and political rights. Section 1 of the Women's Equal Rights Law, 5711–1951, which is the keystone of its legislation in this matter, provides: "A man and a woman shall have equal status with regard to any legal act; any provision of law which discriminates, with regard to any legal act, against women as women, shall be of no effect." The Israeli legislator, for obvious reasons, could hardly adopt the legislative technique of the *talfiq* customary in Arab countries, intented to give the reforms the character of an internal refurbishing of religious law.[11] Out of regard for the legal systems of the various religious communities, the Knesset subjected its legislation to two severe restrictions: abstention from interfering with any religious prohibition or permission as to marriage and divorce and adoption of procedural provisions and penal sanctions as deterrents in preference to substantive provisions which would have invalidated the relevant religious law; and, in matters for which provisions superceding religious law were enacted, the parties were usually given an option to litigate in accordance with religious law.[12]

In sum, the position of Muslim women in Israel in matters of personal status was thus determined by two legal systems, a religious one and a secular one, based on different social philosophies. Only in matters of succession has there been since 1965 a clear demarcation between the religious judicial authority, which applies religious law, and the civil judicial authority, which applies secular law. In other matters of personal status, the *sharīʿa* court must, in the absence of consent of the parties, apply Knesset legislation specifically addressed to it.[13] Disregard of this legislation is excess of authority and a ground for intervention by the High Court of Justice. Disregard of other secular legislation or of the religious law of the community does not constitute excess of authority but is at most a mistake of law.[14]

Social, Economic and Cultural Pressures for Change

The position of Muslim women, as of the general population in Israel, has been determined not only by progressive Knesset legislation but also by demographic, economic, cultural and social factors.

In 1968 the Muslim population of Israel formed about three-quarters of the total non-Jewish population. From 112,000[15] in 1949 it had increased to 301,000. Sources of this increase were the approximately 40,000 refugees, mostly Muslims, who had entered Israel under the family reunion scheme, and especially, infiltrators whose residence had been approved *ex post facto* in the first years after the establishment of the State, as well as the 69,000 inhabitants of East Jerusalem (over 80% Muslims), added on the reunification of the city following the Six-Day War. But about half the additional population stemmed from natural increase, which was one of the largest in the world (43 per mille in 1968, as against 23 per mille among the Arab Christians).

The equilibrium, characteristic of traditional society, between a high birth rate and a high death rate had been drastically upset. The death rate had dropped to one-third of what it had been at the end of the Mandate period and had become equal to that of the Jewish population (six per mille). This was due to an improvement of the health services. On the other hand, the birth rate remained high, as is usual in traditional society (about 50 per mille). The overall fertility of the Muslim woman was nine children (as against four for the Christian woman). Early marriage lengthens the period of fertility; the average age of marriage of the Muslim woman in 1968 was almost 21 years, the median age of marriage almost 20 years (as against 23 years and more than 22 years, respectively, for the Christian woman). The fertility of the urban woman, especially in the mixed towns, was considerably lower than that of the village woman, and the higher a woman's education, the lower her fertility; of course, besides the type of settlement account should also be taken of religious affiliation. Until recent years, the birth rate was steadily rising, which was probably due to the youthful age structure of Muslim society (average age 21 years, median age 16 years[16] in 1961, as against 25 years and 21 years, respectively, among the Christians) and to the improvement of women's state of health. A decline has recently been noticeable in this rate, and hence also in the natural increase, but it is too early to say whether this tendency will be of any lasting significance.[17]

The Muslim population was a definitely rural one. In 1961, only about one-sixth was concentrated in towns (as against 60% of the Christians): in Nazareth (half of the population), Shafā ʿAmr (one-third) and mixed towns (Acre, Haifa, Tel Aviv-Jaffa, Lod and Ramla). About two-thirds or, together with the Beduin (an additional sixth), over four-fifths of the Muslims lived in rural areas (as against some two-fifths of the Christians). About half of the Muslim population was concentrated in Galilee (Northern District) and about 30% in the Little

Triangle. The rural population in these two areas was almost equal (over 50,000 in 1961). About two-thirds of the Beduin lived in the surroundings of Beersheba and south of it and about one-third in different places in Galilee.[18]

Distribution according to type of settlement had lost its significance in many respects. The Beduin, especially those in Galilee, were at an advanced stage of sedentarization; some of them even skipped the rural stage and became town dwellers in every respect (for example, the inhabitants of the Beduin settlement at Bosmat Tivᶜon). The gap between the rural and the urban population had narrowed considerably. The village had undergone radical changes: the irrigated area had been enlarged, a variety of market crops had been introduced, cultivation methods had been improved (mechanization); the agrarian system had been completely transformed; large-scale basic investments had been made in approach roads, drinking water, electricity, educational institutions, health services and the like.

As a result of all these and other circumstances, Israeli Arab laborers commuting from home localities to centers of employment in Israel amounted to half of the Israeli Arab labor force in 1961, and in some villages the proportion of commuters reached two-thirds or more.[19] The Arab town, on the other hand, dwindled owing to the exodus of the élite strata to Arab countries in the 1948 War. Urban settlement did not increase significantly after the establishment of the State despite increasing numbers of commuters. Social, economic, cultural and political factors militated against urbanization. In fact, A. Cohen has found that not only did the urbanization process cease in the Little Triangle villages, but villagers who had settled in towns during the Mandate returned to their villages in the first years of the State, and the balance of migration was also negative in Nazareth between 1954 and 1964.[20] As a result of these developments the differences in standard of living, level of education, occupational structure and social stratification between towns and villages were blurred considerably.[21] This applied especially to the villages of the Little Triangle, which had known economic prosperity since the late 1950s, and to villages near large, well-established urban centers. Several large villages, such as Ṭayyiba and Umm al-Faḥm[22] in the Little Triangle, outstripped towns such as Jaffa, Lod and Ramla (especially as to the Muslim population of these towns). In many respects Shafā ᶜAmr had a definitely rural character.

The rate of participation of Muslim women in the civil labor force in 1961 was 11% of the total number of Muslim women from the age of 14 upward (the corresponding figure for Christian women was 17% and for Jewish women 29%).[23] The causes of this low rate were the youthful age structure of the Muslim population, the early age of marriage of women, the high rate of fertility, the low level of education, but above all, the severe restrictions imposed by traditional society on women's work, especially as regards married women and work outside the localities where they lived.[24] Cohen, who studied Little Triangle villages in the late 1950s, notes that most women who worked in agriculture ceased to do so after marrying and veiling their faces.[25] The rate of participation of women in the labor force was higher in the towns, especially the mixed towns, than in the villages, because of a higher standard of education, religious affiliation, and the greater opportunities of non-agricultural employment, in the towns.[26]

About two-thirds of the women employed in the Arab sector worked in agriculture (double the percentage of the men). Agriculture afforded solutions to some of the limitations on women's work in traditional society. Owing to the increase of commuting, the demand for female workers had grown; Cohen and H. Rosenfeld found that for this reason many women preferred to marry landless men or were not willing to marry peasants at all. On the other hand, there were also relatively more women than men in the professions, especially in teaching.[27] Several dozen women worked in the civil service as welfare and health officials. An isolated few worked in journalism. Muslim women were not represented in medicine or advocacy. Women's share in handicrafts and industries was small owing to the organization of the work (shifts, work together with men).[28] The Arab section of the Working Women's Council has in recent years made great efforts to train Arab women as nurses and thus to enable them to earn a living in permanent employment outside their homes.[29]

Forty-four percent of the female Arab labor force worked outside their home localities, most of them young and single. They usually did seasonal work in agriculture. The fact that women worked outside their own locality does not mean that they enjoyed freedom of movement. Their outside work was organized by a middleman (*raʾīs*), who kept their movements under strict supervision. This arrangement was an old-style solution to a modern problem which had evolved following changes in the rural employment structure.[30] The rate of women's participation in the upkeep of the family was low. A sample taken in

Nazareth in 1964–65 showed that the average annual income of the wife of the family head from wages was about 4% of the gross income of the family from all sources. The woman's contribution to the family income was the greater the higher the family head's level of education, and the smaller the more children there were; it was also affected by the rural nature of the Muslim population.[31] The relative share of women in the labor force had been steadily increasing since the late 1950s, and it was estimated that with the spread of education, the rise of the age of mariage, the progress of family planning, the improvement in economic opportunities, the growth of the demand for labor and the loosening of family and clanship ties, its future increase would be greater than that of the relative share of men.[32]

About 14% of Muslim women could read and write at the time of the 1961 census (as against 66% of Christian women and 61% of Muslim men). The level of education was the lower the older the age. About one-quarter of Muslim women of the 14–29 age group could read and write (as against 84% of Christian women and 76% of Muslim men), but only 2% of the 65-and-over age group could do so (as against 41% of Christian women and 22% of Muslim men). The relatively high percentage among the young was chiefly due to the implementation of the Compulsory Education Law. Moreover, those under 14 years of age, the overwhelming majority of whom received an elementary education, were about one-half of the population in that year. The number of Muslim female pupils in the State educational system rose from 6,400 in 1951–52 to 28,000 in 1969–70. Hundreds of girl students attended secondary schools and dozens teachers' colleges. Some trailblazers appeared in the institutions of higher learning.[33]

The patriarchal extended family in Israel was rapidly disintegrating and was being superseded by the nuclear family.[34] Rosenfeld found that the number of married sons in Ṭurʿān village leaving their father's house before his death increased from 50% in 1954 to two-thirds in 1966,[35] and that the proportion of nuclear families in that village increased from 75% to 88% during the same period. Cohen found that the proportion of nuclear families in Bint al-Ḥudūd village reached 84% in the late 1950s,[36] and an economic survey carried out in Nazareth in 1965 revealed that 80% of the local Muslim families were nuclear ones.[37] Rosenfeld notes a tendency in recent years of sons to leave their father's house even before their marriages. In mixed towns, the extended family was probably still rarer. The causes of this development were the large-scale commuting of manpower to centers of employment in the Jewish sector, which ended the economic dependence of the sons on the head of the family[38]; the fragmentation of landed property by inheritance,[39] and its curtailment by large-scale nationalization[40]; the lessening importance of extensive farming as a source of income, resulting in large areas being left uncultivated; disputes within the extended family arising from disharmony between the division of labor on the family farm and the complex of property relations in which the women played a major role; the spread of education and the adoption of modern standards (such as heightened economic expectations on the part of young couples, and improved housing). Most of these factors were not new,[41] but their intensity and extent in Israel were unique. The transition from the extended to the nuclear family largely liberated women from dependence on the husband's family, with all that this implies in terms of kinship and property relations, self-sufficiency and freedom of movement.

Paradoxically, however, despite the disintegration of the extended family, endogamous marriages in Israeli Muslim society were on the increase compared with earlier periods, mainly as a result of the numerical growth of families and clans. In the Galilean village of Ṭurᶜān, studied by Rosenfeld, the rate of intra-clan and cousin marriages was 80% in the years 1954–63, and in the Little Triangle village of Bint al-Ḥudūd, studied by Cohen, 57% in the years 1953–59. A high percentage was observed by E. Marx in a sample taken among peasant Beduin in the Negev.[42]

The findings with regard to women's social status are meagre and do not convey a comprehensive picture. Rosenfeld says that village women were restricted in their movements and required the permission of men even for the purposes of supplementary vocational training; the sexes were separated in entertainment and in what little other social activity there was in rural areas.[43] As against this, Yūsuf Dasūqī, Secretary of the *Sharīᶜa* Court of Ṭayyiba, found instances of women's freedom of movement: they traveled alone, unveiled, visited places of entertainment and maintained social contact with men.[44] The choice of the mate was still a family matter, and a woman's modesty was still judged by traditional standards, although deviations from these norms did occur here and there; expectations as to the marriage partner's education were rising[45]; a woman might refuse to marry the man chosen for her by her father and might complain to the *qāḍī* that she was being pressed to marry someone she did not want.[46] Cohen lengthily describes the case of a woman who married the man of her choice in open defiance of her father's wishes.[47] Although no research has been conducted as to the townswomen in Israel, it may be assumed that, especially in the mixed towns, they enjoyed a greater measure of freedom of movement and other benefits of social liberation than their sisters in the coutryside.

NOTES

1. The remarks concerning communal organization are mainly based on Layish, *Communal Organization.*
2. See Layish, *Waqf.*
3. See Layish, *Communal Organization*, pp.51–61.
4. See Layish, *Jurisdiction*, pp.50–60; *idem, Waqf*, pp.43–7.
5. Succession Law, 5725–1965, secs.151(a), 155(a). See Yadin, *Reflections,* p.133.
6. See Gibb, pp.233–45; Goitein and Ben-Shemesh, pp.83–4, 124–6, 134–5; Levy, pp.91–5, 121; Anderson, *Patriarchal Family*, pp.221–2; Lecerf, p.306; Schacht, p.161; for pre-Islamic marriage customs in Arabia see Robertson Smith, ch.3.
7. See Anderson, *Islamic Law*, pp.26–7, 54, 91–3. For an Arabic text of the Family Rights Law, in use in *sharīʿa* courts, see Goitein and Ben-Shemesh, pp.290–311.
8. For the title of the collection see Qadrī. See Schacht, p.100; Layish, *Qāḍīs*, pp.241, 249; Maḥmūd al-Māḍī, *AI*, vol.11(1968), Nos.1–2, p.15.
9. See Baer, p.77.
10. Criminal Code Ordinance, 1936, secs.181(c), 182, 183. See Eisenman, pp.155–83, 258–63, 307–12; Dykan, p.437.
11. To the extent that he did so, he was guided by the norms of Jewish law. See Layish, *Qāḍīs*, p.239; Eisenman, p.386.
12. Cf. the remarks of the Minister of Justice in the Knesset on presenting *IFB*, *KP*, vol.20, p.1929 col.1.
13. See Layish, *Jurisdiction*, pp.60–79; *idem, Qāḍīs*, pp.238–9, 255. Some uncertainty exists as to the applicability of the Capacity and Guardianship Law in the religious courts. For a detailed discussion of the reforms made by the Knesset in the various fields of personal status see the introductions to the relevant chapters.
14. M. Silberg, pp.172–7, 421–3; High Court of Justice No.187/54, Ḥalīma

Sulaymān Barriyya vs. *Qāḍī* of the *Sharīʿa* Court of Acre, *PD*, vol.9, p.1193. Parts of the said judgment are quoted by Goitein and Ben-Shemesh, pp.242–5; cf. Vitta, pp.123–4, 129–30.

15. This figure includes the 31,000 inhabitants of the Little Triangle, which was incorporated into Israel by the Rhodes Armistice Agreement in 1949.
16. In other words, nearly half of the Muslims were born in the State of Israel.
17. The data are based on the following sources: *Census Publication No. 17*, pp.XXIX, XL, 3, 6, 43–5; *DCPI*, p.58; *Vital Stats. 1965; 1966*, p.18; *Vital Stats. 1967; 1968*, pp.6, 36, 105; *SAI*, 1970, No.21, pp.63, 69, 85; *SAP 1944–45; GMBCS*, 1948; Layish, *Changes*, pp.2–6; Ben-Amram; Stendel; Shidlovsky, pp.1–14; Ben-Porath, p.13 *seq*.
18. *Census Publication No.17*, pp.11–12, 18–19. The rural population in Galilee includes also Beduin.
19. *Ibid.*, pp.LVI, LVII, 74 *seq.;* Ben-Porath, p.59 *seq.; NzDS*, p.13; Cohen, pp.30, 34, 38; Rosenfeld, *Peasants*, p.47; Shidlovsky, pp.15–27; Stendel, pp.57–9. The proportion of commuters declined in 1967 to 40%; *Labor Force, 1963–1967*, p.23.
20. Cohen, pp.21, 24. Only one resident of the Little Triangle village of Bint al-Ḥudūd, studied by Cohen, migrated to town in the ten years last preceding the study (*ibid.*, p.52). See *NzDS*, pp.14–15; Ben-Porath, p.67; Layish, *Changes*, pp.4–5; Stendel, pp.59–62.
21. See Rosenfeld, *Change and Conversation,* pp. 208–9.
22. In recent publications of the Central Bureau of Statistics, these two villages are treated as urban settlements, the criterion being size of population.
23. Ben-Amram, p.22.
24. See Ben-Porath, pp.20–4; *NzDS*, pp. 40, 57.
25. Cohen, p.35. See also *ibid.*, pp.41, 47.
26. Ben-Porath, p.24. This rate of participation of Arab women in the labor force in 1967 ranged from 7% for those with 0–4 years' schooling to 40% for those with nine years' schooling. See *Labor Force, 1963–1967*, pp.16–17.
27. See Ben-Porath, pp.28–9, 33; Cohen, pp.34–6, 50; Rosenfeld, *Peasants*, pp.67, 192–4; *NzDS*, pp.54, 57, 69.
28. Women of Bāqa al-Gharbiyya in the Little Triangle were unwilling to work in the local canning factory (together with men), preferring to work in agriculture or take jobs outside the village. Only five Arab women worked in a factory in Upper Nazareth in 1965 (none of them married); *NzDS*, pp.57, 69, 70.
29. In the years 1960–65 630 vocational courses were held, attended by some 9,000 women, and a women's dressmaking cooperative was set up in Nazareth. See Katsab. See also Rosenfeld, *Peasants*, pp.198–9, 209–10.
30. See Ben-Porath, pp.56–7, 66–8; Cohen, pp.39, 49; Rosenfeld, *Peasants,* pp.167–8.

31. The share of the wife of the Muslim family head was greater than that of her Christian counterpart: 5.6% as against 2.4%; but the contribution of Christian girls to the family income was considerably greater than that of Muslim girls owing to different attitudes of the two communities to the gainful employment of girls, the high proportion of Christian women teachers and the different age structures of the two communities. *NzDS,* pp.164–70.
32. Ben-Porath, pp.24–6; Ben-Amram, p.22; *NzDS,* pp.39, 40, 57, 143, 165–6, 170.
33. *Census Publication No.17,* pp.XLIII–XLV, 50; *SAI,* 1970, No.21, p.561; Ben-Porath, pp.18–19; Stendel, pp.69–71. Interviewee Suʿād Qaramān said that the liberation of woman would be achieved by education and the acquisition of vocational skills, which would make her economically independent.
34. Unless otherwise indicated, the data on the fragmentation of the extended family and the analysis of its causes are based on Rosenfeld, *Peasants,* pp.21–45, 74–92, 142–54; *idem, Recent Changes,* pp.21–30; *idem, Change and Conservation,* pp.208–17; Cohen, pp.50–9, 108; *NzDS,* pp.146–8.
35. In one of the villages studied in 1944 in a survey of five Muslim villages, only one-third of the sons left their father's houses after their marriages. Rosenfeld, *Peasants,* p.78, quotes that survey.
36. Cohen apparently includes among the nuclear families those independent families which maintain separate households but continue for a time to live under one roof. The proportion of such families was 9%; Cohen, pp.58–9. In the five Muslim villages studied in 1944, nuclear families were 56% of the total number of families; Cohen, p.51, Table 6.
37. This includes 8% of married couples without children and 3% of unmarried persons living alone. *NzDS,* p.148.
38. If commuting eventually led to urbanization, this undoubtedly accelerated the passage from the extended to the nuclear family.
39. Granott, pp.205–6.
40. Layish, *Absentees,* pp.191–2. Cohen found that all the landless families at Bint al-Ḥudūd were nuclear families; see Cohen, pp.50, 53.
41. See Baer, pp.59–61.
42. See Rosenfeld, *Peasants,* pp.116, 137; Cohen, p.93; Marx, *Bedouin,* pp.111–13; *idem, Marriage Patterns,* pp.397–8.
43. Rosenfeld, *Peasants,* pp.209–11.
44. *AI,* vol.8(1962), Nos.1–2, p.4.
45. See Rosenfeld, *Peasants,* pp.67–8; Cohen, pp.126, 135.
46. The author was present on such an occasion at the *Sharīʿa* Court of Ṭayyiba on May 21, 1971. The girl, who was not yet 17, said that her parents, and especially her mother, were putting pressure on her to marry her maternal

uncle, and the *qāḍī* ordered them to desist. See *JfQ2*, p.310:no.480–f.23/58 (the daughter, aged 13, had been married against her will and had run away from home). Suʿād Qaramān knew of several cases of girls committing suicide because they were told to marry someone they did not want. Shaykh Mūsā al-Ṭabarī instructed that it first be ascertained that the bride indeed agreed to marry the groom. *AI*, vol.8 (1962), Nos.1–2, p.13.

47. Cohen, pp.78–88. In one case, a woman committed suicide because she was not allowed to marry the man of her choice, a member of another clan; *ibid.*, p.123. See also *NzI4*, p.231 : no.2/28–f.94/67 (the couple had married without the permission of the parents; a month later, the fathers gave their consent).

Chapter One
AGE OF MARRIAGE

I. LEGAL BACKGROUND

Orthodox Islamic law imposes no age qualification whatever for marriage, and there is thus no bar to the marriage of minors. The provisions as to competence for marriage in the Ottoman Family Rights Law are based on the puberty rules of the *Mejelle,* the Ottoman civil code, which follows the Ḥanafī school of law, though with some material differences: the minimum age of puberty of the *Mejelle*—nine years for girls and 12 for boys (article 986)—has become the minimum age of marriage (article 7); a marriage below that age is considered irregular (*fāsid*) (article 52) and must therefore be terminated. The condition of competence that the groom should be at least 18 and the bride at least 17 (article 4) is an innovation as against the *Mejelle,* which provides that the maximum age of puberty for both sexes is 15 years completed (articles 986 and 987). At the same time, the Ottoman legislator left a wide loophole for circumvention of that condition by giving the *qāḍī* discretion to approve the marriage of a bride and groom below the said ages on the grounds of early physical maturity; in the case of the bride, the consent of the marriage guardian is also required (articles 5 and 6)—these provisions, too, being modeled on the *Mejelle* (articles 985, 988 and 989). The plea of physical maturity may thus be made in respect of boys between the ages of 12 and 18 and, until the repeal of this part of the provision, it might formerly have been made in respect of girls between the ages of nine and 17.[1]

Though trying to find warrant for these reforms in the Islamic legal heritage, the Ottoman legislator was guided by social considerations, and especially strove to improve the position of women. The fixing of a minimum age of marriage was prompted by abuse, for economic reasons, of the legal permission to marry off minors without limitation of age. The raising of the age of puberty from 15 to 17 and 18 was prompted by the heavy responsibility resting on the family as the basis of society, a responsibility immeasurably greater than that attaching to the capacity for owning property under the *Mejelle*. Especial concern was shown for the girl's physical and mental health, for fear of possible defects in the physical or mental health of the offspring.[2]

In regulating the marriage of minors within the framework of the Criminal Code Ordinance, the British Mandatory legislator followed the *Mejelle*. He fixed the minimum age of marriage at 15 years completed and prescribed a penalty of six months' imprisonment for marrying or solemnizing or assisting in the solemnization of the marriage of a girl under that age. At the same time, a good defense to such a charge was provided along the lines of the Ottoman Family Rights Law: physical maturity of the girl, a medical certificate that sexual intercourse would not damage her health, and the consent of her parents and guardians.[3]

The Knesset considered that a girl of 15 was not fit for marriage because physical maturity was not sufficient and psychological maturity and vocational training were also to be taken into account. Nor was the Knesset prepared to accept consent of the parents as a criterion of marriageability, because parents frequently bore the chief responsibility for pressuring a girl into an early marriage against her will.[4] The Age of Marriage Law, 5710–1950, raised the minimum age of the bride from 15 to 17 years, as in the Ottoman Family Rights Law (which applies only to Muslims), but in addition—and this is the main point—the Knesset abolished the Mandatory good defense and thus eliminated the principal means of circumventing the provisions relating to the age of marriage. The penal sanction was made still more severe: a person who marries, or solemnizes, or assists in solemnizing marriage of a girl under 17 or who, being her father or guardian, marries off such a girl, is liable to imprisonment for up to two years, or to a fine of up to IL 600, or to both.[5] Where a girl has given birth or is pregnant, the district court (but not the religious court) may permit her to marry the father, and a marriage performed under these circumstances is not considered a criminal offense (section 5). In 1960, the district court was empowered to permit the marriage of a girl of 16 even if she had not given birth or become pregnant, provided that special circumstances existed which in the opinion of the judge justified the grant of such permission.[6]

II. MARRIAGES OF MINOR GIRLS

The *sijill*s of the *sharīʿa* courts reveal hundreds of offenses against the Age of Marriage Law, especially in the first years after its passage. Most of them became apparent in the immediate context of the performance of the marriage, others in proceedings concerning various matrimonial matters.[7] There is also evidence of girls being married off at a very early age.[8] Moreover, the offenses are reflected—though not fully—in the data of the Central Bureau of Statistics. The Population and Housing Census of 1961 indicates a relatively high percentage of Muslim women married at an early age, as shown in Table I.

TABLE I: AGE OF MARRIAGE OF WOMEN ACCORDING TO RELIGION (IN PERCENTAGES) IN 1961[a]

Age at time of (first) marriage	Jewish[b]	Muslim	Christian	Druze
Up to 15	2.9	21.6	11.4	22.2
16 to 17	6.4	21.1	15.4	20.3
Up to 17	9.3	42.7	26.8	40.5
Up to 21	60.5	77.6	62.5	76.7

a) *Census Publication No.17*, Table XVIII, p.XXXVIII.
b) Provisional data.

Twenty-two percent of Muslim married women in 1961 had been married by the age of 15, as against 11% of the Christians and 3% of the Jewesses. Forty-three percent had been married by the age of 17, as against 27% of the Christians and 9% of the Jewesses. The percentage of Muslim women who married at an age up to 15 in the years 1951 to 1961, that is, in the first decade after the enactment of the Age of Marriage Law, was 7 as against 2.5 for Christians.[9] These data are underestimates; the rate of offenses against the Age of Marriage Law was undoubtedly higher than is reflected in the official statistics, since the Bureau's data are based on the marriage registers. They do not reflect marriages confirmed *ex post facto* by the courts (by declaratory judgment) nor, of course, marriages performed without resort to a court or its agents.[10]

The Age of Marriage Law was circumvented in various ways: for instance, through the mechanism provided by the Ottoman Family

Rights Law: a girl under 17 would ask the *qāḍī* to permit her to marry on the grounds of physical maturity and consent of the marriage-guardian. The accepted criterion of physical maturity is menstruation. The girl sometimes supported her application with various documents, such as a *maḍbaṭa* (petition) signed by the village *mukhtār* (a functionary appointed by the Government from among local notables) and others, and a medical certificate attesting that she was able to have sexual intercourse and conceive without injury being caused to her, and with the testimony of persons who knew her. The court would grant the application if the applicant's submissions were proved to its satisfaction. This was the principal means, under the Mandate and in Israel, of circumventing the provisions of the Criminal Code Ordinance as to the age of marriage before the enactment of the Age of Marriage Law, and this method was also applied for a time to circumvent the latter. Thus, from the enactment of this law to the end of 1951, the *Sharīʿa* Court of Ṭayyiba issued 80 marriage permits for women in reliance on article 6 of the Ottoman Family Rights Law, including several dozen for girls under 17.[11] These offenses were probably committed in good faith since there was no attempt to conceal the fact that the girl was not yet 17. The loophole was stopped after less than a year, when the *qāḍī*s ceased to grant marriage permits under these circumstances.

Another means of circumventing the Age of Marriage Law, which likewise involved reliance on the Family Rights Law, does not seem to have always been adopted in good faith: the girl would declare in the court that she had completed her 17th year or was of marriageable age and that statements in various documents making her out to be younger were erroneous. She would apply for and obtain a marriage permit on the basis of article 6 of the Family Rights Law. If her claim that she was over 17 was correct, she did not have to prove physical maturity and did not need a permit. In the first year after the enactment of the Age of Marriage Law, 120 marriage permits for girls were issued under these circumstances in the *Sharīʿa* Court of Nazareth and more than 20 in the *Sharīʿa* Court of Ṭayyiba. Most of the women in these cases had no official birth certificates, and this was probably why the *maʾdhūn liʿuqūd al-ankiḥa al-sharʿiyya* (authorized *sharʿī* marriage notary, hereinafter referred to as *maʾdhūn*) refused to solemnize and register the marriage and a permit from the *qāḍī* had to be sought.[12] To prove the allegation as to the women's ages, extensive use was made of the *maḍbaṭa,* and the testimonies and medical certificates, in which the estimated ages were indicated.[13] It has happened that signatories to the *maḍbaṭa* "assumed responsibility toward the law in case a religious-legal or secular-legal impediment to the marriage was discovered."[14] Though it may be supposed that errors in indicating the date of birth in official documents did occur, this method of proving age was probably used deliberately to obtain marriage permits so as to avoid a criminal charge. This method, too, was no longer available once the Population Registry had advised the public, shortly after the enactment of the law, that the date of birth might only be corrected on the basis of an official birth certificate and a medical certificate from the Government Health Office, accompanied by a sworn declaration by the father or marriage guardian.[15]

A third method of circumventing the law was recourse to an official correction of the date of birth. From early in 1951 there are to be found dozens of cases in the Nazareth *sijill*s where a marriage permit was issued after correction of the date of birth. The correction was made, without great formality, in a magistrates' court, whereupon the permit was obtained from the *sharīᶜa* court. In one case, a girl, her father and her fiancé's father appeared in the *sharīᶜa* court and declared that the girl wished to be married to her fiancé, that her father agreed to the marriage and that the fiancé had already prepared the prompt dower, but that they had all agreed to postpone the marriage until the girl's age had been corrected "in accordance with the truth."[16]

Also resorted to was solemnization of the marriage without a *maʾdhūn,* and, after the girl had reached the age of marriage, receipt of a declaratory judgment from the *sharīᶜa* court as to the validity of the marriage, in other words, a confirmation of the marriage (*ithbāt al-zawāj*) retroactively to the date of solemnization. The provisions of the Family Rights Law as to the solemnization of marriages are not of a substantive character, and a deviation from them does not affect the validity of the marriage so long as it is solemnized in accordance with the *sharᶜī* rules as to offer and acceptance (*ījāb waqabūl*) and the presence of witnesses.[17] The court is not debarred from granting relief under these circumstances.[18] It is indeed not always possible to prove intent to circumvent the law in this manner; the applicants may have acted in good faith, in ignorance of the need to register the marriage. But there can be no doubt that in many cases this method was used to circumvent the law. The more than 200 marriage confirmations issued by the *Sharīᶜa* Court of Jaffa up to the beginning of 1970 included 30 clear cases of marriages of girls under 17.[19] It has happened that a couple applied to the court several years after the marriage, when they already had children, to confirm the marriage and declare that the children were theirs.[20]

In dozens of other cases in Jaffa, there is a suspicion that the marriage confirmation was obtained in circumstances involving an offense against the Age of Marriage Law. No definite proof is provided by the judicial findings because basic data, such as the wife's age, exact date of marriage, and age of the children, are lacking. The suspicion arises precisely from what appears to have been a systematic attempt to blur the evidence. Thus, some couples asserted in court in 1960 and 1961 that they had been married "for about ten years," but it is impossible to tell from this finding whether they were married before or after the enactment of the Age of Marriage Law.[21] In other cases, when a marriage was contracted before the Age of Marriage Law, but a suspicion might have arisen that an offense had been committed, the date of the marriage was exactly stated so as to remove all doubt.[22]

The *sijill*s of Nazareth and Acre also record many dozens of marriage confirmations, but in these cases, too, it is almost impossible to trace offenses against the Age of Marriage Law owing to the lack of sufficient data in the judgments. The *Sharīʿa* Court of Ṭayyiba issued five marriage confirmations, two of which indicated the clear intent to circumvent the Age of Marriage Law. In the first case, the couple alleged that the *maʾdhūn* had solemnized the marriage when the bride was "a few months" short of the legal age. The *maʾdhūn* denied this emphatically (the marriage had not been registered). An examination of the identity booklets revealed that the woman had married at the age of 15. In the second case, the couple admitted that they had married without having the marriage registered because the wife had been under 17 at the time; but they added that they had not known then of the legal prohibition. In another case, the couple said that they had cohabited (and had a child) without marriage because the woman had not reached the legal age at the time.[23]

The *sharīʿa* courts issue certificates of marital status (*ithbāt ḥāla madaniyya*) which include certificates given to women for the purpose of establishing that the holder is single and that there is no religious-legal or secular-legal bar to her marrying. Certificates of the latter kind usually indicate that they were required for the purpose of marriage. Some such certificates were issued to girls under 17.[24]

At least in the first year after the enactment of the Age of Marriage Law, its circumvention was facilitated by the fact that *maʾdhūn*s were not particularly strict about the bride's age. Though the *sijill* usually attests that the *maʾdhūn* refused to solemnize the marriage on the ground that the bride's competence with regard to age had not been proven to his satisfaction,[25] there is also evidence of several cases where a *maʾdhūn* lent his hand to the marriage of a girl below the legal age.[26] Incomplete and faulty entries in birth certificates and identity booklets provided favorable opportunities for such offenses. Until the end of 1950, many residents, especially Negev Beduin, had no identity documents at all, and the provisional documents issued by the military authorities gave estimated dates of birth on the strength of the testimony of *mukhtār*s, shaykhs and local notables. In 1951, *maʾdhūn*s were forbidden to regard the temporary documents as evidence of a woman's age; they were requested to rely on official birth certificates or, failing these, on identity booklets issued by the Ministry of the Interior.[27] The transition period, of course, facilitated circumvention of the legal age of marriage. Commissions consisting of regional *qāḍī*s and representatives of the Muslim Division of the Ministry of Religious Affairs inspected the records of the *maʾdhūn*s from time to time to try to discover to what extent religious and secular law was being complied with.[28] Especial care was taken to give guidance to *maʾdhūn*s recruited from among Negev Beduin shaykhs and tribal chiefs.[29] The *Qāḍī* of the *Sharīʿa* Court of Jaffa, in whose area of jurisdiction the Beduin were located, met with them from time to time for this purpose. Despite all these measures, the official statistics disclose offenses as to the age of marriage even in the most recent years. As these statistics are based on the marriage registers, the inescapable conclusion is that the offenses were committed with knowledge of the *maʾdhūn*s.

Yet another method of circumvention consisted in the drawing up of the terms (*shurūṭ*) of the marriage of a girl under 17 by the *maʾdhūn* on the strength of an assurance that the wife would only take up residence with the husband after reaching the legal age. The Muslim Division made it clear to the *maʾdhūn*s that the drawing up of the terms of a marriage was tantamount to a marriage within the meaning of the law and that it made no difference whether the couple established their joint residence immediately or after a lapse of time.[30]

The only lawful way of by-passing the restrictions as to the age of marriage in certain circumstances is, as stated, the receipt of a marriage permit from the district court, but the author found no indication that Muslims availed themselves of this opportunity, although in many cases it would not have been difficult to obtain this relief, especially where there were children born out of wedlock.[31] Muslims preferred in such circumstances to obtain a marriage confirmation[32] or at any rate not to have recourse to a civil court.

Offenses against the Age of Marriage Law are encountered especially in periods of transition from one political regime to another: in the first years after the establishment of the State of Israel and since the reunification of Jerusalem[33]—when people had not yet become acquainted with the law and learned to adjust to it or to circumvent it. Marriages of minor girls were widespread in all types of settlements, including the towns.[34] At the same time, they were particularly frequent among the Negev Beduin, as Shaykh Tawfīq ᶜAsaliyya confirmed; according to him "they unfortunately do not know the elementary rules concerning marriage although *maᵓdhūns* are distributed among their encampments."[35] There is a great deal of evidence of Beduin girls getting married at the ages of 12 and 13.[36]

With a few exceptions, offenses and reasonably suspected offenses against the Age of Marriage Law involved completely illiterate women. This appears from the fact that instead of their signatures they affixed their thumbprints (*baṣma*) to the court judgments.[37] The type of marriage may also have something to do with the age at which women marry. Marriages between cousins or within the clan and exchange marriages (*tabādul al-zawjāt, shighār*) may create strong family pressures to circumvent the legal age of marriage. In one case, for example, the couple explicitly admitted that the reason for the wife's marrying below the legal age was their common family background (*ḥasab*).[38] Other cases involved a combination of exchange marriage and clan endogamy or cousin marriage.[39] This is perhaps the situation most conducive to the generation of structural pressure to circumvent the Age of Marriage Law, because of the combination of property and relationship considerations involved in these types of marriage. However, the rate of such marriages, in violation of the Age of Marriage Law, was not particularly high, whence it may be concluded that the type of marriage was not a decisive factor with regard to marriages of minor girls. The occurrence of such marriages was no doubt favored by the fact that Islamic law knows no age qualification for marriage, as well as by the personal example of the Prophet Muḥammad. Thus, in one case, a man contended that it was permissible to marry off a nine-year-old girl, adducing the marriage of Muḥammad and ᶜĀᵓisha as evidence.[40]

III. RISE IN THE AGE OF MARRIAGE

The rate of marriages of minor girls has dropped drastically in Israel as compared with the period of the Mandate as is clear from Table II.

TABLE II: GIRLS MARRYING UP TO THE AGE OF 15 ACCORDING TO TIME OF MARRIAGE AND RELIGION (IN PERCENTAGES)[a]

Religion	Time of Marriage			
	Up to 1930	1931–40	1941–50	1951–61
Muslim	33.4	31.1	27.0	6.8
Christian	22.0	16.9	8.2	2.5
Druze	33.8	34.6	21.0	4.0

a) *Census Publication No.17*, Table XIX, p.XXXIX.

Although a decrease was already noticeable during the Mandate, it is particularly striking in the first decade of the State. During that decade, the percentage of Muslim minor brides dropped to one-quarter of the figure of the preceding decade: from 27 to 7 (the same applies, more or less, to the other communities). In some years of the second decade of the State, the number of Muslim girls marrying below the legal age did not exceed a few dozen.[41] The data in Table II may tempt one to jump to the conclusion that the main cause of the steep decline in the number of marriages of minor girls was Israeli legislation, but it seems that this proposition must be considerably qualified in the light of a number of factors.

The registration of the marriages of minor girls after the enactment of the Age of Marriage Law is incomplete owing to a desire to avoid penal sanctions (as far as they have a deterrent effect). The deterrent effect of these sanctions was rather limited; they were seldom applied, and then only in the form of fines that were small in relation to the dower.[42] The rate of marriages of Muslim minor girls was already on the decrease in Mandatory times, when the age qualification of the Criminal Code Ordinance could be circumvented without great difficulty through the mechanism provided by the Ottoman Family Rights Law. Then again, in other communities in Israel as well, the rate of marriages of male minors has dropped drastically (as against a moderate decline under the Mandate) although the Age of Marriage Law does not apply to the groom.[43]

The decline in the rates of marriage of both male and female juveniles must therefore be attributed in part—perhaps even mainly—to factors other than penal legislation. The effect of these factors was particularly noticeable in the age-groups over 17–18, which were not affected by the Age of Marriage Law or the Criminal Code Ordinance. The median age of marriage of Muslim women rose from 19 in 1951–1955 to 20 years in 1968.[44]

The main factors tending to raise the age of marriage were economic, cultural and social[45]: changes in the occupational structure and women's increasing participation in economic life; the increase in the amounts of dower[46]; the spread of education (there was a distinct correlation between women's level of education and the age of marriage)[47]; the rapid disintegration of the extended family and transition to the nuclear family; the adoption of modern concepts of marriage, such as the right of a free choice of partner for marriage and the necessity of mutual maturity, under the influence of Israeli society; increased expectations as to the marriage partner, as well as economic requirements (a dwelling with all modern comforts) as a necessary condition for marriage. These factors are reflected in the statistics of women's ages of marriage according to type of settlement, as is shown in Table III.

TABLE III: AVERAGE AGE OF MARRIAGE OF MUSLIM WOMEN ACCORDING TO TYPE OF SETTLEMENT IN 1960[a]

	Towns			Villages			Beduin	
National Average	Nazareth	Shafā ʿAmr	Mixed Towns	Northern District	Haifa District	Central District	Galilee	Negev
20.5	20.0	19.7	21.2	20.3	20.5	20.4	19.9	20.8

a) *AI*, vol.8(1962), Nos.1–2, p.15. For explanatory note to table see English Summary, *ibid.*, p.4.

The age of marriage was highest in mixed towns, owing to direct contact with Jewish society. The age of marriage in Arab towns was not materially different and might be earlier than that in the villages of the Haifa and Central Districts. The data concerning the Beduin are implausible. According to all the evidence, marriages of minor girls were more common among them than in any other ecological group. The explanatory note to these data states that the late age of marriage among the Beduin is due to "late registration of marriages concluded in earlier years."[48]

In sum, although the Age of Marriage Law undoubtedly contributed to the drop in the rate of marriages of minor girls,[49] the factors mentioned above were the main causes of this phenomenon and of the rise in the age of marriage of both bride and bridegroom.[50] If marriages of minor girls still occur in certain areas, it is not only because the authorities are unable to punish offenders wherever they are, but mainly because social and cultural conditions in those areas have not yet radically changed.

IV. THE *QĀḌĪ*S AND THE AGE OF MARRIAGE

Since the Knesset's interference in the matter of the age of marriage was not of a substantive character, and did not *invalidate* the marriage of a girl under 17, the *qāḍī*s were put to no severe test, especially as the minimum age of marriage prescribed by the Ottoman Family Rights Law remained unchanged. At their first conference in 1950, the *qāḍī*s resolved that "the age of marriage shall be 17 years in accordance with the Family Rights Law and the law passed by the Knesset."[51] This vague resolution blurred the material differences between the two laws as regards both the possibility of circumventing their provisions and the criminal sanctions they impose. Shaykh Ṭāhir al-Ṭabarī and Shaykh Ḥasan Amīn al-Ḥabash granted marriage permits to minor girls on grounds of physical maturity and consent of the marriage-guardian. The *qāḍī*s were no sticklers for documents but relied on witnesses and their own visual impressions. If the external appearance of the girl supported her plea of maturity, the *qāḍī* would declare that she was marriageable and that there was no religious-legal or secular-legal bar to her marriage, and would order the *maʾdhūn* to solemnize it. In several cases, Shaykh Ṭāhir al-Ṭabarī issued a marriage permit to a girl after it had been ascertained that she was "about the age of competence [for marriage]."[52] In other cases, when a girl had been married under 17, the *qāḍī* declared that the *maʾdhūn* should not have solemnized the marriage "without a *sharʿī* permit"[53] (within the meaning of the Family Rights Law but not the Age of Marriage Law). But apart from a few exceptions, the *qāḍī*s ceased to issue marriage permits for minors after a transition period of less than one year.

Shaykh Ṭāhir Ḥamād and Shaykh Tawfīq ᶜAsaliyya issued marriage confirmations frequently and even in cases involving offenses against the Age of Marriage Law. Other *qāḍīs* did so to a varying extent. This method, as stated, has been and still is one of the principal means of circumventing the Age of Marriage Law, either deliberately or in good faith. In both cases, the *qāḍīs* validated the marriage retroactively insofar as it was valid according to the *sharīᶜa*. Shaykh Ṭāhir Ḥamād proposed at the first *qāḍīs*' conference that the marriage of a girl under 17 "should be brought before the *sharīᶜa* court, which should pronounce on its legality; it should be possible to impose punishment, but on no account should the marriage be terminated."[54] Already in one of his first judgments, this *qāḍī* held that "age does not affect the validity of the marital bond." The only impediment to the marriage of a minor girl was, in his opinion, her sexual immaturity.[55] This had indeed been his guiding principle in day-to-day practice. Neither he nor other *qāḍīs* had ever raised the question of the criminality of solemnizing the marriage of a minor or of the prosecution of offenders under the Age of Marriage Law. If, on the retroactive validation of a marriage it appeared that it had been solemnized in contravention of the law and constituted a criminal offense, the *qāḍīs*, apparently for fear of disrupting the couple's married life, did not bring this fact to their attention or to that of the competent civil authorities. This attitude of the *qāḍīs* was probably one of the reasons why Muslims did not apply to a civil court for a marriage permit.

NOTES

1. See Anderson, *Contract of Marriage*, pp.114, 116 *seq.*; Coulson, *History*, p.194; Fyzee, p.90; Levy, pp.106–7, 140–2; Eisenman, p.118; Qadrī, arts.140–2; *FRL* arts.75–7. No age qualification exists as to betrothal (*khuṭba*), since neither it nor the promise of marriage (*waᶜd*) creates a marital bond (*FRL*, art.1).
2. *ENFRL*. See also Goitein and Ben-Shemesh, pp.215–6.
3. Criminal Code Ordinance, sec.182(a) and (b), sec.183.
4. The immediate cause of the Knesset's interference in the matter of the age of marriage was the great number of marriages of minor girls among Oriental

Jewish immigrants. See *KP*, vol.5, p.1703 col.1, p.1704 col.2. See also *KP*, vol.4, p.638 col.2, p.639 col.1.

5. Age of Marriage Law, secs.1, 2, 6 (repeal of pars.(*b*) and (*c*) of sec.182, and of sec.183 of the Criminal Code Ordinance). See Criminal Code Ordinance (Amendment) Bill, 5710–1950, *Bills*, No.31 of January 15, 1950, pp.77–8.
6. Age of Marriage (Amendment) Law, 5720–1960, sec.1. See Explanatory Note to Age of Marriage (Amendment) Bill, 5719–1959, *Bills*, No.339, p.415; *ha-Aretz* of July 21, 1960. For the reasons for this amendment see the remarks of the Minister of Justice in the Knesset, *KP*, vol.28, p.10 col.1.
7. See, e.g., *JfQ3*, p.331:no.472–f.8/67; *JfQ4*, p.113:no.126–f.82/68; *JfQ5*, p.49:no.85–f.89/69; *NzḤ20*, p.10:no.4/105 and p.11:no.5/106 (the *qāḍī* ordered the *tafrīq* of the couple because they had not been married in accordance with the *sharīʿa*, and on the same day the man applied for a marriage permit, alleging that the woman was "about marriageable age"); *AcṬ3*, p.192:f.35/60.
8. See, e.g., *JfQ1*, p.175:no.289–f.19/55 (a Beduin girl alleged that her father had married her to a relative "while still a little child"); *AcD4*, p.69:f.114/65 (girl married off at 12).
9. See Table II. For further data see *SAI*, 1967, No.18, p.49; *AI*, vol.7 (1959), Nos.1–2, p.34.
10. The *sijill*s record hundreds of instances of marriages concluded according to local custom (not according to the rules of the *sharīʿa*), which mostly involved minor female partners. See Layish, *Custom*, pp.380–3.
11. For instances of this kind of circumvention of age of marriage legislation under the Mandate see *NzḤ14*, pp.1, 4, 5, 9, 29, 30, 36, and in Israel (about a hundred cases) see *NzḤ14*, pp.76–126; *NzḤ15*, pp.4–104; *ṬbḤ1*, p.6: no.3/11, p.39:no.23/69, p.83:no.19/34, p.95:no.11/57.
12. See, e.g., *NzḤ16*, p.38:no.263/62 (the woman alleged that she was over 16 and that the entry in the identity booklet giving her age as 12 was erroneous).
13. See, e.g., *NzḤ15*, p.126:no.4/180; *NzḤ16*, p.1:no.11/212 (according to the identity booklet, the girl was 14; the medical certificate said she was 17); *ṬbḤ1*, p.35:no.16/62 (the woman alleged that she was between 17 and 18 and produced a medical certificate to this effect; the *maḍbaṭa* said that according to an official birth certificate she was over 14; and according to the testimony of the *mukhtār* and others "her appearance shows conclusively" that she was over 16).
14. See, e.g., *ṬbḤ1*, p.78:no.8/23.
15. *AI*, vol.2 (1951), No.2, p.27.
16. *NzḤ17*, p.134:no.34/285. See also *NzḤ16*, p.97:no.53/35 (the girl alleged that she had completed her 17th year and that the entry in the identity booklet giving her age as 13 was erroneous; she and her mother went to

the magistrates' court, where the mother swore to her true age), p.120: no.14/85 (a medical certificate and a sworn declaration as to the girl's age made by her father in the magistrates' court, were submitted to the *sharīʿa* court).

17. A *sharʿī* marriage not solemnized by the *maʾdhūn* is popularly called a *barrānī* (external) marriage. According to interviewee Suʿād Qaramān and others, it serves, *inter alia*, to circumvent the Age of Marriage Law.
18. As it is, e.g., in Egypt under modern legislation. See Anderson, *Islamic Law*, p.48.
19. See, e.g., *JfQ2*, p.310:no.480–f.23/58 and p.315:no.490–f.27/58 (in the course of the proceedings, it was incidentally discovered that the wife had been 13 years old at the time of her marriage); *JfQ3*, p.145:no.231–f.125/64 (the father admitted marrying off his daughter at the age of 13, and witnesses stated that she had been "a minor below the legal age"), p.204:no.336–f.12/66, p.258:no.398–f.86/66 (the wife had been 15 at the time of the marriage).
20. See, e.g., *JfQ3*, p.166:no.270–f.24/65, p.204:no.12/66, p.257:no.397–f.84/66, p.258:no.398–f.86/66, p.337:no.477–f.42/67 (the wife had been 12 at the time of the marriage; she received confirmation of the marriage 15 years later, when she had seven children).
21. *JfQ2*, p.454:no.461–f.34/60, p.509:no.471–f.107/61, p.510:no.472–f.108/61. See also *JfQ2*, p.599:no.642 (the couple alleged in 1963 that they had been married for 13 years; the husband's year of birth is given, but not the wife's), p.289:no.448–f.66/57 (the couple's years of birth are given, but the year of the marriage is not); *JfQ5*, p.16:no.29–f.121/69 (the wife was born in 1952; the year of the marriage is not given, but the marriage was confirmed on June 8, 1969).
22. See, e.g., *JfQ1*, p.224:no.347–f.8/52, p.229:no.355–f.19/59, p.328:no.515–f.67/58; *JfQ5*, p.11:no.21–f.110/69, p.13:no.23–f.113/69.
23. *ṬbḤ4*, p.48:no.5, p.74:no.39, and p.77:no.42, respectively. The Knesset was told of hundreds of Israeli couples cohabiting without marriage until the girl reached the age of 17. *KP*, vol.28, p.24.
24. See, e.g., *JfQ4*, p.10:no.10–f.106/67 (it expressly indicated that the certificate was for purposes of marriage), p.81:no.77–f.36/68; *AcD8*, p.15: f.15/68.
25. See, e.g., *NzḤ16*, p.112:no.2/73 (the bride's date of birth was not indicated); *ṬbḤ1*, p.16:no.50/31 (the bride was under 17); *JfQ3*, p.194:no.320–f.45/65 (the *maʾdhūn* saw from the identity booklet that the girl was a minor and not permitted for marriage).
26. See, e.g., *NzḤ15*, p.124:no.2/178 (the *qāḍī* found that the *maʾdhūn* should not have performed the marriage because the bride had been under 17); *NzḤ16*, p.6:no.18/219 (the marriage was performed by the *maʾdhūn*

"regardless of the fact that according to the identity booklet the bride was under 17").

27. *AI*, vol.1(1950), No.7, p.5; *AI*, vol.2(1950), No.1, pp.6–7.
28. *Yediᶜon*, vol.1(1950), No.1, pp.1–2; *AI*, vol.2(1951), No.2, pp.18–19.
29. For a list of their names see *AI*, vol.2(1951), No.2, p.20.
30. *AI*, vol.2(1951), No.1, pp.6–7.
31. This mode of circumventing the law was particularly common in Jewish society. In many cases, pregnancy was deliberately brought about so that it might be possible to obtain a marriage permit. Sometimes a fictitious medical certificate attesting pregnancy was submitted. See *KP*, vol.28, pp.10, 24, 28; *KP*, vol.29, p.1929.
32. See, e.g., *ṬbḤ4,* p.77:no.42.
33. About a third of the approximately 100 marriage confirmations issued by the *Qāḍī* of Jaffa to residents of East Jerusalem (the city and the villages in its area of jurisdiction) were clear cases of offenses against the Age of Marriage Law or of reasonable suspicion of such offenses.
34. For the causes of early marriages of women in traditional society see Baer, p.23; Rosenfeld, *Peasants*, pp.65–6.
35. *AI*, vol.11(1868), Nos.1–2, p.12.
36. See, e.g., *JfQ2*, p.310:no.480–f.23/58, p.315:no.490–f.27/58; *JfQ3*, p.6: no.10–f.90/63, p.145:no.231–f.125/64 (the husband was from ᶜArab al-Jawārīsh, Ramla), p.156:no.253–f.160/64, p.337:no.477–f.42/67; *JfQ5*, p.22:no.39–f.135/69, p.66:no.112–f.222/69. Cf. Marx, *Bedouin*, p.103–6; *idem, Marriage Patterns*, p.398.
37. See, e.g., *ṬbḤ1*, p.25:no.1/47, p.75:no.4/19. For rare instances of a woman's signature see, e.g., *NzḤ15*, p.120:no.18/173; *NzḤ17*, p.41:no.45/169 (in both cases the women were from Nazareth).
38. *ṬbḤ4*, p.74:no.39. See also *ṬbḤ4*, p.48:no.5 (marriage within the *ḥamūla*).
39. *ṬbḤ1*, p.55:no.21/93 and p.56:no.1/94, p.90:no.1/47 and p.91:no.2/48.
40. *JfQ1*, p.41:no.70–f.39/51.
41. *AI*, vol.8(1962), Nos.1–2, p.15; *ibid.*, Nos.3–4, p.32; *AI*, vol.9(1964), Nos.1–2, p.51; *ibid.*, Nos.3–4, p.23; *AI*, vol.10(1966), Nos.1–2, p.94; *AI*, vol.11(1968), Nos.1–2, p.93. As to the years 1968 and 1969, see unpublished data of the Central Bureau of Statistics.
42. See, e.g., *ha-Aretz* of July 14, 1970 (the husband and the father of a minor girl of the al-Huzayyil tribe were each sentenced to a fine of IL 500 or 60 days' imprisonment; in passing sentence, the judge had regard to the custom of minor girls' marriages among the Beduin). See also *ha-Boqer*, *Lamerḥav* and *The Jerusalem Post* of June 2, 1964.
43. See *Census Publication No. 17*, Table XIX, p.XXXIX.
44. *Ibid.*, pp.39–40; *SAI*, 1970, No.21, p.69.

45. Where no other source is indicated, the analysis of the factors is based on Rosenfeld, *Peasants*, pp.66–7, and *NzDS*, pp.38–40.
46. See Marx, *Social Structure*, p.4. See also the chapter "Dower," pp.41 *seq.*
47. See *Census Publication No.32*, p.22. Cf. Woodsmall, p.95.
48. *AI*, vol.8(1962), Nos.1–2, p.15; explanatory note in English see *ibid.*, p.4. Cf. Muhsam, *Marriage Habits*, pp.64–6; Marx, *Social Structure*, p.3.
49. *AI*, vol.5(1957), Nos.1–2, p.25.
50. Rosenfeld, on the other hand, holds that despite the Knesset legislation the early age of marriage of women in rural areas has not materially changed. Rosenfeld, *Peasants*, pp.29, 65.
51. *AI*, vol.1(1950), No.7, p.4.
52. See, e.g., *NzḤ16*, p.23:no.40/241. In one case, this *qāḍī* estimated the woman's age at her request and decided on the basis of her appearance that she had completed her 17th year. See *NzḤ15*, p.41.
53. See, e.g., *NzḤ15*, p.124:no.2/178.
54. *Yediʿon*, vol.1(1950), No.7, p.3.
55. *JfQ1*, p.50:no.79–f.38/52 (the girl had married during the Mandate).

Chapter Two

STIPULATIONS INSERTED IN CONTRACTS OF MARRIAGE

I. LEGAL BACKGROUND

Stipulations in the marriage contract are a means of improving the status of women in so far as they enable marital rights and duties anchored in the *sharīʿa* to be circumvented or varied. The stipulation is a relatively convenient means since it involves no express derogation from substantive provisions of the *sharīʿa* by a legislative or judicial act. On the face of it, all that is required is agreement between the parties as to the contents of the stipulation at the time of the conclusion of the marriage. However, the Ḥanafī doctrine, which provides the theoretical basis for this mechanism, leaves little scope for flexibility. For according to this doctrine, only those stipulations are valid and enforceable which reaffirm ordinary legal effects of the marriage, for example with regard to the dower. Stipulations quite inconsistent with the nature of the marital bond, such as a time-limit to the marriage, are inoperative and render the marriage null and void. Stipulations that would alter the marital rights or duties of one of the parties, for instance, that the wife need not obey the husband, that the husband need not pay dower or shall not exercise unilateral right of *ṭalāq* (dissolution of marriage without resort to legal proceedings), are void but leave the marriage contract valid.

The Ottoman legislator established (in article 38 of the Family Rights Law) that the wife may stipulate in the marriage contract that the husband may not take an additional wife and that if he infringes this stipulation she or her rival shall be considered divorced. For this provision, which is inconsistent with the husband's *sharʿī* right, support may be found in Ḥanbalī doctrine, and the legislator stressed that polygamy, though permitted, is not commanded, by religious law. At the same time, he did not go so far as to turn the stipulation into an instrument for improving the status of women in other matrimonial matters, as was done later in several Arab countries.[1]

II. RESORT TO THE STIPULATION

Resort to the stipulation in the marriage contract was not particularly frequent among Israeli Muslims.[2] The *sijill*s record only about 30 instances, although the actual figure is undoubtedly higher. The practice seems to have increased in recent years. In 1962, stipulations were inserted in approximately 100 marriage contracts, 6% of the total for that year, and in 1968 the figure was twice as high, making up about 10% of the year's total.[3]

Stipulations made on the wife's initiative included a separate conjugal dwelling (away from the families of both spouses), the establishment of the dwelling in the wife's home locality, the vesting of ownership of the dwelling in the wife[4]; a specific mode of payment of the prompt dower (*mahr muʿajjal*—dower paid immediately on marriage)[5]; the gift of household utensils, jewelry and the like as part of, or in addition to, the dower; abstention from forcing the wife to go out to work; maintenance and kind treatment of the wife[6]; an undertaking by the husband to support the wife's children by another man[7]; provision of a maidservant (*khādima*) in the case of a veiled townswoman[8]; the fulfilment of the *kafāʾa* principle requiring that the family background and economic position etc. of the husband be at least equal to those of the wife[9]; payment of compensation to the wife by the husband in the event of his taking an additional wife[10]; delegation to the wife of the power to divorce herself ("delegated repudiation") at any time or under certain circumstances, as in the event of the husband leaving the country without her consent or deserting her or making her live in another locality than the one chosen by her or taking an additional wife; the obligation of the husband to pay the wife a sum of money "in consideration of the education of her children" or a fine (*gharāma*) in the event of his divorcing her against her will.[11] Stipulations by the husband included the obligation of the wife to obey him; a prohibition against her leaving the town in which they were living, without his consent, on pain of losing all her matrimonial rights[12]; his right to divorce her at any time[13]; the affiliation of her children to the Muslim faith (in the case of a (Christian?) woman who had converted to Islam).[14]

About two-thirds of the stipulations made in 1968 concerned the dwelling; next came matters of work of the wife, dower and jewelry, and lastly matters of divorce. About two-thirds of the stipulations were legitimate from the point of view of the Ḥanafī school. Stipulations such as a completely furnished room, a separate dwelling within the husband's family residence, a specific mode of paying the dower, jewelry, maintenance, kind treatment of the wife and delegation to the wife of power to divorce herself, were designed to assure, or add to, the wife's matrimonial rights under the *sharīʿa* without prejudicing the husband's rights. On the other hand, stipulations such as a completely separate dwelling for the couple and its location in the wife's home town or village were inconsistent with the law of legal dwelling (*maskan sharʿī*), and stipulations prohibiting the husband from taking an additional wife or from leaving the country without the wife's consent infringed his religious-legal rights. The wife's stipulation that if the husband takes an additional wife the latter shall be regarded as divorced [15] is indeed supported by article 38 of the Family Rights Law, but it is doubtful whether in the one case of this kind encountered by the author Ottoman legislation was relied on. In similar circumstances, the wife tried to protect herself against polygamy by other means: the right to divorce herself by delegation, or to claim a large monetary compensation from the husband, if the husband took an additional wife.[16] It thus seems that the stipulation in the marriage contract was essentially a matter of social custom. Its dissociation from the Ḥanafī school might to some extent have been facilitated by the fact that most of the population did not belong to that school. Indeed, in certain localities, such as some Little Triangle villages, the population—including *maʾdhūn*s—belonged to the Ḥanbalī school.[17]

Stipulations were not always actually written in the marriage contract, not even at the stage of solemnization of the marriage. Occasionally it was considered sufficient to mention them orally[18]; in one case, the stipulation was mentioned at the time of the betrothal, which does not create a marital bond.[19] Sometimes the matter of the stipulation came up during the existence of the marriage and was thus unconnected with the marriage contract. In such cases, which were not particularly frequent, the stipulation consisted chiefly in the delegation to the wife of power to divorce herself under certain circumstances agreed on between the parties in the light of their experience of married life; for instance, if the husband did not provide the wife with a dwelling agreeable to her, did not supply her requirements with regard to clothing and footwear, discriminated against her in favor of her rival[20] or delayed the payment of her maintenance even for a single day.[21] The wife occasionally forewent the realization of the stipulation.[22]

There appears to be a causal connection between the type of settlement, the wife's education and occupation and the type of marriage on the one hand, and resort to stipulations in the marriage contract on the other. Such resort was particularly frequent where the spouses, or at least the wife,[23] originated from a mixed town: in 1968 this was so in more than half the cases where marriage contracts contained stipulations.[24] To assess the significance of this proportion, the Israeli Muslims' small share in the urban population should be borne in mind. As for the rural areas, resort to stipulations was more frequent in the Little Triangle than elsewhere; 60% of the cases occured there and only 40% in all the villages in the areas of jurisdiction of the *Sharīʿa* Courts of Jaffa (countryside near Jerusalem), Acre and Nazareth together. This distribution seems to be due to the relatively favorable socio-economic position of women in the Little Triangle villages and to the high concentration of followers of the Ḥanbalī school in that region. Resort to stipulations was very rare in Arab towns (two cases) and in the villages near Nazareth, and was practically non-existent in Beduin society; two isolated instances concerned Beduin who had settled in Ramla.[25]

In only one-sixth of the cases involving stipulations in 1968 did the wife have no education at all. In 70% of the cases she had had at least five years' schooling; this includes 14% of cases where the wife had a secondary education. The distribution according to the wife's education largely coincided with that according to type of settlement: the level of education of women was higher in towns than in rural areas and higher in the Little Triangle villages than in villages in other regions.[26] In some cases, there is express evidence that the wife worked away from home in jobs requiring an education—as a teacher, nurse, clerk or club manageress.[27]

Resort to stipulation was particularly frequent in the case of exogamous marriages, which made up about four-fifths of the cases involving stipulations in 1968. This is especially noticeable in the Little Triangle villages, where more than half of all marriages in the late 1950s were endogamous,[28] while the proportion of endogamous marriages involving stipulations in this area did not exceed one-quarter;

at the same time it seems that the low national rate of endogamous marriages involving stipulations was principally a reflection of the distribution of these marriages according to type of settlement; in other words, stipulations prevailed mainly in mixed towns where endogamous marriages were rare. The woman's personal status had no bearing on the resort to stipulations; she had generally not been married before, although there were cases involving women previously divorced or widowed.[29]

III. THE *QĀḌĪ*S AND STIPULATIONS

In the attitude of the *qāḍī*s to the stipulation in the marriage contract, two diametrically opposed positions may be distinguished: a formalistic one, consonant with the Ḥanafī view which, as stated, negates the validity of a stipulation designed to alter the rights and obligations of the spouses; and a pragmatic view, which recognizes a stipulation as valid in so far as it corresponds to social custom. Moreover, there was a tendency to turn the stipulation into an instrument for the improvement of the status of women as long as it was not inconsistent with the essential nature of marriage. Shaykh Ṭāhir Ḥamād decided in one case that a husband's undertaking on conclusion of the marriage to support the wife's children by another man was an "irregular stipulation, inoperative according to the *sharīʿa*."[30] In another case, where the wife had stipulated that the conjugal dwelling should not be in the husband's village, Shaykh Mūsā al-Ṭabarī decided that the wife must "follow the husband . . . and a stipulation in the marriage contract must not be contrary to the provisions of the *sharīʿa*."[31] A woman's application to dissolve her marriage because she and her husband "curse each other at home and outside" was dismissed by Shaykh Ḥasan Amīn al-Ḥabash on the ground that the marriage contract contained no stipulation as to divorce and that the wife's claim was not based on a ground recognized by the *sharīʿa* or "a stipulation to be acted on by virtue of law, such as article 38 of the Family Rights Law."[32] Shaykh Tawfīq ʿAsaliyya hinted on one occasion that the wife might insert stipulations in the marriage contract in order to protect herself against polygamy, and it appeared that he was referring to article 38 of the Family Rights Law.[33]

As a rule, however, the *qāḍī*'s attitude to the stipulation was not tied to the doctrine of the Ḥanafī school. For instance, two *qāḍī*s fully agreed with a clause in the Egyptian Personal Status Bill of 1966 designed to validate a stipulation concerning the conjugal dwelling and wife's occupation in so far as it was not inconsistent with the essential nature of marriage. Shaykh Ḥusnī al-Zuᶜbī considered that each of the spouses might make any stipulation not inconsistent with the essential nature of marriage, and Shaykh Amīn Qāsim Mudlij thought that the Egyptian amendment "conforms with the personal status law applied by the *sharīᶜa* courts in Israel and that any stipulation by either spouse is considered valid [under the *sharīᶜa*] and must be implemented."[34] Needless to say, had this been the accepted Ḥanafī position, the proposed Egyptian amendment (and similar amendments in several other Arab countries) would have been unnecessary. The *qāḍī*s did not hesitate to confirm the validity of stipulations infringing the husband's personal rights, especially one to the effect that the conjugal dwelling should be in the wife's home locality. Shaykh Tawfīq ᶜAsaliyya and Shaykh Amīn Qāsim Mudlij repeatedly decided accordingly.[35] In one case, Shaykh Ṭāhir Ḥamād decided that the wife was divorced because it had been stipulated that the husband should divorce her if he fell behind with the maintenance payments even for a single day.[36] In several cases, the wife's application to confirm the validity of a stipulation invalid under the Ḥanafī doctrine was refused by the *qāḍī*s merely because it was not written in the marriage contract. Once, for example, a wife had stipulated that the conjugal dwelling should be with her family, but Shaykh Tawfīq ᶜAsaliyya ordered obedience to the husband because the stipulation had been made at the time of the betrothal.[37]

The deviation of the *qāḍī*s from the Ḥanafī school suggests that the insertion of stipulations in the marriage contract might be basically a social custom supported in certain regions by the Ḥanbalī school and to which the *qāḍī*s gave the sanction of the *sharīᶜa*. They generally did not examine the substance of the stipulation (but they insisted on its being written in the marriage contract, although this was of no legal significance).[38] Particularly instructive is the *qāḍī*s' endeavor to turn the stipulation into an instrument for improving the status of women. At conferences held from time to time to discuss legal questions arising during court proceedings, they made various proposals to this end. Some stipulations confirm the customary legal effects of the marital union, for instances, as regards the mode of payment of the dower. At a *qāḍī*s' conference in 1966, it was resolved that the indication of the deferred (*muʾajjal*) dower—dower paid at the termination of the marriage on divorce or death of one the spouses—in the marriage contract in addition to the prompt (*muʿajjal*) dower should be insisted on in order to assure the wife's future in the event of divorce or widowhood and to discourage hasty *ṭalāq* divorces.[39] At a *qāḍī*s' conference in 1963, it was resolved to exhort *maʾdhūn*s to set out in the marriage contract clear stipulations safeguarding the wife's rights, such as to compensation on divorce. This resolution was prompted by the consideration that the wife's legal right to maintenance during the waiting-period (*ʿidda*) was not sufficient to assure her subsistence after divorce.[40] Shaykh Ḥusnī al-Zuʿbī stated that he would tell *maʾdhun*s to insert any stipulation desired by one of the spouses, but especially stipulations desired by the wife designed to assure her future.[41] Shaykh Amīn Qāsim Mudlij suggested that the wife stipulate that a dwelling near that of the husband's relatives should not be considered legal, so as to eliminate a frequent source of conflict.[42]

The *qāḍī*s regarded the stipulation as a legitimate device not affecting the substantive validity of the religious law; the deviation from Ḥanafī doctrine did not worry them unduly. This may be because personally they did not all belong to the Ḥanafī school (for instance, in matters of worship and religious duties), though as *qāḍī*s they were bound to treat matrimonial matters in accordance with Ḥanafī doctrine. Moreover, it is certainly more convenient to improve the status of women by this device than by Israeli secular legislation. Knesset interference is likely to be particularly unwelcome in matters in which express provisions exist in the textual sources of Islamic law. This is why the *qāḍī*s opposed, for example, the limitation of dower by legislation, suggesting other ways of solving the problem.[43] In sum, by their pragmatic approach, the *qāḍī*s have succeeded in extending the scope of the stipulation in such measure that any stipulation beneficial to the wife was valid and enforceable, even if it curtailed the husband's rights under the *sharīʿa*, as at times indeed it did, so long as it was not inconsistent with the essential nature of marriage. A similar extension of the scope of the stipulation has only been achieved in Syria by secular legislation. The Syrian Personal Status Law of 1953 validates every stipulation beneficial to the wife which is not inconsistent with the essential nature of marriage; if the stipulation curtails the husband's rights under the *sharīʿa* it does not bind him, but its infringement is a ground for dissolution of the marriage on the wife's initiative.[44]

NOTES

1. See Anderson, *Contract of Marriage*, pp. 122–4; *idem, Islamic Law*, pp. 50–1; Coulson, *History*, pp.189–90; *idem, Conflicts*, pp.28–30; *ENFRL;* Goitein and Ben-Shemesh, pp. 218–19.
2. Cf. Woodsmall, p. 127.
3. The data on marriages are based on *AI*, vol.8(1963), Nos.3–4, p.30; *AI*, vol.11(1969), Nos.3–4, p.86.
4. A detailed analysis of stipulations according to contents, with source references, is given in the relevant chapters.
5. E.g.: The husband shall pay the wife the remainder of the prompt dower "whenever she demands it." *JfMC62*, no.20183; *JfQ1*, p.77 : no.120–f.90/52.
6. E.g.: The husband shall pay the wife a sum of money if he annoys her. *JfMC62*, no.20194.
7. See, e.g., *JfQ1*, p. 164 : no.272–f.66/54 (the stipulation was that if he deserted her children without paying maintenance for them he should pay her IL 300); *AcI3*, p.50:no.12–f.2/57.
8. *NzI4*, p.53:no.1/16–f.27/49.
9. See, e.g., *AcMC62*, no.21226.
10. *JfMC68*, no.10313.
11. *AcṬ2*, p.96; and *AcṬ1*, p.15, respectively. Shaykh Ḥusnī al-Zuᶜbī thought that the payment of compensation to the divorced wife was ensured in advance by a stipulation in the marriage contract. But apart from the references in these two cases, the author has found no confirmation of this in the *sijill*s or marriage registers for the years 1962 and 1968.
12. *JfMC62*, no.20079.
13. *AcṬ3*, p.2; *AcI3*, p.43:no.4–f.9/57.
14. *JfMC62*, no.20069.
15. *AcMC68*, no.3441.
16. *JfMC68*, nos.9515, 10313.
17. This appears from research currently conducted by the author on Muslim religious functionaries in Israel. Anyhow, Yūsuf Dasūqī, Secretary of the *Sharīᶜa* Court of Ṭayyiba, believed that the stipulations in marriage contracts were not framed in accordance with any school but with local custom (*ᶜurf*, *ᶜāda*)—his letter to the author of February 28, 1973. Moreover, the *maᵓdhūn*s who belonged to the Ḥanbalī and Shāfiᶜī schools declared that in matrimonial matters they followed the Ḥanafī school, which corroborated the view that the stipulations were based on custom alone.
18. *ṬbI1*, p.202 : no.24–f.36/62, p.249 : no.5–f.8/64.
19. *JfQ3*, p.370 : no.511–f.80/67 (the wife alleged that she had stipulated at the time of the engagement that the conjugal dwelling should be near to her family in the city and that she had repeated this stipulation when

"she was angry once"). Under modern legislation in Iraq, the wife may demand dissolution of the marriage if the husband fails to fulfil a stipulation of the marriage contract. But this innovation has proved ineffective because the men use various devices in order not to bind themselves by such a stipulation. Among other things, they make separate agreements (outside the marriage contract), the fulfillment of which does not entitle the wife to dissolve the marriage. See el-Naqeb, pp.88, 94.

20. For references see the chapter "Divorce," pp.153 *seq.*
21. *JfQ1,* p.65 : no.104–f.1/52. See also *Ṭb I1,* p.238 : no.26–f.28/63 (the wife sought, through a lawyer, to stipulate that if the husband fell behind with the payment of her maintenance for a week he should have to divorce her).
22. *JfQ1,* p.77 : no.120–f.90/52; *AcṬ1,* p.15; *AcṬ2,* p.96.
23. In the area of jurisdiction of the *Sharīʿa* Court of Jaffa, there were cases where the wife came from an urban and the husband from a rural or Beduin type of settlement.
24. Cf. Anderson, *Jordan,* p.193.
25. *JfMC68,* no.10135 (the couple's address: tent of hair *(bayt al-shaʿr),* Ramla, formerly of the Abū ʿAmār tribe), no.10278 (wife from the ʿArab Jawārīsh housing estate, Ramla).
26. The two isolated cases in which the wife had a post-secondary education were in Little Triangle villages.
27. *JfMC68,* nos.9513, 10284; *ṬbMC68,* nos.8114, 8124; *AcMC68,* nos.2426, 2428. The marriage contract usually stated that the woman was a housewife, but this does not prove that she did not work away from home—in agriculture or some other branch of employment. See Ben-Porath, p.24.
28. See Cohen, p.112.
29. See, e.g., *JfMC68,* no.10277 (the divorced woman made the same stipulations as she had in the earlier contract), no : 10094; *ṬbMC68,* no. 8258; *AcMC68,* nos.1850, 2630, 2848 (divorced woman doing office work).
30. *JfQ1,* p.164:no.272–f.66/54.
31. *AcI3,* p.58 :no.23–f.59/57 (the wife was from Acre, the husband from Majd al-Kurūm village).
32. *ṬbI1,* p.246:no.2–f.4/64.
33. *AI,* vol.10(1967), Nos.3–4, p.18.
34. *AI,* vol.10(1967), Nos.3–4, pp.5, 9, 14.
35. See, e.g., *JfQ4,* p.117 :no.132–f.84/68, p.141 :no.168–f.135/68; *AcD7,* p.13 : f.48/66, p.52 : f.11/67.
36. *JfQ1,* p.65 : no.104–f.1/52.
37. *JfQ3,* p.370 : no.511–f.80/67.
38. Cf. Anderson, *Jordan,* pp.193–4.
39. *AI,* vol.10(1966), Nos.1–2, p.83; see English Summary, *ibid.,* p.6. For more details see the chapter "Dower," p.63.

40. *AI,* vol.9 (1964), Nos.1–2, p.11. See also Advocate Maḥmūd al-Māḍī, *ibid.,* pp.7–8. For more details see the chapter "Divorce," pp.214 *seq.*
41. Shaykh Ḥusnī al-Zuᶜbī's letter to the author of November 22, 1970.
42. *AI,* vol.11 (1968), Nos.1–2, pp.8–10.
43. See the chapter "Dower," pp.62–3.
44. Syrian Personal Status Law of 1953, sec.14. The achievements of the Jordanian Law of Family Rights of 1951 are more modest. See Anderson, *Syria,* pp.35–6; *idem, Jordan,* pp.193–4; Coulson, *History,* p.191. The Iraqi Personal Status Law of 1959 provided that the wife might make a "legal stipulation" in the marriage contract and that its fulfillment should entail dissolution of the marriage on her initiative. But since it is not indicated what a legal stipulation is, the *qāḍī*s find themselves at a loss. They do not, as the legislator expected, apply the Ḥanbalī norm and are careful not to deviate from the Ḥanafī norm in respect of the Sunnites or from the Jaᶜfarī norm in respect of the Shīᶜites. In other words, they act as they did prior to the reform. See el-Naqeb, pp.88, 90, 91, 94. See also Fyzee, pp.119–22.

Chapter Three
DOWER

I. LEGAL BACKGROUND

According to the customary law prevailing before Islam, marriage was the sale of a woman, in return for whom her father or guardian received a dower. Muḥammad changed the wife from a mere object of sale into a party to the marriage contract, enabled her to own property and prescribed that the dower should be given to *her* in return for marital relations[1]; the husband has no status with regard to the dower. Islamic law knows no community of property between spouses. Property relations are based on the principle of separation of the property of husband and wife. Each remains the owner of the property he or she acquired before, in consequence of, or during the marriage and manages it independently.[2] The Ottoman Family Rights Law stresses that the dower belongs to the wife and that she cannot be forced to spend it on the acquisition of *jihāz* (equipment, clothing and household effects). Moreover, the parents and relatives of the bride are forbidden to accept money or any other consideration for giving her in marriage or handing her over to her husband. The wife may deal with the dower in the manner of an owner, transmit it by way of inheritance and perform any act of transfer in respect of it.[3]

According to the Ḥanafī school of law, the minimum dower payable to the wife is ten dirhams. In view of the small purchasing power of this sum, the Ottoman legislator, relying on the Ḥanbalī school of law, ignored this question completely.[4] The Family Rights Law distinguishes between a specified (*musammā*) dower, stipulated in the marriage contract, and a fair (*mithl*) dower, equal to that of another woman of her father's kin similar to the bride in social status and personal (physical and moral) qualities or, in the absence of such a woman, equal to the dower of residents of her locality. In accordance with the Ḥanafī school, the law provides that the specified dower may be wholly or partly paid as a prompt dower (*mahr muʿajjal*), that is, dower payable immediately on marriage, or after a time. Where no date has been fixed for its payment, it is assumed to be payable on divorce or on the death of one of the parties as a deferred dower (*mahr muʾajjal*). The amount of the dower due to the woman depends on the type of dower (specified or fair), the type of marriage (*ṣaḥīḥ*, valid, or *fāsid*, irregular), on whether the marriage has been consumated, and the like. Thus, for instance, if in the case of a valid marriage the amount has not been agreed on, and divorce takes place before valid privacy (*khalwa ṣaḥīḥa*), the woman is entitled to *mutʿa,* an indemnity fixed in accordance with custom, consisting of a set of clothing, provided that its value does not exceed half the amount of the fair dower.[5] The marital bond requires the husband to pay his wife the dower, but the dower is not a condition of the validity of that bond. If the prompt dower has not been paid, the wife is not bound to share the husband's dwelling and may refrain from intercourse with him, provided the marriage has not been consummated.[6]

The Knesset has not intervened in the matter of the dower in any way. Section 2 of the Women's Equal Rights Law was implicitly intended to make Jewish women capable of owning and disposing of property and to introduce for them the system of separation of the property of the spouses.[7] These reforms brought nothing new to Muslim married women.[8] In 1966, the Knesset debated a private member's bill designed to prohibit the taking of a dower exceeding IL 50. The bill was rejected.[9]

II. PROMPT DOWER

The prompt dower has increased enormously since the establishment of the State of Israel in 1948, as the Tables I and II indicate. In the two decades from 1950 to 1969, the average prompt dower increased from IL 230 to IL 3,700, that is, about sixteenfold. Even allowing for the decline in the purchasing power of the Israel pound, it is no overstatement to say that the dower went up by leaps and bounds. Using the consumer price index as a measure of the real increase of the dower, it works out at 300%.[10] Rosenfeld found that the real value of the dower in the villages was two-and-a-half times as great in the early 1960s as compared with 30 to 40 years earlier. Y. Ben-Porath found that in the decade from 1950 to 1961 the dower increased faster than

TABLE I: AVERAGE PROMPT DOWER BY DISTRICTS AND SUBDISTRICTS SELECTED YEARS, 1950–61[a]

District and Subdistrict	Average Amount of Dower in IL 1950	1955	1958	1961
National Average	229	1,187	1,603	1,974
Northern District	237	1,160	1,486	2,666
Safad Subdistrict	–	–	1,762	2,064
Kinneret Subdistrict	222	1,362	1,486	1,847
Jezreel Subdistrict	218	1,199	1,552	2,068
Acre Subdistrict	250	1,088	1,427	2,066
Haifa District	257	1,400	1,792	1,923
Haifa Subdistrict	–	1,130	1,838	2,095
Hadera Subdistrict	257	1,500	1,785	2,451
Central District	200	1,315	1,880	2,405
Sharon Subdistrict	211	1,396	1,764	3,031
Petah Tikva Subdistrict	163	1,195	2,545	–
Ramla Subdistrict	170	980	1,346	1,870
Rehovot Subdistrict	–	–	1,000	–
Tel Aviv-Jaffa District	171	708	1,386	1,400
Jerusalem District	238	836	1,433	1,381
Southern District	–	–	–	–
Ashkelon Subdistrict	–	–	1,500	–
Beersheba Subdistrict	–	–	1,315	2,188

a) Data of the Central Bureau of Statistics, as published (with slight variations) in *AI*, vol.5(1957), Nos.1–2, pp.23–4; *AI*, vol.7(1959), Nos.2–3, p.35; *AI*, vol.8(1963), Nos.3–4, p.34; *Marriages, 1957–1958*, p.54.

the gross national product per capita: its average annual increase was 8.8% as against 5.5% annual increase of the gross national product in the years 1950–1960.[11] This was due to the improvement of the economic situation in Israeli Muslim society. The phenomenon is especially striking in the villages of the Central District and in the Hadera Subdistrict of the Haifa District, i.e., in the villages of the Little

TABLE II: AVERAGE PROMPT DOWER BY TYPE OF BRIDE'S SETTLEMENT SELECTED YEARS, 1960–69[a]

Type of Bride's Settlement	Average amount of Dower in IL				
	1960	1962	1965[c]	1967	1969[d]
National Average	1,196	2,341	3,114	3,267	3,654
Urban National Average	1,088	2,079	2,596	2,411	2,469
Nazareth and Shafā ʿAmr	–	2,338	2,537	2,080	2,558
Mixed Towns	845	1,796	2,687	2,671	2,273
Jewish Settlements	–	2,900	1,000	2,740	5,333[e]
Rural National Average	1,221	2,405	3,195	3,383	3,826
Northern District	1,088	2,344	3,191	3,329	3,860
Haifa District	1,426	2,466	3,236	3,738	3,737
Central District	1,526	2,642	3,702	3,509	4,239
Ṭayyiba and Umm al-Faḥm[b]	–	–	–	2,963	3,399
Jerusalem District	2,167	2,220	2,824	2,667	4,000[f]
Beduin National Average	–	–	–	–	4,436
Negev	1,756	2,344	3,110	4,416	4,632
Galilee	144	2,224	2,979	3,612	3,727

a) Data of the Central Bureau of Statistics, as published (with slight variations) in *AI*, vol.8 (1962), Nos.1–2, p.16; *AI*, vol.9 (1964), Nos.1–2, p.49; *AI*, Nos.3–4, p.24; *AI*, vol.10 (1966), Nos. 1–2, p.93; *AI*, vol.12 (1970), Nos.1–2, p.54 (variations in accordance with unpublished data of the Bureau).

b) These two villages are treated as urban settlements under the new classification.

c) See also *Vital Stats., 1965; 1966*, p.62, where there are slight differences from the material published in *AI*, due to different definitions of the settlements.

d) Based on unpublished data of the Central Bureau of Statistics. See also *AI*, vol.12 (1971), Nos.3–4, p.67 (amounts rounded off; differences due to different definitions of the settlements).

e) Based on the average of three cases.

f) Based on one case.

Triangle.[12] Throughout the period the average amount of the dower was higher in the villages than in the towns, and highest in the villages of the Central District, where in 1969 it was IL 4,200 as against a national average of IL 2,500 in urban settlements and of IL 3,800 in rural settlements.[13] The differences in the amount of the dower in the Northern and Haifa Districts are without significance. The amount for Ṭayyiba and Umm al-Faḥm, IL 3,400, was considerably smaller than that for the Central District.

The amounts of the prompt dower in the towns were the lowest in the whole country throughout the period under review; in the mixed towns, the amount was smaller than in Nazareth and Shafā ʿAmr—IL 2,300 as against IL 2,600.[14] This seems to be mainly due to the deferred dower customary in the towns: its amounts were inversely proportional to those of the prompt dower.[15]

The most impressive discovery is that of the large amounts of prompt dower among the Beduin. In fact, in recent years, the amounts among the Negev Beduin have approximated and even exeeded those in the villages of the Central District; in 1969, the respective figures were IL 4,600 and IL 4,200. The average amounts among the Galilee Beduin exceeded those in the towns and in recent years have not been much smaller, and sometimes even larger, than the average for all types of rural settlements; the respective figures are IL 3,600 and IL 3,400 for 1967 and IL 3,700 and IL 3,800 for 1969.[16] It should, of course, be remembered that the registration of marriages among the Beduin was not complete, and it may be assumed that the amounts of dower were larger in the case of registered marriages than in the case of marriages performed in accordance with custom, without resort to the *maʾdhūn,* on the fringe of Beduin society. In 1969, 191 marriages were registered among Negev Beduin and 53 among Galilee Beduin. The average dower thus reflects the position as to a relatively small, unrepresentative sample of marriages and so quantitative conclusions should be guarded against.

Nevertheless, there can be no doubt that these data are significant and that there is one basic fact which accounts for them: the registered marriages were largely those of members of the ruling class in Beduin society: shaykhs, heads of clans and tribes. Marx, in his study on the Negev Beduin, notes that the shaykhs frequently contracted short-term marriages (in addition to polygamous unions) in order to have more children.[17] The economic position of the Beduin shaykhs in the Negev was among the best of any section of Israeli Muslim society. They had grown rich in various ways since the establishment of the State. Hundreds of thousands of dunams of land in the areas where the Negev Beduin were concentrated had been leased to the farmers among them through the intermediary of the tribal chiefs; large amounts of drought compensation were until recent years paid to the shaykhs; they enjoyed what amounts to a monopoly on agricultural machinery (tractors etc.)[18];

they maintained close relations with real estate dealers and various agrictultural companies; moreover, there were certain highly lucrative pursuits traditionally engaged in in this transit zone. Since the shaykhs, the tribal chiefs, served as *maʾdhūn*s in their tribes, it may be assumed that they also registered their own frequent marriages, for which they paid large sums as prompt dower. Large sums are also not unexpected in view of the fact that the Negev Beduin quite often married town girls, for whom they paid handsomely. There is much evidence of this in the marriage contract registers and in the *sijill*s.[19]

The dower was usually paid in money,[20] sometimes by instalments, and by means of promisory notes.[21] It might take the form of a plot of land, an olive grove, or a vegetable garden (*ḥakūra*), a house,[22] or livestock.[23] The wife frequently inserted in the marriage contract stipulations (*shurūṭ*) to the effect that the husband must give her various household articles (*athāth*, *ʿafsh al-bayt*), such as furniture and bedding, or jewelry and ornaments (*ḥaly*, *maṣāgh*), a room of a house, livestock and the like; the things themselves were likewise referred to as stipulations. Such stipulations were part of,[24] or additional to, the prompt dower.[25] The wife was sometimes careful to note that they were *her* property. The monetary value of the stipulations was occasionally indicated alongside the prompt and deferred dowers and included in the total amount of the dower.[26] The Central Bureau of Statistics estimates that the custom of indicating the monetary value was much more widespread than is reflected in the marriage contracts and that it mainly related to gold coins and gold jewelry.[27] The marriage contract registers of 1968 show more than 130 stipulations, which constitute about 70% of all stipulations inserted in marriage contracts in that year. Stipulations were especially customary in mixed towns and in the Little Triangle villages—more than in villages in other areas. The author did not come across a single instance of such stipulations among Negev or Galilee Beduin.

The Central Bureau of Statistics, which had examined this question both by interview and in the marriage contracts, found that it was usually the wife who had to bring the household effects and the bedding and that the stipulations in marriage contracts imposing this duty on the husband were contrary to accepted practice.[28] From research and various sources it is known that the practice with regard to the purchase of household effects, jewelry and clothing varied from place to place. According to one view, it was customary for a woman to leave her father's house and join her husband with the *jihāz*, which included bedding and various utensils.[29] Rosenfeld found that part of the prompt dower which did not remain with the bride's father was expended on the requirements of the young couple.[30] A survey in Nazareth in 1965 revealed that prompt dower was not as common in that town as in the the villages but that, on the other hand, the economic demands made by the bride's family in return for its consent to the marriage were much weightier than the dower payments; an appartment and most modern conveniences had to be assured prior to the marriage.[31]

It was customary for the groom to pay the prompt dower at or before the drawing up of the marriage contract. There were differences in this respect between different types of settlement. In 1968, prompt dower was paid in full in four-fifths of the marriages contracted in the towns (including Ṭayyiba and Umm al-Faḥm) as against two-thirds in the villages (including Beduin settlements in the Negev and in Galilee). It was partly paid in 13% of the marriages in the towns as against 9% in the villages, and it was not paid at all in 8% of the marriages contracted in the towns as against one-quarter of the marriages in the villages.[32] It seems that in the towns the wife and her family were more insistent about receiving the whole or part of the prompt dower than in the villages or in Beduin society. At the same time, the mode of paying the prompt dower was essentially a custom varying from place to place.[33]

The *sijill*s contain a fair amount of evidence of women not receiving the whole or part of the prompt dower. The fact emerges at the hearing of actions for maintenance, obedience, divorce and the like.[34] A woman might allege that she had not received the prompt dower although her husband would assert that he gave it to her.[35] There was sometimes a discrepancy between the amount indicated in the marriage contract and that claimed by the wife.[36] All the foregoing shows that although the wife was careful to stipulate her rights to prompt dower in the marriage contract and usually in fact obtained it, there were cases when it was not paid, and it might happen that the wife sought to realize her right years after the marriage, sometimes at the very moment of divorce. The parties might agree at the time of the marriage that the prompt dower should be paid a specified time after the signing of the marriage contract.[37] Sometimes a divorced woman was entitled to half the specified dower or waived this right; this refers to cases where a divorce was performed before consummation of the marriage or valid privacy. Hence it may be deduced that a woman was not always ready to move into her husband's house before the prompt dower had been paid to her.[38]

There is a definite connection between dower customs and the type of marriage, especially exchange marriage (*tabādul al-zawjāt*, *shighār*). The *raison d'être* of this institution is the mutual waiver of the dower for the two exchanged women. According to customary law, each of the two women constitutes the substance (*ᶜayn*) of the dower of the other. This type of marriage creates a mutual dependence between the two women and is very injurious to family life. Islam sought to eradicate exchange marriage indirectly by laying down that the dower belonged to the wife; according to the Ḥanafī school, where no dower was agreed on at the time of the marriage, each of the two exchanged wives was entitled to a fair dower. In other words, the exchange marriage was incorporated into Islamic law and at the same time distorted and emptied of its main content.[39] But social custom is stronger than religious law. In many of the approximately 100 exchange marriages which the author came across in the *sijill*s,[40] the two women received no dower. Thus, in one case, it was stated in court that a girl had been given to a man, in a gift (*ᶜaṭāʾ*) marriage, by way of exchange for the man's sister, who was given to the girl's brother, without anything being paid to either bride. In another case, in which the husband demanded that his wife should obey him, the wife replied that she was prepared to do so if her exchange partner (*badīla*) did likewise or, alternatively, if she received her dower.[41] Of course, it was usual to indicate in the marriage contracts identical amounts of dower for the two brides, but it seems that this was a fiction and that in reality the two dowers cancelled each other out. Thus, in one case, the *maʾdhūn* testified that no dower had been paid in his presence although identical amounts of dower had been indicated in the marriage contracts.[42] In another case, a woman renounced the whole (including the deferred) dower on divorce, alleging that she had not received the prompt dower—"not one mil"—because it had been an exchange marriage.[43] The wife's renunciation of the dower on divorce by mutual consent was frequent in exchange marriages and may support the assumption that she did not really receive the prompt dower at the time the marriage was contracted.[44]

At the same time, there is evidence, though not much, of exchanged wives receiving all or part of the dower. Thus, in one case, two such wives were divorced on the same day and it was decided that each should receive the balance of the prompt dower, since the total prompt dowers had not been received at the signing of the marriage contracts. In another case, it was noted in the marriage contract that the wife's father had received half the dower on contraction of the marriage and that it had been stipulated that the husband should pay a certain sum as deferred dower. In a further case of divorce by agreement between the parties to an exchange marriage, it was stated that the wife had received the whole dower at the time of contraction of the marriage and that the husband had waived its return.[45] In several cases, the marriages of the two couples were not consummated and the exchanged wives waived half the dower, from which it may perhaps be concluded that they had received one-half.[46] In one case, one of the wives was divorced, while her *badīla* received the prompt dower and remained with her husband.[47] Payment of dower to one of the exchanged wives infringes the principle of equality of treatment for them; the dissolution of the marriage of one of the couples does not automatically entail the dissolution of the marriage of the other.[48] It might happen that instead of the dower the wife was given or promised its equivalent in clothing (*jihāz*), jewelry (*maṣāgh*), household effects and the like.[49]

Many researchers have found that in marriages of paternal cousins the dower was smaller than in exogamous marriages.[50] The author came across only one express testimony to a reduction of the dower under these circumstances. A witness testified in court that the girl's father had said: "I allow my brother's son a reduction of IL 200 [on a dower of IL 2,500]."[51] The author did indeed come across many cases of dissolution of cousin marriages by consent of the parties where the wife waived both the prompt and deferred dowers,[52] as well as cases where the dower was not mentioned at all in the terms of divorce,[53] but such phenomena were not peculiar to cousin marriages and do not permit the conclusion that this type of marriage had any effect on the amount or mode of payment of the dower.

According to religious law, as stated, the dower belongs to the wife. To what extent did she enjoy this property right in practice? An exhaustive reply to this question cannot be obtained from the sources because a woman was generally given in marriage by a marriage guardian, who might be her father or brother or another relative, and who received the dower on her behalf.[54] Hence, it cannot be ascertained whether the dower was given to the bride or what became of it. At the same time, scattered evidence permits one at least to say that the wife did not always enjoy this right. Sometimes a woman declared in court, during the hearing of some matrimonial matter, that the dower had been given to her father or brother.[55] In several cases, a woman alleged that she had not received the whole or part of the dower, and afterward it appeared that her father had received it without her knowledge.[56] In one case, a woman alleged that she had received the dower, and afterward it appeared that her father had received it.[57] In another case, the dower was given to the woman, who declared before the court that she was making it over to her father as a *sharᶜī* gift (*hiba*) and was not allowed to revoke this act.[58] There is also express evidence of husbands taking control of their wives' dower without their consent. In one case, the husband took back the whole dower and spent it on his farm and on medical treatment for himself. In other cases, he reassumed possession of a plot of land or of some goats or olive trees that had been given the wife as part of the dower.[59]

On the other hand, there is a great deal of evidence in marriage contracts of women receiving the dower either directly or through a marriage-guardian. When a woman married without a guardian, she took the dower herself. This was usually a widowed or divorced woman,[60] but sometimes even a spinster married without a guardian and the dower was given her without an intermediary.[61] There is evidence also in the *sijill*s of women receiving the dower from their guardians after the marriage, or "through" their guardians, but it is not always certain that they actually got it.[62] In one case, a man alleged that his deceased wife's father had appropriated her estate (dower and gifts) and asked that it be distributed in accordance with *sharᶜī* rules, whence it may be deduced that in the wife's lifetime the dower was in her possession.[63]

There is a great deal of evidence of women insisting on their rights to dower and the stipulations connected with it. In many cases, women left their husbands' houses on the ground that they had not been paid the whole or part of the dower and that the *jihāz* and various stipulations connected with the dower, such as household effects and jewelry and other ornaments, had not been delivered to them; they refused to return until they had received these things and in the meantime they claimed maintenance from their husbands. In one case, a woman of Jaffa contended that the household effects "belonged to her personally and were bound up with the dower in accordance with accepted custom." She also alleged that the husband had given her two radio sets, a piano and other articles, but had not yet registered them in her name. She asked the court to decide that these articles were hers and that her husband be forbidden to use them without her consent.[64] As stated, the wife sometimes refused from the outset to move into the husband's house before she had received the dower, but it seems that as a rule she wished to realize her right to dower after the marriage had been consummated and offspring born. Non-payment of the whole or part of the dower was a frequent cause of divorce on the wife's initiative. Instances of the wife's struggle for realization of her property rights were common in urban and rural, but not in Beduin, society.[65]

Most of the women who married without a guardian and received dower directly came from urban types of settlement, especially from mixed towns,[66] and the same applies in cases where the dower was given through a guardian. There is less evidence of rural women receiving dower, and the author found only one instance of a woman being given dower in Beduin society (in Galilee).[67] These findings are confirmed by other sources. Rosenfeld found that among the Muslims of Ṭurᶜān 40% of the dower was given to the wife for the purchase of clothing and gold and the remainder was left to her father. Cohen found that in 56% of the cases surveyed in a sampling carried out in the late 1950s in the village of Bint al-Ḥudūd, the dower was given to the wife's father or brother and that the wife was sometimes given monetary compensation by the person who had taken the dower.[68] Yūsuf Dasūqī, Secretary of the *Sharīᶜa* Court of Ṭayyiba, reported in 1965 that the practice of the bride's father pocketing the dower was diminishing in the Little Triangle villages. Fathers, except the very poor, wished to help the young couple at its first steps and therefore generally returned the dowers to the daughters.[69] Marx notes that among the Negev Beduin the whole or the largest part of the dower was given to the bride's father or brother.[70] G. Kressel found that in the ᶜArab Jawārīsh housing project in the Ramla municipal area many fathers returned the whole or part of the dower in the form of gold jewelry or furnishings for the daughter's home.[71] In a survey conducted in Nazareth in 1965, it appeared that in most cases the dower was given to the daughter for her personal requirements and for domestic arrangements and did not remain with her father.[72] Shaykh Muḥammad Ḥubayshī reported that in Acre it was usual for the daughter to receive the whole dower, while in rural areas the father took part of it and used the remainder to buy her jewelry and clothes.[73] There are also indications—though not in the *sijill*s—that beside the dower, the institution of the dowry (the contribution of the bride's father to the marriage) was spreading. Rosenfeld found such indications in several places.[74]

What did the wife do with the dower she received? The author could discover information as to this in only one instance. A woman who had married at the beginning of the 20th century had received 5,000 Turkish Kurush as dower, partly in cash and partly in the shape of seven olive trees; with the cash she had bought gold coins, for which her husband had sold her six olive trees in the village.[75]

III. DEFERRED DOWER

Deferred dower (*mahr muʾajjal*) and its proportion to the whole dower are not matters of law but of custom recognized by the Ḥanafī school. If the deferred dower was of a considerable amount, it might deter the husband from hasty or arbitrary divorce and also give a certain measure of economic security to the wife after divorce,[76] for according to the *sharīʿa* she is only entitled to maintenance during the *ʿidda* (the waiting-period of a woman after termination of the marriage), which is normally three months.[77] According to the testimony of Shaykh Muḥammad Ḥubayshī, it was then usual to regard the deferred dower as the wife's insurance policy. In several cases, the wife, on contraction of the marriage or subsequently, demanded that the deferred dower should be increased.[78] In functional respect, there is thus a distinct material difference between prompt and deferred dowers.

Until recently, deferred dower was not an object of study[79]; this was chiefly on account of its rarity. It was not accounted in the sense that its realization was a matter for the future. Table III shows that deferred dower was not particularly frequent in Israeli Muslim society.

Nearly 60% of the national total of marriages were concluded without deferred dower. At the same time, there are noticeable differences in the frequency of this practice between and even within the various ecological groups. Deferred dower was particularly frequent in urban society: more than three-quarters of the total number of cases. It was more usual in mixed than in purely Arab towns: 87% as against 69%. In rural society it was comparatively rare: one-quarter of the total number of cases; there were no significant differences between villages in different areas. The frequency of the deferred dower in the large villages of Ṭayyiba and Umm al-Faḥm (12%) was below the national average. Surprisingly enough, it was widespread among the Negev Beduin. Although caution is required in evaluating the phenomenon there

TABLE III: MUSLIM MARRIAGES WITHOUT DEFERRED DOWER IN 1969 BY TYPE OF BRIDE'S SETTLEMENT[a]

Type of Bride's Settlement	Total Number of Marriages	Marriages without Deferred Dower Number	% (rounded off)
National Total	1,910	1,117	58
Total Urban	355	83	23
Nazareth and Shafā ʿAmr	212	65	31
Mixed Towns	143	18	13
Total Rural	1,295	981	76
Northern District	712	541	76
Haifa District	278	230	83
Central District[a]	304	210	69
Jerusalem District	1		
Total Beduin Tribes	244	53	23
Negev	191	3	2
Galilee	53	50	94

a) Including Ṭayyiba and Umm al-Faḥm.

on the basis of percentage figures,[80] there can be no doubt that its extent was significant: it occurred in almost all the marriages performed by the *maʾdhūn*. This seems mainly to be due to marriages between Beduin and women from mixed towns—as is also the case with large amounts of prompt dower.

Considerable differences between the various types of settlement (urban, rural, and Beduin), and within each type, existed also with regard to the amounts of deferred dower, as is illustrated in Table IV. The amounts of the deferred dowers were larger in towns than in villages—IL 2,700 as against IL 950—and slightly larger in mixed towns than in Nazareth and Shafā ʿAmr. The rural sector showed striking differences in different districts. The amounts of deferred dower were smallest in Ṭayyiba, Umm al-Faḥm and the villages of the Haifa District (about IL 400) and largest (IL 2,700) in the Central District of the Little Triangle, where they approximated to the average of the mixed towns

TABLE IV: AVERAGE AMOUNTS OF PROMPT DOWER AND DEFERRED DOWER IN 1969 BY TYPE OF BRIDE'S SETTLEMENT[a]

Type of Bride's Settlement	Average Amount of Dower in IL		
	Prompt	Deferred	Ratio of Prompt to Deferred Dower
Overall National Average	3,654	1,247	2.9
National Average, Urban	2,469	2,694	0.8
Nazareth and Shafā ʿAmr	2,558	2,660	0.9
Mixed Towns	2,273	2,767	0.8
Jewish Settlements	5,333[b]	1,667	
National Average, Rural	3,826	943	4.0
Northern District	3,860	855	4.5
Haifa District	3,737	439	8.2
Central District	4,239	2,727	1.5
Ṭayyiba and Umm al-Faḥm	3,399	421	8.0
Jerusalem District	4,000	4,500[c]	
Beduin National Average	4,436	694	6.2
Negev	4,632	822	5.6
Galilee	3,727	231	16.1

a) Derived from unpublished data of the Central Bureau of Statistics.
b) Based on three cases.
c) Based on one case.

The deferred dower was smallest among the Beduin (IL 700), but three-and-a-half times as large among the Negev Beduin as among the Galilee Beduin (IL 820 as against IL 230, approximately equal to that customary in the villages of the Northern District), which was probably due to the sizeable representation of shaykhs in registered marriages.

On the national average, the prompt dower was about three times as large as the deferred dower (IL 3,600 as against IL 1,200), but there were differences as to the ratio of the two kinds of dower between and within the various types of settlement. In the towns, the deferred dower slightly exceeded the prompt dower (IL 2,700 as against IL 2,500). On the other hand, in the villages and among the Beduin, the prompt dower was four and six times, respectively, as large as the deferred dower; the gap was particularly wide in the villages of the Haifa District and in Ṭayyiba and Umm al-Faḥm (eight times) and among the Galilee Beduin (16 times).[81] In the Little Triangle villages, the prompt dower exceeded the deferred dower by only 50%; the ratio between the two kinds of dower was here nearest to that customary in the towns. The two kinds of dower were inversely proportional: the larger the deferred dower, the smaller the prompt dower, and vice versa. This is clearly apparent in all types of settlement. In the mixed towns were found the largest deferred dowers side by side with the smallest prompt dowers: IL 2,800 as against IL 2,300, and among the Beduin, the smallest deferred dowers alongside the largest prompt dowers: IL 700 as against IL 4,400. Exceptions to this rule were the Little Triangle villages (not including Ṭayyiba and Umm al-Faḥm), where the amounts of deferred and prompt dower were the largest in the country: IL 2,700 as against IL 4,200.

The negative correlation between prompt and deferred dower arose from different conceptions of the function of dower. In the villages and in Beduin society, where the traditional conception was still very much alive, the amount of deferred dower was but a small fraction of that of prompt dower. In the towns, where women's freedom is greatest, the idea that the main object of the dower is economic security for divorced and widowed women was gaining ground, and as a result, deferred dower was eclipsing prompt dower to the extent of reducing it to a mere token payment. In the Little Triangle villages, which had enjoyed increasing prosperity since the late 1950s, the two conceptions, the traditional and the modern, seemed to exist side by side, which probably accounts for the large amounts of both prompt and deferred dower. Rather surprisingly, in Ṭayyiba and Umm al-Faḥm, two of the most developed and progressive villages in Israel, a small deferred dower was found beside a large prompt dower (IL 400 as against IL 3,400).

The negative correlation between the two kinds of dower becomes clear if the dower is viewed in connection with women's education, one of the accepted criteria of their social liberation.[82] Table V shows that where the wife was completely uneducated the prompt dower was largest and the deferred dower smallest: IL 4,000 as against IL 600, whereas in the case of a woman with a secondary education the prompt dower was smallest and the deferred dower largest: IL 2,900 as against

TABLE V: AVERAGES OF PROMPT AND DEFERRED DOWERS IN 1969 BY NUMBER OF YEARS OF SCHOOLING OF THE BRIDE [a]

Number of Years of Schooling	Average Amount of Dower in IL		Ratio of Prompt to Deferred Dower
	Prompt	Deferred	
Overall Average	3,654	1,247	2.9
0	3,964	626	6.3
1–4	3,923	948	4.1
5–8	3,365	1,712	1.9
9–12	2,941	3,145	0.9
13+[b]	4,333	1,667	2.5

a) Derived from unpublished data of the Central Bureau of Statistics.
b) The averages in this group are based on six cases.

IL 3,100. The gap between the two kinds of dower narrowed the better the woman's education: where she had had no schooling at all, the prompt dower was six times or more the amount of the deferred dower, and where she had had nine to 12 years of schooling, the two dowers were almost equal.

An anomaly exists with regard to the relation between dower and higher education of the wife: the prompt dower was largest (IL 4,300) and the deferred dower comparatively small (IL 1,700). Although caution is needed in drawing conclusions as to this group in view of the small number of cases, it may be significant that both the smallest[83] and the largest amounts of prompt dower were to be found here (the median prompt dower being IL 750 in 1966 and IL 4,500 in 1969). This phenomenon may be due to the bride's family background. A woman with a higher education is likely to be among the most liberated socially—to have adopted (and imparted to her family) the modern conception of the choice of the marriage partner and the function of the dower, but on the other hand, she may belong to a prominent, wealthy family which has preserved the traditional approach to marriage; such families tend to be punctilious about social origin and economic status, one of the symbols of which is the fair dower. Some researchers have already noticed that upper-class women tend to be less liberated than their middle-class sisters.[84]

IV. THE PROBLEM OF EXCESSIVE DOWER

The problem of the soaring dower never ceased to exercise the Muslim public, and some considered it "the most serious problem facing a Muslim youth in Israel on reaching maturity."[85] The young men complained that they had to incur heavy debts, at usurious interest, or work for years to save up money for the dower, the gifts for the bride and her family, the wedding festivities and the dwelling with all the necessary equipment. Especial criticism was levelled at the increase of the dower in the Little Triangle villages: it was contended that fathers sold their daughters like cattle to the highest bidder, that young men had to forego their betrothed because the fathers had withdrawn their consent to the marriages and demanded exorbitant dowers.[86] As a result of all this, the young men were utterly bewildered. Some of them accused the Government of encouraging the prevailing practice in order to limit the Arab birth-rate. The marriage rate in Muslim society was generally on the decline: it had dropped from eight per mille in 1953 to six per mille in 1968, and in some years, there had even been an absolute decline in the number of marriages.[87] One of the causes of this phenomenon was the enormous increase in the prompt dower.[88]

The young men reacted to this irksome problem in different ways. According to one, there were three courses open to them: old bachelorhood, theft (to finance the dower), or abduction of the girl of their choice. Some of them had threatened to declare a marriage strike "in order that the fathers might learn a lesson and let them marry their daughters free of charge."[89] There were several criminal cases and acts of despair in this connection.[90] Many had asked the Ministry of Religious Affairs to intervene, for example, by introducing criminal legislation to prohibit excessive dower.[91]

The first organized expression of the young men's point of view occurred early in 1960. Intellectuals from the Little Triangle villages held a meeting in Ṭayyiba to create an organizational framework for a movement to fight excessive dower. One of the leaders of this movement, ᶜAbd al-Salām Yūsuf Maṣārwa, opened the conference "in the name of Allāh and tortured humanity, which collapses under the yoke of reaction" and read out letters of encouragement from Shaykh Mūsā al-Ṭabarī and from Knesset Members and other public figures, Muslim and non-Muslim. The local *imām* quoted passages denouncing excessive dower from the Qurʾān and *ḥadīth*s (formal traditions) attributed to the Prophet.

The young men made it clear that they did not intend to abolish dower altogether, since it was ordained by religion, but to reduce it to token proportions. They demanded that it should be limited by legislation to a minimal amount. A young teacher asked excitedly "How can such a disgraceful trade [in daughters] be carried on in the 20th century, the era of the conquest of space?" The meeting decided to convene a national Muslim conference to discuss measures for a reduction of the dower, and to conduct a large-scale propaganda campaign in the press and at local, regional and national meetings. A second rally of the movement took place soon afterward on a Friday at the mosque of Kafr Qāsim, when the villagers were urged to content themselves with a token dower after the manner of the Prophet and the Caliphs and to contribute to a fund to finance the activities of the movement. Following this rally, ᶜAbd al-Salām estimated that "our victory is near, for among the Muslim public, and especially the intelligentzia, support and solidarity are forthcoming which in part already found practical expression at Kafr Qāsim." About two months later, a national rally was held at the Israel Labor Federation's club in Jaffa, attended by youths from Galilee, the Little Triangle, Jaffa and Ramla. For the first time, girls had been invited to take part actively in discussing means to reduce the dower. The rally was under the patronage of Shaykh Ṭāhir Ḥamād.[92] The movement continued its activities for some time longer. Thus, for instance, the Minister of Religious Affairs was asked to ensure, by criminal legislation, full freedom for women in the choice of their spouses, to assist in a large-scale propaganda campaign among the general public, and to urge that the *qāḍī*s support the movement both materially and morally.[93]

However, the great enthusiasm that had seized the public subsided quickly. ᶜAbd al-Salām emigrated to the United States, and so ended the movement. From time to time, young people attempted to revive it, as in Majd al-Kurūm in 1965, but afterward feelings cooled again.[94] The expected response from wide sections of the public and assistance from the Government did not materialize.[95] The Minister of Religious Affairs did not bring in a bill to limit the amount of the dower. On the contrary, he strongly opposed the initiative of Knesset Member U. Avneri, whose private member's bill entitled the Prohibition of Dower Bill, 5726–1966, was designed to impose a penal sanction for taking dower of a value exceeding IL 50. Mr. Avneri thought that the problem could not be solved by public action but only by legislation, as according to him had been done by the revolutionary regime in Egypt.[96] The Knesset rejected the bill. The Minister of Religious Affairs based its rejection on social, legal and practical considerations. In his opinion, limiting dower by legislation would not have stood the test of reality and the law would have been ridiculed; the problem could only be solved by a change in social habits. He added that Knesset intervention would produce angry reactions from the Arab states and Israel would be accused of attacking the *sharīʿa*. Knesset Member ʿAbd al-ʿAziz al-Zuʿbī denounced excessive dower, but expressed the view that it should not be combatted by legislation forbidding something permitted by the Qurʾān and warned that there might be those who would say that "the Jews want to change the Qurʾān."[97]

Though the movement for the fight against excessive dower did not succeed in getting the Knesset to introduce prohibitive or restrictive legislation, it probably contributed, by influencing public opinion, to the speeding-up of far-reaching changes in dower practices in Israeli Muslim society. There is evidence of a number of instances of token prompt dower, usually amounting to IL 10, alongside deferred dower running into thousands of pounds, sometimes IL 10,000 or more.[98] This arrangement placed no financial obstacle in the way of marriage, and on the other hand provided a deterrent to arbitrary divorce, and was a means to ensure the wife's subsistence in the event of divorce or the husband's death. Still, the token prompt dower might become meaningless, for the husband sometimes undertook in the marriage contract to give the wife, in addition to the prompt dower, various household effects, high-quality furniture for their dwelling, jewelry, and occasionally even an appartment or house, of an aggregate value exceeding the average amount of the prompt dower. Thus, in one case, the prompt dower was IL 5, but in addition, the wife received a fully appointed house worth IL 15,000 and was, moreover, promised a deferred dower of IL 10,000.[99] From the point of view of the husband, this arrangement was thus not always advantageous. But neither was it from the point of view of the wife: instead of the prompt dower, which passed into her ownership for her own exclusive use, she received its equivalent in property used by the whole family. In places where custom required the husband to provide the household effects at his own expense, the wife was deprived in that they were bought with her money.

Though not particularly frequent, the token prompt dower seems to have become established in Israeli Muslim society. In 1968, it occurred in about 140 marriages, i.e., about 7% of the total number, in amounts up to IL 10, but there were remarkable differences in this respect between different types of settlement. About one-fifth of the marriages in towns involved token prompt dower, as against approximately 4% in villages.[100] Token dower was a recent phenomenon (since the mid–1950s), found especially in Acre, or where at least the bride was from that town, among intellectuals and members of relatively prestigious callings[101]; the author came across some instances also in exchange marriages.[102] In such cases, token prompt dower met the demands of both social custom and religious law.

Since the early 1960s, a new practice has emerged in Israeli Muslim society: marriage with no dower at all, prompt or deferred. The press gave great prominence to "the first case" of this kind in Mazraᶜa village near Acre. The bride's family agreed to take no dower from the groom, a member of the "Arab pioneer youth," and the *qāḍī* did not believe his ears. This was regarded as "an historic precedent in the fight against excessive dower."[103] Thirteen dowerless marriages took place in 1968, all in urban types of settlement.[104] Instead of paying dower, the groom probably bought household effects, clothes and the like for the bride with his own money, as he often did in cases of token prompt dower.

Militating against renunciation of the dower were not only consideration of finance, but also of status and prestige. A small dower, let alone the total lack of dower, was apt to impair a woman's standing, which was identified with the family honor (*ᶜird*).[105] This notion underlay the fair dower, i.e., the dower to be given to a woman according to her value by criteria of a traditional society. There is evidence of dozens of girls imploring families to forego the dower and let them marry the penniless boys they loved and not some wealthy old man, and quite often the family would have been ready to comply but for the fear that this would mean a loss of face.[106] To overcome this obstacle, the bride and her family sometimes contributed to the dower or even paid the whole of it or secretly returned it to the groom after he had paid it in the presence of many people.[107] Methods of circumventing the dower with the consent of the girl but against the will of the family included the borrowing of equipment and jewelry, to be returned to the owners after the marriage,[108] and the abduction of the bride.[109] Informed persons pointed out a further way of circumventing the problem: marriage to Jewish and Christian girls. Such marriages had the added advantage of providing educated brides, who were in great demand in

Muslim society.[110] Marriages between Muslim men and non-Muslim women (but not the other way round) were widespread in Israel, but the evidence of the *sijill*s does not convey the impression that they were contracted without dower.[111] Relief to those wrestling with the problems of excessive dower came from an unexpected quarter. After the Six-Day War of 1967, many dozens of brides began to be imported from the West Bank, the Gaza Strip and East Jerusalem and its rural vicinity at comparatively low rates of dower.[112]

The *sijill*s mention hundreds of cases in which women renounced their right to dower, viz., prompt dower (the whole or the outstanding part), deferred dower, or half the specified dower where the marriage had not been consummated; in almost all cases, the renunciation was made on divorce by mutual agreement of the parties.[113] In other words, the divorced woman did not in fact enjoy her right to deferred dower[114] or even, sometimes, to the whole or part of the prompt dower. In this context, it is significant that the *sijill*s afford no evidence of widows realizing or demanding the realization of their right to dower out of the estates of their late husbands before distribution thereof among the heirs. Renunciation of the dower was frequent in all ecological groups and must be understood in the light of changes in the status of women, of which the extremely widespread dissolution of marriage on the wife's initiative was one of the most notable manifestations. The wife was ready to forego monetary and other rights in order to obtain her freedom.[115]

V. THE *QĀḌĪ*S AND DOWER

As a rule, the *qāḍī*s sought to apply the religious-legal norm which made the dower the exclusive property of the wife and rejected social custom as far as it was inconsistent with this conception. This approach was of course in keeping with the wife's interest. In one case Shaykh Ṭāhir al-Ṭabarī rejected a husband's demand that his wife obey him when he became aware that theirs was an exchange marriage and the wife had not received her dower.[116] In another case, in which a man contended that the marriage had been contracted without dower with the wife's consent, Shaykh Ṭāhir Ḥamād decided that a *fair* dower was obligatory whether dower was agreed on or not. In yet another case, he decided that the dower belonged to the wife and that the husband should not use it without her permission. On the other hand, he once dismissed a wife's contention that a clause in the marriage contract concerning dower was fictitious and that neither of the two exchanged wives had received anything.[117] In similar circumstances, Shaykh Ḥusnī al-Zuᶜbī dismissed a woman's claim for dower on the ground that a wife's contention that she had not received the whole dower should not be heard after she had given herself to her husband.[118]

Shaykh Ḥasan Amīn al-Ḥabash once declared that he insisted on the dower being given to the wife and not to anyone else.[119] He ordered a woman to return to her deserted daughter-in-law a cupboard the latter had bought with her dower, and a husband to pay his wife the balance of the prompt dower.[120] In another case, he rejected a wife's demand that her husband pay her the balance of the dower and took no account of the fact that the dower had been handed to a proxy (*wakīl*), who had not transmitted it to the wife.[121] Shaykh Amīn Qāsim Mudlij considered that the dower belonged to the wife alone and that neither her father nor her husband had any share in it. The dower, he believed, was in part designed to enable the wife to buy jewelry and clothes, and in part to be saved for emergencies, such as divorce or the husband's death. In his opinion, a wise father would give his daughter money to supplement her dower.[122] But these sentiments were not reflected in his judgments. Shaykh Mūsā al-Ṭabarī stated that according to custom prevailing in Muslim localities of Israel a woman moved from her father's house to that of her husband equipped with various household effects.[123] When a woman was divorced before consummation of the marriage, the *qāḍī*s took care to ensure that she was aware of her entitlement to one-half of the specified dower.[124] They did not intervene in any way when a woman renounced the dower—prompt or deferred—in the event of divorce.[125]

The problem of excessive dower frequently preoccupied the *qāḍī*s outside their judicial activity. They renounced excessive dower on religious and social grounds. Shaykh Ṭāhir Ḥamād thought that this problem did not exist at the inception of Islam or in the days of the *tābiᶜūn*, the followers of the Prophet. At the same time, both he and Shaykh Ḥasan Amīn al-Ḥabash quoted *ḥadīth*s attributed to the Prophet and the earliest Caliphs deprecating excessive dower. Shaykh Mūsā al-Ṭabarī revealed that he was "greatly perturbed by the position with regard to excessive dower and the heavy burden it imposed on the husband because of debts or the necessity to sell his property in order to finance the dower. . . ." He also stressed that he wholeheartedly supported the movement for the fight against excessive dower.[126] Shaykh Amīn Qūsim Mudlij, in one of his Friday sermons, expressed the view that excessive dower was "contrary to honor (*sharaf*) and religion"; he attacked the fathers who "make their daughters objects of trade and treat them like cattle" for monetary gain, who exposed them to contempt and humiliation by their husbands, who later blamed them for their economic straits. In his opinion, excessive dower corrupted morals and encouraged prostitution and suicide among women, as well as marriages between Muslims and Jewish and Christian girls, which were foredoomed to failure. He, too, invoked *ḥadīth*s in repudiating excessive dower.[127]

At the same time, all the *qāḍī*s, for religious and practical reasons, categorically rejected a solution of the problem by means of legislation forbidding or limiting dower. Shaykh Ḥasan Amīn al-Ḥabash thought that dower "was not set an upper or lower limit by the *sharīʿa*" and relied in this connection on interpretations of the term *qinṭār* (a measure mentioned in Qurʾan IV: 19 and in *ḥadīth*s attributed to the Prophet). Shaykh Ṭāhir Ḥamād voiced the opinion that a law fixing grades for dower—high, medium and low—would be of no practical value.[128] At the first *qāḍī*s conference in 1950, proposals were made to limit dower and were all rejected.[129] The question was again discussed at a conference in 1966 following the tabling of Knesset Member U. Avneri's bill. The *qāḍī*s sharply objected to Knesset interference in Islamic custom and law.[130] The only means they thought they could adopt without fear of infringing religious law was to exhort fathers to agree of their own free will not to demand excessive dowers for their daughters. The 1950 conference resolved that *qāḍī*s and religious functionaries should advise *maʾdhūn*s to persuade those concerned to exert moderation with regard to dower. Such activities were indeed conducted from time to time by mosque functionaries, *maʾdhūn*s[131] and also *qāḍī*s. Shaykh Ṭāhir Ḥamād said, on the one hand, that "the best method is to point out to preachers (*wāʿiẓ*s) and instructors (*murshid*s) that they should urge the people to follow the straight path." On the other hand, he doubted the effectiveness of such activities in view of the experience of the Supreme Muslim Council in Mandatory times. Shaykh Ḥasan Amīn al-Ḥabash called for the "launching of a campaign" (*shann ḥamla*) of enlightenment against excessive dower; he participated personally in such a campaign. In 1950, Shaykh Mūsā al-Ṭabarī called on *imāms* to urge people to reduce dower and fix limits for it: a lower limit of IL 500 and an upper limit of IL 1,000; he declared his willingness to conduct a campaign in the villages for this purpose.[132] In 1966, Shaykh Amīn Qāsim Mudlij undertook a campaign in Galilee villages to combat excessive dower. He reportedly intended to propose the introduction of fixed norms for dower on the basis of voluntary arrangements.[133]

The fact that the problem remained on the agenda of the *qāḍī*s for years suggests that propagandistic activities against excessive dower bore no real fruit. It is doubtful whether the *qāḍī*s were in fact capable of solving this problem. Their personal authority was not sufficient to uproot a social custom supported by religious law. Moreover, this was not a question of a legal norm, religious or secular (it is also doubtful whether intervention by the Knesset would be of use), but of a social norm, which by nature changes slowly, in the course of a long period. The *qāḍī*s were aware of this, and at their 1966 conference they expressed the view that the problem would find its solution with the passage of time.[134] They seemed to have had in mind the token prompt dower alongside a large deferred dower, an arrangement which, as noted, has begun to evolve in recent years. This was a practical solution which involved no violation of Islamic law. Such, at any rate, was the view of Shaykh Amīn Qāsim Mudlij.[135]

Shaykh Ḥasan Amīn al-Ḥabash advocated increasing the specified dower beyond the *qinṭār* mentioned in the Qurʾān as deferred dower, so as to discourage divorce.[136] At their 1966 conference, the *qāḍī*s recommended that the provision in the marriage contract providing for deferred dower be strictly adhered to in order that it might assure the wife's future in the event of divorce or the husband's death.[137] This recommendation sprang from a new social motive, not rooted in Islamic law. At the same time, it is very doubtful whether the *qāḍī*s had any influence on contemporary practices with regard to deferred or token dower. It seems more likely that they desired to give such practices *sharʿī* sanction. Thus, for instance, Shaykh Ḥasan related how during a visit to a village the people who had gathered on that occasion told him that the Ministry of Religious Affairs ought to limit prompt dower; they stressed that there was nothing to prevent deferred dower being three or four times as large as prompt dower. The *qāḍī* transmitted their wish to the Ministry of Religious Affairs with the remark that it seemed reasonable to him.[138]

NOTES

1. The origin of dower has been variously explained by reference to marital, kinship or property relations, matters of manpower, etc. See Robertson Smith, pp.93–6; Gibb, p.237; Anderson, *Islamic Law,* pp.40–1; Coulson, *History,* p.14; Schacht, p.161; Abu Zahra, p.144; Levy, pp.95, 115; Baer, p.41; Granqvist, vol.1, pp.132–4, 139, 145–7; Rosenfeld, *Peasants,* pp.117, 136, 166, 187.
2. Schacht, p. 167; Qadrī, art.206; Goitein and Ben-Shemesh, p.223.
3. *FRL,* arts.89–90; Qadrī, arts.97, 99; Fyzee, pp.134–6, 374–5.
4. The Qurʾān, IV:20, mentions the *qinṭār*. The Ḥanbalī and Shāfiʿī schools do not recognize a lower limit for dower. No school recognizes an upper limit. Qadrī, art.70; *ENFRL;* Linant de Bellefonds, pp.207–8; Coulson, *History,* p.40; Abu Zahra, pp.141–2.
5. *FRL,* arts.80–8; Qadrī, arts.70–111; Linant de Bellefonds, pp.213 *seq.*; Schacht, pp.167, 191–2; Fyzee, pp.131–2; Goitein and Ben-Shemesh, pp.130–1. The matter of the *mutʿa* is based on Qurʾān, II:236, and other verses.
6. *FRL,* arts.69, 71; Qadrī, art.104; Linant de Bellefonds, pp.201–2; Abu Zahra, pp.141–2; Fyzee, p.135; Levy, p.114; Schacht, p.197.
7. Silberg, p.400; Zadok, pp.67, 69; Women's Equal Rights Bill, 5711–1951, *Bills,* No.75 of 1951 (5711), p.191; remarks of the Minister of Justice in the Knesset, *KP,* vol.9, p.2005 col.1, p.2171 col.2; remarks of Knesset Member Jarjūra, *ibid.,* p.2089 col.1.
8. The position is not clear with regard to unmarried women. See Gibb, p.240.
9. See Prohibition of Dower Bill, 5726–1966, *Private Members' Bill,* No.26; *ha-Aretz* of June 23, 1966. See above, pp.57–8.
10. The calculation is based on Table IX/I, *SAI,* 1970, No.21, p.241.
11. Rosenfeld, *Peasants,* pp.66–7, 117, 138; Ben-Porath, pp.78–9. Cf. Marx, *Bedouin,* p.159.
12. See Ben-Porath, pp.72, 78. See also *AI,* vol.5(1959), Nos.1–2, p.25. Shaykh Amīn Qāsim Mudlij explained the increase of dower as a consequence of competition, especially in recent years, for educated brides, who are few, and in great demand. *Maʿariv* of July 3, 1966.
13. Cf. Chatila, pp.184, 192, 195; Granqvist, vol.1, pp.122, 124, 132.
14. See *AI,* vol.9(1964), Nos.1–2, English Summary.
15. For deferred dower see above, p.51.
16. Cf. Marx, *Bedouin,* p.159; Granqvist, vol.1, p.124.
17. Shaykh Salmān al-Huzayyil, e.g., was married 39 times, and shaykhs had an average of eight living children as against three to four for Beduin generally. Marx, *Bedouin,* pp.139–40.

18. Marx, *Bedouin,* pp.42–5. See also the appendix relating to leased lands. *Ibid.,* p.244.
19. See, e.g., *JfMC68,* no.10132 (husband of the al-Huzayyil tribe, wife of Jaffa; total dower IL 10,000, prompt IL 5,000, deferred IL 1,000, value of household effects forming part of the dower IL 4,000), no.10032 (husband of the Abū Ruqayyiq tribe, wife of Jaffa; total dower IL 7,500, prompt IL 7,000). For references to *sijill* entries concerning marriages between Beduin and town women see the chapter "Maintenance and Obedience," pp.96 *seq.*
20. It may be paid in foreign currency. See, e.g., *JfQ1,* p.131 : f.112/52 (Egyptian pounds) ; *JfQ5,* p.86 : no.146–f.219/69 (300 Jordanian dinars).
21. See, e.g., *JfQ2,* p.567 : no.578–f.88/62; *NzḤ24,* p.216 : no.1/28–f.64/69.
22. See, e.g., *NzḤ15,* p.46 : no.20/73; *AcṬ2,* p.120; *AcṬ1,* p.10. Cf. Granqvist, vol.1, p.119; Chatilla, p.193.
23. *NzḤ19,* p.160 : f.5/52. Cf. Granqvist, vol.1, p.120; al-ᶜĀrif, pp.130–1; Chatila, pp.193, 195.
24. See, e.g., *JfMC68,* nos.10033, 10147, 10149; *ṬbMC68,* nos.8027, 8028, 8037; *AcMC68,* nos.2636, 2848.
25. See, e.g., *JfMC68,* nos.10163, 10027; *ṬbMC68,* nos.8030, 8040; *AcMC68,* no.3022.
26. See, e.g., *JfMC68,* nos.9520, 10132, 10315.
27. See Palmon.
28. *Ibid.*
29. *AcI2,* p.21 : no.18–f.1/51.
30. Rosenfeld, *Recent Changes,* p.23. Cf. al-ᶜĀrif, pp.130–1; *Maᶜariv* of July 3, 1966.
31. *NzDS,* p.39. Cf. Granqvist, vol.1, p.126; Chatila, pp.185–6, 194; Baer, p.41.
32. Derived from unpublished data of the Central Bureau of Statistics.
33. See Rosenfeld, *Peasants,* pp.121–2. Among Negev Beduin it is usual to pay the whole dower before consummation (not on contraction) of the marriage, and the father does not agree to hand over his daughter before receiving the dower. Marx, *Bedouin,* pp.104, 159. Cf. Granqvist, vol.1, p.111; Chatila, pp.192–3.
34. See, e.g., *JfQ1,* p.116 : no.198–f.62/53; *JfQ4,* p.102 : no.114–f.70/68; *NzḤ20,* p.128 : no.2/56 (the wife alleged at the time of the divorce that she had received nothing of the prompt dower) ; *NzḤ22,* p.133 : no.3/28–f.52/64; *NzḤ24,* p.93 : no.10/64–f.136/67; *NzI4,* p.108 : no.2/20–f.76/51 ; *AcI2,* p.26 : f.32/51; *AcṬ3,* p.12 : f.7/57; *ṬbI1,* p.15 : no.1–f.1/51, p.175 : no.16–f.38/60.
35. See, e.g., *JfQ1,* p.101 : no.163–fs.63/52, 12/53; *JfQ3,* p.359 : no.501–f.31/67.
36. See, e.g., *AcD6,* p.15 : f.29/65.
37. See, e.g., *JfQ4,* p.88 : no.87–f.3/68.

38. *FRL,* art.83. See, e.g., *ṬbI1,* p.5 : no.713–f.17/50, p.266 : no.17–f.22/64 and p.280 : no.1–f.51/64; *JfQ4,* p.126 : no.146–f.119/68 and p.138 : no. 165–f.126/68. In one case, the husband was given time to prove his virility, and he agreed that if he did not succeed in doing so within a month the wife should be regarded as divorced and be entitled to receive back one-third of the prompt dower. See *AcI1,* p.85 : f.59/50.
39. See Qadrī, arts.15, 76; Ibn ᶜĀbidīn, p.361; Linant de Bellefonds, pp.209 *seq.* See also Levy, p.105; Robertson Smith, p.112; Granqvist, vol.1, pp.111–17, 136, 140; *ibid.,* vol.2, p.13; Rosenfeld, *Peasants,* pp.117, 122–5, 136; Marx, *Bedouin,* p.121; al-ᶜArif, pp.131–2; Shaykh Ḥasan Amīn al-Ḥabash, *AI,* vol.11(1968), Nos.1–2, p.3. See also *AD,* vol.3(1966), Nos.1–2, p.14.
40. See the chapters "Divorce," pp.129–30, and "Maintenance and Obedience," pp.100–1.
41. *AcD6,* p.19 : no.58/65; and *NzI4,* p.87 : no.4/45–f.114/50, respectively.
42. *ṬbMC68,* nos.8045, 8046. See also *JfQ5,* p.102 : no.171–f.258/69.
43. *AcṬ3,* p.172 : f.15/60.
44. See, e.g., *NzḤ18,* p.212 : no.9/34 and p.212 : no.10/34; *JfQ5,* p.26 : no.46–f.144/69 and p.27 : no.47–f.145/69.
45. *ṬbḤ1,* p.103 : no.2/70 and p.103 : no.3/71; *AcMC68,* nos.2694, 2695; and *ṬbḤ1,* p.108 : no.1/78 and p.109 : no.2/79, respectively.
46. But this is not certain; it is perfectly possible that the waiver of half the dower is purely formal, devoid of practical significance. See, e.g., *AcṬ4,* p.4 : fs.7/64, 8/64, p.6 : f.12/64, p.8 : f.15/64, p.10 : f.20/64, p.11 : f.22/64 and p.12 : f.23/64.
47. *AcṬ3,* p.172 : f.15/60.
48. For instances of equal treatment in various spheres, of the wives in exchange marriages, see the chapters "Maintenance and Obedience," pp.100–1, and "Divorce," pp.100–1.
49. *JfQ3,* p.97 : no.154–f.21/64; *NzI4,* p.284 : no.1/6–f.165/65.
50. Granqvist, vol.1, pp.70, 122–3; Rosenfeld, *Peasants,* p.117; Chatila, pp.184, 192; Kressel, p.25; Baer, p.66 and the sources indicated there.
51. *AcD6,* p.71 : f.177/64.
52. See, e.g., *NzḤ23,* p.16 : no.6/92–f.157/64.
53. See, e.g., *ṬbḤ2,* p.53 : no.19; *NzḤ18,* p.160 : no.6/262; *JfQ4,* p.65 : no.61–f.12/68.
54. Cf. Chatila, p.185.
55. See, e.g., *NzḤ23,* p.163 : no.2/22–f.32/66; *ṬbI1,* p.10 : no.1/11–f.25/50; *JfQ1,* p.8 : no.15–f.13/51, p.94 : no.150–f.74/52.
56. See. e.g., *JfQ2,* p.520 : no.495–f.6/61; *NzI4,* p.59 : no.2/26–f.43/49, p.126 : no.24/4–f.102/52 (the groom had paid the dower to the bride's father in two instalments, and the bride did not know of the second instalment). See the remarks of the Minister of Justice in the Knesset in the debate on

U. Avneri's private member's bill for the limitation of dower; *KP,* 74th meeting of June 22, 1966.

57. *NzḤ22,* p.82 : no.2/75–f.127/63.
58. *NzḤ17,* p.133:no.34/285 the girl, of the ᶜArab al-Ṣubayḥ tribe, was not yet 17 years of age, and it had been agreed to marry her to her fiancé, who had paid the dower, after her age had been corrected to 17 years; in the meantime, the dower was to remain "until called for" with two persons with whom the father had deposited it).
59. See, e.g., *Ṭbl1,* p.25 : no.9–f.24/51; *NzḤ15,* p.46 : no.20/73; *NzḤ19,* p.160 : no.5/52; and *NzI4,* p.61 : no.5/59–f.?/49, respectively.
60. See, e.g., *JfMC68,* nos.10094, 10148, 10149, 10291; *AcMC68,* nos.2834, 3445.
61. See, e.g., *JfMC68,* nos.9520, 10080, 10081, 10097, 10098, 10150, 10166, 10279, 10299, 12561, 12601, 12606, 12610, 12615, 12617, 12621, 12623, 12624; *ṬbMC68,* no. 9399 (the dower was handed to the wife and the proxy *(wakīl)*); *AcMC68,* nos.2828, 2831, 2835, 3022.
62. See, e.g., *Ṭbl1,* p.249 : no.5–f.8/64 (the wife received the dower through her father and was only then asked to let herself be conducted to the husband's home); *JfQ2,* p.323:no.505–f.53/58 (received the dower "by the hand of" her father); *NzḤ23,* p.43:no.4/24–f.48/65; *NzḤ24,* p.35:no.4/84–f.147/66, p.95 : no.11/65–f.137/67, p.114 : no.4/4–f.5/68.
63. *Ṭbl1,* p.5 : no.3/7–f.17/50.
64. *JfQ2,* p.403 : no.565–f.55/59. Cf. Granqvist, vol.1, p.145.
65. For more details, and source references, see the chapters "Maintenance and Obedience," pp.92–3, and "Divorce," p.131.
66. This statement is based on marriage contracts in which the wife made some stipulation.
67. *NzI4,* p.44:no.4/4–f.147/67 (the wife, of the ᶜArab al-Ṣubayḥ tribe, affixed her signature to the judgment for divorce).
68. Rosenfeld, *Peasants,* pp.117, 166, 187; *idem, Recent Changes,* p.23; *idem, Change and Conservation,* p.211; Cohen, pp.87–8.
69. D. Goldstein, *Maᶜariv* of June 25, 1965. See also interview with Shaykh Ḥasan Amīn al-Ḥabash, Z.Laviʾ, *Maᶜariv* of June 12, 1970. Cf. Granqvist, vol.1, pp.128, 132, 139–40; Chatila, p.194.
70. Marx, *Bedouin,* pp.159, 199; *idem, Social Structure,* p.3. Cf. Canaan, p.194; Chatila, p.196; Baer, p.40.
71. Kressel, p.25.
72. *NzDS,* p.39. Cf. Chatila, p.185.
73. Interview with Shaykh Muḥammad Ḥubayshī.
74. Rosenfeld, *Peasants,* p.166. This was confirmed by the *Mukhtār* of Bayt Ṣafāfā, Muṣṭafā ᶜAlayān. See also *Maᶜariv* of June 25, 1965. Cf. Chatila, pp.185–94; Abu Zahra, p.144.
75. *NzI4,* p.61 : no.5/59–f.?/49. Cf. Granqvist, vol.1, p.146. For the use of the

dower by the bride's father see Rosenfeld, *Peasants*, pp.23–4, 117–9; Granqvist, vol.1, pp.135, 137; Baer, p.41, and the sources indicated there.

76. *FRL*, art. 71. See Coulson, *History*, pp.207–8; Schacht, p.167; Abu Zahra, p.142; Fyzee, pp.134–6, 140, 374–5; Chatila, pp.184, 191, 199; E. Hareʾuveni, *Maʿariv* of July 3, 1966 (quotes persons who held that a connection exists between the amount of dower and the rate of divorces).
77. See the Chapter "Divorce," p.177.
78. See, e.g., *AcI3*, p.43: no.4–f.9/57; *AcQ5*, p.31: f.63/63.
79. See Chatila, p.190. The author is indebted to Messrs. Ziyon Rabi and Refaʾel Palmon, of the Demographic Section of the Central Bureau of Statistics, for allowing him to use their statistical analysis, the first of its kind, on deferred dower in marriage contracts in Israel, prepared on the basis of unpublished data of the Bureau for the year 1968.
80. The performance of marriages without registration and without observing the niceties of the *sharīʿa* is particularly widespread among the Negev Beduin. See Layish, *Custom*, pp.381–3.
81. Cf. Chatila, pp.185, 191–3, 195.
82. Dower is fixed according to the status and personal qualities of the bride and not according to the financial ability of the groom.
83. In 1966, the average prompt dower was smallest in the highest educational group—smaller by IL 100 than in the group with nine to 12 years of schooling. See *AI*, vol.11 (1968), Nos.1–2, p.94.
84. Cf. Berger, p.128; Baer, p.52 n.1.
85. *ha-Aretz* of May 7, 1956.
86. See, e.g., *AI*, vol.3 (1955), No.4, p.13; *AI*, vol.5 (1957), Nos.1–2, p.26; *AI*, vol.7 (1959), No.4, pp.4–8; *ha-Aretz* of May 7, 1956; Suʿād Qaramān and Aḥmad Ṣafadī, Beyt ha-Gefen of May 16, 1968. Cf. Rosenfeld, *Peasants*, p.187; Chatila, pp.188–9.
87. See *Marriages, 1957–1958*, p.46; *Vital Stats. 1967; 1968*, p.6.
88. See *AI*, vol.5 (1957), Nos.1–2, Hebrew Summary, p.3.
89. Y. Hameʾiri, *Yediʿot Aḥaronoth* of August 17, 1956. Cf. Chatila, p.197.
90. See, e.g., *ha-Aretz* of May 7, 1956; *ha-Tzofeh* of December 12, 1960.
91. See, e.g., an appeal by the Imām Ghālib Aḥmad Shibl, *AI*, vol.1 (1950), No.6, pp.8–9; a letter from a young man to the Minister of Religious Affairs, *AI*, vol.5 (1957), Nos.1–2, p.27; *Lamerḥav* and *ʿAl ha-Mishmar* of October 10, 1955, *Davar, Lamerḥav, ha-Boqer* and *Ḥerut* of March 17, 1956.
92. *ʿAl ha-Mishmar* of February 1, 1960; *Davar, ʿAl ha-Mishmar* and *ha-Boqer* of January 6, 1960; *Ḥerut* of February 24, 1960; *Yediʿot Aḥaronoth* of March 16, 1960.
93. *Davar* and *ha-Boqer* of March 24, 1960. Cf. Chatila, pp.187–91, 197.
94. D.Goldstein, *Maʿariv* of June 25, 1965 (ʿAbd al-Salām's sister was married off with a large dower).

95. See Rāshid Ḥusayn, *al-Mirṣād* of January 11, 1960, and January 21, 1960.
96. Prohibition of Dower Bill, 5726–1966 (Private Member's Bill No.26), secs.1, 3–6, 10; *KP*, 74th meeting of June 22, 1966. Neither Egypt nor any other Arab state has prohibited or limited dower. On the contrary, the relevant legislation was designed to increase the rates of dower by bypassing the minimal amounts, devoid of real value, prescribed by the Ḥanafī and Mālikī schools. See Linant de Bellefonds, pp.251–2.
97. *KP*, 74th meeting of June 22, 1966. Knesset Member E. Ḥabībī, a Christian and a Communist, likewise said that the Knesset was not the appropriate place for solving the problem of excessive dower, for which he held the Government responsible (*loc. cit.*). Interviewee Judge Eliyās Kteylī thought that the problem would not be solved, as demanded by the young, by legislation, but by change from below, and especially by education.
98. See, e.g., *AcMC68*, no.3441 (IL 5 prompt, IL 10,000 deferred), no.2644 IL 10, IL 5,000), no.2426 (IL 10, IL 12,000), no.2848 (IL 10, IL 15,000), no.2946 (IL 1.60, IL 3,000), no.2432 (10 agorot, IL 5,000); *ṬbMC68*, no.18304 (IL 5, IL 10,000); *NzḤ23*, p.131: no.7/111–f.173/65 (IL 10, IL 10,000); *JfMC68*, no.10083 (IL 50, IL 2,000).
99. *ṬbMC62*, no.18304. See also *AcMC68*, nos.2644, 2826, 2841, 2848 (IL 10 and IL 15,000; the wife stipulated that the house with all its contents should be registered in her name as part of the prompt dower), no.2432. Cf. E. Hareʾuveni, *Maʿariv* of July 3, 1966.
100. According to unpublished data of the Central Bureau of Statistics. The category "villages" includes over 200 Beduin marriages, a few of them with token dower. See Palmon.
101. See, e.g., *AcMC68*, no.2426 (the spouses had a secondary education and were employed as teachers), no.3441 (the husband had a secondary education and was employed as a clerk; the wife had an elementary education), no.2848 (the husband had a university education and the wife a secondary education; the husband was a teacher and the wife a clerk); *ṬbMC62*, no.18304 (the husband was a school principal and the wife a teacher). See ʿAbd al-ʿAzīz al-Zuʿbī in *ʿAl ha-Mishmar* of July 17, 1966; E. Hareʾuveni, *Maʿariv* of July 3, 1966 (interview with Shaykh Amīn Qāsim Mudlij). See also the remarks of the Minister of Religious Affairs in the debate on U. Avneri's private member's bill; *KP*, 74th meeting of June 22, 1966. In Iraq, too, token dower (commonly of one dinar) is a new phenomenon, having developed in recent years in the educated strata; on the other hand, the groom is expected to prepare the dwelling at his expense, while the bride shares in the cost only if she is a woman of means; see el-Naqeb, p.62. Cf., on the other hand, Chatila, p.191.
102. See, e.g., *NzḤ23*, p.131 : no.7/111–f.173/65, p.158 : no.11/15–f.20/66 and

p.159 : no.12/16–f.21/66; *NzḤ24,* p.106 : no.2/79–f.169/67 and p.107 : no.3/80–f.170/67.

103. *Davar* and *Lamerḥav* of June 30, 1960. For further instances, see *Davar* of November 7, 1960, and *al-Yawm* of January 28, 1963 (both quoted from *AI,* vol.8(1963), Nos.3–4, p.48). See also Baer, p.62 and the sources indicated there.
104. According to unpublished data of the Central Bureau of Statistics.
105. Cf. Berger, p.108.
106. Knesset Member U.Avneri, *KP,* 74th meeting of June 22, 1966. Cf. Granqvist, vol.1, pp.120–2.
107. See E. Hareʾuveni, *Maʿariv* of June 3, 1966. Yūsuf Dasūqī reported that youths in Little Triangle villages tended to marry girls with occupational skills "in order to recoup themselves for the dower they pay to them." See *AI,* vol.8(1962), Nos.1–2, pp.4–5. Cf. Chatila, pp.191, 195.
108. In one case, the deception came to light when the bride's mother visited the young couple a week after the wedding "and saw that her daughter's hands were bare." The bride's family was convinced that the young man had duped them, relations between the two families became strained, and the bride was regarded as a traitress by her family. The younger generation, at any rate, admired the couple's pluck. *ha-Aretz* of August 31, 1960.
109. Interviewee Judge Eliyās Kteylī knew of many abductions in which the woman consented and waived the dower. Cf. Granqvist, vol.1, pp.153–4.
110. See, e.g., *Maʿariv* of June 3, 1966, and ʿAṭallāh Manṣūr, *ha-Aretz* of January 19, 1968. In one case, a well-known Muslim public figure converted to Judaism in order to marry a Jewess and afterward returned to Islam. See *al-Ittiḥād* of March 18, 1960.
111. The dower question is referred to in many cases. See, e.g., *JfQ1,* p.106 : no.169–f.47/53; *NzḤ22,* p.150 : no.13/46–f.78/64.
112. See, e.g., ʿAṭallāh Manṣūr, *ha-Aretz* of January 19, 1968, February 5, 1969, and March 13, 1970; Z. Laviʾ, *Maʿariv* of June 12, 1970, *al-Anbāʾ* of November 4, 1970. Jalāl Abū Ṭuʿma, former Chairman of the Council of Bāqa al-Ghrabiyya, reported that dozens of young men of his village had since the Six-Day War brought brides from the West Bank for the low rate of dower of IL 2,000. See also *JfQ4,* p.175 : no.220–f.73/69; *JfQ5,* p.53 : no.89–f.194/69; and the chapter "Polygamy," p.76.
113. See, e.g., *JfQ1,* p.76 : no.118–f.88/52, p.196 : no.318–f.60/55; *JfQ5,* p.138 : no.229–f.6/70; *AcṬ2,* p.7; *AcṬ3,* p.32 : f.23/57, p.162 : f.5/60, p.173 : f.16/60; *AcṬ4,* p.16 : f.31/64; *AcI3,* p.71 : f.7/58.
114. There is only sporadic evidence of divorced women insisting on realizing their right to deferred dower. See, e.g., *JfQ2,* p.498 : no.458–f.75/61 (a divorced woman sued her ex-husband for deferred dower after a lapse of years, when he had remarried and had children by his new wife); *JfQ4,* p.162 : no.199–f.25/69; *ṬbI1,* p.8 : no.1/9–f.22/50.

115. See the chapter "Divorce," p.159.
116. *NzI4,* p.87: no.4/45–f.114/50.
117. *JfQ1,* p.6 : no.12–f.10/51; *JfQ2,* p.403 : no.565–f.55/59; and *JfQ3,* p.97 : no.154–f.21/64, respectively.
118. In reliance on art.104 of Qadrī's collection. *NzI4,* p.284 : no.1/6–f.165/65.
119. Interview with Shaykh Ḥasan Amīn al-Ḥabash. See also Z. Laviʾ, *Maʿariv* of June 12, 1970.
120. *NzI4,* p.54 : no.2/17–f.28/49; and *ṬbI1,* p.175, respectively.
121. *NzI4,* p.59 : no.2/62–f.43/49.
122. *AI,* vol.1 (1950), No.8, p.9.
123. *AcI2,* p.21 : no.18–f.1/51.
124. See, e.g., the decisions of Shaykh Tawfīq Maḥmūd ʿAsaliyya. *JfQ4,* p.126 : no.146–f.119/68, p.138 : no.165–f.126/68.
125. See the chapter "Divorce," p.198.
126. *AI,* vol.3 (1955), No.4, pp.13–14; *Davar, ʿAl ha-Mishmar* and *ha-Boqer* of January 8, 1960.
127. *AI,* vol.1 (1950), no.8, pp.9–11; *Maʿariv* of July 3, 1966.
128. *AI,* vol.3 (1955), No.4, pp.13–14. Shaykh Ḥasan Amīn al-Ḥabash's opinion as to minimum dower was inconsistent with the view of the Ḥanafī school (but conformed with those of the Shāfiʿī and Ḥanbalī schools. See Linant de Bellefonds, pp.207–8). On the other hand, he declared during an interview that the *qāḍī*s had opposed the limitation of dower by legislation on the ground that the *qinṭār* mentioned in the Qurʾān constituted a minimum quota.
129. *AI,* vol.1(1950), No.7, p.4.
130. *AI,* vol.10 (1966), Nos.1–2, English Summary, p.6. *KP,* 74th meeting of June 22, 1966. In a letter to the Minister of Justice of March 13, 1966, the Minister of Religious Affairs said that the *qāḍī*s regarded the bill as contrary to Islamic law because dower is mentioned many times in the Qurʾān and therefore cannot be banned or limited in any religious-legal way and that any interference by the Knesset in the matter of dower would be considered by them interference in religious affairs. See also Z. Laviʾ, *Maʿariv* of June 12, 1970.
131. *AI,* vol.1 (1950), No.7, p.4; *AI,* vol.6 (1958), No.4, pp.8–9.
132. *AI,* vol.1 (1950), No.5, p.5; *AI,* vol.3 (1955), No.4, pp.13–14; *AI,* vol.11 (1968), Nos.1–2, p.5; *ʿAl ha-Mishmar* and *Lamerḥav* of October 10, 1955.
133. See E. Hareʾuveni, *Maʿariv* of May 31, 1966, and July 3, 1966.
134. *AI,* vol.10(1966), Nos.1–2, English Summary, p.6.
135. See E. Hareʾuveni, *Maʿariv* of July 3, 1966.
136. *AI,* vol.9(1964), Nos.1–2, p.11.
137. And also act as a bar to rash *ṭalāq* divorces. *AI,* vol.10 (1966), Nos.1–2, p.83. See *ha-Tzofeh* and *ha-Yom* of July 19, 1966; *ha-Aretz* of July 22, 1966.
138. *AI,* vol.1 (1950), No.5, pp.14–15.

Chapter Four
POLYGAMY

I. LEGAL BACKGROUND

Polygamy in Islam is a right reserved to men. It was adopted as part of the legacy of patriarchal Arab society. The Qurʾān does not unequivocally limit the number of wives a Muslim is permitted to have, but all the schools of law agree that no more than four legal wives may be kept at one time. The Qurʾānic verses relating to polygamy (IV: 3 and 129) stress the need for equal and just treatment of the wives as a condition of polygamy, but orthodox interpretation confines equality to measurable technical criteria, such as the provision of maintenance (*nafaqa*) and the apportionment (*qasm*) of the husband's time among the wives; as for the "inclination of the heart" (*mayl al-qalb*), it is not treated as a condition with binding legal effects but as a matter of ethics, left to the individual conscience. The Ottoman legislator, who sought to improve the position of women in this sphere, did not dare to tackle polygamy by a substantive provision; he reaffirmed it by laying down that "it is forbidden for a man with four wives, married to him or in the waiting-period (*ʿidda*), to take an additional wife." On the other hand, he sought to circumvent it by the device of the stipulation in the marriage contract,[1] in reliance on Ḥanbalī doctrine in this matter and on the fact that the Qurʾānic provision is permissive and not mandatory. Article 38 of the Ottoman Family Rights Law permits the wife to stipulate in the marriage contract that her husband may not take an additional wife and that if he does she or her rival shall be regarded as divorced. The legislator assumed that no wife would agree to her husband taking an additional wife and so the mechanism of the stipulation seemed sufficient to him. He was also careful to restate the husband's duty of treating his wives equally and justly, but this time, too, the injunction was without teeth.[2]

The Mandatory legislator, who regulated the question of polygamy in the Criminal Code Ordinance, gave a "good defense" to this charge to non-Jews whose personal law permitted polygamy.[3] This defense was, in fact, meant only for Muslims or, more exactly, for Muslim men because, as stated, Islamic law does not recognize polyandry. The intention was to exempt Muslims *qua* Muslims from the criminal sanction provided for polygamy by the Ordinance (five years' imprisonment).

In 1951, the Knesset abrogated the "good defense" available to Muslims against the charge of polygamy.[4] The intention was to adjust Muslims to the monogamous form of marriage accepted in Israeli society.[5] As a result, Muslim men were given the defense intended until then for non-Muslims: absence of the spouse for a consecutive period of seven years without her being known to be alive.[6] In 1959, Muslims were given an additional defense: inability of the spouse by the earlier marriage to agree to its dissolution or annulment owing to mental illness.[7] These two defenses are conditional on receipt of a judgment of the religious court permitting the new marriage.[8] In other words, the *qāḍī* is empowered to permit polygamy on either of two grounds: absence or mental illness. These two defenses are essential to the Muslim because the Knesset also forbade him to divorce his wife against her will without a court judgment.[9] The Knesset's intention, at any rate, was to give Muslims the same defenses as are available to Jews.[10]

From the point of view of the equality of Muslim women, the abrogation of the defense available to Muslim men under the Criminal Code Ordinance against the charge of polygamy did not remove the traditionally basic discrimination between men and women given religious sanction in the Qurʾān. True, both men and women are exempt from criminal responsibility in the event of their taking a spouse in addition to the one who is a absent or ill, but while the man's new marriage is valid according to religious law, the woman's is not, and the Israeli legislator was not prepared to interfere with any religious-legal prohibition or permission relating to marriage or divorce.[11]

In effect, the Knesset did not abolish polygamy but prohibited its practice. Islamic law in this matter remains in force. If a man takes an additional wife, the additional marriage is valid as far as it is so under the *sharīʿa*, but he is liable to the secular criminal sanction provided for that offense. At the same time, the Knesset made it possible to circumvent the prohibition in the above-mentioned cases. The same technique was used by countries such as Syria and Iraq: they, too, prohibited polygamy but did not abolish it, and infringers of the prohibition are liable to statutory sanctions; but Syrian and Iraqi *qāḍī*s have wider discretion than their Israeli colleagues to permit polygamous marriages.[12]

II. CONTRAVENTION OF THE BAN ON POLYGAMY

There are no official statistics of polygamy in Israel. The official data on marriages are indeed based on the registers of marriage contracts, but infringers of the ban on polygamy were not anxious to incriminate themselves, and in so far as they married with the participation of a *maʾdhūn*, they were careful, as far as possible, to conceal their true marital status in various ways, as will be seen below. The detection of polygamous marriages through the *sijill*s is also difficult, because this type of marriage was not as such a subject-matter of court actions. Polygamous marriages are discovered incidentally, in the course of the hearing of other matters, especially actions for the confirmation of marriages (*ithbāt nikāḥ*), maintenance, obedience and divorce. In this way, the author came across more than 70 instances.[13] The number was undoubtedly greater than is reflected in the *sijill*s, but this does not seem to alter the basic finding that polygamy was not widespread among Israeli Muslims. This finding is confirmed by field research in different regions.[14] The cases ascertained mostly involved two wives, but there were men who had three or even four.[15]

Polygamous marriages are found in all ecological groups. Particularly striking was their frequency among Beduin—about 40% of all cases discovered in the *sijill*s. Another 40% occurred among the rural population, half of this in the Little Triangle villages. Polygamy was also still extant in urban areas, though on a smaller scale: some 16%,[16] which included Beduin who had recently settled in towns such as Lod, Ramla and Jaffa.[17] Polygamy was thus a problem for urban women as well. In some cases, they tried to protect themselves against it by a stipulation in the marriage contract. In one case, the wife stipulated that the husband should not take an additional wife so long as she was able to fulfil her marital duties and that if he did he should pay her IL 5,000. In two other cases, the stipulations were respectively that the wife should be delegated by the husband the power to divorce herself if he took an additional wife, and, in the second case, that any additional wife the husband might take should be regarded as divorced.[18]

In about 30% of the cases of polygamy discovered through the *sijill*s, there is express evidence or a reasonable suspicion that the marriage was contracted in contravention of Israeli law.[19] There can be no doubt that the actual proportion of offenses was higher. Thirteen persons were convicted of polygamy in district courts in 1966 and nine in 1969.[20] These data indeed do not necessarily relate to offenses committed in those years, but on the other hand it may be supposed that not all offenders were caught and brought to trial. Two-thirds of the offenses discovered through the *sijill*s were committed by Beduin, mostly in the Negev. Most of the offenses in rural areas were committed in the Little Triangle. Polygamy thus occurred in Israel despite its prohibition by law (and there were those who said that it was more frequent than divorce).[21] Three years after the passage of the law by the Knesset 13 tribal chiefs in the Negev sent a petition to the Prime Minister declaring that the ban on polygamy was a disaster the like of which had never befallen Muslims before and that the Beduin could not endure it.[22]

There were a number of different ways of circumventing the ban on polygamy. One of the commonest methods was the performance of polygamous marriages otherwise than by a *maʾdhūn*. In this way, the question of criminality did not arise. The Negev Beduin did not appear to be prompted by the wish to circumvent the law[23] and their polygamous, as well as their first, marriages were performed in good faith in accordance with tribal custom; only later, when some occasion arose for the updating of their identity booklets, did they apply to the *sharīʿa* court for confirmation of the marriage.[24] But deliberate circumvention was practiced in other regions. Thus, for instance, a woman from a Little Triangle village alleged that her husband had left her and taken a second wife "without a legal tie."[25] Suʿād Qaramān, a well-known figure active in women's affairs, and social workers in the Haifa and northern regions, attested that the circumvention of the ban on polygamy by *barrānī* (external) marriages, i.e., marriages performed without the participation of a *maʾdhūn*, was a familiar feature in Muslim society.[26] This was confirmed to the author by Judge Muḥammad Nimr al-Hawwārī of the District Court of Nazareth. According to him there were *maʾdhūn*s who charged twice as much for the performance of marriages without registration as for the regular procedure because of the risk of prosecution involved.[27]

A man might cohabit with an additional woman without a proper marriage having been performed, in a kind of common-law marriage. This phenomenon in Muslim society was probably a consequence of the ban on polygamy. It is true that cohabitation without a *sharʿī* marriage was widespread among Beduin and also among the recently settled rural population, which had not yet been fully absorbed into orthodox Islam but still adhered to their tribal customary law in matters of personal status. The occurrence of common-law marriages as deliberate means to circumvent the ban on polygamy was confirmed to the author by the Central Bureau of Statistics.[28] There are also some indications of it in the *sijill*s. In one case, a wife alleged that she had been compelled to leave her husband's house because he had taken another wife. The husband admitted that the other woman was at his house, together with the first, but denied that he had married her.[29]

Obtaining the first wife's consent to the new marriage was another means of circumventing the ban on polygamy. Although this was not a "good defense" to a charge of polygamy it did afford some assurance that the party most interested in preventing that marriage would take no legal steps.[30] In one case, a wife alleged that her husband had told her to sign a document confirming that she agreed to the second marriage, and that when she refused, he began to ill-treat her and to lock her up in the house.[31] The husband may have honestly believed that, as in the case of divorce, the wife's consent released him from criminal responsibility, and it is easy to imagine that under certain circumstances the wife would prefer acceptance of the second marriage to divorce.

After the Six-Day War, some men resorted to importing a second wife from the Israel-administered areas.[32] Although the chief reason for marrying a Gaza Strip or West Bank woman seems to have been the smaller dower she commanded,[33] the possibility cannot be ruled out that the choice of such a woman as an additional wife was also prompted by a desire to evade the penal sanction. For polygamy is not prohibited in the Israel-administered areas, where Israeli law does not apply. (In East Jerusalem Israeli law has applied since the reunification of the city in 1967.) The law indeed says that an Israeli national or resident who marries an additional wife abroad is also liable to punishment,[34] but this provision was not known among the general public.[35]

Yet another device resorted to was to repudiate one's wife by revocable divorce (*ṭalāq rajʿī*) and to take her back after marrying an additional wife. A revocable divorce does not undo the marital bond immediately, and the husband may take the divorced woman back during the waiting-period (*ᶜidda*) without need for a new union or a new dower. As far as secular law is concerned, the husband was in the clear on notifying the divorce and amending the marital status entry in the identity booklet. The reinstatement of the wife did not involve legal proceedings; a verbal utterance, or significant conduct, of the husband was sufficient. The divorced wife remained in the husband's house throughout the *ᶜidda*. It was very difficult to prove an offense of this kind because the husband could always say that he admitted his former wife into his house out of pity.[36] In one case, a man declared, after divorcing his wife, that he was free of wives, including wives in the *ᶜidda* following a revocable or other divorce, and there was no wife in his "protection" (*ᶜiṣma*); he was seeking confirmation of the divorce for the purpose of changing the description of his marital status in the Population Register.[37] One *qāḍī* sometimes warned a man who had divorced his wife not to take her back so long as he had another wife, in view of the ban on polygamy.[38]

Another method of evading legal punishment, and which indeed involved a certain risk, was to divorce one's wife without her knowledge, amend the marital status entry in the Population Registry, take another wife, and continue living with the first wife as well without a formal marital bond. The author discovered only one case of this kind, but it sheds light on a mechanism for protection against the Knesset's innovations which was sometimes developed with the cooperation of the *maʾdhūn*. In this particular case, the wife (both she and the husband being of the Abū Ruqayyiq tribe) alleged that her husband had divorced her at a date unknown to her, concealed this from her and continued to have marital relations with her until she learnt of the divorce. The husband denied that he had divorced her, but admitted taking an additional wife. In fact, it transpired that the husband, who had wished to take an additional wife, had told the *maʾdhūn* that his wife agreed to his doing so. The *maʾdhūn* thereupon said to him: "When I ask you in the presence of people: 'Are you divorced?' you must say: 'Yes, I am.' The certificate of divorce which I shall make out will be quite worthless; its only purpose will be to convince the Government." The *maʾdhūn* sent the certificate of divorce to the Population Registry, and the divorced man took another wife. The *qāḍī* found that the man had circumvented the law by concealing the divorce from the wife "in order that he might be able to live with her as well as take another wife."[39]

III. THE DECLINE OF POLYGAMY

From a variety of sources it may be inferred that polygamy is on the decline in Israel. About 70% of the cases discovered during the hearing of various actions in court involved marriages concluded before the establishment of the State.[40] The prohibition of polygamy by criminal legislation has undoubtedly made its mark on whatever inclination toward polygamy still exists. Witness the various means employed to circumvent the ban. But quantitatively the most significant manifestation of the deterrent effect of the criminal sanction is that the traditional motives for polygamy, viz., barrenness of the wife, lack of male issue, advanced age of the wife or illness incapacitating her for sexual intercourse, the desire for a young wife as a symbol of status and social prestige, etc.,[41] had now become frequent causes of divorce.[42]

As will be seen below, the Knesset's ban on polygamy, well-intentioned though it certainly was, did women more harm than good because divorce was considered by most worse than polygamy. If there is no normative or economic bar to a polygamous marriage, there is no reason for a husband to divorce his first wife when wishing to take a second; on the contrary, he has good reason for not divorcing her: if he does, he will lose her working power and have to pay her the deferred dower in addition to maintenance for the waiting-period.[43] There is express evidence that men who desired another wife instead of one who was old, barren or away in some Arab country were reluctantly compelled to divorce the first wife for no reason but the ban on polygamy. This happened especially in the Little Triangle villages, where the inclination to marry young wives had increased because of economic prosperity. Since polygamy was prohibited, it became usual to divorce the ageing wife, pay her what was due to her under matrimonial law and even compensate her in various ways.[44]

But Israeli legislation was not the only, or even the principal, cause of the decline of the polygamy rate. In most of the cases in which a person was convicted of polygamy, the law was not applied with full rigour; small fines were imposed which could have no deterrent effect. A judge of the District Court of Beersheba, whose attitude toward polygamy in Beduin society was one of tolerance, remarked in one of his judgments: ". . . it may be said that there is actual disregard of the law here and perhaps that the risk is worthwhile and not deterrent. A man who pays several thousand pounds for a new wife will not mind paying several hundred or even more as a fine; the fine at most puts the price up a little."[45] The author found only one case of a man applying to the *sharīʿa* court for permission to take a second wife on one of the grounds recognized by the Knesset. He contended that his wife was mentally ill and had been in hospital for a long time, and that there was no hope of recovery. In another case, a man applied to the court for registration of his second marriage on the ground that his first wife had borne him six daughters and no son and that he had been "compelled to take a second wife in order that Allāh might bless me with a son who would bear my name after my death"[46]; this was of course an application for confirmation of a polygamous marriage *ex post facto*. Muslims did not seem to be aware of the grounds recognized by the Knesset or at any rate did not use them. In some of the dozens of cases in which a man divorced a wife absent from the country a good defense could have been set up to a charge of polygamy.[47] Except for one case,[48] there is no evidence of a wife intending to bring a criminal action against her husband in the event of his taking an additional wife. Women seemed to be unaware of this right, or in so far as they were aware, not to have attained a degree of social freedom enabling them to take criminal proceedings. Divorce probably worried them more than polygamy.[49]

The decline of polygamy has become a general phenomenon in the Middle East, known also in countries where polygamy is not prohibited by law.[50] The causes of this decline should therefore be sought, first and foremost, in economic, cultural and social factors: in the spread of education and in the resulting change in the normative values and in attitudes toward the institution of marriage; in the rise in the standard of living and in the economic expectations of both spouses; in the increase in the amounts of the dower; in the transformation of traditional society, and especially in the liberation of woman.[51] Owing to these factors, polygamy would have receded even if it had not been prohibited. In sum, the decline of polygamy has not necessarily been a boon to women as far as the balance-sheet of marriages and divorces is concerned. Indeed, there was a correlation between the decline of polygamy and the rise of the divorce rate.[52] This was particularly noticeable in the Little Triangle villages, where according to Shaykh Ḥasan Amīn al-Ḥabash the rate of divorces exceeded that of marriages.[53]

In several cases, a woman had two husbands at one and the same time.[54] This does not indicate a material change in the position of women, but laxity in compliance with the law of marriage and divorce. This phenomenon was found especially among Beduin, but also in recently-settled rural society and even among the urban population.[55] The polyandrous marriage is irregular (*fāsid*) and liable to immediate termination under religious law[56]; it is criminal under general law. In one case, a woman was punished for polyandry.[57]

IV. THE *QĀḌĪ*S AND POLYGAMY

The attitude of the *qāḍī*s to polygamy in the context of religious and secular law was perplexed and ambivalent. On the one hand, they welcomed the ban imposed by the Knesset; they even tried to find support for it in the Qurʾān and for this purpose adopted elements of modernistic interpretation in the spirit of Muḥammad ʿAbduh (1849–1905), who led the movement to adapt Islam to modern Western civilization, and who with regard to polygamy attempted to interpret the Qurʾānic verses as a legally binding injunction in favor of monogamy. On the other hand, they were concerned for the substantive validity of religious law in this matter and at times even found some social justification for it. Shaykh Ṭāhir Ḥamād held that the treatment of polygamy in the Qurʾān expressed a subtle intent in favor of monogamy since it was usually impossible to maintain justice and equality between several wives in all circumstances and the *sharīʿa* itself contends that if one can not do so one should content oneself with one wife. Shaykh Tawfīq ʿAsaliyya said that the Qurʾān ordered fair treatment of one's wives and that polygamy was conditional on one's ability to treat them justly.[58] Both referred to the well-known "polygamy verses" in the Qurʾān. They made their remarks in connection with the Knesset's ban on polygamy in order to show that secular legislation in this matter was consonant with the spirit of the *sharīʿa*. But it seems that the *qāḍī*s did not, like the modernists, mean to go so far as to give binding legal validity to the Qurʾānic moral prohibition.[59] Shaykh Ṭāhir Ḥamād stressed that the Knesset's ban on polygamy sprang from the same religious-legal consideration as was expressed in the Qurʾān, but that the Knesset could not "attack the *sharīʿa* or the heavenly laws," i. e., detract from the substantive validity of the Quarʾānic permission. The idea that the Knesset's legislation is intended to strengthen the validity of the Qurʾānic norm recurs in various formulations. Shaykh Ṭāhir

Ḥamād considered that the ban on polygamy (like other prohibitions in criminal legislation) not only did not abrogate the religious law but strengthened it by means of the penal sanction, because the moral command, being without teeth, was ineffective. Shaykh Tawfīq ᶜAsaliyya was likewise careful to point out, praising the Knesset's criminal legislation in matters of marriage and divorce, that it was framed "whilst maintaining the validity of the religious law."[60]

In 1954, Advocate Muḥammad Nimr al-Hawwārī applied to the Supreme Court sitting as the High Court of Justice for an order against the *qāḍī* of the *Sharīᶜa* Court of Acre to show cause why he should not agree to the bigamous marriage of a certain man. Shaykh Mūsā al-Ṭabarī had refused to do so on the ground that although there was no bar to such a marriage under the *sharīᶜa* it was forbidden by secular law. Advocate al-Hawwārī contended in the High Court of Justice that the Knesset's ban on polygamy constituted an infringement of the freedom of religion of the Muslims and that it conflicted with section 5 of the Women's Equal Rights Law, which provides that "this Law shall not affect any religious-legal prohibition or permission relating to marriage or divorce." The court rejected these arguments, holding, *inter alia*, that freedom of religion (within the meaning of the general law) was the freedom to do what religion commands, and not what it permits, and that, since Islam did not command, but merely permitted polygamy, its prohibition did not infringe the freedom of religion. In this connection the Indian modernist Ameer Ali was mentioned, who tried (like ᶜAbduh) to prove by reference to Qurʾānic verses that Islam forbids polygamy.

Shaykh Ṭāhir Ḥamād was not satisfied with this judgment. In a letter to the President of the Supreme Court, he maintained that the orthodox interpretation of the "polygamy verses" should be adhered to and stressed that the main criterion of equality was economic; although it was not possible to adopt the same emotional attitude toward several wives, he said, the resulting restriction was merely moral, not legally binding—a matter of piety (*waraᶜ*), left to the individual conscience. Shaykh Ṭāhir utterly rejected Ameer Ali's interpretation, since Allāh could not have permitted and forbidden polygamy at the same time. Lastly, Shaykh Ṭāhir held that freedom of religion was not only freedom to do what religion commanded, but also what it permitted; more exactly, the Muslim marriage should be considered in terms of the five religious qualifications under which any aspect of Muslim behavior is categorized (*al-aḥkām al-khamsa*—obligatory, recommended, indifferent, reprehensible, and forbidden). In his opinion, the Knesset's ban on polygamy conflicted with all but the last (*ḥarām*) of these qualifications and therefore constituted an infringement of the freedom of religion promised in the Declaration of Independence.[61]

Shaykh Ḥusnī al-Zuᶜbī also welcomed the ban on polygamy, but considered that the range of "good defenses" should be widened. He suggested adding in the Penal Law Amendment (Bigamy) Law, 5719–1959, a provision to the effect that the wife's refusal to comply with a judgment for obedience, her chronic illness, barrenness "and the like" should entitle the husband to take an additional wife without this being considered a criminal offense. The ban on polygamy and on divorce against the wife's will had barred the two traditional remedies available to the husband against a disobedient wife, and the *qāḍī*'s proposal was intended to restore the equilibrium upset by the secular law, which, in his opinion, was misused by the wife.[62] Shaykh Amīn Qāsim Mudlij shared the view that rebelliousness of the wife should be a justification for polygamy.[63] In effect, the *qāḍī*s asked for the legalization of what were the commonest reasons for polygamy in traditional society.

The Egyptian Personal Status Bill of 1966 would not have abolished polygamy (had it been approved), but entitled the first wife to demand dissolution of the marriage (*tafrīq*) on the ground of *ḍarar* (damage, legal cruelty), which was in itself a new ground for dissolution. The *qāḍī*s rejected the proposed reform most categorically because, in their opinion, it expressly contradicted the *sharīᶜa*. Shaykh Tawfīq ᶜAsaliyya thought it impossible to regard the taking of an additional wife, which is expressly permitted by the Qurᵓān, as causing damage to the first wife; he suggested some orthodox remedies instead. Shaykh Amīn Qāsim Mudlij held that any allegation of damage was a matter of "discord" within the meaning of article 130 of the Ottoman Family Rights Law and should be dealt with by arbitration. Shaykh Ḥusnī al-Zuᶜbī added that the problem of the ban on polygamy had found its solution within the framework of the "existing law," in other words, by means of criminal legislation.[64]

Polygamy as a type of marriage, apart from the criminal aspect, did not preoccupy the *qāḍī*s in their day-to-day practice. In their view, polygamy was a legitimate institution, anchored in the *sharīᶜa* and in social reality. Where between the spouses questions arose that were rooted in this type of marriage, such as allegations of deprivation or discriminatory treatment of one of the wives as to maintenance, housing or conjugal rights, the *qāḍī*s dealt with them in the context of the rights and duties of the spouses under the *sharīʿa*.[65] They were well aware of the Knesset's ban on polygamy. Thus, in one case of a polygamous marriage in East Jerusalem, Shaykh Tawfīk ʿAsaliyya was careful to indicate in the record that while the marriage was contrary to Israeli law, it had been concluded when the latter was not yet in force there, before the Six-Day War.[66] Shaykh Amīn Qāsim Mudlij once noted, when about to confirm a marriage, that no other wife had remained in the husband's *ʿiṣma* since his first wife's death.[67] Moreover, when about to confirm the divorce of one of the wives in a polygamous marriage, he was accustomed to warn the husband not to take the divorced wife back so long as there was another wife in his *ʿiṣma*, "having regard to the Women's Equal Rights Law" or "in order that he might not incur the legal liability" attached to such a marriage.[68]

On application for confirmation of a marriage concluded without registration and in violation of the ban on polygamy, the *qāḍī*s would validate the marriage retroactively if it was valid under the religious law and confirm the *nasab* (blood-relationship) between the children and the parents. As stated, most of these offenses were committed by Negev Beduin, in whose case some *qāḍī*s either ignored the offense completely or treated it with leniency. In one instance, Shaykh Amīn Qāsim Mudlij, on confirming the marriage of Beduin of the al-Huzayyil tribe, remarked: "These two do not know the law that forbids polygamy because life in the desert makes it impossible to know the laws that are to be observed in this country, especially the recently enacted ones."[69] According to one source, Shaykh Ṭāhir Ḥamād used to advise men who wanted to take an additional wife to do so in a ceremony performed in accordance with the *sharīʿa* but not before the *maʾdhūn*, and then to apply to the *sharīʿa* court for a declaratory judgment. In one case, he advised a man who had taken an additional wife to have her sue him for maintenance and then to agree to pay maintenance while admitting her to be his wife, whereupon the *qāḍī* would award maintenance while incidentally confirming the marriage on the basis of his admission. In this way, the question of the criminality of the polygamous marriage would not arise.[70]

On the other hand, there were *qāḍī*s who, with certain differences in style and wording, took care to note the fact of the offense in the record. Shaykh Tawfīq ʿAsaliyya did so on several occasions. He would confirm the validity of the polygamous marriage, but add at once that it had been performed in contravention of Israeli legislation.[71] In one case, the man applied for confirmation of his marriage while his identity booklet already described him as married. He alleged that he had divorced his first wife but had not amended the entry of his marital status in the Population Register owing to ignorance of the law. The *qāḍī* confirmed the second marriage, adding that it had been performed in contravention of the law and that the man was obliged to prove that he had divorced his first wife or face the legal penalty.[72] In the case of the man who had divorced his wife without her knowledge so as to be able to take another wife and at the same time keep the first one, Shaykh Ṭāhir Ḥamād found that the use of this device involved two offenses: polygamy and divorce against the wife's will, and that the man was liable to the legal penalties.[73]

All these cases, in which the *qāḍī*s evinced sensitivity to the question of the criminality of polygamy, were actions for confirmation of a marriage (or divorce). The *qāḍī*s seemed to be less sensitive where the offense was disclosed incidentally to the hearing of some matrimonial claim, as for maintenance or obedience. The reason for this may be a purely formal one, viz., that in the latter kind of case the legality of the marriage was not at issue, so that the *qāḍī*s were not obliged to take a stand on it. But it is also possible that the *qāḍī*s were not anxious to upset the life of the family where it seemed to them that the first wife had accepted the situation. Thus, in one case, a woman claimed maintenance until such time as her husband would agree to provide a legal dwelling (*maskan sharᶜī*) for her. She contended that he had installed her rival in close proximity to her, remarking in this connection that he had married the other woman illegally. The husband maintained that he had married the second wife "in accordance with the *sharīᶜa* and the general law, under special circumstances," which he did not specify, and voluntarily agreed to pay maintenance to the first wife until he had provided her with suitable accommodation. The wife agreed to the amount of the maintenance, and the *qāḍī*, Shaykh Ḥasan Amīn al-Ḥabash, confirmed it without in any way referring to the question of the criminality of the second marriage.[74] In several actions for maintenance heard by Shaykh Tawfīq ᶜAsaliyya, the husband did not deny the offense at all, but this question was not dealt with by the court. Thus, in one case, a woman claimed maintenance on the ground that her husband had badly treated her, thus compelling her to return to her father's house. The husband replied that his wife had left him not because of any ill-treatment but because he had taken another wife (from Gaza). The *qāḍī* awarded maintenance.[75] In another maintenance claim, it appeared during the inspection (*kashf*) of the dwelling that the man's first wife and her grown-up children were living in one of the rooms, whereupon the *qāḍī* declared that the dwelling was not legal and ordered the man to pay maintenance. The couple later reached a compromise and the wife asked the *qāḍī* to quash the claim, which he did.[76]

Although the grounds recognized by the Knesset as justifying polygamy are technical and do not leave much scope for judicial discretion, the manner in which the *qāḍī*s relied on them is a significant criterion of their attitude toward polygamy; but they had little opportunity to invoke them for the simple reason that Muslims, as stated, did not usually ask permission for polygamy. In one case, Shaykh Ḥasan Amīn al-Ḥabash, in express reference to the law of 1959, permitted an additional marriage on the ground that the wife suffered from an incurable mental illness. In another case, a man's application to approve and register his polygamous marriage because his wife had borne him no son (though she had borne him daughters) was dismissed by Shaykh Ḥasan on the unprecedented grounds that polygamy was forbidden by law and that the registration of marriages was not his business but that of the *maʾdhūn*, who would register a marriage after it had been proved to his satisfaction that there was no bar to it under the *sharīʿa* or secular law.[77] In other words, Shaykh Ḥasan refused relief in these circumstances because an offense had been committed and apparently also because the plea of lack of male issue did not satisfy him.[78]

NOTES

1. See the chapter "Stipulations Inserted in Contracts of Marriage," pp.30–1.
2. *FRL,* arts.14, 74. See Qadrī, arts.19, 30; *ENFRL;* ʿAbduh and Riḍā, pp.348–9; Amīn, pp.139–40; Linant de Bellefonds, pp.134–6; Hinchcliffe, *Polygamy,* pp.13–16; Anderson, *Contract of Marriage,* pp.122–4; *idem, Islamic Law,* pp.41–2, 46, 49; Coulson, *History,* pp.18–19, 208; *idem, Conflicts,* pp.30, 93; Meron, pp.515–16, 519, 521; Goitein and Ben-Shemesh, pp.132–3, 218–19; Levy, pp.101–2.

3. Par.(c) of the proviso to sec.181 of the Criminal Code Ordinance, 1936. See Meron, p.516.
4. Women's Equal Rights Law, 5711–1951, sec.8 (repeal of par.(c) of the proviso to sec.181 of the Criminal Code Ordinance).
5. During the debate on the Bill in the Knesset, the Prime Minister said: "We regard polygamy as an insult to the human race, an insult to woman as a human being. If we permit polygamy among Muslims, it means that we abandon the Muslim woman and discriminate between women, and as we are pledged to grant equal rights to women, we must not retain discrimination against the Muslim woman." *KP,* vol.9, p.2191 col.1; see also the remarks of the Minister of Justice in the Knesset, *ibid.*, p.2006 col.2; the Explanatory Note to the Women's Equal Rights Bill, 5711–1951, *Bills,* No.75 of 1951 (5711), p.192; Silberg, pp.426–7; Meron, p.530 *seq.*
6. Par.(*b*) of the proviso to sec.181 of the Criminal Code Ordinance. This defense was reformulated in the Penal Law Amendment (Bigamy) Law, 5719–1959 (in connection with the repeal of the said sec.181), as follows: "the spouse by the earlier marriage is missing under circumstances raising a reasonable presumption of his [or her] death, and all trace of him [or her] has been lost for at least seven years." (*Ibid.*, par.(2) of the proviso to sec.6).
7. Penal Law Amendment (Bigamy) Law, 5719–1959, par.(1) of the proviso to sec.6.
8. *Ibid.*, sec.6.
9. Absence and mental illness of the spouse are grounds for dissolution of the marriage on the wife's initiative. See the chapter "Divorce," pp.199 *seq.*
10. See Glasner, pp.276, 279–80. The Minister of Justice told the Knesset that it appeared from an opinion submitted to the Ministry of Religious Affairs by a *qāḍī* that although there might seem to be no need to permit polygamy in the event of mental illness of the spouse because of the ease with which divorce could be effected, it was repugnant to the humane outlook of the Muslims to divorce a wife who was mentally ill and that they therefore sought something like a *hetter de-meʾa rabbanim* (permit signed by a hundred rabbis). *KP,* vol.23, pp.263–6, 313.
11. This attitude is expressed in sec.5 of the Women's Equal Rights Law, 5711–1951. See Silberg, p.428; Zadok, pp.74–6.
12. They are guided in their decisions by considerations such as the man's ability to support his wives and treat them impartially, and the benefit to be expected from the polygamous union. See Linant de Bellefonds, pp.137–8; Hinchcliffe, *Polygamy*, p.19 *seq.*; Coulson, *History*, pp.208–13; *idem*, *Conflicts*, p.93; Anderson, *Islamic Law*, pp.48–50; *idem*, *Syria*, pp.36–8; *idem*, *Tunis*, pp.267–9; Meron, pp.527–8; Fyzee, pp.60, 93.
13. For polygamous marriages revealed on dealing with the confirmation of a marriage see, e.g., *JfQ3*, p.156: no.253–f.160/64 (the man contended that

since the death of one of his wives he had had only one wife), p.297: no.437–f.133/66 (the *qāḍī* noted that the marriage was contrary to the Women's Equal Rights Law); *NzI4*, p.368: no.3/33–f.89/68 and p.368: no.4/34–f.68/90 (two women applied for confirmation of their marriages to the same deceased man); *AcQ5*, p.84: f.230/63 (a man said that he had divorced one of his wives and had only one wife left in his *ᶜiṣma*). For references to *sijill* entries relating to polygamy disclosed in the course of actions for maintenance, obedience or divorce see the chapters "Maintenance and Obedience," pp.98–9, and "Divorce," p.129.

14. See Rosenfeld, *Peasants*, p.126; Marx, *Bedouin*, p.139.
15. *AcṬ4*, p.79: f.17/67, p.94: f.32/67, p.139: f.28/68; *ṬbḤ1*, p.182: no.11 (four wives). Cf. Marx, *Bedouin*, p.139; Muhsam, *Marriage Habits*, pp.71–2.
16. Cf. Marx, *Bedouin*, p.139; *idem, Marriage Patterns,* pp.405–6; *idem, Social Structure,* p.6; al-ᶜĀrif, p.133; Baer, pp.37–8.
17. See, e.g., *JfQ1*, p.63: no.101–f.14/52 (the husband lived in a tented camp (*mukhayyam*) at Ramla); *JfQ4*, p.113: no.126–f.82/68 (the wife, from Lod, the husband from Ramla, both of Negev Beduin origin).
18. *JfMC68*, nos.10313, 9515, and *AcMC68*, no.3441, respectively. The author has not found such stipulations in other types of settlement. See also *JfQ3*, p.145: no.230–f.108/64 (the wife stipulated that if the husband preferred her rival to herself, she might divorce herself by delegation). See the chapter "Divorce," pp.153 *seq.*
19. See, e.g., *JfQ3*, p.155: no.251–f.150/64 (the second marriage was concluded in 1959), p.374: no.515–f.95/7; *ṬbI1*, p.188: no.9–f.15/61 (the wife revealed in an action for maintenance that her husband had "illegally" taken another wife). Cf. Anderson, *Islamic Law,* p.88.
20. Unpublished data of the Central Bureau of Statistics. See also *Criminal Stats.* 1968, pp.34–5. Cf. Meron, p.524; *The Jerusalem Post* of June 15, 1971.
21. Rosenfeld, *Peasants*, pp.39–40, 141.
22. The petition was of September, 1954. See the Archives of the Bureau of the Adviser on Arab Affairs, Prime Minister's Office. In the Little Triangle villages, there were those who interpreted the ban as a deliberate attempt to reduce the natural increase of the Israeli Arab population. See Cohen, p.135.
23. Cf. Marx, *Bedouin*, p.139.
24. See, e.g., *JfQ3*, p.297: no.437–f.133/66, p.312: no.451–f.5/66. See Layish, *Custom*, p.382. To conceal polygamy offenses, it is usual in Turkey to register the children in the name of only one wife. See Dirks, p.80.
25. *ṬbI1*, p.160: no.1–f.3/60.
26. They said so at a symposium at Beyt ha-Gefen in Haifa on May 26, 1971.
27. Interviewee District Judge Muḥammad Nimr al-Hawwārī explained that the expression *barrānī* was borrowed from the terminology of the land

registry: a *barrānī* transfer of land is made outside the land registry by consent of the parties, while a transfer made at the registry is described as *jawwānī* (internal).

28. Through the head of the Demography Section, interviewee Zion Rabi.
29. *AcD8*, p.97:no.14/70–f.125/69. See also *Ṭbl1*, p.226:no.18–f.14/63; *JfQ4*, p.94:no.97–f.38/68; *AcD8*, p.76:f.97/69 (the wife alleged that her husband had deserted her and was living with a young woman on the West Bank).
30. Sec.9 of the Penal Law Amendment (Bigamy) Law, 5719–1959, permits a wife to testify against her husband concerning an offense under this law, but does not require her to do so, and in the absence of such testimony it is difficult to prove the offense.
31. *Ṭbl1,* p.278:no.26–f.33/64 (at the time of the hearing, the man had not yet taken a second wife).
32. See, e.g., *JfQ4*, p.84:no.83–f.16/68, p.185:no.239–f.57/69.
33. See the chapter "Dower," p.60.
34. Penal Law Amendment (Bigamy) Law, 5719–1959, sec.4(3).
35. District Judge Muḥammad Nimr al-Hawwārī refused to hear such a case on the plea of lack of jurisdiction because the offense had been committed outside Israel, but the Supreme Court directed him to hear it and the man was convicted. Particulars were given by interviewee Judge al-Hawwārī. See *AI,* vol.12(1970), Nos.1–2, p.119–26; Meron, p.525. See also *ha-Aretz* of February 9, 1970, and *Maᶜariv* of February 3, 1970.
36. The author was told about this subterfuge by S. Nawi. The *sijill*s contain evidence that a divorced wife sometimes remained at the house of the husband, who provided for all her needs. See the chapter "Divorce," pp.147–8.
37. *JfQ5*, p.124:no.210–f.2/70.
38. See, e.g., *AcṬ4*, p.38:f.3/66, p.107:f.45/67.
39. *JfQ2*, p.401:no.564–f.12/59.
40. Cf. Rosenfeld, *Peasants*, p.126. See there for data on polygamy at Arṭās, studied by Granqvist, and in five Muslim villages in Palestine studied in the 1940s.
41. See Rosenfeld, *Peasants*, pp.39–40, 64, 127–8, 136, 150; Granqvist, vol.2, pp.174, 208–12; Marx, *Bedouin*, pp.139–40; Muhsam, *Polygamy*, pp.88–90; Baer, p.37; *Maᶜariv* of February 3, 1970 (the man said the reason for his second marriage was that his first wife had borne him two daughters, while the second wife had borne her former husband four sons).
42. See the chapter "Divorce," pp.125 *seq*. and *Maᶜariv* of February 3, 1970 (the man took a second wife only after the first wife had refused to agree to a divorce).
43. Cf. Rosenfeld, *Peasants,* p.131.
44. See the chapter "Divorce," pp.143 *seq*. Cf. Cohen, p.72.
45. Quoted from Meron, pp.524–5. See also *ibid*., p.539. The person guilty of bigamy is liable to five years' imprisonment and the person who solemnizes

the marriage is liable to six months' imprisonment. Sec.181 of the Criminal Code Ordinance and sec.8(a) of the Penal Law Amendment (Bigamy) Law, 5719–1959. District Judge Muḥammad Nimr al-Hawwārī said that the court usually sentenced such offenders to small fines and up to three months' imprisonment. He personally imposed a fine of IL 2,000 on a man who had contracted a polygamous marriage on the West Bank. The District Court of Haifa sentenced a resident of Kafr Qarᶜ to six months' imprisonment for polygamy. The prosecution maintained that polygamy was widespread in Israel and that a heavy penalty should therefore be imposed as a deterrent, but the court took into account the pregnancy of the second wife, who asked clemency for her husband. Judgment 13/59, *AI,* vol.7(1959), no.1, p.28.

46. *ṬbḤ4,* p.65:no.26; and *ṬbḤ2,* p.90:no.1, respectively.
47. See the chapter "Divorce," p.131.
48. *JfQ2*, p.528:no.510–f.93/61. Cf. Marx, *Bedouin*, p.139 n.1.
49. In Iraq, too, women rarely invoke the penal sanction attached to polygamy. This is because disputes in matrimonial matters are frequently settled out of court—by arbitrators—and custom and conditions in traditional society assign a passive role to women. el-Naqeb, pp.57–9.
50. See Baer, p.38.
51. See Rosenfeld, *Peasants*, p.126; Marx, *Social Structure*, p.6; Baer, p.37; Levy, p.101; Anderson, *Patriarchal Family*, p.231; Woodsmall, p.117; Granqvist, vol.1, p.138.
52. Cf. Baer, p.38 and the sources indicated there; Woodsmall, pp.125–6.
53. See the chapter "Divorce," pp.180 *seq.*
54. See, e.g., *JfQ2*, p.290:no.451–f.63/57; *AcD6*, p.48:no.49–f.124/64; *NzI4*, p.49:no.1/9–f.14/49; *NzḤ20*, p.75:no.6/68 (the wife married another man while the husband was in prison).
55. See, e.g., *JfQ1*, p.94:no.150–f.74/52 (a woman married a well-known public figure in Lod before her earlier marriage had been properly dissolved).
56. *FRL*, arts.13, 54.
57. *Ha-Aretz* of June 7, 1966 (a Jewess converted to Islam and married a Muslim before her marriage to a Jew had been terminated).
58. *AI*, col.9(1964), Nos.1–2, p.9; and *AI*, vol.11(1968), Nos.1–2, p.11, respectively.
59. See ᶜAbduh and Riḍā, pp.350–1; Amīn, pp.139–40; Shafik, pp.43–9; Goitein and Ben-Shemesh, pp.133, 218–19.
60. *AI,* vol.8(1963), Nos.1–2, pp.1–2; and *AI,* vol.11(1968), Nos.1–2, pp.10–11, respectively.
61. Shaykh Ṭāhir Ḥamād remarked incidentally that keeping a common-law wife was a form of polygamy not subject to legal punishment. The correspondence between him and the President of the Supreme Court was published in *AI*, vol.7(1959), No.4, pp.1–9. The case in question was High Court of Justice 49/54, Mulḥim Nāʾif Mulḥim vs. the Religious Judge

in Acre, *PD*, vol.8, pp.910, 913–14. Parts of the judgment are quoted by Silberg, pp.419–20, 427–8, and by Goitein and Ben-Shemesh, pp.239–41. See also Arami, pp.116–17. For Knesset Member A. Jarjūra's objection to the withdrawal of permission for polygamy among Muslims see *KP*, vol.9, p.2189. See also Schacht, pp.120 *seq.*; Meron, pp.517 *seq.*, 526–7.

62. *AI*, vol.8(1963), Nos.3–4, pp.1–2; *AI*, vol.9(1964), Nos.1–2, p.8; *AI*, vol.11(1968), Nos.1–2, p.6. For a more extensive discussion see the chapter "Maintenance and Obedience," pp.110–11.
63. So did Advocate Maḥmūd al-Māḍī, a former director of *sharīʿa* courts. Shaykh Amīn Qāsim Mudlij suggested that disobedience of the wife should also be a "good defense" to the charge of divorcing her against her will. *AI*, vol.9(1964), Nos.3–4, pp.2–3, 8–9.
64. *AI*, vol.10(1967), Nos.3–4, pp.7–8, 12–13, 18.
65. See the chapter "Maintenance and Obedience," pp.98–9.
66. *JfQ4*, p.137:no.164–f.148/68.
67. *JfQ3*, p.156:no.253–f.160/64. See also *AcṬ4*, p.57:f.27/66.
68. *AcṬ4*, p.38:f.3/66, and p.80:f.18/67, respectively. See also *AcṬ4*, p.50: f.17/66 (the *qāḍī* confirmed the divorce, adding that the man might only marry his divorced wife again "after he had become single"), p.88:f.26/67 (the reinstatement of the divorced wife was "prohibited by law"), p.94: f.32/67 (the *qāḍī* warned the man not to take his divorced wife back so long as he had two wives in his *ʿiṣma*), p.98:f.36/67, p.107:f.45/67 (the *qāḍī* explained that although the man might take back his divorced wife according to the *sharīʿa*, he might not do so according to secular law so long as he had another wife).
69. *JfQ3*, p.155:no.251–f.150/64.
70. Based on information supplied by Advocate S. Darwish.
71. *JfQ3*, p.297:no.437–f.33/66, p.312:no.451–f.5/67.
72. *JfQ3*, p.374:no.515–f.95/67.
73. *JfQ3*, p.401:no.464–f.12/59.
74. *ṬbI1*, p.188:no.9–f.15/61.
75. *JfQ4*, p.84:no.83–f.16/68. See also *JfQ4*, p.185:no.239–f.57/69.
76. *JfQ4*, p.92:no.95–f.121/67 and p.133:no.158–f.130/68. See also *JfQ4*, p.113:no.126–f.82/68; *JfQ5*, p.133:no.218–f.317/69.
77. *ṬbḤ4*, p.65:no.26; and *ṬbḤ2*, p.90:no.1, respectively. Permission for polygamy sought from *qāḍī*s in Iraq on the plea of "legal benefit" is granted automatically and the law is thus made a mockery. Also, ignoring offenses subject to penal sanctions (imprisonment up to one year and a fine up to 100 dinars), the *qāḍī*s confirm polygamous marriages *ex post facto;* el-Naqeb, pp.51–4, 58.
78. For his attempt to turn the mechanism of registration into an effective bar to divorce against the wife's will see the chapter "Divorce," pp.191*seq.*

Chapter Five
MAINTENANCE AND OBEDIENCE

The complex of rights and duties assigned to the wife by virtue of the marriage reflects a balance adapted to the patrilineal and patriarchal structure of the family. The wife is obliged to move to the husband's dwelling, to stay at his house (*mulāzamat baytihi*) and not leave it without his permission; to obey him (*ṭāᶜa*); to fulfil her marital duties (*istimtāᶜ*); to bring up the children, and attend to the household. On the other hand, she has property rights *vis-a-vis* the husband. She is entitled to maintenance; to kind treatment (*ḥusn al-muᶜāshara*); to the legally specified number of visits to and from her relatives, and such like.[1]

I. LEGAL BACKGROUND

Maintenance (*nafaqa*) includes food (*ṭaᶜām*), clothing (*kiswa*) and a legal dwelling (*maskan sharᶜī*). As between the spouses, the right to maintenance is vested in the wife alone. She is not required to bear the cost of her and her children's subsistence and of the household, even if the husband is unable to do so and she has means of her own. According to Islamic law, the property of the spouses is separate and the wife may manage her property independently.[2]

The amount of maintenance is fixed by agreement between the spouses or, in the absence of agreement, by the *sharīᶜa* court. The *qāḍī* appoints experts (*mukhbirūn*)—representatives of the parties and of the court—to assess the amount. They are religious functionaries and public figures of accepted authority, such as *imām*s, *mukhtār*s, heads of local councils, advocates and secretaries of *sharīᶜa* courts.[3] The amount is fixed in accordance with the economic position of the spouses, the cost of living and the needs of the wife and the family. The concept of maintenance has greatly widened in present-day Muslim society: it now comprises also the cost of the education of the children, medical treatment, including sick-fund dues, expenditure in connection with childbirth, traveling expenses, etc.[4] Maintenance was usually paid in money, but occasionally in kind, in the shape of staple foods (such as oil) and essential household articles (such as soap). Sometimes it consisted in property bearing a yield (such as olive trees). Payment might also be made in promissory notes.[5]

The wife can enforce a judgment for maintenance by execution, but few instances are attested of her doing so.[6] On the other hand, numerous cases are on record of husbands failing to comply with the judgment. Such failure is apparent from recurrent actions for maintenance and from judgments for divorce by agreement, by which the wife waived maintenance accumulated in her favor since the judgment awarding it.[7] If the husband is unable to support the wife or is absent, having left her without maintenance, the wife may, with the approval of the court, borrow money (*istidāna*) in his name which he will have to repay. Cases are recorded where a relative of the wife, who, but for her marriage, would have owed her maintenance, granted her a loan at her request[8] or where she collected maintenance out of her absent husband's property.[9] If the woman left her husband for any reason, she commonly went to the house of her father or some other agnatic relative, who supported her until she returned to her husband's house.[10] A frequent way of collecting maintenance was by transferring the insurance pension of the children or the old-age pension from the husband to the wife.[11] In urban areas, sometimes it was found that wives were the supporters of the family, including, in some cases, the husband.[12] There were instances of wives being compelled to work because the maintenance paid by their husbands was insufficient for their upkeep.[13]

II. CAUSES OF CLAIMS FOR MAINTENANCE AND OF DISOBEDIENCE

The wife's duty of moving into the husband's dwelling is conditional on receipt of the prompt dower. If the dower is not paid, she may leave his house without his permission without being regarded as a rebellious wife (*nāshiza*), in which case she would lose her right to maintenance.[14]

In many cases, the wife left the husband's house on the ground that all or part of the prompt dower or some stipulations connected therewith, such as household effects and various appurtenances, had not been forthcoming[15]; she claimed maintenance, refusing to return until she had received her due. In some instances, it was expressly stated that the wife had not moved in with the husband (*zifāf*) at all and that the marriage had not been consummated.[16] But usually the wife left the husband after *zifāf* had taken place and sometimes even after children had been born.[17] Other property items which frequently gave rise to a claim for maintenance and to disobedience were the *jihāz* (equipment, clothing and household effects which the wife brought with her from her father's house on her marriage),[18] the *maṣāgh* (jewelry) and the *ḥaly* (ornaments). A wife would claim ownership thereof, accuse the husband of taking them from her against her will, sometimes by force, and demand their return.[19] The aforesaid grounds obtained in towns and villages, where women were alive to their property rights, but not in Beduin society.

Non-receipt of maintenance was, of course, the principal motive for a claim. A wife might sometimes allege that her husband was delaying (*yumāṭil*) her maintenance,[20] that the amount of maintenance was insufficient and that an addition (*ziyāda* or *rafᶜ*) was required,[21] or that her husband had left the house and gone to live elsewhere without arranging for her maintenance.[22]

Disputes concerning the dwelling were another cause for claims. The husband is obligated to provide the wife with a legal dwelling (*maskan sharᶜī*), containing all the equipment she requires, at a place chosen by him. A legal dwelling is a separate house (*dār ᶜalā ḥidatihā*; i.e., separate from the house of the husband's family) if the couple are well off, and a separate apartment within the husband's family's house (*bayt min dār ᶜalā ḥidatihi*) if they are not. The dwelling must have all the legally required facilities, as well as neighbors of a social level which accords with the couple's standing. The husband must not accommodate his relatives—except an undiscriminating (*ghayr mumayyiz*) minor—in the dwelling without the wife's consent, nor may the wife accommodate therein her children (even minor) by another husband or her relatives without the husband's consent. If the husband installs his wife in a separate dwelling in his family's house, she is not entitled to demand a different dwelling unless his relatives "harass her by word or deed."[23] In fact, the characteristics of the legal dwelling correspond to the principle of patrilocality (dwelling within the husband's family's residence).[24]

Hundreds of maintenance and obedience judgments indeed reflect a complex set of relationships between the spouses within the framework of the extended family, with all its typical manifestations and tensions. The wife might assert that the dwelling was not legal, i.e., that it was not a separate entity within the husband's family's dwelling[25]; that the catering and meals were shared—in other words, that she was completely dependent on her mother-in-law[26]; or that some household utensils, clothing and other appurtenances were lacking.[27] But her main complaints in this connection were that her husband's relatives (her mother-in-law, father-in-law, brothers-in-law, sisters-in-law, etc.) "harass her by word and deed," i.e., insulted and beat her (sometimes so seriously as to force her to flee the house); locked her up in the house; turned her out of the house; prevented her from entering the house or her room; charged her with immoral conduct, and so forth. The wife frequently demanded that the husband prevent his relatives from entering her dwelling and interfering in her life.[28]

Tensions between the wife and the husband's relatives were important factors in the disintegration of the extended family.[29] There is evidence of this and especially of attempts by the wife to achieve a structural solution by which she would escape the control of her in-laws: she might leave the husband's house and refuse to return to him and obey him until he provided her with a dwelling away from his family, in a house owned by him; there were cases in which such attempts were successful.[30] Sometimes a woman made her consent to the marriage conditional on the husband providing her with a separate dwelling; this mostly meant a dwelling in the house (*dār*) of the husband's family, but occasionally express stipulation was made for a "completely separate house."[31] The wife at times agreed to live in her husband's father's house, but stipulated that "if anger erupts" between her and the husband's family or "if she is compelled to leave the house for any reason" the husband should provide her with a dwelling "away from the family" or pay her a sum of money with which to build a new house.[32]

The practice of making the marriage conditional on the provision of a separate dwelling was particularly widespread in urban types of settlement and in the Little Triangle villages. Cohen in his study of Bint al-Ḥudūd in the Little Triangle found that the wife demanded a separate dwelling when there was no blood-relationship between her and her husband,[33] that is to say, that the grip of the extended family was stronger in the case of endogamous marriages. This finding is not confirmed by the sources of the present work. On the contrary, in more than half the cases in which the wife stipulated for a separate dwelling the spouses belonged to the same clan (*ḥamūla*) or were even first cousins.[34] The endogamous marriage was thus no serious obstacle to the wife's striving for a separate dwelling, i.e., to the breakup of the extended family. The stipulation in the marriage contract was particularly widespread in relation to the contents of the dwelling, viz., the various household effects (*ʿafsh al-bayt*, *athāth*): furniture, bedding, a sewing-machine, "a complete drawing-room suite," bedroom and kitchen equipment, and all this "after the latest fashion."[35] The value of the household equipment usually ranged between IL 1,500 and IL 2,000.

The wife sometimes refused to move into a dwelling because in her opinion it did not suit her social status or might lower her prestige. Thus, in one case, a woman contended: "[Girls] who are my equals (*mathīlātī*) obtained separate conjugal dwellings," and in another case the woman said that the *maskan* was not legal "considering their status and the kind of people they are"; she asked that a house of concrete be built for her. In yet another case, the wife refused to live in the *maskan* because it was situated in the village main street, "lest her good name be impaired."[36] In several cases, the wife alleged that her husband would leave her in the house by herself so that she felt lonely (*tastawḥish*). This, too, is a legal ground for maintenance in certain circumstances, and the husband must either provide a female companion (*muʾnisa*) to keep her company and cheer her up or transfer her to a place where she will not feel lonely.[37] In one case, a woman from Ramla said that her husband went to his other wife in Gaza every Saturday morning and returned only on Monday, leaving her to herself in the meantime; "and there are no neighbors nearby so that I am afraid." In a further case, a woman from Galilee reported that her husband went to work near Jerusalem, leaving her to herself, and that she "felt lonesome." The husband provided a *muʾnisa* to relieve her boredom on the nights when he was away from home, but the wife refused to accept her because she belonged to the husband's *ḥamūla* and harassed her.[38]

The wife is bound to follow the husband to whatever locality he chooses.[39] She generally raised no objection as to the type of settlement, the neighborhood or the like. But in several dozen cases wives did raise objections although their dwellings were legal and their husbands had not withheld any of their conjugal rights or ill-treated them, but on the contrary, had been kind to them. However, these women were not willing to live with their spouses in certain localities or geographical areas even if they were treated "in the best possible way" and provided with "the best of dwellings."[40] The chief cause of this phenomenon was the unwillingness of the wives to change the way of life, habits, standards, type of housing, etc., to which they had been accustomed before their marriages. Two-thirds of the cases involved townswomen who were not prepared to live in the country,[41] in a Beduin encampment[42] or even in a town regarded as inferior in social, economic or other respects.[43] Sometimes a townswoman was unwilling to move to another quarter of the same town.[44] A countrywoman might not be prepared to live in a village less developed or farther from urban centers than her home village or might wish to live in another quarter of the same village.[45] In one case, a Beduin woman who had married a Beduin of another tribe refused to live in his encampment.[46] A countrywoman might refuse to live in town, despite better housing conditions, and a higher standard of living, because of her attachment to her original environment and her family and because of her fear of change, and of confrontation with a modern way of life.[47]

A townswoman married to a Beduin or villager could stipulate in the marriage contract that the conjugal dwelling should be in her home locality.[48] She sometimes added that if the husband infringed this stipulation he should have to pay her a sum of money for the purchase of a dwelling there.[49] In isolated cases, countrywomen stipulated that their townsmen husbands reside in their villages.[50] In one case, the couple lived for a time near the residence of the wife's family at Lod. Because of disputes between the husband, a Negev Beduin, and the wife's family, and because he worked near Beersheba, he suggested that they go to live with his tribe, but she would have none of it "even if he gives me a palace."[51] This case is instructive because it involved a phenomenon approximating matrilocality. It was a consequence of intensified commuting of rural and Beduin manpower to urban and economic centers, especially since the late 1950s, when restrictions on movement imposed by the Military Government were gradually relaxed and eventually abolished. In the encounter between rural and Beduin commuters and urban women, the latter had the upper hand, and as a result, the couples took up residence in town. Significant in this connection, though rare, was the husband's resort to a stipulation in the marriage contract in order to ensure that the conjugal dwelling be in his home locality,[52] although the *sharīʿa* already required it to be there.

Sometimes a wife reached a goodwill agreement—without binding force—with the husband establishing the conjugal dwelling in her home locality. Thus, in one case, the couple lived for a time in the husband's village but then, following a quarrel, they made an agreement under which the permanent dwelling was to be in the wife's township and she was to supply his meals when he was staying with her in return for a fixed maintenance payment. In another case, the spouses agreed to move from the countryside to the city where the husband worked. He sold his property, but at the last moment he changed his mind, whereupon the wife left his house and went to live in the city. In a further case, the husband moved to the wife's dwelling in a Beduin settlement after she had repeatedly left his house, situated in a village. Later he was compelled to return to his village, but his wife refused to follow him.[53]

In several cases, the husband lived in the wife's dwelling (not in her family's); in almost all such cases she was a townswoman and he from some other type of settlement.[54] Sometimes the wife stipulated in the marriage contract that the dwelling should be her property or the common (*mushtarak*) property of the spouses or that half of the house should be her property as part of, or in addition to, the dower.[55] In all these cases, the wife came from one of the mixed towns (Jaffa, Ramla, Lod) or from a Little Triangle village. In one case, the spouses were first cousins who had inherited the plot and house where they lived from their parents. In another case, the wife required the husband to register the dwelling in her name and to give her "whatever she might demand in the future, without any restriction."[56]

Cruelty toward the wife or "lack of good treatment" by the husband was frequently a cause of disobedience. A wife might complain that her husband ill-used her in various ways: cursed her, humiliated her, treated her rudely and harshly, burdened her with work beyond her strength, beat her violently, sometimes to the point of grievous injury necessitating medical attendance and hospitalization, or even threatened or attempted to kill her.[57] Sometimes women called the police or filed actions in the civil courts.[58] Under such circumstances, the wife mostly left the husband's house and refused to obey him on the ground that she was not "safe in the dwelling with him."[59] The husband frequently ejected the wife from the house, alone or with her children.[60] Occasionally he himself left the house and disappeared without leaving a trace[61] or stayed away for a long time, especially for purposes of work. In one case, the wife said that the husband spent five hours every day traveling to work and back to his village and that damage was caused her thereby[62]; such disruption of family life was typical of the increased commuting of manpower from towns and villages to centers of employment.[63] Imprisonment of the husband or his confinement, by police order, to a place outside the locality in which the couple lived could also be a ground for a claim for maintenance.[64] Sometimes the wife complained that her husband was insulting her by charging that she "loved someone else" or was unfaithful to him.[65] In one case, the wife took offense at the fact that her husband had not himself come to take her to his house "in accordance with custom and tradition"; had he done so, she said, she would have willingly obeyed him. In another case, the wife had waited three years in vain at her brother's house for the husband to ask her personally to return to him; then she had sued him for maintenance.[66]

It has happened that a husband forced his wife to work and hand over her earnings to him and beat her soundly when she started out late for work.[67] A wife might assert that she was ill and unable to work.[68] In the Little Triangle villages, the wife frequently stipulated in the marriage contract that she would go "veiled or keep indoors" (*mukhaddara*) and "not have to work away from home."[69] Changes in the occupational structure, especially the large-scale commuting of rural manpower, had caused a serious shortage of agricultural labor. As a result, there was an increased need for the employment of women and children, and since agricultural work was hard, many women preferred to marry landless men. The liberation of women from agricultural work has in recent years become a matter of prestige. A woman who did not work away from home, or who in consequence of her marriage had stopped doing so, covered her face with a veil.[70] The author did not encounter conditions of this kind in other parts of the country, except for one case involving a woman from Acre.[71] The fact that this custom was peculiar to the Little Triangle was probably due to the advanced social position of women in this area compared with other agricultural regions. In most cases, the women in question had had an elementary or secondary education.[72]

Polygamous marriages were another cause of claims of maintenance and disobedience. Islamic law requires the husband to practice justice and equality (ʿ*adl*) toward his wives as regards maintenance and the apportionment (*qasm*) of his time between them. He must also install each of them in a separate dwelling. This applies even in so far as a wife does not claim that a rival in the same house (*dār*) harms her by word or deed.[73] Wives often complained of discrimination as to maintenance or marital relations.[74] Another frequent complaint by a wife was that the husband had installed her and her rival in the same dwelling or adjoining dwellings and that this caused her so much suffering or injury that she sometimes fled from the house; her flight might also be a means of exerting pressure on the husband to grant her a separate dwelling.[75] There have been cases in which a husband, after taking a second wife, turned the first wife out of the house[76] or left the house and went to live elsewhere with the other.[77] It has also happened that a wife left her husband's house because of his taking another wife, with the declared intention of not returning to him and without claiming maintenance.[78]

One of the commonest causes of the wife's leaving the husband's house and refusing to return to him—sometimes despite numerous approaches by the husband through mediators (*wusaṭāʾ*) and "people of good will" (*ahl al-khayr*)[79]—were disputes between the two families and interference by them in the life of the couple. The dispute could be quite unconnected with the spouses themselves; it might be over some criminal matter or some land.[80] Then, again, it might be between the husband and the wife's family.[81] Shaykh Ḥasan Amīn al-Ḥabash said that most of the disputes were due to incitement (*taḥriḍ*) by the wife's family.[82] Shaykh Amīn Qāsim Mudlij, on the other hand, tended to stress the role of the husband's relatives. The latter seemed to think that since the wife was bought with their money, she ought to be their slave (*ʿabda*) and servant (*khādima*) rather than serve and obey her husband. They regarded themselves as "a political and legislative authority and the son [the husband] as an executive authority" whose task was to implement the decisions of his family regarding his wife. The wife's relatives, on the other hand, were distressed about her being severed from her family and felt that she was entitled to a married life in freedom, without outside interference. These opposing views might even find expression on the very first day of the marriage, especially among unintelligent people. The immediate cause of disputes of this kind was the proximity of the conjugal dwelling to the residence of the husband's family.[83]

In such circumstances, the wife usually displayed loyal, sometimes even fanatical, attachment to her family. Thus, in one case, a wife who had left her husband's house contended: "My children's honor is not greater than that of my brothers."[84] Sometimes the wife was not prepared to return to the husband's house until the families had made peace (*taṣāluḥ*) or her father had given his consent.[85] But it also happened that she might openly admit that her father or brother forced her to leave her husband's house, that she did not deny that the dwelling was legal and that her husband had given her everything due to her, and that she wanted to return to him but was afraid that her relatives would harm her.[86] In one case, the wife said that her father "will slaughter her if she crosses him" and asked that the court issue an order for obedience and that she be handed over to her husband by the police "so as to escape punishment by her father."[87]

In the case of exchange marriages (*shighār*, *tabādul al-zawjāt*) it is difficult in everyday life to maintain strict equality between the exchanged women as to food, housing, clothing, and so on. Shaykh Ḥasan Amīn al-Ḥabash said that it was sufficient for one of them to think that she was less favorably off than her *badīla* (the one for whom she had been exchanged) to make jealousy and envy spring up immediately, which would in turn lead to a distorted outlook and spoil relations between the spouses.[88] Exchange marriage created a mutual dependence between the two families: the falling out, for any reason whatsoever, of one couple, as a result of which the wife left the husband's house and he applied for a judgment for obedience or she claimed maintenance, would almost automatically entail similar steps on the part of the other couple. A wife frequently admitted that she had no complaints against her husband regarding the dwelling, dower, or any other matter, and that she only left his house because her *badīla* had quarreled with *her* husband and because "according to custom," when one *badīla* left her husband, the other was expected to do likewise.[89] A woman sometimes stipulated that she would only return to her husband on the condition that her *badīla* return to hers.[90] And indeed, if and when the first couple made up its quarrel, the other wife would also return to her husband.[91]

Other manifestations of the mutual dependence created by exchange marriages were the payment of maintenance at like rates to the two wives[92] and actions for maintenance and obedience between the respective partners, ending in the divorce of both wives at the same time and on the same terms.[93] The women were pawns in the game between the families: their moves were usually determined against their will.[94] In only one case did a woman seek release from the rules of mutual dependence, but the matter ended in divorce contrary to her wishes.[95]

The only way to break the dependence between the two marriages was to pay dower, and in several cases a *badīla* in fact announced her willingness to return to her husband if dower was paid.[96] Exchange marriages were particularly frequent in rural and Beduin society, but did occur in urban society as well.[97]

Chief among the causes of non-payment of maintenance, and of claims for obedience, were conditions in which the wife had left the house without the husband's permission and gone to see her father, brother, mother, children or other relatives or her neighbors,[98] refused to return to the husband and to obey him,[99] was "rebellious," did not fulfil her duties toward the husband, the children and the household,[100] gave her own family and her children preference over the husband,[101] had her children by another man live in her husband's house,[102] or had misbehaved herself[103]; sometimes the husband was unable to pay maintenance or to provide a separate dwelling to the wife owing to poverty, unemployment, or insufficient income.[104] The wife might work away from home against the husband's will[105] or demand to live in her original locality.[106] Some of these causes attest to innovations in the status of women, such as their working away from home and supporting their families.[107]

III. THE REBELLIOUS WOMAN

A wife who leaves her husband's house without his permission and without a legal reason is considered rebellious (*nāshiza*) and loses the right to maintenance for the duration of her rebelliousness (*nushūz*).[108] The declaration of a wife as rebellious is the customary legal sanction against her refusal to obey. The concept of the *bayt al-ṭāᶜa* (house of obedience) does not exist in Israel, where a judgment for obedience is not legally enforceable.[109] Moreover, the prohibition of polygamy and of divorce against the wife's will had deprived the husband of two severe sanctions that once would have deterred the wife from disobedience. Shaykh Ḥusnī al-Zuᶜbī and other *qāḍī*s were of the opinion that women now took unfair advantage of the reforms in their legal status and that the rules of obedience were no longer effective.[110]

The *sijill*s do not contain many declarations of rebelliousness, but many women were actually in a state of rebellion in the sense that they did not obey their husbands and did not receive maintenance. In many cases, though women told the courts that they would not obey their husbands, they were nevertheless not declared rebellious; and many judgments for obedience were not enforced for many years, if at all.[111] For both traditional and modern reasons, the economic sanction did not seem to deter women from disobedience. As stated, a woman who left her husband usually went to her agnatic relatives, who provided for her and for her children (if she had taken them with her) until she became reconciled with her husband and returned to him. If the dispute ended in divorce, the burden of maintenance devolved on her family until she was remarried. Sometimes a wife made her return to her husband conditional on his reimbursing the maintenance paid by her father during her stay with him.[112] Moreover, the urban woman enjoyed a sense of economic security. She was not dependent on her father; she worked for her living and was able to support her children and might even live alone.[113] She might waive maintenance for herself and her children and undertake to provide for her children "at her own expense."[114]

Furthermore, in some cases the wife, on her own initiative, demanded to be considered rebellious and denied the right to maintenance.[115] In about half the cases in which the wife was declared rebellious, the spouses, or at least the wife, came from an urban type of settlement. Reasons for the wife's being declared rebellious included unwillingness of a townswoman to live in the husband's home locality (if rural or a Beduin encampment)[116]; disputes between the spouses over property, such as jewelry, livestock and immovables[117]; the wife's working away from home; her living in a separate dwelling with her children by another man[118]; and her reaction to being ill-treated by the husband in various ways.[119] In one case, the husband alleged that the wife's father incited her against him "for reasons of village party politics."[120] In the vast majority of cases, there was no blood relationship between the spouses, and it seems reasonable to assume that in an exogamous marriage the wife enjoys greater freedom in her relations with the husband than in an endogamous one.

The traditional equilibrium between the rights and duties of husband and wife had thus been greatly upset in Israeli Muslim society. This was due to the disintegration of the extended family, to the changes in the position of women and to the intervention of the Knesset. It seems that more than in the past the husband in recent times has resorted to legal action to get his wife to obey him. It is characteristic that in one case the husband sought a judgment for obedience because he feared that the wife was about to slip across the border into some Arab country; he asked for her to be tied to him by a IL 3,000 guarantee and with the help of the police.[121] However, since judgments for obedience were not enforceable, the husband had no choice but to apply the traditional methods of establishing domestic peace by means of arbitrators and mediators.

Sometimes disputes between spouses were indeed terminated by reconciliation. An important part was played in this connection by arbitrators, mediators, "people of good will," the children of the spouses, and *qāḍī*s.[122] In the case of reconciliation, the wife withdrew her claim for maintenance or asked that the judgment for maintenance given in her favor be rescinded,[123] and the husband withdrew his action for obedience.[124] Reconciliations were sometimes accompanied by detailed agreements between the spouses, specifying the duties and rights of each toward the other. The husband might undertake not to be late in paying maintenance to his wife and children; to assure their subsistence and well-being; to allot a specific daily amount to the wife for household expenses (to be supplemented by him if insufficient, while any surplus was to be kept by her in a special fund); to treat the wife well; not to beat or curse her; to prevent his relatives attacking her or interfering in her life; to divide his time equitably between his wives; to provide a separate dwelling for his wife, to build her a new house with a kitchen and modern facilities, to set up a partition between her dwelling and that of his family, to provide a separate entrance to her dwelling; to permit the wife to visit her relatives from time to time. On the other hand, the husband was entitled to bring up his children and ensure that they obeyed him, and to determine the location of the dwelling. The wife would undertake to be "extremely courteous" toward the husband, not to annoy him "and to remember that he is the head of the family"; not to interfere in matters pertaining to his personal freedom, such as the times of his going out and coming home; to obey him, not to go out without his permission; to fulfil her marital duties; to manage the household, cook his meals and look after the children; to see that her relatives did not call without his invitation or consent, and so on.[125] Sometimes it was provided that one of the wife's relatives should offer surety for the fulfilment of her obligations under the agreement or that if the husband infringed a condition of the agreement he should pay maintenance or—which was very rare—the wife might be delegated by the husband to divorce herself.[126] On the basis of such agreements, the *qāḍī* would give a judgment for obedience by mutual consent of the parties.[127]

IV. MAINTENANCE OF WOMEN WITHIN THE WIDER FAMILY CIRCLE

Maintenance out of the estate is unknown in Islamic law. The widow is not entitled to maintenance out of her husband's estate; according to the *sharīʿa*, she takes a share of it.[128] Her maintenance is the responsibility of her children. However, unlike the wife's right to maintenance, which exists even where she is rich and the husband poor, the mother's maintenance is fixed in accordance with her economic position: only a destitute mother is entitled to maintenance, and on the other hand, children are only liable to pay it if they have the necessary means.[129] The Knesset interfered in the matter of maintenance as far as the wider family circle is concerned, which includes the parents and grandparents of the spouses, the grown-up children and their spouses, the grandchildren, and the brothers and sisters of the spouses. There was no interference as to maintenance within the immediate family (i.e., the spouses and their minor children), to which religious law continues to apply. The Family Law Amendment (Maintenance) Law, 5719–1959, provides, *inter alia*, that the extent, measure and modes of provision of maintenance within the wider family circle shall, in the absence of agreement between the parties, be prescribed by the court "according to the need of the person entitled and the ability of the person liable." This principle is consonant with the Islamic legal concept. Another section provides that the law "shall add to, and not derogate from, maintenance rights accruing under any law administered by a religious court, or under the personal law applying to the parties."[130]

More than 200 claims for maintenance within the wider family circle were filed in *sharīʿa* courts in the period under review. About one-third were filed by the widowed mother, the remainder by the father (sometimes maintenance was sought by both parents) and other relatives. All the applications by widows were directed against sons, not one against daughters. The mother based her application on the plea that she was old, ill and poor, that she had no property or source of income, that the National Insurance pension was insufficient, that she was incapable of earning a living, that she had no supporter and that no one but her son (or sons) owed her maintenance.[131] She sometimes alleged that her son had seized control of the family property and thereby deprived her of her means of subsistence.[132]

Some of the actions ended with maintenance being awarded to the mother by mutual agreement of the parties. The sons might undertake to provide their mother, in addition to maintenance, with a suitable dwelling in which to spend the rest of her days.[133] Failing mutual agreement, the rate of maintenance was fixed by *mukhbirūn* (experts). Sons who refused to pay maintenance to their mothers contended that their commitments toward their own families did not allow them to assume additional burdens and that their mothers had property—shares in the estates of their family heads—sufficient for their subsistence.[134] There was a definite correlation between the extent of the sons' readiness to pay maintenance to their mothers and the state of property relations after the death of a family head: where the mother held the family property or her share in the estate, the sons were less ready to grant her economic assistance. A similar attitude governed relations between sons and their aged father. In some cases, a father claimed maintenance from his sons on the ground that he had registered all his property in their names.[135] In one case, the sons made it an express condition for their paying maintenance to their father that he should transfer part of his property to them, and in another case they rejected their father's claim for maintenance on the ground that he had registered all his property in the name of his wife, their mother.[136] All the maintenance claims of widowed mothers arose in rural or urban, but not Beduin, types of settlement.

A small number of maintenance claims were filed by women of other degrees of relationship: by sisters against brothers, by nieces against paternal uncles, by granddaughters against grandfathers and so forth. The maintenance claim of a minor in the custody of her mother was usually filed by the latter,[137] but sometimes by the claimant herself.[138] In claims by sisters, it was occasionally contended that the brother had usurped their share in the father's estate.[139] In some cases men were ordered to pay maintenance to their daughters-in-law or granddaughters because their husbands were unable to support them; the maintenance was then regarded as a debt of the husbands.[140]

V. THE *QĀḌĪ*S AND MAINTENANCE AND OBEDIENCE

The salient feature in the *qāḍī*s' dealing with maintenance and obedience claims was their effort to reconcile the spouses and restore domestic peace. This sprang from their deep-rooted belief in the importance of the marital union and family life. Shaykh Tawfīq Maḥmūd ᶜAsaliyya stressed the heavy responsibility of the courts in this connection: "The family is the nucleus of society, and the greater its integrity and inner equilibrium, the cooperation between its members, and its purity, the greater is the *umma's* [Muslim community's] progress on the road of civilization."[141] Shaykh Ḥusnī al-Zuᶜbī said that "the marital bond is a solid bond between the spouses, and the *sharīᶜa* wants it to subsist and the comradeship and love between the spouses to endure."[142] Shaykh Amīn Qāsim Mudlij, Shaykh Mūsā al-Ṭabarī and observers close to *sharīᶜa* court affairs likened the *qāḍī* to the family doctor.[143] Almost all maintenance and obedience judgments note that the court made efforts to bring about reconciliation and compromise settlement between the spouses. Frequently the hearing was adjourned in the hope that the spouses would meanwhile reach agreement.[144] The *qāḍī* might invoke the blood-relationship of the spouses to smooth out their differences.[145] Indeed, his efforts were sometimes successful without his having to render judgment for maintenance or obedience.[146] The striving for compromise was probably connected with an established tradition of avoiding application of the *sharīᶜa* for fear of distorting it.[147] This tendency turned the *sharīᶜa* court into a kind of arbitral agency, as customary in traditional society; in fact, the *qāḍī*s occasionally called in outside arbitrators to settle disputes between spouses.[148] They refrained as far as possible from handing down decisions and applying legal sanctions. The judgment was very often intended to validate an agreement or compromise reached by the parties.[149]

If the court's efforts to reconcile the parties failed and there was no escape from passing judgment, the *qāḍī* did so reluctantly.[150] He might add that the judgment for obedience was conditional on the husband's treating the wife well and fulfilling all his conjugal duties, or he might warn the husband not to ill-use his wife in any way, to respect her rights, not to touch her property, to grant her "full freedom so long as no infringement of Islamic law is involved," to enable her to visit her relatives, not to force her to wait on him or his relatives and to avoid petty jealousy, malicious gossip and the like.[151] He would sometimes threaten that if the husband did not comply with his directions he would award maintenance to the wife or permit her to act against the husband's will, for instance, in the matter of visits to relatives.[152] Sometimes the *qāḍī* exhorted both spouses to fulfil their mutual duties, to prevent their respective families from meddling in their affairs.[153] Shaykh Mūsā al-Ṭabarī and Shaykh Tawfīq ᶜAsaliyya occasionally made a judgment for obedience conditional on the husband's providing sureties for good behaviour toward the wife.[154]

The *qāḍī*s' approach in judgments was extremely formal; they decided in scrupulous adherence to the provisions of the *sharīᶜa* and sometimes invoked Qurᵓānic verses and commentaries to support their judgments.[155] With regard to maintenance, this approach was usually favorable to the wife. The *qāḍī*s took no account of changes in the social and economic status of women and continued to regard the husband as the head and supporter of the family. Thus, in one case, Shaykh Ṭāhir Ḥamād awarded maintenance to the wife although she had admitted that she was well-off and lived without assistance from her husband, "because maintenance is one of her legal rights and the husband is not exempt from providing it." In another case, he ordered the husband to pay maintenance "because according to the *sharīᶜa* a wife cannot be forced to put up the husband in her house . . . if she does not do so of her own free will."[156] Shaykh Ḥasan Amīn al-Ḥabash decided that maintenance of the wife was the responsibility of the husband alone even if he was poor.[157] Shaykh Tawfīq Maḥmūd ᶜAsaliyya held that unemployment of the husband did not relieve him of the duty to provide maintenance to the wife.[158] These decisions conformed to the spirit of Islamic law. The foregoing also applied whenever the husband failed to fulfil one of his other obligations toward the wife, such as the payment of prompt dower, or to conform to any stipulations connected therewith, the provision of a legal dwelling, good treatment of the wife, and so on; in all these cases, the *qāḍī*s were careful to award maintenance to the wife.[159]

On the other hand, the formal approach was sometimes to the wife's disadvantage. Thus, the claim of a woman in the last month of pregnancy for maintenance from the day, six months earlier, when she had been driven from her husband's house was dismissed by Shaykh Amīn Qāsim Mudlij on the ground that according to the *sharīᶜa* maintenance is not awarded for the time preceding the filing of the application.[160] Shaykh

Ṭawfīq Maḥmūd ᶜAsaliyya distinguished between wife-beating "contrary to the principles of the *sharīᶜa*" and wife-beating "after the manner of husbands." He accordingly awarded maintenance to a wife who left her husband's house only in the case of the former type of wife-beating.[161]

Nevertheless, in some cases the *qāḍī*s deviated from the rigid formal approach in view of the husband's economic position. Thus, for instance, Shaykh Mūsā al-Ṭabarī directed a wife to file a claim for maintenance for herself and her children against her grown-up sons and dismissed her application for maintenance from her husband because the latter was poor and unemployed, had no property and was supported by his sons. In another case, he ordered the husband's father to pay maintenance to his daughter-in-law and her children because the husband worked for his father as a shepherd and was not able to support his family.[162] The *qāḍī*s at times had recourse to the welfare services of the State rather than to the institutionalized organs entrusted with the provision of maintenance to the wife and family in traditional society. In some cases, they took into account pensions from the National Insurance Institute or the Ministry of Social Welfare or even asked that such pensions be increased to make things easier for husbands who found it difficult to meet their obligations.[163]

The *qāḍī*s usually heeded the wife's troubles concerning the dwelling as far as was consistent with the *sharīᶜa*, and when they departed from this practice it was not necessarily to her advantage. They decided that the dwelling was not legal when it was not separate *within* the house (*dār*) of the husband's family, as when sanitary facilities were shared, where there was no separate entrance to the wife's dwelling, when there were no decent neighbors, or when furniture and other essential accessories were lacking. They also decided so when physical or mental injury was caused to the wife or when her safety was threatened.[164] The husband was sometimes ordered to provide a dwelling *outside* his family's residence when his relatives harassed his wife in any way, as he was indeed required to do according to the *sharīᶜa*.[165] Nonetheless, in several such cases, the *qāḍī*s sought solutions within the joint dwelling of the extended family, having regard to the husband's circumstances and the housing shortage.[166] On some occasions, they were in favor of a separate dwelling even though no legal grounds for it existed. Shaykh Amīn Qāsim Mudlij was alert to the fact that interference in the couple's life by the husband's parents caused great suffering to the wife and that it was difficult for her to find witnesses to her harassment since the husband's relatives were not usually eager to testify against him. He therefore suggested that if the *qāḍī*, by examining the spouses (and not by evidence required under the *sharīʿa*), gained the impression that the proximity of the dwelling to the residence of the husband's parents was the direct cause of the disputes between the spouses he should have to decide that the dwelling was not legal.[167] This suggestion was not reflected in judgments, and its very making seems to indicate that the *qāḍī*s did not follow it.[168] The same *qāḍī* suggested that the wife stipulate in the marriage contract that a dwelling near the residence of the husband's parents shall not be legal.[169] Such stipulations, though invalid according to the Ḥanafī school,[170] have met with the full support of the courts, and so have stipulations to the effect that the conjugal dwelling shall be situated in the wife's home locality.[171]

The question of the separate dwelling was particularly serious in the case of a polygamous marriage. The *qāḍī*s usually insisted on a separate dwelling (*dār*) for each wife,[172] although there were deviations from the *sharīʿa* in this matter: for instance, Shaykh Ṭāhir Ḥamād decided that the dwellings of the rival wives need not be fully separate unless the spouses were people of means,[173] and Shaykh Ḥasan Amīn al-Ḥabash rejected an application by a wife for a separate dwelling although her rival was living in an adjoining room.[174]

The *qāḍī*s' approach to the question of obedience was likewise formal. They were careful to order obedience (*ṭāʿa*) when the wife had *prima facie* obtained all her matrimonial rights, such as dower and a legal dwelling, and there was no legal ground for her leaving the husband's house.[175] Wife-beating "for the purpose of chastisement" (*biqaṣd al-taʾdīb*) was considered legitimate from the *sharīʿa* point of view and not a sufficient reason for leaving the conjugal dwelling.[176] The *qāḍī*s were not prepared to recognize the departure of one *badīla* in an exchange marriage from her husband's house as a legal ground for the other to do the same; in each case they ordered obedience[177] unless it was proved that the wife had not received dower.[178] Shaykh Ḥasan Amīn al-Ḥabash sharply attacked this type of marriage, calling it "a malignant disease" since, in his opinion, it was a cause of trouble, of disputes between the families and of divorce: as the couples could not, by the nature of things, be alike in character, temper and economic circumstances, there would always be jealousy and resentment between the two women. He recommended a form of marriage not linking the two couples to each other.[179] The exchange marriage is a striking example of a clash between social custom and religious norm. The *qāḍī*s sided with the *sharīʿa*, which in this case represents a more progressive concept than custom. A more frequent example is the conflict between the wife's loyalty to her father's house, which did not cease after her marriage, and her loyalty to her husband, enjoined on her by the *sharīʿa*. Here, too, the religious norm did not stand the test of reality owing to the strength of the blood-tie, and here, too, the *qāḍī*s sided with the religious norm. When a wife refused to return to her husband's house on the ground that her brothers were no less important to her than her children, Shaykh Tawfīq Maḥmūd ʿAsaliyya said that "such a viewpoint is recognized neither by the *sharīʿa* nor by the [secular] law."[180]

The *qāḍī*s were chary of judging a woman rebellious (*nushūz*) even when required to do so according to the *sharīʿa*. In such circumstances, they contented themselves with a judgment for obedience; in fact, even when it was apparent that the wife did not comply with the judgment, they were in no hurry to subject her to the full rigor of the law. It seems that they did not wish to exacerbate relations and give a kind of legitimation to their severance. Moreover, they were aware that the denial of maintenance to a rebellious wife was no longer a deterrent. Shaykh Ḥusnī al-Zuʿbī said so expressly,[181] and this awareness was probably the reason why he had not given a single *nushūz* judgment. In some cases, the *qāḍī*s contented themselves with a threat that if the wife did not obey the husband she would be declared rebellious, but when she persisted they did not carry out their threat.[182] In other cases, they rejected the wife's claim for maintenance "because of her rebelliousness" or because she had failed to comply with an order for obedience, but still did not positively declare her rebellious.[183] Only in about a score of cases was the wife actually declared rebellious, and this mostly at her own request[184] or because she had failed to comply with an order for obedience.[185] Most of the *nushūz* judgments were rendered by Shaykh Mūsā al-Ṭabarī,[186] who sometimes gave as the reason his inability to compel the wife's obedience.[187]

The *qāḍī*s were alive to the fact that judgments for obedience were practically meaningless because they could not be enforced. Shaykh Mūsā al-Ṭabarī would explain to the husband that he had no power over the wife after passing a judgment for obedience or *nushūz* and was not allowed to interfere in her affairs.[188] Shaykh Ḥusnī al-Zuʿbī considered that the Knesset should intervene with regard to obedience since its criminal legislation in matters of marriage and divorce had deprived the husband of the two sanctions traditionally available to him against the rebellious wife in addition to denial of maintenance. Shaykh Ḥusnī suggested inserting a provision in the Penal Law Amendment (Bigamy) Law, 5719–1959, to the effect that if the wife did not comply with a judgment for obedience this should be a good defense for the husband to a charge of polygamy. He believed that such a sanction would deter the wife and cure her waywardness.[189] Shaykh Amīn Qāsim Mudlij suggested enacting a provision whereby rebelliousness of the wife should also be a good defense to the charge of divorcing her against her will if the divorce were to take place under a special permit from the *sharīʿa* court.[190] Shaykh Ḥasan Amīn al-Ḥabash also noted the helplessness of the husband where the wife refused to comply with a judgment for obedience, rebelled and transgressed "the bounds of the *sharīʿa*, good sense, reason, and benevolence." "There are women," he said, "whose extortion must be guarded against," who "are instigated to rebellion by human beings and demons," and for whom detailed and precise laws must be devised in accordance with each kind of rebelliousness.[191]

With regard to maintenance within the wider family circle, there is no clear distinction between positive, legally-binding norms and ethical norms, the latter being more in the nature of charity.[192] This encouraged *qāḍī*s to forego the exercise of judicial power and to try and settle claims by way of compromise and agreement between the parties. They often acted as real arbitrators[193] and, when an agreement had been reached, gave it the force of a judgment.[194] It was only when the parties did not reach agreement or when the defendant did not appear in court that the *qāḍī* was compelled to exercise his power and have maintenance fixed by *mukhbirūn*.[195] Almost all the maintenance suits filed by widowed mothers or other women in the wider family circle were allowed. The *qāḍī* might also decide, for instance, that a grown-up son should provide a suitable dwelling for a widowed mother or separate his dwelling from hers.[196] Only in a few cases did the *qāḍī* dismiss a woman's maintenance claim after it had been found that she had property, a share in an inheritance or an income sufficient for her livelihood.[197]

NOTES

1. See *FRL,* arts.69–74. For more detail see Qadrī, arts.17, 150–9, 206–16.
2. See Qadrī, art.150; Linant de Bellefonds, pp.258 *seq.*; Schacht, p.167; Abu Zahra, p.145; Fyzee, p.203.
3. See, e.g., *Ṭb11,* p.157:no.21–f.23/59, p.160:no.1–f.3/60, p.167:no.8–f.15/60, p.170:no.11–f.22/60; *AcD8*, p.97:no.14/70–f.125/69; *JfQ4*, p.103:no.115–f.83/68.
4. See, e.g., *AcI3*, p.28:no.17–f.47/56, p.29:no.19–f.55/56, p.85:no.19–f.78/58; *AcQ5*, p.45:f.109/64; *AcD8*, p.39;no.39–f.77/68; *NzI4*, p.195:no.1/5–f.13/59; *JfQ2*, p.590:no.623–f.29/63. Cf. the Syrian Law of Personal Status, No.59 of September 17, 1953, art.71(1).
5. See, e.g., *AcI2*, p.5:f.3/51; *AcD6*, p.51:f.121/64; *NzI4*, p.141:no.6/2–f.15/53 (the husband undertook to give the wife a promissory note for the balance of maintenance due to her for one year and she "is free to use it as she pleases . . .").
6. See, e.g., *AcD6,* p.41:f.94/65; *JfQ3,* p.131:no.206–f.82/64; *JfQ5,* p.4:no.7–f.12/69.
7. See the chapter "Divorce," p.159.
8. *FRL*, arts.96, 98. See Abu Zahra, p.145; Goitein and Ben-Shemesh, p.225. See, e.g., *AcD7*, p.62:f.21/67.
9. See, e.g., *NzI4*, p.62:no.1/1–f.2/50, p.67:no.1/13–f.25/50.
10. See, e.g., *Ṭb11*, p.156:no.20–f.3/59, p.281:no.2–f.4/65.
11. See, e.g., *JfQ4*, p.2:no.2–f.80/65, p.134:no.160–f.125/68, p.145:no.174–f.134/68; *Nz14*, p.289:no.4/14–f.64/66.
12. See, e.g., *JfQ1*, p.216:no.338–f.48/55 (the husband had a pension insufficient even for coffee and tobacco; he was unfit for heavy physical work and the wife was a seamstress); *JfQ2*, p.432:no.418–f.12/60; *JfQ4*, p.55:no.51–f.97/67 (the wife went out to work and was the sole supporter of the family; the husband had another wife in Gaza), p.130:no.153–f.132/68 (the wife said that she did not want the husband and that "he provides support [for himself] and I provide support [for myself]"), p.134:no.160–f.125/68.
13. See, e.g., *NzI4*, p.227:no.1/19–f.60/63.
14. *FRL*, art.71; Qadrī, art.214.
15. See, e.g., *JfQ2*, p.335:no.527–f.5/85, p.406:no.570–f.35/59.
16. See, e.g., *JfQ4*, p.108:no.122–f.77/68; *AcD6*, p.12:no.12/65–f.174/64; *AcD7*, p.23:f.132/65; *Ṭb11*, p.10:no.1/11–f.25/50.
17. See, e.g., *JfQ1*, p.6:no.12–f.10/51; *AcI2*, p.45:f.42/53. Cf. Granqvist, vol.2, p.226.
18. See, e.g., *NzI4*, p.53:no.1/16–f.27/49, p.98:no.3/8–f.17/51, p.113:no.5/5–f.14/52 (the wife was willing to obey if the husband gave her *nuqūṭ* (bridal gifts) to replace those he burnt); *AcD8*, p.17:no.17/68–f.143/67.

19. See, e.g., *JfQ2*, p.529:no.583–f.39/62; *AcD6*, p.28:f.24/65 (the husband complained that the wife had fraudulently taken jewelry from him that belonged to him), p.71:f.71/64; *NzI4*, p.139:no.2/4–f.8/53; *Ṭbl1*, p.156: no.20–f.31/51 (unless the husband returned to her her gold, of which he had possession, the wife would not obey him in any house "even though his house were of gold"), p.224:no.16–f.15/63 (the wife refused to hand over her jewelry to the husband and he beat her and locked her up in his house until she was rescued by the police; he was arrested and she brought a criminal action against him).
20. See, e.g., *JfQ4*, p.2:no.2–f.80/65 (the husband delayed maintenance so long that the grocer, contrary to his habit, refused to give the wife credit; the husband neither gave her money nor bought the commodities himself); *AcD7*, p.62:f.21/67.
21. See, e.g., *AcI1*, p.82:f.54/50 (the wife contended that she "also smokes"); *AcD6*, p.65:f.153/65.
22. See, e.g., *JfQ3*, p.310:no.449–f.130/66; *NzI4*, p.345:no.10/47–f.138/67.
23. *FRL*, arts.70–2; Qadrī, arts.184–8; See Fyzee, pp.119–22.
24. See Baer, p.64.
25. See, e.g., *JfQ4*, p.46:no.46–f.123/67 (the husband's mother slept in the passage, which also served as kitchen, to the couple's room); *Ṭbl1*, p.232: no.21–f.36/63 (the doorway between the wife's room and the residence of the husband's relatives was not properly stopped up; she asked for it to be stopped up with stones and clay and that none of the husband's relatives should come near it); *NzI4*, p.85:no.1/42–f.110/50 (the wife had been installed near the room in which the husband's parents and relatives lived), p.119:no.2/15–f.59/52 (shared sanitary facilities), p.272:no.2/26–f.89/65 (no partition or roof separating the wife's dwelling from the residence of the husband's relatives), p.290:no.5/15–f.50/66 (no separate entrance to the wife's dwelling), p.307:no.2/37–f.154/66 (the husband had established a barber shop in the dwelling); *AcD7*, p.13:f.48/66 ("a place dark in the daytime," not fit for permanent residence), p.55:no.14–f.?/67 (no running water in the kitchen; the landlord, a bachelor, lived on the premises and there were no separate sanitary facilities).
26. See, e.g., *JfQ4*, p.94:no.97–f.38/68 (the wife alleged that the husband supported her through the intermediary of her mother-in-law, who "gave her food when she wanted to and none when she did not"); *NzI4*, p.127: no.25–f.98/52); *Ṭbl1*, p.261:no.14–f.28/64 (the wife wanted no "partnership (*shirka*) with the husband's relatives in kitchen and household because it gives her headaches").
27. See, e.g., *JfQ3*, p.266:no.406–f.24/66; *JfQ4*, p.94:no.97–f.36/68; *JfQ5*, p.132:no.217–f.263/69; *Ṭbl1*, p.139: no.2–f.43/58.
28. See, e.g., *NzI4*, p.128:no.26–f.104/52 (the father-in-law had cursed the

wife and sworn a *ḥarām* oath that she would not enter his house), p.136; no.4/36–f.121/52 (the mother-in-law accused the wife of adultery with the father-in-law and of being pregnant by him), p.139: no.1/3–f.12/53 (the son of her rival insulted and beat the wife), p.188: no.1/7–f.25/58 (the dwelling was near the residence of the husband's relatives and not near that of Muslim neighbors who might save her when she cried for help or was attacked), p.358: no.7/21–f.39/68 (the wife's brother-in-law frequently chased her out of the house; her husband did not protect her because he was under his brother's thumb); *AcI1*, p.76: f.47/50 (the husband and mother-in-law beat the wife); *JfQ1*, p.34: no.58–12/52 (the wife was "harmed by the proximity" of the residence of the husband's relatives and asked for them to be warned and ordered to use the back door); *ṬbI1*, p.69: no.7–f.8/55 (the mother-in-law and sister-in-law forbad the wife to enter her room "and to make use of my freedom . . . their behavior is such that even an animal could not endure it"), p.102: no.10–f.29/57 (the wife and her sister were married to cousins of theirs (brothers), and the two couples lived in the same house, together with the father of the husbands, who was mentally ill and had committed a heinous crime on her sister; the wife feared for her life).

29. See Rosenfeld, *Peasants*, pp.32–3, 87–9; Cohen, p.54.
30. See, e.g., *NzI4*, p.360: no.9/23–f.49/68 (the husband left his family's home and rented a separate house to bring his wife back to him and "ensure a quiet married life"); *ṬbI1*, p.122: no.10–f.4/58, p.208: no.4–f.39/62; *AcD8*, p.17: no.17/68–f.143/67.
31. *JfMC68*, no.9513 (special dwelling—*maskan khāṣṣ*), no.12617; *ṬbMC68*, no.8276 (a room and sanitary facilities), no.8278 (a stipulation that the husband should have the upper storey of his father's house); *AcMC68*, no.2437 (separate legal dwelling—*maskan sharʿī mustaqill*); *NzMC68*, no.6110 (separate house standing by itself—*dār mustaqilla waḥdahā*). Cf. Cohen, p.54; Rosenfeld, *Peasants*, p.36; Yūsuf Dasūqī, *AI*, vol.8(1962), Nos.1–2, p.3.
32. See, e.g., *JfQ3*, p.363: no.504–f.60/67; *AcMC68*, no.2612 (the husband undertook to pay the wife IL 10,000 for the construction of a house in the village if she should be compelled to leave his house for any reason).
33. Cohen, p.54.
34. See, e.g., *ṬbI1*, p.122: no.10–f.4/58, p.202: no.24–f.36/62, p.208: no.4–f.39/62.
35. See *JfMC68*, no.10316. See also *AcMC68*, nos.2636, 2644, 2830.
36. *ṬbI1*, p.249: no.5–f.8/64, p.164: no.5–f.9/60; and *NzI4*, p.297: no.8/24–f.82/66, respectively. See also *NzI4*, p.139: no.2/4–f.8/53.
37. See Qadrī, art.187.
38. *JfQ4*, p.185: no.239–f.57/69; *NzI4*, p.135: no.3/35–f.3/52. In another case,

the *qāḍī* ordered the husband to spend every night at home "to allay the wife's fear of attacks." See *AcQ5*, p.65:f.71/63.

39. *FRL*, arts.70–1.
40. *AcQ5*, p.74:f.192/63. See also *NzI4*, p.101:no.1/14–f.99/51, p.182:no.1/12–f.43/57.
41. See, e.g., *JfQ2*, p.475:no.499–[f.39/60] (a woman from Jaffa refused to live at Bāqa al-Gharbiyya. She contended that life was penurious there, that she went hungry and, in addition, the dwelling was shared with her husband's parents); *AcI3*, p.68:no.40–f.85/57; *AcQ5*, p.74:f.192/63; *AcD8*, p.50:f.50/68 (a woman from Acre refused to live in Qalansuwa village "because of the discrepancy between her habits and the traditions of the village people"); *NzI4*, p.117:no.1/12–f.53/52, p.300:no.1/27–f.106/66.
42. *JfQ2*, p.545:no.543–f.68/62 (wife from Jaffa, husband from the al-Huzayyil tribe; the husband was willing to provide her with a dwelling at her choice in Ramla, Jaffa or any of several other places).
43. See, e.g., *JfQ4*, p.34:no.32–f.102/67, p.126:no.145–f.104/68 (the husband had moved from Jaffa to Lod for reasons of work); *NzI4*, p.101:no.1/14–f.49/51 (wife from Nazareth not willing to live at Shafā ᶜAmr).
44. See, e.g., *NzI4*, p.182:no.1/12–f.43/57 (Nazareth).
45. *ṬbI1*, p.7:no.4/8–f.16/50, p.89:no.9–f.31/56; *AcD8*, p.5:f.5/68; *NzI4*, p.122:no.1/18–f.74/52.
46. *NzI4*, p.358:no.7/21–f.39/68.
47. See, e.g., *AcD8*, p.29:f.29/68; *NzI4*, p.107:no.2/18–f.72/51, p.297:no.9/25–f.74/66, p.328:no.4/24–f.88/67 (the wife refused to move from the eastern Muslim quarter of Nazareth to a relatively luxurious quarter mostly inhabited by Christians).
48. See, *JfQ4*, p.88:no.87–f.3/68, p.117:no.132–f.84/68, p.141:no.168–f.135/68; *AcD6*, p.71:no.71–f.138/64; *AcD7*, p.13:f.48/66, p.52:f.11/67; *AcMC68*, nos.2846, 2945; *NzMC68*, no.6539; *JfMC68*, nos.10132, 10294.
49. See, e.g., *JfMC68*, no.10132 (wife from Jaffa, husband from the al-Huzayyil tribe; the amount to be paid to the wife in the event of an infringement of the stipulation was IL 10,000).
50. *JfMC68*, no.10099; *AcMC68*, no.2987 (it was stipulated that so long as the husband was tied to Nazareth by his work they would live in town, but that when he had to leave town because of his work they would both make their permanent home in her village).
51. *JfQ3*, p.370:no.511–f.511/67.
52. *AcMC68*, no.2937 (husband from Nazareth, wife from Haifa), no.1850; *NzMC68*, no.6380.
53. *AcI3*, p.50:no.12–f.2/57; *NzI4*, p.287:no.1/10–f.48/66, and p.382:no.5/52–f.173/68, respectively.
54. *JfQ1*, p.88:no.138–f.8/53; *JfQ2*, p.434:no.421–f.27/59; *JfQ3*, p.137:

no.214–f.?/64 (the wife lived on the ground floor of the house and the husband on the upper floor; the wife paid rent out of her own money); *JfQ4*, p.117: no.132–f.84/68.

55. *JfMC68*, nos.10027, 10291, 10322; *ṬbMC68*, nos.8030, 8047, 8049; *AcMC68*, no.2848.
56. *AcQ4*, p.8:f.2/61 (each of the spouses had rights in the property in accordance with his or her share in the inheritance); and *AcD6*, p.15:f.29/65, respectively. See also *ṬbI1*, p.273:no.21–f.39/64 (the wife refused to obey the husband because the house was not registered in her name).
57. See, e.g., *JfQ1*, p.57:no.91–f.30/51 (the wife demanded a separate bedroom during her menstrual period), p.107:no.172–f.48/53 (the husband beat the wife till she bled because she was negligent in her housework and reviled him); *JfQ2*, p.405:no.568–f.50/59 (the husband beat and reviled the wife; she would not be content with a "certificate of guarantee for her life" from the police); *JfQ3*, p.239:no.377–f.49/66 (the husband beat the wife "after the manner of husbands"); *JfQ4*, p.46:no.46–f.123/67 (the husband beat the wife while the court proceedings were in progress); *ṬbI1*, p.24:no.8–f.21/51 (the husband threatened to kill the wife), p.167:no.8–f.15/60 (the husband beat the wife severely and burdened her beyond her capacity with work "contrary to humanity, religion and law"), p.173:no.14–f.34/60 (the wife fled the husband's house after he had tried to set her alight and strangle her), p.259:no.12–f.25/64 (the spouses accused each other of attempting to set the other alight), p.260:no.13–f.31/64 (the husband spent his time gambling in coffee-houses); *NzI4*, p.62:no.2/2–f.4/50 (the wife said that her husband beat and harassed her "when I have done wrong and when I have not"), p.127:no.25–f.98/52 (the husband beat the wife until she had a miscarriage); *AcI2*, p.10:no.8–f.10/51 (the husband got drunk and beat the wife).
58. See, e.g., *JfQ4*, p.46:no.46–f.123/67; *ṬbI1*, p.173:no.14–f.34/60, p.259: no.12–f.25/64; *NzI4*, p.127:no.25–f.98/52, p.256:no.1/9–f.39/66.
59. See, e.g., *ṬbI1*, p.173:no.14–f.34/60; *NzI4*, p.88:no.6/47–f.118/50, p.107: no.2/18–f.72/51, p.127:no.25–f.98/52; *AcD6*, p.50:f.120/65.
60. See, e.g., *JfQ3*, p.287:no.427–f.80/66; *JfQ4*, p.46:no.46–f.123/67; *NzI4*, p.53:no.1/16–f.27/49, p.218:no.1/11–f.8/62; *ṬbI1*, p.18:no.4–f.10/51, p.225:no.17–f.7/63.
61. *JfQ3*, p.310:no.449–f.130/66; *JfQ4*, p.78:no.74–f.141/68; *NzI4*, p.371: no.7/37–f.81/68, p.383:no.2/55–f.125/68.
62. *NzI4*, p.88:no.47/6–f.118/50.
63. See, e.g., *JfQ4*, p.7:no.7–f.94/67; *JfQ5*, p.33:no.56–f.141/69 (the couple lived in Abū Ghūsh; the husband worked in Jerusalem and Bethlehem and spent one night a week at home; his brother provided the wife's maintenance and received a monthly payment from him); *NzI4*, p.287:no.1/11–f.53/66

(the husband worked in Tel Aviv and came home to his Galilee village once a week, as he used to do before his marriage), p.345: no.10/47–f.138/67.

64. See, e.g., *JfQ1*, p.68: no.6–f.2/55; *AcI3*, p.59: no.26–f.82/57; *Ṭbl1*, p.271: no.20–f.5/64.
65. *NzI4*, p.60: no.4/28–f.49/49 (in consequence of his accusation, she was "not respected by the people"), p.329: no.5/5–f.96/67; *Ṭbl1*, p.18: no.4–f.10/51 (the husband denied having accused the wife of prostitution and said that she was "modest and pure").
66. *NzI4*, p.181: no.3/11–f.38/57; and *JfQ4*, p.85: no.84–f.22/68, respectively. See also *AcD8*, p.1: no.1/68–f.146/67. For the ill-tempered woman (*ḥardāna* or *zaᶜlāna*) see Granqvist, vol.2, pp.218 *seq.*; Rosenfeld, *Peasants*, pp.43–5, 145–6; Cohen, p.124; *JfQ1*, p.273: no.422–f.19/57, p.282: no.436–f.30/57.
67. *JfQ2*, p.300: no.464–f.5/58; *AcI3*, p.13: no.16/55–f.49/55.
68. *AcI2*, p.13: no.10–f.15/51; *Ṭbl1*, p.33: no.17–f.41/51.
69. See, e.g., *ṬbMC68*, nos.8101, 8119, 8227, 9318.
70. See Cohen, pp.34–6, 50.
71. *AcMC68*, no.2631 (the veiling of the face and the confinement of the wife to the house are not referred to).
72. See, e.g., *ṬbMC68*, nos.8114, 8115, 8119, 9323.
73. *FRL*, art.74; Qadrī, arts.152–5, 186.
74. See, e.g., *JfQ1*, p.61: no.97–f.50/51, p.273: no.422–f.19/57 ("the rival wife is bitter"—*al-ḍarra murra*); *JfQ4*, p.55: no.51–f.97/67, p.84: no.83–f.16/68, p.94: no.97–f.97/68, p.185: no.239–f.57/69; *AcI2*, p.5: f.3/51 (the wife at first demanded that the husband exercise justice and equality as to marital relations, housing conditions and subsistence, but later declared that she accepted the existing rate of maintenance provided he exercised justice as to marital relations).
75. *JfQ1*, p.273: no.422–f.19/57; *JfQ3*, p.311: no.450–f.135/66; *JfQ4*, p.92: no.95–f.121/67, p.113: no.126–f.82/68 (the wife had been installed in her rival's house and "ate out of her hand"); *Ṭbl1*, p.127: no.15–f.3/58, p.131: no.19–f.20/58 (when one of the wives was talking in her room, the other heard her, which was a source of incessant quarrels between them), p.188: no.9–f.15/61, p.201: no.13–f.34/62 (a partition two metres high should be erected between the wives' rooms); *NzI4*, p.32: no.47–f.86/47, p.121: no.4/17–f.58/52 (the wife asserted that at the time of the inspection (*kashf*) the husband had deceived the court emissaries as to the legality of the dwelling, for all the furnishings had been borrowed from her rival's quarters, to be returned after the inspection); *AcD7*, p.11: no.11/66–f.165/65. Cf. Granqvist, vol.2, pp.191–2.
76. See, e.g., *JfQ4*, p.92: no.95–f.121/67; *Ṭbl1*, p.12: no.4/14–f.28/50, p.42: no.1–f.6/53; *NzI4*, p.373: no.3/40–f.98/68 (the wife had found shelter with one of her children).

77. *Ṭb11*, p.160:f.31/60; *Ac12*, p.18:no.15–f.19/51; *AcD8*, p.76:f.97/69.
78. *JfQ3*, p.32:no.54–f.111/63, p.340:no.470–f.12/67; *JfQ4*, p.94:no.97–f.38/68; *JfQ5*, p.103:no.172–f.244/69.
79. See, e.g., *Ṭb11*, p.180:no.1–f.40/60.
80. See, e.g., *AcQ5*, p.30:no.20–f.121/62, p.70:f.182/63; *Ṭb11*, p.91:no.12–f.37/56; *Nz14*, p.314:no.3/4–f.8/67 (the wife was beaten and expelled from the husband's house "because of a family quarrel unconnected with her"), p.372:no.1/38–f.110/68.
81. See, e.g., *Ṭb11*, p.151:no.9–f.16/57.
82. See, e.g., *Nz14*, p.321:no.6/13–f.49/67, p.327:no.3/23–f.85/67, p.343:no.7/44–f.147/67, p.360:no.9/23–f.49/68; *JfQ5*, p.70:no.121–f.140/69.
83. *AI*, vol.11(1968), Nos.1–2, pp.3, 8–10.
84. *JfQ5*, p.65:no.110–f.198/69.
85. See, e.g., *Nz14*, p.161:no.1/9, p.245:no.6/16–f.75/64.
86. See, e.g., *JfQ3*, p.32:no.54–f.111/63, p.113:no.177–f.66/64 (the wife was turned out of her house "screaming" by her brother).
87. *JfQ2*, p.523:no.501–f.65/62.
88. *AI*, vol.11(1968), Nos.1–2, p.3.
89. *Nz14*, p.125:no.3/23–f.96/52, p.127:no.25–f.98/52, p.288:no.2/12–f.49/66 (the wife left the husband's house "in return" for her *badīla* having done so); *Ṭb11*, p.88:no.8–f.30/56 and p.89:no.9–f.31/56; *AcQ5*, p.41:f.120/61. Cf. al-ᶜĀrif, p.132.
90. *Nz14*, p.360:no.9/23–f.49/68; *JfQ4*, p.174:no.219–f.90/68; *JfQ5*, p.119:no.201–f.177/69; *Ṭb11*, p.31:no.16–f.38/51; *AcD7*, p.31:f.31/66 [71/66], p.49:f.8/67.
91. See, e.g., *JfQ4*, p.115:no.130–f.71/68 and p.116:no.131–f.74/68; *Ṭb11*, p.31:no.16–f.38/51 (after the man had taken back his wife, who was his daughter's *badīla* and whom he had repudiated by revocable divorce, his daughter also returned to her husband).
92. See, e.g., *Ṭb11*, p.213:no.8–f.32/62 and p.214:no.9–f.48/62; *Nz14*, p.131:no.1/30–f.129/52 and p.132:no.2/31–f.130/52.
93. See the chapter "Divorce," pp.129–30.
94. See, e.g., *JfQ3*, p.172:no.282–f.159/64.
95. *JfQ4*, p.174:no.219–f.90/68 (after the wife had learnt that her father, who was her *badīla*'s husband, wished to divorce his wife, she declared that she objected to a divorce and that, as far as she was concerned, there was nothing to prevent her from returning to her husband; the *qāḍī* ordered obedience, but the matter ended with the divorce of both women). See *JfQ4*, p.184:no.238–f.88/69 and p.184:no.237–f.87/69.
96. *Nz14*, p.87:no.4/45–f.114/50; *JfQ3*, p.97:no.154–f.21/64. Cf. al-ᶜĀrif, p.132.
97. Cf. Rosenfeld, *Peasants*, pp.108, 122–5, 136, 138; Cohen, pp.113–14; Marx, *Bedouin*, pp.102, 121, 150, 160.

98. See, e.g., *JfQ1*, p.59:no.93–f.39/51 and p.270:no.418–f.25/57; *Ṭbl1*, p.30: no.15–f.35/51, p.126:no.14–f.17/58, p.256:no.10–f.13/64, p.258:no.11–f.20/64; *NzI4*, p.268:no.3/19–f.65/65, p.271:no.2/24–f.61/65.
99. See, e.g., *NzI4*, p.299:no.2/26–f.13/66; *JfQ4*, p.103:no.115–f.53/68.
100. See, e.g., *JfQ4*, p.32:no.31–f.128/67 (the wife did not live maritally with him and did not prepare his meals).
101. See, e.g., *NzI4*, p.94:no.2/3–f.10/59 (the wife distributed the food the husband gave her to *her* family, neglecting *his* family).
102. See, e.g., *NzI4*, p.193:no.1/1–f.2/59.
103. See, e.g., *Ṭbl1*, p.4:no.1/5–f.15/50 (the wife "ill-treats me by word and deed, by curses and spitting in my face, and this is contrary to the *sharīʿa*"); *NzI4*, p.306:no.2/35–f.137/66; *JfQ3*, p.128:no.201–f.83/64 ("because of her long tongue"), p.310:no.499–f.130/66 (she used "ugly expressions"); *JfQ4*, p.1:no.1–f.81/67 (she beat her husband), p.64:no.109–f.195/69.
104. See, e.g., *NzI4*, p.93:no.1/2–f.4/51, p.355:no.1/15–f.33/68; *JfQ2*, p.437: no.424–f.2/60; *JfQ3*, p.202:no.333–f.1/66, p.250:no.389–f.42/66, p.333: no.473–f.29/67; *JfQ4*, p.2:no.2–f.80/65.
105. *Ṭbl1*, p.4:no.1/5–f.15/50 (the wife worked in the fields "like the other village women"), p.173:no.14–f.34/60, p.207:no.3–f.44/62 (wife working as a schoolteacher); *JfQ1*, p.246:no.382–f.36/56 (the husband was willing to increase the wife's maintenance on condition "that she stops working as a hired employee and stays at home"); *JfQ4*, p.55:no.51–f.97/67 (wife worked as a poultry plucker). See Rosenfeld, *Peasants*, p.37.
106. In one case, the husband gave as the reason for his inability to provide his wife with a dwelling separate from that of his family that as the eldest son he could not leave his parents and brothers. See *NzI4*, p.310:no.5/40–f.159/66. Cf. Rosenfeld, *Peasants*, p.85.
107. See, e.g., *Ṭbl1*, p.271:no.20–f.5/64; *JfQ4*, p.122:no.144–f.103/68 (the husband said that the wife wasted all his earnings by issuing cheques).
108. *FRL*, art.101; Qadrī, arts.166–71. Cf. Schacht, p.168.
109. *JfQ4*, p.146:no.5/17–f.111/68. See Yūsuf Dasūqī, *AI*, vol.7(1959), Nos.2–3, p.14; *AI*, vol.10(1966), Nos.3–4, p.3; Baer, p.35.
110. *AI*, vol.8(1963), Nos.3–4, pp.1–2; *AI*, vol.9(1954), Nos.1–2, p.8; *AI*, vol.11(1968), p.6.
111. See, e.g., *Ṭbl1*, p.30:no.15–f.35/51, p.69:no.8–f.11/55 (the wife was not prepared to return to the husband's house "for the time being"; she wished to "chastise him properly" but considered the possibility of returning to his house in a year "if he treats me better"), p.70:no.9–f.12/55 (the husband undertook to treat the wife well "and to honor her as his life companion," but she refused to return to him on the ground that she had heard such promises before), p.153:no.17–f.28/59, p.180:no.1–f.40/60 ("my blood and body do not match and do not mix with his"; she "will never" return

to him); *JfQ4*, p.173:no.217–f.65/69; *AcQ5*, p.5:no.5/63–f.26/62; *AcD6*, p.6:f.8/65. See Shaykh Ḥusnī al-Zuᶜbī, *AI*, vol.11(1968), Nos.1–2, pp.6–7.

112. See, e.g., *NzI4*, p.157:no.2/4–f.1/54.
113. *AcI2*, p.32:f.76/51 (the wife worked and deposited her money in a bank); *AcI3*, p.10:no.13/55–f.33/55 (the wife worked "independently of him" and lived alone with her daughter); *JfQ1*, p.62:no.98–f.56/51.
114. See, e.g., *JfQ1*, p.228:no.353–f.15/56; *JfQ2*, p.545:no.543–f.68/62; *JfQ3*, p.327:no.468–f.16/67; *NzI4*, p.163:no.1/12–f.47/54.
115. See, e.g., *NzI4*, p.140:no.1/5–f.13/53, p.52:no.2/19–f.58/53, p.156:no.2/2–f.4/54, p.161:no.3/8–f.17/54, p.169:no.1/2–f.4/56, p.186:no.2/4–f.16/58, p.188:no.1/7–f.25/58; *JfQ1*, p.186:no.307–f.36/55.
116. *NzI4*, p.140:no.1/5–f.13/53, p.169:no.1/2–f.4/56; *AcI2*, p.38:f.125/51.
117. See, e.g., *AcI2*, p.37:f.116/52, p.39:f.133/52, p.71:f.34/54; *AcI3*, p.4:no.4/55–f.9/55 (a village woman was unwilling to accept that the property should belong to her townsman husband; she claimed five cows); *AcD6*, p.15:f.29/65.
118. *AcI2*, p.32:f.76/51; and *ṬbI1*, p.54:no.5–f.8/54, respectively.
119. *ṬbI1*, p.39:no.8–f.19/52 (her husband beat her and she refused to return to his house "even if it were a palace in Paradise"), p.234:no.23–f.42/63; *AcI2*, p.33:f.84/51; *AcI3*, p.1:no.1/55–f.3/55.
120. *ṬbI1*, p.152:no.16–f.27/59.
121. *JfQ2*, p.552:no.552–f.73/62. In another case, a husband whose wife had fled to Shaykh Salmān al-Huzayyil sought to get her back by an order for obedience for fear that she was "to be divorced from him and married to another man." See *JfQ2*, p.528:no.510–f.93/61.
122. See, e.g., *JfQ3*, p.145:no.230–f.108/64 (arbitrator—*ḥakam*); *TbI1*, p.180:no.1–f.40/60 (mediators—*wusaṭāʾ*), p.186:no.7–f.14/61; *NzI4*, p.194:no.3/4–f.12/59 (men of good will—*ahl al-khayr*), p.220:no.2/7–f.21/63 (the arbitrators' agreement included IL 50 "reconciliation fee"—*badal muṣālaḥa*); *AcD6*, p.1:no.1/66–f.172/65. On the *qāḍī*s see below, p.106.
123. *JfQ4*, p.133:no.158–f.130/68. See also *JfQ4*, p.72:no.68–f.20/68, p.92:no.95–f.121/67; *NzI4*, p.46:no.1/3–f.7/49; *AcQ5*, p.19:f.61/61.
124. See, e.g., *JfQ4*, p.133:no.158–f.130/68.
125. See, e.g., *JfQ3*, p.145:no.230–f.108/64; *ṬbI1*, p.239:no.27–f.75/63; *NzI4*, p.220:no.2/4–f.32/63, p.231:no.5/25–f.75/63, p.253:no.2/31–f.141/64, p.253:no.3/23–f.137/64, p.262:no.1/8–f.1/65; *AcQ5*, p.15:f.59/62; *AcD6*, p.76:f.188/64.
126. See, e.g., *JfQ3*, p.145:no.230–f.108/64; *NzI4*, p.220:no.2/4–f.32/63; *AcQ5*, p.15:f.59/62. For delegated repudiation see the chapter "Divorce," pp.153 *seq.*
127. See, e.g., *NzI4*, p.236:no.1/1–f.1/64, p.243:no.3/13–f.65/64; *AcQ4*, p.29:f.12/59, p.51:f.188/59.

128. *FRL*, art.152. See Fyzee, p.204.
129. For more details see Qadrī, arts.408 *seq.*
130. Family Law Amendment (Maintenance) Law, 5719–1959, *SCH,* No.276 of March 12, 1959, secs.1–6, 19(b). See also Explanatory Note to Family Law Amendment (Maintenance) Bill, 5716–1956 (*Bills*, No.267 of June 4, 1956, p.126), and Explanatory Note to secs.122–36, 198 of *IFB*.
131. See, e.g., *JfQ3*, p.251:no.390–f.61/66; *JfQ4*, p.28:no.27–f.104/67; *Ṭbl1*, p.49:no.10–f.24/53; *NzI4*, p.248:no.4/22, p.308:no.3/38–f.160/66; *AcI1*, opposite p.25:f.12/49, p.47:no.40–f.28/49.
132. See, e.g., *Ṭbl1*, p.194:no.15–f.25/61 (the widow had three daughters).
133. See, e.g., *Ṭbl1*, p.85:no.4–f.7/56.
134. *JfQ1*, p.78:no.121–f.91/52; *JfQ3*, p.199:no.327–f.84/65; *Ṭbl1*, p.49: no.10–f.24/53, p.196:no.18–f.25/61; *AcI2*, p.64:f.26/54 (the sons contended that the mother could sell her share in the estate of the family head).
135. *JfQ4*, p.173:no.216–f.117/69; *Ṭbl1*, p.53:no.3–f.4/54, p.256:no.9–f.12/64.
136. *JfQ2*, p.316:no.493–f.40/58; and *JfQ3*, p.199:no.327–f.84/65, respectively.
137. See, e.g., *JfQ2*, p.336:no.528–f.7/59; *Ṭbl1*, p.194:no.15–f.25/61, p.253: no.7–f.3/64; *NzI4*, p.149:no.1/15–f.43/53, p.172:no.1/6–f.31/56, p.288: no.3/13–f.56/66; *AcI2,* p.35:f.4/52; *AcI3,* p.17:no.21/55–f.88/55, p.21: no.30–f.105/55.
138. See, e.g., *JfQ1*, p.218:no.341–f.80/55 (the brothers said they were prepared to pay their sister a higher rate of maintenance than she demanded if she would live with them again in the same house; she and her small daughter were living at a strange woman's house).
139. See, e.g., *AcQ5*, p.9:f.16/63.
140. See, e.g., *AcI3*, p.60:no.28–f.62/57; *NzI4*, p.1:no.9–f.12/47, p.20:no.34–f.60/47.
141. *AI,* vol.11(1968), Nos.1–2, p.10.
142. *NzI4*, p.223:no.1/10–f.2/63. See also *NzI4*, p.220:no.1/2–f.5/63; *AI*, vol.8(1963), Nos.3–4, p.1.
143. *AI*, vol.11(1968), Nos.1–2, pp.9–10; *AI*, vol.6(1957), Nos.1–2, p.15; *AI*, vol.7(1959), Nos.2–3, p.16; *AI*, vol.1(1950), No.2, p.4. For a more extensive discussion see the chapter "Divorce," pp.180–1.
144. See, e.g., *JfQ1*, p.284:no.442–f.33/57; *JfQ2*, p.477:no.503–f.48/60; *NzI4*, p.254:no.5/34–f.146/64.
145. See, e.g., *JfQ3*, p.266:no.406–f.24/66; *JfQ4*, p.122:no.141–f.103/68.
146. See, e.g., *JfQ4*, p.32:no.31–f.128/67; *JfQ5*, p.7:no.11–f.100/69; *JfQ1*, p.477:no.503–f.48/60; *NzI4*, p.200:no.1/3–f.13/60; *JfQ3*, p.273:no.412–f.94/66.
147. See, Goitein and Ben-Shemesh, pp.39–40.
148. See, e.g., *NzI4*, p.220:no.2/7–f.21/63; *AcQ4*, p.51:f.188/59; *AcD6*, p.1:

no.1/66–f.172/65; *JfQ3*, p.145:no.230–f.108/64 (in the event of an infringement of the terms of the agreement brought about between the spouses by the *qāḍī* and a Beduin shaykh, the latter was to serve as an arbitrator between them and his decision was to be final); *JfQ4*, p.116:no.131–f.74/68.

149. See, e.g., *AcI2*, p.50:f.88/53, p.71:f.81/54; *AcI3*, p.16:no.20/55–f.56/55, p.26:no.12/56–f.31/56; *AcQ4*, p.64:f.231/59; *AcQ5*, p.15:f.59/62; *AcD6*, p.76:f.188/64; *NzI4*, p.220:no.2/4–f.32/63, p.231:no.5/25–f.75/63; *JfQ3*, p.145:no.230–f.108/64; *ṬbI1*, p.239:no.27–f.50/63.

150. See, e.g., *JfQ3*, p.128:no.201–f.83/64, p.145:no.230–f.108/64; *JfQ4*, p.1:no.1–f.81/67; *AcD6*, p.71:no.71–f.159/65 (Shaykh Amīn Qāsim Mudlij ordered obedience only after the wife had rejected reconciliation—*muṣālaḥa*—with the husband "even on terms which she might propose"); *AcD7*, p.8:f.37/66; *AcD8*, p.59:no.120/68 (obedience was ordered because the wife refused to appoint a family council for the purpose of reconciliation—*ṣulḥ*).

151. As did especially Shaykh Ḥusnī al-Zuʿbī. See, e.g., *NzI4*, p.264:no.1/13–f.33/65, p.270:no.2/21–f.75/65, p.271:no.1/31–f.80/65, p.304:no.4/32–f.31/66.

152. See, e.g., *NzI4*, p.307:no.1/36–f.158/66; *AcI2*, p.46:f.48/53; *AcI3*, p.27:no.14–f.37/56, p.40:no.39–f.127/56, p.51:no.13–f.33/57, p.82:no.15–f.72/58; *ṬbI1*, p.195:no.16–f.28/61.

153. See, e.g., *NzI4*, p.220:no.1/2–f.5/63; *ṬbI1*, p.4:no.1/5–f.15/50; *AcI2*, p.35:f.93/51.

154. *AcI3*, p.55:no.19–f.67/57; *NzI4*, p.206:no.1/4–f.10/61; *JfQ3*, p.116:no.131–f.74/68 (the surety also served as arbitrator—*ḥakam*—between the spouses).

155. See, e.g., *JfQ1*, p.57:no.91–f.30/51, p.279:no.432–f.36/57; *AcQ5*, p.72:f.176/63.

156. *JfQ3*, p.30:no.49–f.7/52; and p.88:no.139–f.10/53, respectively.

157. *ṬbI1*, p.205:no.2–f.30/62.

158. *JfQ3*, p.333:no.473–f.29/67; *JfQ4*, p.7:no.7–f.94/67, p.20:no.18–f.114/67, p.118:no.134–f.91/68.

159. See, e.g., *JfQ1*, p.37:no.64–f.21/52, p.128:no.217–f.17/54; *JfQ2*, p.559:no.466–f.62/62; *NzI4*, p.73:no.3/22–f.57/50, p.119:no.2/15–f.59/52; *ṬbI1*, p.5:no.2/6–f.16/50; *AcI2*, p.38:f.117/52.

160. *FRL*, art.95; *AcD8*, p.1:no.1/68–f.132/67.

161. *JfQ3*, p.239:no.377–f.49/66; *JfQ4*, p.103:no.115–f.53/68.

162. *AcI4*, p.16:f.74/59; and *AcI3*, p.51:no.14–f.35/57, respectively.

163. See, e.g., *JfQ4*, p.2:no.2–f.80/65; *AcI4*, p.92:f.94/60; *AcD8*, p.37:f.37/68.

164. See, e.g., *NzI4*, p.99:no.1/10–f.27/51, p.119:no.2/15–f.59/52, p.127:no.25–f.98/52, p.219:no.1/1–f.1/63; *JfQ1*, p.57:no.91–f.30/51 (the wife lacked

cosmetic equipment); *JfQ2*, p.472:no.493–f.30/61, p.498:no.458–f.75/61 (a dwelling not owned by the husband was not legal); *JfQ3*, p.287:no.427–f.80/66, p.291:no.431–f.120/66; *JfQ4*, p.34:no.32–f.102/67, p.88:no.87–f.3/68; *ṬbI1*, p.126:no.14–f.17/58, p.149:no.12–f.20/59; *AcI3*, p.18:no.23–f.73/55, p.49:no.11–f.31/57; *AcQ5*, p.72:f.176/63 and p.82:f.201/63; *AcD7*, p.13:f.48/66.

165. See, e.g., *JfQ2*, p.414:no.582–f.74/59, p.431:no.417–f.81/59; *ṬbI1*, p.102:no.10–f.29/57, p.122:no.10–f.4/58.

166. *AcQ4*, p.95:f.127/60 (Shaykh Mūsā al-Ṭabarī dismissed the wife's claim for a separate dwelling "because dwellings are scarce these days and involve high key-money . . . and there is nothing wrong with a *maskan sharʿī* housing two or three families, with shared sanitary facilities"). See also *JfQ1*, p.100:no.161–f.37/53 (Shaykh Ṭāhir Ḥamād); *ṬbI1*, p.162:no.3–f.8/60 (Shaykh Ḥasan Amīn al-Ḥabash directed the husband to provide provisional dwelling arrangements until he was better off).

167. *AI*, vol.11(1968), Nos.1–2, p.8–10.

168. See, e.g., *AcD6*, p.71:f.138/64 (Shaykh Amīn Qāsim Mudlij himself dismissed a wife's claim for another dwelling because she had not succeeded in proving (by witnesses) that the husband's relatives harassed her).

169. *AI*, vol.11(1968), Nos.1–2, pp.8–10.

170. See the chapter "Stipulations Inserted in Contracts of Marriage," p.30.

171. For references to *sijill* entries concerning stipulations as to the dwelling see above, pp.95 *seq.*

172. See, e.g., *ṬbI1*, p.12:no.4/14–f.28/50, p.42:no.1–f.6/53, p.127:no.15–f.3/58; *AcD7*, p.11:no.11/66–f.165/65.

173. The judgment was set aside by the Court of Appeal. *JfQ1*, p.273:no.422–f.19/57; *Ap1*, p.25:no.31.

174. *ṬbI1*, p.131:no.19–f.20/58.

175. See, e.g., *ṬbI1*, p.25:no.9–f.24/51; *AcQ5*, p.65:f.71/63; *AcD8*, p.17:no.17/68–f.143/67.

176. See, e.g., *JfQ1*, p.107:no.172–f.48/53 (the wife alleged that the husband had beaten her until she bled, but Shaykh Ṭāhir Ḥamād, accepting the husband's plea that he had struck her with his hand "in order to chastise her" and not for revenge, ordered obedience).

177. *ṬbI1*, p.31:no.16–f.38/51, p.88:no.8–f.30/56 and p.89:no.9–f.31/56; *AcQ5*, p.41:f.120/61; *AcD7*, p.31:no.31/66–[f.71/66]; *JfQ4*, p.174:no.219–f.90/68; *JfQ5*, p.119:no.201–f.177/69; *NzI4*, p.125:no.3/23, p.288:no.2/12–f.49/66, p.360:no.9/23–f.49/68.

178. See, e.g., *NzI4*, p.87:no.4/45–f.114/50; *JfQ3*, p.97:no.154–f.21/64 (the wife alleged that she had not received the dower, but Shaykh Ṭāhir Ḥamād ordered obedience because the marriage contracts indicated that the two *wakīl*s of the *badīla*s had received the dower).

179. *AI*, vol.11(1968), Nos.1–2, pp.3–5.
180. *JfQ5*, p.65: no.110–f.198/69.
181. *AI*, vol.8(1963), Nos.3–4, pp.1–2.
182. See, e.g., *JfQ1*, p.34: no.58–f.12/52, p.186: no.307–f.36/55; *JfQ3*, p.131: no.206–f.82/64; *AcI3*, p.95: f.127/60; *AcQ5*, p.7: f.5/61, p.17: f.50/61; *NzI4*, p.205: no.1/18–f.90/60.
183. See, e.g., *Ṭbl1*, p.39: no.8–f.19/52, p.54: no.5–f.8/54, p.132: no.21–f.27/58, p.176: no.17–f.43/60; *NzI4*, p.169: no.1/2–f.4/56, p.250: no.4/28–f.80/64.
184. See, e.g., *NzI4*, p.152: no.2/19–f.58/53, p.188: no.1/7–f.25/58.
185. See, e.g., *AcQ5*, p.2: f.2/63; *AcI2*, p.29: f.61/51.
186. See, e.g., *AcI2*, p.32: f.76/51, p.72: f.85/54; *AcI3*, p.1: no.1/55–f.3/55; *AcD6*, p.15: f.29/65 (Shaykh Amīn Qāsim Mudlij); *Ṭbl1*, p.207: no.3–f.44/62, p.234: no.23–f.42/63, p.273: no.21–f.39/64 (Shaykh Ḥasan Amīn al-Ḥabash).
187. See, e.g., *AcI3*, p.4: no.3/55–f.7/55.
188. See, e.g., *AcI3*, p.4: no.4/55–f.9/55.
189. *AI*, vol.8(1963), Nos.3–4, pp.1–2; *AI*, vol.9(1964), Nos.1–2, p.8; *AI*, vol.11(1968), Nos.1–2, p.6. Such an amendment in the law was also urged by Advocate Maḥmūd al-Māḍī, then director of *sharīʿa* courts: see *AI*, vol.9(1964), Nos.1–2, p.9.
190. *AI*, vol.9(1964), Nos.1–2, pp.2–3. Cf. Yūsuf Dasūqī, *AI*, vol.7(1959), Nos.2–3, pp.13–18.
191. *AI*, vol.9(1964), Nos.1–2, pp.5–10.
192. See Fyzee, p.202.
193. See, e.g., *JfQ2*, p.336: no.528–f.7/59 (in a woman's action for maintenance against her sons, both sides asked Shaykh Ṭāhir Ḥamād to act as arbitrator).
194. See, e.g., *JfQ1*, p.277: no.427–f.43/57; *Ṭbl1*, p.48: no.8–f.22/53; *NzI4*, p.374: no.4/41–f.117/68; *AcI1*, p.92: f.67/50.
195. See, e.g., *JfQ3*, p.251: no.390–f.61/66; *JfQ4*, p.119: no.136–f.101/68; *Ṭbl1*, p.253: no.7–f.3/64, p.59: no.11–f.21/54; *NzI4*, p.190: no.2/10–f.31/58.
196. *JfQ1*, p.218: no.341–f.80/55; *AcQ4*, p.61: no.29–f.130/57.
197. *Ṭbl1*, p.196: no.18–f.25/61; *AcQ4*, p.59: no.25–f.46/57.

Chapter Six
DIVORCE

I. CAUSES OF DIVORCE

The causes of divorce on the husband's initiative, some traditional and some modern, are rooted in socio-economic, legal and political circumstances. The main purpose of marriage, according to a conception deeply rooted in traditional society, is the production of offspring, especially sons. Where this purpose is not achieved, the marriage has no *raison d'être.*[1] Thus, in one case, a man asked permission to divorce his wife because she was barren and "the legal object of marriage is the bringing forth and raising of children," and in another case, a husband told the court that since his wife had borne him no children he was "compelled, in order to ensure progeny, to dissolve the marriage. . . ." In some further cases, the husband wished to divorce the wife either because she had borne him no children at all or because "she had borne him no male children."[2] The *sijills* contain many instances of barrenness, childlessness[3] or of the birth solely of daughters being the reason for divorce.[4] In several cases, the marriage was dissolved after the couple had had half a dozen or more daughters.[5] It might happen that a mother of girls was divorced during pregnancy.[6] The wife often admitted that failure to bear children or sons was a ground for dissolution of the marriage,[7] which might account for the high proportion (90%) of divorces by mutual agreement under these circumstances.[8]

In the traditional view, barrenness or the absence of male issue is not necessarily a ground for divorce since the position may be remedied by taking a second wife without divorcing the first,[9] unless the husband is unable to support two wives or is unwilling to do so for other reasons. One such reason was provided by the Knesset, which prohibited polygamy. If the husband did not wish to run foul of the law, the only way for him to have children was by his divorcing his wife and taking another wife. There are clear cases of the Knesset's ban being the direct cause of the divorce of a barren woman. Most of them occurred in the Little Triangle villages. Thus, one man sought to divorce his barren wife in order to take another wife because "her [the first wife's] remaining within my ᶜ*iṣma* prevents me from doing so."[10]

In many cases, the wife on divorce was of advanced age or had been married a long time (20 years or more). As a rule, no definite reason for the divorce was given but vague formulas were used, such as "incompatibility" or "lack of normal matrimonial relations."[11] But from various indications it appears that one of the main reasons for divorce under such circumstances was the husband's wish to take a young wife to replace his aging one.[12] This was indeed a common motive for polygamy, but since the latter had been forbidden by the Knesset (and for other reasons), the husband was now compelled to divorce his first wife in order to take a second. He sometimes explained that the wife had "aged and [was] unable to fulfil her marital duties," or that she was "unable to serve him,"[13] but he might say quite openly that the purpose of the divorce was to enable him to take another wife.[14]

Divorce of an elderly wife in order to take a young one was particularly widespread in the Little Triangle villages, probably owing to the economic prosperity of the region. Men suddenly grown rich wished to marry young women of a social status appropriate to their new economic position. Shaykh Ḥasan Amīn al-Ḥabash dwelt disapprovingly on this phenomenon. Frequently, he said, the cause of divorce was "the lightheadedness that seizes him who has become rich after having known poverty; he has a sudden feeling of ease; it spreads and pulsates powerfully in his veins, and this is the source of the evil. Instead of being thankful for the ease and wealth that has been vouchsafed him he becomes ungrateful, Heaven forfend, and chooses to divorce the wife who has been his partner in times of trial and borne him children; after becoming rich, he repays her by divorcing her for a strange, astonishing reason: love for another woman. This phenomenon is unfortunately a frequent subject of court cases." In this connection, Shaykh Ḥasan quoted a *ḥadīth* with the moral that there were people whom wealth corrupted and for whom it would have been better to be poor.[15] The phenomenon in question was also clearly reflected in the testimony of some women. In one case, a woman said that her husband was trying to get rid of her by various devices "because he has become wealthy after knowing dire poverty, which I shared with him during the best years of my youth . . . After he had become one of the well-known, rich people in the village, he cut himself off from me, who had borne him seven children, because I had in his eyes become unworthy of one like him, one of the rich people in the village. . . ." In another case, a woman asserted that "people talked him [her husband] into taking another wife because I am old."[16]

But for the Knesset's ban on polygamy, sudden wealth would probably have caused an increase in the polygamy rate. Paradoxically, this ban, prompted by good intentions, led to an increase in the divorce rate[17] and thus harmed more than helped women. As regard the legal and financial consequences, divorce was apt to be much worse for them than polygamy.[18]

The husband might be dozens of years—sometimes half a century[19]—older than the wife, and there were cases when the wife was considerably older than the husband.[20] Great age differences tend to disrupt married life; in some cases, the marriage was probably never consummated owing to the husband's advanced age.[21] Other instances of incompatibility involved differences as to type of settlement, education, or religion. A townswoman might be loath to move to her husband's village, tribe or even town for reasons of status and prestige.[22] Sometimes the wife was better educated than the husband, which might become apparent in cases in which the divorce judgment bore the wife's signature beside the husband's fingermark (*baṣma*).[23] In marriages of a Muslim man and a Jewish or Christian woman, the difference in religion usually involved also social, economic and cultural differences, and although the wife sometimes adopted Islam to facilitate integration within her husband's environment, this formal act could not obliterate or blur those differences. Many dozens of marriages failed for this reason.[24]

In many cases, divorce took place after the wife had claimed maintenance or been awarded maintenance for non-payment of dower, non-provision of a legal dwelling or the like.[25] In one case in which a wife was divorced in the course of the hearing of her maintenance claim the *qāḍī* remarked that "it seems the husband meant to get rid of her in the hope that he would not have to pay maintenance to her and her daughters."[26] The very fact of litigation over maintenance might lead to divorce. Sometimes feelings ran so high in the course of the hearing that the husband divorced the wife spontaneously[27] or the spouses reached the conclusion that it was impossible or pointless to continue their marriage and decided on divorce by mutual agreement.[28] The wife might be alive to this possibility and therefore delay the filing of the maintenance claim, sometimes for years, "in order to preserve our marriage."[29]

More frequent causes of divorce were the wife's disobedience and rebelliousness: her leaving the husband's house without his permission and without a legal reason, for instance, in order to visit her relatives at other than the permitted and agreed times[30]; her going out to work against the husband's will[31]; the dismissal of the husband's claim for obedience[32]; the wife's refusal to comply with a judgment for obedience[33]; her rebelliousness or her having been declared rebellious (*nāshiza*).[34] Under such circumstances the husband divorced the wife because he did not agree to her deviating from the norm accepted in traditional society as regards freedom of movement, economic activity, and so on. Divorce is the husband's last resort when the economic sanction against a rebellious wife (denial of the right to maintenance) does not achieve its purpose, because a judgment for obedience is not enforceable.[35] Rebelliousness was a particularly frequent ground in cases of suspended repudiation, which was intended to deter the wife from doing something (such as going out) or to get her to do something (such as to return home).

Another, less frequent motive for divorce was behavior on the part of the wife which, according to the traditional scale of values, was disgraceful. The reference was mainly to deviation from the accepted norm in relations with the husband or to matters of chastity and female honor (*ʿird*). A man might divorce his wife with the contention that she had caused him humiliation or brought him into contempt, for example, that her behavior toward him was "intolerably" bad; "that she [was] depraved"[36]; that at the time of the consummation of the marriage she had not been a virgin[37]; that she refused to have sexual intercourse with him[38]; that she did not live in his house, loitered, crossed the frontier from time to time or sullied her womanly honor; that she fled from his village home to the city[39]; that she was not faithful to him, that she went with another man for a long trip on the West Bank without his knowledge and consent and thus "impairs my good name and stains my honor"[40]; that she fled with a strange man or a relative to a distant place and he did not even know where she was.[41] The fact that these matters were solved by divorce and not by the traditional methods of dealing with a wayward wife is one of the manifestations of the process of modernization Israeli Muslim society has been undergoing.

Another cause of divorce was polygamy. A man might simply wish to divorce one of his wives "in order that only one wife may remain in his *ʿisma*"[42] or he might explain that "he cannot support both wives"[43] or there might be "constant quarrels between the two rivals."[44] The divorced in these cases were oldish women who had had 20 to 30 years of marriage, which suggests that the man wished to keep the younger woman. At any rate, the divorce of a polygamous wife did not appear to have anything to do with the Knesset's ban on polygamy.

Exchange marriages were a fairly frequent cause of divorce. It has already been noted that this type of marriage creates a mutual dependence between the two wives.[45] The tendency to give them equal treatment found its expression also in the matter of divorce. The divorce of one of them, whatever its cause—barrenness, lack of male offspring or anything else—was in itself an incentive for divorcing the other even if no such disability attached to her.[46] In one instance, a man divorced his wife conditionally on another man's divorcing her *badīla*, who was the first man's sister, that is to say, the divorce was to become effective automatically on the *badīla*'s divorce.[47] There were indeed cases where the very same cause, viz., the wife's having left the husband's house, was invoked in the divorces of both *badīla*s, or where actions for obedience or maintenance ended with the simultaneous divorce of both couples,[48] but it seems that even in these cases only one of the women had a concrete reason for acting the way she did, while the other merely reacted to the behavior of the first. Only in one case did the dispute not end with the dissolution of both marriages. One woman was divorced and waived both dowers, while her *badīla*, who insisted on staying with her husband, received the prompt dower.[49]

Characteristic features of exchange marriages were a relatively high proportion (25%) of cases in which the union was never consummated and the short duration of such marriages (usually between one and four years). In other words, exchange marriages appear in many instances to have been doomed in advance to failure. This has also been noted by Shaykh Ḥasan Amīn al-Ḥabash,[50] and there is also evidence from some of the parties concerned which confirms that a form of marriage that links the fates of the two couples or the two wives leads to quarrels and conflicts and makes divorce almost inevitable.[51] Another characteristic of exchange marriages was that the divorces all involved mutual renunciation of matrimonial rights—dower and maintenance during the *ʿidda*[52]—and, ostensibly, mutual agreement of the parties. The dissolution of exchange marriages, similarly to their contraction required the prior definition of the rights of the two women on a basis of equality. Almost two-thirds of the divorces of exchange marriages occurred in rural settlements, one-half in the Little Triangle villages. Particularly striking is the comparatively large share (more than one-quarter) of the Negev and Galilee Beduin.[53] About one-tenth of the cases occurred among the urban population.

Another type of marriage particularly likely to end in divorce was the cousin marriage. Dissolutions of marriages of this kind, though not very frequent, are significant in the context of the modernization of Israeli Muslim society, a principal manifestation of which has been the disintegration of the extended family. Cousin marriages have many advantages in terms of kinship and property relations,[54] but these advantages accrue to the two families concerned and not to the spouses themselves. In fact, since the individual has a natural tendency to seek his mate outside his near kin, marriage within the extended family, the basic unit of traditional society, is likely to be less than successful. The following case is symptomatic: after a marriage had not been consummated for five years, the husband wished to dissolve it with the wife's consent, *inter alia,* on the ground that "we, I and my wife, have lived together all our lives within the same family."[55] The *sijill*s record further cases of cousin marriages that were never consummated.[56]

A dispute between the spouses into which the two families were drawn or a "family rift" (*khilāf ʿāʾilī*)[57] with which the spouses had in fact nothing to do might also be a cause of divorce. Sometimes there was serious inter-family fighting, involving bloodshed, which left no alternative to the dissolution of the marriage.[58]

A physical defect, chronic or mental illness of the wife or her invalidity as the result of an accident, preventing normal marital relations, were further causes of divorce. The husband might contend that the wife was unable to fulfil her marital duties, serve him, raise the children; that relations between them had deteriorated owing to her defect or illness and that he wished to take another wife in her place.[59] A defect preventing marital relations, or mental illness, as grounds for judicial dissolution of marriage, were reserved to the wife[60]; moreover, they were not good defenses to a charge of divorce against the wife's will. In 1959, the law was amended to the effect that the wife's mental illness should be a good defense to a charge of polygamy, but the *sijill*s reflect a tendency of men in such circumstances to resort to divorce rather than take an additional wife.[61] In a case of a different kind, a man wished to dissolve his marriage on the ground that he had fraudulently been married to a wife with an eye defect, having been promised that the eye could be cured, while afterward it transpired that it could not.[62]

In numerous cases, the ground for divorce was the wife's being in a neighboring Arab country. This situation was basically a consequence of the 1948 War: either the family had been separated by the new border or the husband had married his wife in an Arab country and then somehow entered Israel, while the wife had remained in her country of origin. The problem was largely solved by the family reunion scheme, but in several dozen cases the wife refused to rejoin the husband although he had obtained permission for her to come to Israel. The main reason for her refusal was unwillingness to leave her family (her father's house) and especially her grown-up children, who were not included in the reunion scheme.[63] Other cases concerned women who fled from their husbands to an Arab country after the 1948 War and there joined their relatives, and especially their children; sometimes all trace of them was lost.[64]

The husband usually stated as the reason for the divorce that he could not live alone, that he needed a wife to serve him, to run the household, to raise his children, and the like[65]; that his marriage to the absent woman had never been consummated[66]; that the divorce was necessary in order for him to take another wife because of the Knesset's ban on polygamy.[67] Here, too, the tendency was to divorce one's wife rather than take an additional one, even in those cases where it would have been possible to invoke the Knesset's good defense that the wife had been absent for a consecutive period of seven years and that her whereabouts were unknown.[68] It sometimes happened that a man divorced his wife when she insisted on leaving Israel for an Arab country to join her kinsfolk and children there.[69]

The causes of dissolution on the wife's initiative were, briefly, as follows[70]: non-payment of the whole or part of the prompt dower, appropriation of household articles (*ʿafsh al-bayt*), clothing and jewelry bought by the wife with her dower[71]; location of the wife's dwelling in the house of the husband's family[72]; non-provision of maintenance to the wife and children[73]; non-provision of maintenance to a deserted wife and fear for her good name and chastity owing to the husband's absence; the husband's being outside Israel[74] or in prison[75]; cruelty and injury (*ḍarar*) to the wife, such as beating, assault and locking her up in the house[76]; charges of immoral conduct, such as infidelity and adultery, against the wife and disownment of the children[77]; the wife's being forced to work away from home[78]; social, cultural or religious incompatibility of the spouses[79]; inability of the wife to fulfil her marital duties owing to advanced age, illness, infirmity and the like[80]; impotence, various defects and diseases preventing marital relations or endangering the wife[81]; reprehensible conduct of the husband, such as depraved habits or transgression of Qurʾānic and other prohibitions[82]; religious-legal defects in the marriage, such as incest, and difference of religion (*ikhtilāf al-dīn*).

II. DIVORCE ON THE HUSBAND'S INITIATIVE

1. LEGAL BACKGROUND

Islamic law recognizes dissolution of a marriage without legal proceedings. The right to this mode of divorce (*ṭalāq*) is reserved to the husband. The wife is a passive party to such a divorce; her consent is irrelevant. The husband may divorce her in her presence or in her absence; the *sharīʿa* court has no standing in a *ṭalāq* divorce. The wife is thus under a permanent threat of divorce, whereas the husband is liable to no legal sanction, although arbitrary divorce is disapproved by the *sharīʿa*.[83] True, Muḥammad introduced several important reforms in this institution, such as the *ʿidda* (waiting-period), which enables the husband, in the case of a revocable divorce (*ṭalāq rajʿī*), to take the divorced wife back without the need for the conclusion of a new marriage, and the *taḥlīl*, designed to discourage hasty divorces by requiring a thrice-repudiated wife to undergo an intermediate marriage before being again permitted to her original husband. But these reforms not only did not affect the husband's unilateral right to divorce the wife, but sometimes aggravated the wife's position, as will be seen below.

Nor did the Ottoman Family Rights Law, which introduced important changes in the law of divorce with a view to improving the status of the wife, abrogate the husband's unilateral right of repudiation. It is true that divorces pronounced in a state of intoxication or under compulsion were declared invalid and that the validity of divorces pronounced in metaphorical expressions was made dependent on proof of intent (*niyya*), but the law reaffirmed the principle that *ṭalāq* divorces do not require legal proceedings and that "explicit utterances or metaphorical expressions the meaning of which is customarily known and clear" are sufficient to make them valid. Suspended repudiation (*taʿlīq al-ṭalāq*) and divorce made effective from a specified future date (*ṭalāq muḍāf ilā al-mustaqbal*) also remained unchallenged by the Ottoman legislator.[84] The Family Rights Law indeed laid down the new provision that the husband must notify the divorce to the *sharīʿa* court, but this is not a substantive but a procedural provision: the husband does not need the *qāḍī*'s consent and the divorce is valid even without notification to the court.[85]

On the other hand, the Muslim woman has no unilateral freedom of divorce in any form. She may indeed obtain her release by mutual agreement with her spouse or by judicial proceedings, but this does not counterbalance the husband's freedom of *ṭalāq*. The seriousness of divorce from the point of view of the wife lies not only in the ease with which the husband can effect it but also in its legal and financial consequences. According to Islamic law, the father alone is the natural guardian of the children, and on the expiration of the period of custody (*ḥaḍāna*) the children pass from the control of the mother to that of the father. Divorce thus means severance of the wife from her children, and this is probably the most serious sanction threatening her. A divorced woman also loses her rights in the family property, although she sometimes had a fair share in its acquisition. She does not succeed her ex-husband. She is entitled to maintenance during the waiting-period (*ʿidda*), which usually lasts three months (*qurūʾ*) or, if she is pregnant, until the birth of the child, to deferred dower and to other connected stipulations if provided for in the marriage contract. Divorce is thus worse from the point of view of the wife than polygamy.[86] The husband's almost unlimited freedom of *ṭalāq* and the adverse consequences of divorce for the wife faithfully reflect the structure of the patriarchal family.

The Women's Equal Rights Law provides that divorce against the wife's will, in the absence of a court judgment imposing divorce on the wife, is a criminal offense carrying a sentence of five years' imprisonment.[87] In other words, the criminality of this kind of divorce does not affect its legal validity insofar as it is valid according to the *sharʿī* personal law applicable to the Muslim parties, but it entails a penal sanction.[88] Although couched in general terms, the provision is intended especially for Muslims.[89] In 1959, section 181A of the Criminal Code Ordinance was replaced by the provision that "where the husband dissolves the marriage against the will of the wife, and there is not, *at the time of the dissolution*, a final judgment of the (civil) court or the competent religious court imposing divorce on the wife, the husband shall be liable to imprisonment for a term of five years" (the italicized words were added to the original section).[90] In this way the Israeli legislator meant to bar the husband from divorcing his wife against her will and afterward obtaining the formal approval of the religious court.[91]

In sum, the Knesset did not intend to negate the validity of the Islamic law which recognizes the dissolution of a marriage by unilateral action of the husband. This finds its explicit expression in section 5 of the Women's Equal Rights Law, which provides that this law is not to affect any legal prohibition or permission relating to marriage or divorce. The intention was to preclude the husband's exercise of the right of *ṭalāq* if the wife did not agree to the divorce, compelling his resort to the court by means of a penal sanction. The question of the wife's consent to divorce by the husband and the dependence of divorce on a judgment making it binding on the wife are elements alien to the spirit of Islamic law.[92] The court's permission provides the husband with a good defense to the charge of divorce against the wife's will, but the divorce is performed by him. If he divorces her without such permission, the divorce is valid, but he is guilty of a criminal offense. Thus, by means of a procedural provision supported by a penal sanction, the Knesset created a mechanism affording the religious court an opportunity to consider each case, in the light of its particular circumstances, whether there was justification for approving the divorce (on other than religious-legal grounds).[93] If the wife agrees to the divorce, there is no room for intervention by the court and so, *ipso facto*, no question of a criminal offense. Knesset Member Uri Avneri proposed by way of a private member's bill that a divorce against the wife's will should be invalid, but his proposal was not adopted.[94]

2. DIVORCE AGAINST THE WIFE'S WILL

More than 1,800 *ṭalāq* divorces have been confirmed and registered since the establishment of the State. Striking among them is the high proportion of the various forms of "renunciation and compensation" divorces (around 1,300) as against other *ṭalāq* divorces (see Table I below); and adding divorces conditional on the wife's renunciation of rights and compensation to the husband, it may be said that about three-quarters (around 1,350) of all *ṭalāq* divorces were by agreement between the parties, whereas unilateral *ṭalāq* divorces made up only about one-quarter (approximately 450; see Table II below). The data on divorces by agreement reflect the position relatively faithfully because the parties were interested in registration.[95] On the other hand, the estimate of *ṭalāq* divorces not by agreement is probably too low for a number of reasons.

Awareness of the duty of registering divorces has not yet taken root in all strata of society. This duty is an innovation introduced in 1919,[96] and has no substantive significance from the *sharʿi* point of view. In the transitional period from the Mandate to the State of Israel,

TABLE I. *Ṭalāq* DIVORCES BY MAIN CATEGORIES AND BY COURTS, DURING THE PERIOD STUDIED IN THE *Sijills*[a]

Court	Total	*Ṭalāq*	*Tafwīḍ al-Ṭalāq*	*Taʿlīq al-Ṭalāq*: Ordinary	*Taʿlīq al-Ṭalāq*: Conditional on wife's Renunciation of Rights	*Taʿlīq al-Ṭalāq*: Total	Renunciation and Compensation Divorces
Jaffa	369	116	7	10	34	44	202
Ṭayyiba	236	65	—	20	—	20	151
Nazareth	488	67	1	17	5	22	398
Acre	714	135	3	7	4	11	565
Total	1,807	383	11	54	43	97	1,316

a) Divorces confirmed by *qāḍīs*, including divorces revealed during the hearing of various matrimonial claims; not including judicial dissolutions and annulments of irregular (*fāsid*) or void (*bāṭil*) marriages (total 80).

TABLE II: *Ṭalāq* DIVORCES BY AGREEMENT BETWEEN THE PARTIES AND OTHERWISE, BY COURTS

Court	Total	*Ṭalāq* Divorces by Agreement	*Ṭalāq* Divorces Otherwise than by Agreement
Jaffa	369	236	133
Ṭayyiba	236	151	85
Nazareth	488	403	85
Acre	714	569	145
Total	1,807	1,359	448

the work of the *sharīʿa* court, including the whole registration machinery, was disrupted and the proper confirmation and registration of divorces was impossible.[97] Since the Six-Day War of June 1967, the Muslims of East Jerusalem have also been in a state of transition; they brought their matrimonial matters before two *sharīʿa* courts, in which differing systems of material law applied.[98]

A divorce was usually registered for a specific purpose, such as realization by the wife of the rights accruing to her in consequence of the divorce; remarriage of one or both of the parties[99]; or an increased old-age pension from the National Insurance Institute for the wife as a lone woman.[100] The motive might arise long after the divorce, and sometimes one or even several decades passed between the divorce and its confirmation.[101] The divorce might not be registered in time because the spouses honestly believed that it was not valid, or were interested in concealing it, and continued to cohabit without a *sharʿī* bond; the divorce might then come to light at a later stage, sometimes during the hearing of another matter, such as a claim for maintenance or obedience.[102] Lastly, the ban on divorce against the wife's will also contributed to the non-registration of divorces (especially since the amendment enacted in 1959), because the husband was not anxious to expose himself to the penal sanction.

Ṭalāq divorces otherwise than by agreement were still, at any rate, a significantly frequent phenomenon. Their rates were lower in the areas of jurisdiction of the *Sharīʿa* Courts of Nazareth (17% of all *ṭalāq* divorces) and Acre (20%) than in those of the *Sharīʿa* Courts of Jaffa and Ṭayyiba (36%). These differences were probably due to the high concentration of an urban population (mixed towns) in the area of jurisdiction of the *Sharīʿa* Court of Jaffa and to the economic prosperity of the Little Triangle villages. Hardly any divorce not by agreement had in recent years been registered at the *Sharīʿa* Courts of Nazareth[103] and Ṭayyiba.

Divorce against the wife's will took various forms: usually she was divorced out of court, sometimes even in her absence, and she might learn of it accidentally or from someone other than her husband[104]; occasionally a husband divorced his wife in court in the presence of the *qāḍī*, but in her absence.[105] It could happen that a wife was divorced in court in her presence without being asked to agree to the divorce and even against her express opposition and without the husband having asked or received permission for the divorce.[106] The husband frequently did not even take the trouble to assign reasons.

One of the most striking manifestations of the husband's freedom of divorce is suspended repudiation (*taʿlīq al-ṭalāq*). The Ottoman legislator did not restrict the husband's right in this matter.[107] Resort to this mechanism has two traditional purposes: the threat of divorce is to get the wife to do or refrain from doing a certain act; the husband may wish to reinforce by an oath a pronouncement he has made in a matter not connected with the wife—that is to say, the element of intent (*niyya*) to divorce is absent here (see below).[108]

Suspended repudiation, usually of the first-mentioned kind, was resorted to in about a hundred cases, that is, about one-quarter of all *ṭalāq* divorces without the wife's consent. It arose out of problems connected with obedience, the dwelling, duties toward the family and the household, property relations between the spouses, family rifts, the type of marriage, etc. Thus, for instance, the husband said ". . . if the wife does not come at once, or at least within the hour, to my house which has been prepared for her, she shall be deemed repudiated by triple repudiation" or "if you do not return to our house by seven o'clock tomorrow morning. . ." or "if you do not return to my house with the bearer of this letter. . . ."[109] The wife's leaving the house without the husband's permission, especially her going to the house of her father, brother or mother or some other relative, was a very frequent ground for suspended repudiation: "if you go to the house of your relatives or your relatives come to you . . . ," "if you leave the house after sunset without my written permission . . . ," "if you leave your home and go outside the village . . . ," "if you go to see the doctor. . . ."[110] Sometimes the husband threatened to divorce the wife if she remained at his house for another night or returned to his house.[111]

Suspended repudiation might be prompted by the wife's refusal to move with the husband to a dwelling in another locality. In some cases, the wife was asked to do so to prevent the splitting up of the family as a result of the 1948 War.[112] Other grounds were the wife's working away from home, for example, as a teacher or laborer[113]; her negligence in the performance of household duties[114]; disputes over financial matters: "if you do not return the money you have taken . . . ," "if you touch it [the money] or use it as you please . . ."[115]; quarrels between the wife and her mother-in-law: "if you cross the threshold of my mother's room . . ."[116]; quarrels between the husband and wife concerning her loyalty to her family: one husband divorced his wife by suspended repudiation, effective if within a stated period she did not give him the power of attorney she had given her brother and undertake in writing never to give a power of attorney in matrimonial matters to a member of her family so long as they were married[117]; in another case, the husband swore an oath [to divorce her] as a chastisement (*yamīn al-taʾdīb*)—"*ʿalayya al-ḥarām*, may she not return to my house until she becomes a human being"[118]; suspended repudiation also occurred in exchange marriage: "if [X] divorces his wife, my sister, then my wife [Y, X's sister] shall be divorced."[119]

Sometimes the fulfilment of the condition of the divorce did not depend on the wife but on the husband; for instance, one stated: "if I beat or humiliate her or ask her a favor, she shall be considered divorced"[120]; another swore not to eat anything his wife had prepared as long as he lived[121] and another not to receive her into his house or take her to the town in which he resided.[122] In one case, the husband did not succeed in consummating the marriage for two years and the wife returned to her father's house; then it was agreed between them that she should return to his house for 30 days and that if he was still unsuccessful at the end of that period she should be considered divorced.[123]

Suspended repudiation as a means to reinforce a pronouncement by the husband unconnected with the wife's behavior was less frequent: a man who had quarreled with his brother swore to leave the house, failing which his wife would be considered divorced (he subsequently returned to the house and the divorce became effective); a man having a fight with another swore to rip his opponent's belly open with a knife (the contestants were separated, but the wife was divorced); a man swore to leave Israel for an Arab country (he gave up the idea when his application for permission to emigrate was rejected, and again the wife was divorced); a man caught a thief in his encampment and when he got away swore that he was a certain person; he was unable to prove the charge because his wife denied having seen the thief, and the divorce became effective.[124]

In dozens of cases the husband declared, sometimes before the court: "If she [the wife] releases me (*idhā abraʾatnī*) [from certain matrimonial obligations, such as deferred dower and maintenance during the waiting-period], I shall be prepared to divorce her."[125] In all these cases, the wife renounced her rights and was divorced. Such a renunciation may play the part of a condition of suspended repudiation, the husband saying: "You shall be divorced . . . if you release me from . . ." and the divorce becoming effective when the wife fulfils the condition.[126] Sometimes suspended repudiation preceded agreement between the parties as to the conditions of divorce and renunciation and might be regarded as an invitation (or pressure[127]) to agree to a divorce on the husband's terms. The process was thus as follows: the husband at first repudiated the wife on certain conditions, and then the wife appeared in court announcing that she agreed to the conditions, whereupon the divorce was complete and effective.[128] Where dissolution involved not only renunciation of rights by the wife but also monetary compensation, the husband expressly stipulated that the divorce should only become effective when the money had been deposited with him.[129] Sometimes several months elapsed before the wife succeeded in raising the money, which she then deposited with the court, whereupon the husband collected it, thus completing the divorce.[130]

In one case, the mechanism of suspended repudiation was applied by arbitrators within the meaning of article 130 of the Family Rights Law. When their efforts to restore domestic peace failed, they decided that the wife should be divorced if the spouses did not become reconciled within six days; they did not, and so the court decided that the wife was divorced.[131] The author did not come across a single case of a wife's being divorced with effect from a specific future date (*ṭalāq muḍāf ilā al-mustaqbal*). Suspended repudiation was particularly frequent in mixed towns and in Nazareth; it was more widespread in the Little Triangle villages of Ṭayyiba, Umm al-Faḥm and Ṭīra than in the villages of Galilee.[132] It was rare in Beduin society.[133] Suspended repudiation, in its various forms, was common also in the Ottoman period, especially in urban society,[134] but, as will be seen below, it received considerable impetus in Israel as a result of the ban on divorce against the wife's will.

There are clear cases of husbands being undeterred by the penal sanction from divorcing their wives against their wills. Sometimes the husband declared in court, before or after the divorce, that he knew that the wife was opposed to it, that he did not care whether or not she agreed, that the divorce was performed before he had received permission for it from a *sharīʿa* court, that he was well aware that it was contrary to secular law and subject to a penal sanction, and that he was "prepared to bear legal responsibility" or "criminal responsibility." The husband might go through with the divorce even after the *qāḍī* had warned him not to divorce the wife against her will.[135] The husband's readiness to bear criminal responsibility is rooted in the belief that the right of *ṭalāq* must not be curtailed in any way because it is given him by the *sharīʿa* or by God. Thus, in one case, the husband declared that he had divorced his wife because "Islamic law has placed the marital bond in the man's charge . . . and in reliance on this legal right granted me by God. . . ." In another case, the husband said he wanted to follow "the path of the *sharʿī* law only."[136] This attitude toward the institution of *ṭalāq* is part of the Muslim's religious belief, which is reinforced by his social outlook. In fact, the borderline between the social and religious was blurred in his consciousness, and he often sought support in the *sharīʿa* for his traditional attitude in social matters.

The restriction of the right of *ṭalāq* by the Knesset is a measure which not all Muslims were able to live with, and under such circumstances social custom reinforced by the *sharīʿa* proved stronger than secular law backed by a penal sanction. There were various ways of circumventing the ban on divorce against the wife's will: until the enactment of the Penal Law Amendment (Bigamy) Law, 5719–1959, it was possible to divorce one's wife and afterward seek permission for the divorce from the court. This was the most usual way of achieving a divorce without becoming guilty of a criminal offense. It is doubtful whether this device was used consciously. It seems rather that application to the court *ex post facto* was not intended to obtain permission but confirmation and registration. In any case, circumvention of the ban diminished greatly after the 1959 amendment, which, as stated, provides that the court's permission must be obtained beforehand.

The simplest way to evade the penal sanction was to divorce one's wife without registering the divorce[137] or to register it after a long time, when the question of the form of the divorce had ceased to be of actual concern. This way was of course effective where the wife was not alert to her rights. Bullying the wife into consenting to the divorce, false pretences, and false and falsified documents as to her consent were also resorted to.[138] Yet another circumvention of the ban on divorce against the wife's will was to drag the wife to court by a ruse, such as by filing an action which required her presence, and in the course of the hearing of that action divorcing her in the presence of the *qāḍī* and ostensibly with his knowledge and permission. It is doubtful whether by such a stratagem the husband really met the requirement of asking the court's permission for the divorce. Thus, in one case, the husband had the wife come to court in connection with a maintenance claim, and then, in the presence of the *qāḍī*, divorced her without having first asked permission. The *qāḍī* entered the divorce in the record and asked the wife to confirm it by her signature. The wife refused to sign and brought a criminal action against the husband for infringing the ban on divorce against the wife's will.[139]

Divorce also sometimes took place before the court in the wife's absence, after she had failed to appear in time for the hearing. Some *qāḍī*s regarded dissolution under these circumstances as lawful.[140] In one case a husband used the mechanism of *tafwīd al-ṭalāq* (delegated repudiation) to make sure that he could divorce his wife against her will without becoming guilty of a criminal offense. He had her sign an agreement to the effect that "he had the right to divorce her . . . with her consent . . . whenever he liked, in her presence or absence."[141]

The most sophisticated, though not widely used, device for circumventing the ban on divorce against the wife's will was suspended repudiation. In many cases, the husband contended that he had not been the active party in giving effect to the divorce, so that there was no basis for charging him with a criminal offense. The choice between continuation and dissolution of the marriage had rested with the wife, he claimed, and if she had opted for the latter alternative she had done so of her own free will. The husband's allegation that the wife had "opted for divorce of her own free will" (*ikhtārat linafsihā hādhā al-ṭalāq wabimaḥḍ irādatihā*) occurred very frequently in different formulations.[142] These formulations were undoubtedly intended to suggest that the situation was one of *tafwīḍ al-ṭalāq*, that is, delegation to the wife of power to divorce herself, and they should be regarded as equivalent to the expressions *takhyīr* and *ikhtārī nafsaki* within the meaning of articles 260 and 261 of Qadrī's collection. This was explicitly confirmed by Shaykh Ṭāhir Ḥamād, who on one occasion used an expression typical of the context of delegated repudiation: *jaᶜala al-amr biyadihā.*[143] In one case, the husband asserted that suspended repudiation was "*sharᶜī*" and "*qānūnī*,"[144] by which he apparently meant that it was valid under the *sharīᶜa* and not contrary to secular law. Some husbands carried out suspended repudiation by means of a letter to the wife with a copy to the court, apparently in order to create a kind of alibi in support of the plea that the wife had known of the divorce "and opted for it."[145] In one case, the wife said that she had asked and received the husband's advance permission for a visit to the pediatrician and that on her return he had told her that she had left the house without his permission and that he had made the divorce contingent on her going out. She said that this had been a "manoeuvre" in order to divorce her so as to be able to marry another woman[146]; she apparently did not think that such a divorce involved a criminal offense since a husband was always able to divorce his wife. The use of suspended repudiation as a means to circumvent the ban on unilateral divorce was particularly widespread in mixed towns within the jurisdiction of the *Sharīᶜa* Court of Jaffa and in the Little Triangle villages.[147]

Those who infringed or circumvented that ban were undoubtedly encouraged by the policy of the competent authorities, who were not unduly anxious to prosecute offenders. Infringements of the ban could without difficulty be traced in the *sijill*s, at any rate, in those cases in which the judge noted expressly in the judgment that the wife had been divorced illegally and the husband admitted this and even declared that he was prepared to bear the criminal responsibility involved. The first trial of a Muslim for divorcing his wife against her will took place as late as 1959,[148] and the number of offenders punished thereafter was very small.

3. THE DETERRENT EFFECT OF THE PENAL SANCTION

On the other hand, there are indications that the penal sanction attached to the ban on divorce against the wife's will had made an impact as will be shown in the following.

a. The Wife's Consent to the Divorce

Divorces with the wife's consent occurred, of course, even before the passage of the Women's Equal Rights Law in 1951, but it seems that her consent related to the mode of settlement of matrimonial rights rather than to the divorce itself.[149] At any rate, up to the prohibition of divorce against the wife's will, obtaining the wife's consent was voluntary, whereas afterward it became a statutory duty. One of the most impressive indications of the deterrent effect of the penal sanction is the husband's tireless effort to obtain the wife's consent in various ways. In hundreds of cases, he renounced his matrimonial rights and paid what was due to the wife; his renunciation related especially to dower. These cases mainly concerned marriages that had not been consummated.[150] Usually it was noted that "each of them [the spouses] renounces matrimonial rights"[151]; occasionally the expression "general renunciation"[152] was used, without any rights or conditions being specified. Sometimes it was noted that the spouses had agreed on the divorce "unconditionally and without qualification."[153] There were cases in which renunciation or other conditions were not referred to even vaguely. This was especially frequent where the marriage had not been consummated and in the case of exchange marriages.[154] These cases may be equated with others in which mutual renunciation of rights had taken place.[155]

The wife's matrimonial rights implemented on divorce by agreement included deferred dower and sometimes also prompt dower or the outstanding balance of it, maintenance for the waiting-period, stipulations connected with the dower, viz., household effects (*ᶜafsh al-bayt*), jewelry, clothing etc.,[156] accumulated maintenance and maintenance for the children left in the custody of the wife[157]; the husband might also renounce *sharᶜī* and civil claims pending in *sharīᶜa* courts and civil courts,[158] promise to relinquish property of the wife and acknowledge the child she was expecting as his.[159] The husband's readiness to discharge all his obligations to the wife at the time of the divorce is extremely significant, even though he would seem bound to do so under religious law; in ordinary *ṭalāq* divorces, the realization of those rights involve legal proceedings.

Another, even more impressive, indication of the deterrent effect of the penal sanction is the compensation paid to the wife for her consent to the divorce. It was usually paid in cash in amounts ranging from several hundred to several thousand Israeli pounds.[160] Shaykh Ḥasan Amīn al-Ḥabash noted that in some cases it reached 15,000 pounds.[161] Occasionally compensation was paid in hard currency, such as pounds sterling, English sovereigns and even Ottoman gold liras, or in jewelry.[162] It was usually paid at the time of the divorce, but sometimes in monthly instalments or in promissory notes payable after several months (or a year) or the wife was left to demand the money "whenever she likes."[163] Frequently the compensation was paid in kind, mostly in immovables: a parcel of land, an olive grove or some fruit trees, a plot in a built-up area, a house or room with a yard, a well, etc. The property was usually transferred to her full ownership, sometimes with an undertaking to register it in her name in the Land Registry.[164] The husband might sell to his divorced wife a parcel of land or a building as part of the compensation arrangement.[165] The compensation might take the form of livestock: goats, sheep, horned cattle, and so forth.[166]

Other arrangements related to the wife's dwelling. The couple might reach an agreement that the house or apartment in which they lived until their divorce should, with all its furniture and appurtenances, serve as dwelling of the woman until her death and that the man might not oust her from it as long as she lived. The man might undertake to leave the house and to pay her a fine (*gharāma*) of several thousand pound if he failed to do so; if he forced her out or if, for any reason, she moved out of her own accord, he was to pay her monetary compensation.[167] The man might undertake to provide a furnished apartment to the woman and to pay the rent for an agreed period.[168] Such arrangements were especially frequent in the towns of Acre and Haifa.

Another way of compensating the woman was by assuring her of an extension beyond the waiting-period of the maintenance which was prescribed by the *sharīʿa* for that period: the husband might undertake to support the woman for life or until she remarried,[169] left the country and rejoined her family,[170] or became entitled to a National Insurance or welfare pension.[171] The principle was that the husband would provide for her upkeep until some other agency assumed that responsibility. Maintenance was often combined with compensation in the form of property or with the provision of living accommodation in the ex-husband's house.[172] Compensation in kind was intended to ensure the ex-wife's subsistence and economic independence.[173]

The chief reason for the payment of compensation to the divorced woman was undoubtedly the Knesset's ban on divorce against the wife's will, which is coupled with a penal sanction. The compensation was intended to secure the wife's consent to the divorce. Evidence of this is to be found in direct references by several *qāḍī*s and in their decisions. Shaykh Ḥasan Amīn al-Ḥabash stated that: ". . . what is called compensation is a quid pro quo given for the wife's consent to her husband's divorcing her, in circumvention of the criminal responsibility incurred in the event of his divorcing her without her consent and without obtaining a judgment of the competent court permitting him to perform the divorce . . . The phenomenon of compensation is clearly a consequence of the law forbidding divorce against the wife's will. . . ."[174] Shaykh Tawfīq Maḥmūd ᶜAsaliyya remarked: "The husband has the right of *ṭalāq* and is therefore not bound to pay compensation to the wife except in the event that the wife does not wish to be divorced and the husband wants to bring her round with money in order to avoid punishment. . . ."[175] Further confirmation that compensation was a consideration for the wife's consent to the divorce was given to the author by Shaykh Muḥammad Ḥubayshī.

In fact, almost all the divorce judgments mentioning compensation state that the wife consented to the divorce. Often they even state expressly that the compensation was a "consideration for her consent"[176] or that the wife made her consent conditional on compensation.[177] Significant in this context is the fact that all the cases in which compensation was paid were divorces by mutual agreement and performed in court. In one case, a man first divorced his wife out of court, but at the time of registration offered to pay compensation as he had done on the divorce of a previous wife.[178] The author did not come across a single instance of payment of compensation to a divorced wife prior to the enactment of the Women's Equal Rights Law on July 17, 1951.[179] Nor did he find any instances in the Ottoman or Mandatory *sijill*s (of several years selected at random).

Some researchers note that the custom of compensating the divorced wife already existed before the establishment of the State, though not on a large scale. The compensation sometimes consisted in a part, usually one-third, of the dower, which had been set aside for the eventuality of divorce or the husband's death.[180] Israeli *sijill*s usually indicate that the compensation was paid in lieu of maintenance for the waiting-period, the dower being rarely referred to[181]; in these few cases, the compensation might have been identical with the dower. In other cases, a clear distinction was made between compensation and dower.[182]

The compensation was often said to be for injury (*ḍarar*) caused to the wife by the divorce.[183] Shaykh Ḥusnī al-Zuʿbī, asked about the origin of the custom of compensation, said that compensation was stipulated in advance in the marriage contract.[184] In fact, at a *qāḍī*s' conference in 1963, it was recommended that *maʾdhūn*s should safeguard the wife's rights in the marriage contract by providing for divorce compensation of an amount to be fixed according to the circumstances or by the court.[185]

But Shaykh Ḥasan Amīn al-Ḥabash, in whose area of jurisdiction compensation was particularly widespread, strongly emphasized that it had nothing to do with dower and that "not a mil" was paid to the divorced wife as compensation before the establishment of the State.[186] Nor is there any evidence in judgments of compensation being stipulated in the marriage contract and its realization sought on divorce; neither did the author find an instance of such a stipulation in the marriage registers of 1962 and 1968. It thus seems that although the practice of paying divorce compensation may not be new, its spread to its present dimensions is at any rate connected with conditions and circumstances which developed in Israel. The stipulation of compensation in the marriage contract must be regarded as still in the recommendation stage, the reference to the injury caused to the divorced woman being, as will be shown below, an attempt to give *sharʿī* legitimation to a custom which has no basis in Islamic law.

The Knesset's ban on polygamy may also have contributed to the spread of the practice of compensation. As stated, the primary intent of the husband who divorced his wife in many cases had been polygamy. But for the ban on the latter, he would not have divorced her; on the contrary, the divorce caused him to lose her working capacity and experience, required him to pay her the deferred dower and maintenance for the waiting-period and might spoil his relations with her family; above all, he might not want to be separated from a wife whom he honored and valued as the mother of his children and to whom he was still emotionally attached.[187] The ban on polygamy thus suddenly placed the husband in a situation where he was reluctantly compelled to divorce his ageing wife in order to be able to marry another younger one, and the compensation under these circumstances may have to be explained not only as the price of her consent to the divorce but also as an expression of his wish to repair the damage he had unwillingly inflicted on her and to provide for her future upkeep. Rosenfeld regards compensation as a structural solution for the elderly divorced woman, who does not return to her father's house.[188]

Support for the view expressed in the foregoing may be found in cases where the husband was willing to enable the divorced wife to reside "temporarily" or to the end of her days near or even in his house. He would build a room for her above his own dwelling, install her in part of his dwelling divided off by a partition "so that they may not see each other" or even allot a room to her within his dwelling without any partition.[189] In rare cases, it was agreed between the parties that the divorced woman should live in her former husband's dwelling and be "under his control." She was to be allowed to use all the household utensils; the ex-husband was to support her and her children; to supply them with food and clothing, provide for their medical needs, and so on. He also undertook "to behave well and properly, displaying all male virtues, be patient and courteous and protect her whenever necessary"; and if they moved elsewhere, it was to be to a dwelling of higher standard than that they had left. On the other hand, the divorced wife was forbidden to be absent from the dwelling without his consent, and if she left the dwelling with her children she was to lose all her rights except the right to maintenance at a specified rate until death or remarriage.[190] It might be agreed that if he ousted her from the dwelling or if for any reason she left of her own accord she should be entitled to monetary compensation.[191]

The divorced wife's living in or near her former husband's house was of no significance where she was elderly, ailing or disabled, and this seemed to be so in most of the cases in question. At the same time, the possibility cannot be ruled out that the divorce was sometimes fictitious in the sense that the couple continued to live maritally together (or that the ex-husband took back or remarried his former wife, which was apt to be in contravention of the ban on polygamy).[192] The author came across a not inconsiderable number of cases in which the divorced wife lived at the former husband's house and maintained marital relations with him without the couple troubling to notify the court of the divorce or to register it until several years later.[193] The facts might come out in court incidentally to the hearing of a claim by the woman for maintenance or by the man for obedience.[194] The divorced wife's living at her former husband's house was more natural and understandable where the parties were cousins who lived in one dwelling-unit within the framework of the extended family. Thus, in one case, a man said that he had divorced his wife by triple repudiation and pointed out to her that her living at his house was prohibited: "I considered her to be living near me [in the dwelling] as my cousin, not as my lawful wife." Four years had passed since the divorce before he decided to apply to the court to make clear to her that she was divorced, so that she might leave his house.[195]

About three-quarters of the cases in which the divorced wife was compensated concerned intra-*ḥamūla* or cousin marriages. Blood-relationship is likely to strengthen a man's inclination to compensate his former spouse owing to family pressures. At the same time it should be noted that the rate of endogamous marriages was high in rural society and had been so even in the past, before the custom of compensating the divorced wife became established. Shaykh Ḥasan Amīn al-Ḥabash remarked that a smaller compensation was paid to a blood-relation than to a stranger and that the rate of compensation was lower in the case of exchange marriages "lest there be a bad influence on the other *badīla*."[196]

About three-quarters of the 120 cases in which compensation was paid were in the Little Triangle villages.[197] Shaykh Tawfīq Maḥmūd ʿAsaliyya confirmed that compensation was not customary in localities in the area of jurisdiction of the *Sharīʿa* Court of Jaffa[198] (in which all types of settlement were represented). The cases with compensation in the Little Triangle constituted almost 60% of divorces by agreement in that region, as against up to 3% in the areas of jurisdiction of the *Sharīʿa* Courts of Jaffa, Nazareth and Acre. The frequency of the practice in the Little Triangle was probably due to the economic prosperity of that region, which fostered the inclination in married men to seek younger wives; polygamy being forbidden, the older woman was divorced with compensation.

The institutionalization of the wife's consent to the divorce found various kinds of formal and structural expression: in most cases of divorce by agreement, it was declared that the parties wished to dissolve their marriage "by voluntary, mutual agreement" (*biriḍāhimā waʾkhti-yārihimā*), and in addition, the *qāḍī* often recorded a statement by the wife, in the first person: "I agree (*rāḍiya*) to this divorce."[199] Occasionally the mechanism of suspended repudiation was used, the wife's consent being one of the conditions, or the only condition, of the validity of the divorce. The husband might say, for instance: "My wife . . . shall be considered divorced . . . if she consents to the divorce and grants me remission of . . . ," and the divorce then took effect as soon as the wife consented to it and renounced various matrimonial rights in accordance with the husband's demand. Divorce conditional on the wife's consent was chiefly practiced in the towns of Jaffa, Lod and Ramla.[200] It was not uncommon to designate the wife's consent as one of the conditions of a comprehensive divorce agreement drawn up in writing with the signatures of the parties.[201] Sometimes it was expressly noted that compensation was paid to the wife "in return for her consent" (*liqāʾ muwāfaqatihā*) or the wife made her consent conditional on receipt of compensation.[202]

The wife's consent to the divorce was undoubtedly meaningful in those cases in which she initiated or demanded the divorce and probably in most of the cases in which she renounced matrimonial rights or even paid compensation to the husband in order to obtain her freedom and in the cases in which divorce was conditional on her consent and the fulfilment of this condition was left to her. But in many other cases in which the wife consented to the divorce, including cases in which she obtained her matrimonial rights and even compensation for her consent, a suspicion arises that she did not always do so of her own free will and in awareness of her status and legal rights. It is often quite clear, especially when the divorce took place out of court, that her consent was given in the innocent belief that the *ṭalāq* was the husband's indisputable *sharʿī* right, given him by Allāh; in other words, she resigned herself to her fate for religious reasons.[203] The wife's submission had also social, traditional causes. In many cases, she gave her consent when she was elderly, disabled or ill, unable to fulfil her marital duties, attend to the household, etc., or when she was barren or had only borne daughters.[204] Shaykh Ḥusnī al-Zuʿbī confirmed that the wife's barrenness or inability to fulfil her duties toward the husband and the family were frequent causes of divorce by agreement. The wife consented to the divorce in order to enable the husband to marry another woman "for a family purpose," i.e., the production of offspring.[205]

Other causes of divorce that the wife regarded as legitimate in view of the norm accepted in traditional society were disputes between rival wives in polygamous marriages,[206] and especially, the divorce of one of the *badīla*s in exchange marriages.[207] Needless to say, the wife's consent to the divorce in cases of exchange marriages was not meaningful in the sense intended by the Knesset. The wife in such a marriage rarely opposed the divorce. The only institutionalized way to preserve the surviving marriage in such cases was by paying dower to the wife who did not wish to leave her husband.[208] Family pressures were also the probable cause of the wife's consent in cases where the spouses were blood-relations, especially where they were cousins,[209] and where there were disputes between the two families.

One may also be sceptical of the wife's consent in cases where she was represented by a proxy (*wakīl*). This proxy, who was usually her father or brother, not only formulated the conditions for her divorce (renunciation, compensation, and so forth) in her name, but also consented in her name to the divorce.[210] She was often not in court on those occasions, and thus her view of the divorce was not heard. The possibility cannot be ruled out that she was forced to appoint the proxy precisely because she was herself opposed to the divorce. The same measure of scepticism should apply in cases where the wife was absent from the session of the court and the husband presented her consent in writing or had people testify to it or alleged that she had consented. It sometimes transpired that she was divorced against her will although the husband alleged that she had consented.[211] In one case, it was ascertained that the wife's signature on the document purporting to attest her consent had been forged and the matter went as far as the Supreme Court sitting as a High Court of Justice.[212] Many cases are on record where the husband put various kinds of pressure on the wife—harassment, humiliating treatment, beating, non-payment of maintenance and ejection from the house—so as to force her to consent to the divorce.[213] In numerous instances, the divorce preceded the wife's consent, which was given only at the registration stage. In other words, she was faced with an accomplished fact and her consent did not relate to the divorce itself but to her matrimonial rights.[214]

Thus, the wife's consent to the divorce should not be taken at face value; the particular conditions under which it was given should be examined in each case. It is much more meaningful in this connection to examine to what extent the wife opposed the divorce in reliance on the secular law. In fact, the author observed the following phenomenon: a wife vehemently opposed the husband's intention to divorce her and when he nevertheless did so "placed on record" that the divorce was against her will[215]; she declared that Israeli law was on her side and that she reserved the right to take legal steps in the competent courts[216]; and in one case the wife threatened to have jailed both her husband who had divorced her, and the *qāḍī* if he confirmed the divorce[217]; she misinterpreted the law to the effect that the divorce was not valid so long as she did not consent to it[218]; in another case, the wife declared that she would only consent to the divorce after she had "scratched his [the husband's] eyes out" and that "Israeli law is on the side of the wife," and in another she opposed the divorce although the husband put pressure on her in various ways and offered her whatever she might ask in return for her consent.[219]

These phenomena are unmistakable signs of a revolutionary change in the traditional mechanism of unilateral divorce by the husband. The requirement of the wife's consent to the dissolution of the marriage has turned her from a passive into an active factor[220]; she has been given a new weapon—the power to threaten the invocation of a penal sanction against the husband. There are clear indications of the wife's growing self-confidence and awareness of her legal rights. The fact that the husband resorted to various devices to obtain her consent is in itself significant. The wife is essentially in a position to refuse her consent, to withhold it as long as she wishes, to attach to it conditions satisfactory to herself and even to retract it.[221] At the same time, the process of change is still in its beginnings. It is particularly widespread in mixed towns, and more so in the villages of the Little Triangle than in those of Galilee. As yet, it is not noticeable at all in Beduin society.

b. Permission for Divorce Granted by the Court

The most significant criterion for the effect of Israeli legislation in the sphere of divorce was the husband's resort to the *sharīʿa* court in order to obtain permission for the divorce where the wife did not consent to it. As stated, what is involved here is a procedural mechanism designed to provide something like a good defense for the husband to the charge of divorce against the wife's will. Requiring the husband to apply to the court in matters of *ṭalāq* was in itself a revolutionary innovation. Only in a few dozen cases did the husband ask the court's permission, and it is not even certain that this was always the real purpose of his application. In some cases, he probably intended to divorce the wife with the knowledge or in the presence of the court, as had already been customary before the enactment of the Women's Equal Rights Law,[222] or to have the divorce registered.[223] Moreover, in a few instances, the wife had consented to the divorce and the court's permission was thus not really needed.[224] There is sometimes the impression that recourse to the court in cases where the wife opposed the divorce was rather in the nature of a request for a religious-legal opinion (*fatwā*); at any rate, the religious and the secular elements were closely linked.[225]

At the same time, there are clear instances of the husband's application for permission being prompted by fear of the penal sanction. Thus, in one case, he made the application "in order to escape legal punishment," and in another case he admitted that he did not wish to divorce his wife out of court, against her will and without a court judgment "for fear of doing something contrary to the law."[226] In a further case, when the court refused permission for the divorce, the husband appealed to the *Sharīʿa* Court of Appeal.[227] Moreover, significant in this context were cases where the husband at first tried to get permission and only when he encountered difficulties contended that he had divorced his wife already, before applying to the court.[228] The chief grounds of applications for permission to divorce a wife were her being an absentee or staying in an Arab country, her barrenness, illness or misconduct, and conflicts arising out of polygamous marriages. The cases of application for permission encountered by the author mark the beginning of a revolutionary change in the sphere of divorce.

c. Reliance on Grounds Provided for Judicial Dissolution

A further indication of the deterrent effect of the penal sanction is the husband's endeavor to dissolve the marriage on one of the grounds provided by the Ottoman Family Rights Law, although they were mainly intended to offset the wife's lack of freedom of *ṭalāq*. The number of cases of this kind is indeed not great but they are symptomatic of the disturbance of the traditional system of balances in the sphere of divorce. Thus, in one case, the husband asked the court to dissolve his marriage on the ground that his wife was mentally ill (article 123 of the Family Rights Law).[229] According to the *sharīʿa*, the husband needs no protection by the court in the event of the wife's disability or illness since he can divorce her by *ṭalāq* or take an additional wife. Mental illness, as stated, is a good defense to the charge of polygamy, but not to the charge of divorce against the wife's will.

Dissolution of the marriage by arbitration (article 130) may release the husband from the obligations to the divorced wife to which he would be subject had he divorced her by ordinary *ṭalāq*, provided that the arbitrators decide that she is responsible for the dissolution.[230] But there were cases in which this mechanism was apparently used in order to obtain dissolution without becoming guilty of a criminal offense through the wife's opposition to the divorce. Thus, in one case, a husband resorted to article 130 after all his efforts to get rid of his wife by "legitimate" methods, such as various harassments and suspended repudiation, had proved unsuccessful. The wife said that the purpose of his application was "obvious," viz., to attempt to rid himself of her "by every possible means."[231]

III. DISSOLUTION ON THE WIFE'S INITIATIVE

The wife's position is reflected not only in her reaction to unilateral divorce; she also plays an active part in dissolving the marriage, trying to obtain her freedom in various ways: by *ṭalāq* and by legal proceedings.

1. *ṬALĀQ* DIVORCES

a. Delegated Repudiation

The most effective means at the wife's disposal to secure a dissolution without recourse to legal proceedings is delegated repudiation (*tafwīḍ al-ṭalāq*).[232] By this mechanism the husband confers on the wife power—a kind of irrevocable power of attorney—to divorce herself in his name and thus to become the active party to the divorce.[233] Of course, the decision as to the delegation itself rests with the husband, who may, in principle, grant it to someone other than the wife,[234] and only the timing of the divorce is left to her or depends on certain pre-agreed conditions. Although according to orthodox doctrine *ṭalāq* is the unilateral privilege of the husband, in actual fact, delegated repudiation is undoubtedly a clear manifestation of the wife's freedom of divorce, albeit limited and structurally controlled.

As far as can be ascertained from the *sijill*s this type of divorce was not frequent in Israeli Muslim society. The author encountered only 11 cases, although, of course, there might be more.[235] The most usual formula for empowering the wife to divorce herself was *takūn ʿiṣmatuhā biyadihā* ("her 'protection' will be in her hands"), whereas the formula customary in *sharʿī* literature, *yakūn amruhā biyadihā* ("she will be responsible for herself"), which is the most serious one as regards the legal effect, since it entails irrevocable or triple repudiation, was rarely employed. The author encountered no other formulas.[236] In most cases, *tafwīḍ al-ṭalāq* was inserted in the marriage contract, in others it was granted in the course of the marriage, following a dispute or crisis between the spouses.

The delegation may be absolute or conditional.[237] An absolute delegation is formulated in a general, indefinite way, and sometimes it is said expressly that the wife may divorce herself whenever she wishes.[238] A conditional delegation becomes operative, for instance if the husband leaves the country without the wife's consent, as during the 1948 War, deserts her, makes her live in another locality than the one chosen by her or takes an additional wife.[239] Other conditions, arising out of the experience of married life, relate to the way the wife is installed in the house of the husband's family, his treatment of the wife, maintenance, equality and justice between rival wives, etc. In all the cases in question, the delegation was the consequence of a dispute between the spouses, the nature of which may be inferred from the conditions. The dispute ended in a compromise, with a saving formula that included empowerment of the wife to divorce herself. Thus, in one case, the wife fled to her father's house and refused to return to the husband's house unless he set up a partition between her dwelling and that of his family, built her a separate kitchen and separate sanitary facilities and paid her a sum of money in cash; if he failed to fulfil these conditions within a week, she was to have the right to divorce herself. The husband accepted the conditions "of his own volition and by free choice" and signed an agreement in court.[240]

In another case, a dispute arose between the spouses and the wife filed a claim for maintenance in the *sharīʿa* court. The *qāḍī* succeeded in restoring domestic peace on the basis of the wife being empowered to divorce herself if the husband did not treat her well, if he beat her, cursed her, did not supply her needs as to clothing and footwear, or gave her rival preference over her in any way. The parties agreed on these conditions thanks to the intervention of Shaykh Salāma al-Huzayyil and also agreed that he should act as arbitrator (*ḥakam*) between them, deciding whether one of the said contingencies had arisen. In yet another case, where after falling out with her husband the wife sued for divorce, the *qāḍī* proposed a reconciliation on the basis of the husband undertaking to pay maintenance to his wife and children. The husband agreed and declared on this occasion: "If I beat or humiliate my wife without there being a good reason for a beating or a humiliation . . . her ᶜ*iṣma* shall be in her hands," but added that a divorce resulting from this should require the consent of the court.[241]

The wife exercised her right to divorce herself on the ground that the husband did not treat her well, that there was no harmony or compatibility between them, or that she was dissatisfied with him.[242] In one case, she did not even trouble to give a particular reason but simply said that according to the marriage contract she was entitled to divorce herself "as she wished."[243] In other cases, the wife exercised her right when the contingency in which she was authorized to divorce herself had in her opinion arisen. Thus, one wife divorced herself as soon as her husband had left the country, and married another man even before the *sharīᶜa* court had confirmed the divorce and before the expiry of the waiting-period.[244] In another case, the wife divorced herself although the husband made desperate efforts to prove that he had fulfilled all the conditions agreed between them and that she, therefore, had no grounds for exercising her right of divorce: the wife emphatically insisted on the divorce and applied to the court to register it.[245] In all these and other cases, the wife effected an irrevocable divorce, i.e., one which did not enable the husband to bring her back to him except by a new marriage contract and a new dower. In one case, she divorced herself by triple repudiation.[246]

In the cases described above, the wife was the active party to the divorce and the husband the passive party, opposing it. This clearly conflicts with the structure of the patriarchal family underlying the *sharᶜī* law. There may be a certain symbolism in the fact that in one case the husband wished to avail himself of the device of *tafwīḍ*, intended for the protection of the wife, to empower *himself* to dissolve the marriage: a year after the wife had been divorced for the first time, the husband wanted to marry her again, but stipulated "that the *ṭalāq* should be in his hands at his will and choice, whether she consents or not." He was probably prompted to do so by the ban on divorce against the wife's will.[247] This is a vivid illustration of the disturbance of the balance of the Israeli Muslim family by the intervention of secular legislation. An anomaly has been created in that, on the one hand, the wife may divorce the husband against his will (in those cases where she has been empowered to do so), and on the other, the husband may not divorce the wife against her will, although this is his elementary right according to the *sharīʿa*, but needs permission from the *sharīʿa* court or her authorization.

As stated, dissolution by way of delegation to the wife was not common in Israeli Muslim society.[248] In most of the cases referred to, the spouses, or at least the wife, originated from urban settlements. One case occurred in the Circassian village of Kafr Kamā[249] and another in the al-Huzayyil tribe in the Negev. No conclusions should be drawn from the latter isolated case as to the status of women in Beduin society; for this was a case not of a stipulation in the marriage contract but of an agreement suggested by the court and a shaykh of the tribe as a solution to a crisis between the spouses[250]; in other words, this was yet another instance of the encounter between *sharīʿa* and custom: a successful linking of a legal device with the institution of arbitration.

b. Suspended Repudiation

Suspended repudiation is indeed one of the most striking manifestations of the husband's freedom of *ṭalāq*. However, this sharp weapon, mainly intended to ensure the wife's obedience and submission, sometimes became a double-edged sword, used by her to obtain her freedom. In many cases, the wife hastened to bring about the fulfillment of the condition and then proceeded forthwith to the *sharīʿa* court to have the divorce confirmed and registered. Thus, in one case, the husband swore that the wife would be considered divorced if she left the house. A quarter of an hour later, she left the house and applied to the court to confirm the divorce.[251] In another case, the husband stipulated that the wife should be considered divorced if she did not return to his house within ten days. Even before the time was up, she informed the court that she refused to return and wanted a divorce.[252]

Occasionally the husband regretted a hasty divorce but could not forestall the wife's prompt action. He would then try to empty the suspended repudiation of its contents by qualifying the condition. Thus, in one case, the husband at first denied having divorced the wife at all, but when she brought witnesses to prove her allegation, he claimed to have stipulated that she should be considered divorced if she spent the night at her mother's house; he added, however, that the condition referred only to the night on which the divorce had been pronounced and that, since she had spent that night at his house, the divorce was ineffective.[253] In another case, the wife alleged that the husband had sworn she would be considered divorced if he ate any food prepared by her and that he had subsequently done so; she accordingly asked that the divorce be declared effective. The husband admitted eating half of some meat she had served him after he took the said oath, but added that he had made the effectiveness of the divorce contingent on "the absence of sincere feelings for him on her part"; he swore that she had again shown tenderness to him but could produce no witnesses to prove it, and she denied it emphatically.[254]

In another case, the wife refused to move into the husband's house after the marriage because she had not received the whole of the prompt dower. The husband stipulated that if she did not move into his house within five days she would be considered divorced. The wife did not move in within the time allowed. In court, the husband contended that the divorce was not effective because, according to him, he had reached an agreement with the wife as to the payment of the balance of the dower. The wife denied the existence of such an agreement and asked the court for "a judgment in accordance with the Muslim *sharīʿa*"; her request was granted. In yet another case, the wife maintained that she should be considered divorced because she had left the house, but her husband contended that he had meant to make the divorce contingent on her re-entering the house, and since she had not yet done so she was still his lawful wife.[255]

The wife sometimes took advantage of a vow of divorce by the husband intended to reinforce a statement in a matter that had nothing to do with her. Thus, a man who had quarreled with his brother swore that if he did not leave the house his wife would be considered divorced; he in fact left the house, but the wife alleged in court that he had returned the same morning, whereby the divorce had become effective.[256] In several cases, the wife alleged that there had been a suspended repudiation, but was unable to prove it.[257] Sometimes there is a distinct impression that the wife resorted to making up a story in order to obtain the dissolution of her marriage.[258]

The stipulation of suspended repudiation in the marriage contract on the wife's initiative was not customary in Israeli Muslim society. The marriage registers of 1968 record only one case of this kind. The wife compelled the husband to stipulate that if he married an additional wife the latter should be considered divorced.[259]

c. Rebelliousness

It sometimes appears that the wife strove to attain the status of *nāshiza* (rebellious wife) in order to wrest a divorce from the husband when she had no legal ground for dissolution or the husband did not agree to divorce her.[260] This impression is particularly strong in those cases in which she initiated the declaration of rebelliousness; she might even openly admit that she did not wish the marriage to continue.[261] In fact, in several instances, the stage of the wife's rebelliousness was followed by divorce.[262] Nor can the possibility be ruled out that a wife might use a maintenance claim as a device to obtain dissolution of the marriage.

d. Divorce Pronounced in a State of Intoxication

The Ottoman legislator, in contrast to the Ḥanafī school, laid down that a divorce pronounced in a state of intoxication was not valid.[263] The plea of the husband's intoxication was provided for the protection of the wife. This plea was in fact made in a few isolated cases (all in urban settlements), but here it was not the wife but the husband who used it to avoid divorce; in some instances, he contended that the wife had extorted the divorce from him by provocation while he was drunk. Thus, in one case, some persons testified that the husband had been sitting in a café, drinking "large quantities of wine until he became besotted," when suddenly the wife appeared, hurled abuse at him and demanded that he divorce her in court. Other people present also urged him to divorce her and be rid of her. Giving in to all this pressure, he had divorced his wife in court. The *qāḍī* accepted the testimony of the witnesses and decided that the divorce was not valid.[264]

In dozens of cases in which the wife sought a judgment confirming her divorce, she did not succeed in proving that a divorce had really taken place.[265] A suspicion sometimes arises that the wife tried to take advantage of the husband's freedom of *ṭalāq* and the lack of formality attending divorce in order to obtain her freedom by falsely claiming that she had been divorced and, by conspiring with false witnesses, getting the court to confirm the alleged divorce.[266] In some cases, in court the wife retracted the allegation that she had been divorced.[267] Occasionally she achieved her purpose during the hearing of her suit by getting the husband to divorce her before the *qāḍī*.[268]

e. "Renunciation Divorces" and "Compensation Divorces"

The means most frequently used by the wife to obtain her freedom was divorce by agreement between the parties. According to traditional classification, this kind of divorce comprises two main varieties: mutual renunciation by the spouses of their matrimonial rights and payment of compensation (*ʿiwaḍ*) to the husband in return for the divorce. Without the husband's consent to the divorce, renunciation and compensation are meaningless. The court cannot compel the husband to divorce the wife or itself dissolve the marriage by *ṭalāq* divorce.[269] It is the husband who performs the divorce, and he does so of his own free will; resort to the court is merely for confirmation of the terms of the divorce with all the attendant effects on legal and property relations.

In "renunciation divorces," the most usual arrangement was for the wife to renounce what would have been due to her by virtue of her matrimonial rights if she had been divorced by ordinary *ṭalāq*. This included maintenance during the waiting-period (*ʿidda*) and—if stipulated in advance in the marriage contract—deferred dower. The wife might also renounce the whole of the prompt dower (if she had not received it) or the balance of it (if she had received part of it on contraction of the marriage).[270] She might renounce half the dower (or half of both dowers); this was mostly in cases where the marriage had not been consummated.[271] She might renounce "the stipulations connected with the dower" enumerated in the marriage contract, such as household effects, *jihāz*, jewelry and clothing.[272] She sometimes forewent the implementation of other provisions of the marriage contract, such as that if the husband divorced her against her will he was to pay her an agreed sum of money "for the education of her children" or a fine (*gharāma*), or her entitlement to a sum of money from him "whenever she demands it."[273]

The wife occasionally renounced maintenance awarded her by the court and accumulated with the husband. She might renounce various claims pending in court and agree to discontinue the proceedings.[274] She often renounced her *sharʿī* right of custody (*ḥaḍāna*), and the children were handed over to their father or some other person. Sometimes the spouses agreed on a division (*taqsīm*, *tawzīʿ*) of the children between them. The wife might retain *ḥaḍāna* but undertake to support the children throughout the legal period and not to claim maintenance for them (suckling and *ḥaḍāna* money) from their father. It might be agreed that the children should remain with the wife until she remarried, or that she should bring up her husband's children by another woman.[275]

The wife's renunciation might relate to rights and claims unconnected with matrimonial matters, such as monetary debts of the husband to her or her family, deposits, promissory notes, and so forth.[276] Often it was stated vaguely that the wife renounced civil (*niẓāmiyya*) claims or claims pending in a civil court. Sometimes reference was made to criminal charges connected with the ban on divorce against the wife's will.[277]

In "compensation divorces" the wife paid compensation to the husband in return for her freedom.[278] It might be in money, in kind or both.[279] It ranged from a few Israeli pounds to several thousand, sometimes 10,000 pounds.[280] Occasionally, it was paid in gold coins, such as Ottoman gold liras.[281] The wife might return the dower, especially in cases where the marriage had not been consummated,[282] the expenses of performing the betrothal and the marriage, or other sums of money received from the husband.[283]

Monetary compensation was normally paid at or about the time of the divorce. In a few exceptional cases, the wife undertook to compensate the husband when she remarried; in one instance, it was expressly stipulated that she was not permitted to remarry before she had paid compensation to her former husband. In most of these cases, security for the payment of compensation was given in the form of an undertaking by the wife's family or of a promissory note signed by the wife's father payable on her remarriage. In one case, the wife undertook to pay an amount equal to half the prompt dower "in order to safeguard her children," who were to be handed over to their father.[284] In two cases, arrangements for deferred compensation were prescribed by arbitrators.[285] It seems that this was because the wife had no money at the time of the divorce and that the intention was that she should compensate the husband out of the dower she would receive on remarriage. This assumption is confirmed by a case in which arbitrators decided on dissolution of a marriage while requiring the wife to pay a certain sum to the husband, and her father promised that on her remarriage he would take some of the prompt dower "and satisfy the [former] husband."[286] Shaykh Muḥammad Ḥubayshī explained that an undertaking to compensate the husband at the time of the wife's remarriage must be honored like a promissory note.[287] What is involved here is a social custom for which there is no support in the *sharīʿa*, but Shaykh Tawfīq ʿAsaliyya attested that the *sharīʿa* court did not interfere in voluntary arrangements of this kind and respected the wishes of the parties.[288]

Compensation was sometimes paid in the form of immovable property: a parcel of land, an olive grove, a house, or a right of the wife in the estate of her father or of members of her original family; the wife undertook to transfer the asset registered in her name in the Land Register to the husband.[289] The asset given as compensation might be the dower she received from him.[290]

In dozens of cases, the parties came to court with the texts of detailed agreements, which they asked to have confirmed as part of the legal effects of the divorce and which thereupon were sometimes attached to the judgment.[291] But it seems that usually the parties formulated the terms of the agreement in court and that immediately afterward the husband divorced the wife and the wife renounced her rights or compensated the husband, or he first divorced her and then she renounced her rights.[292]

Another frequent form of divorce by agreement was, as stated, a combination of renunciation or compensation and suspended repudiation. In this context, the main purpose of suspended repudiation was to ensure in advance that the wife renounced certain rights or compensated the husband before the divorce became effective. Sometimes the wife made her renunciation conditional on the husband's divorcing her. The customary formula was: "I renounce . . . on condition that you divorce me" or ". . . and this renunciation is conditional on divorce. . . ."[293] The act of renunciation or compensation and the divorce might take place on separate occasions. When the wife renounced her rights or deposited a sum of money intended for the payment of compensation, she usually did so at her residence in the presence of the secretary of the *sharīʿa* court, and the husband subsequently divorced her before the court in her absence. The spouses did not meet during these proceedings.[294]

Occasionally the wife was represented by a proxy (*wakīl*) or an advocate authorized to negotiate the terms of the divorce (renunciation, compensation etc.) with the husband and to agree to the divorce in her name.[295] The *wakīl* was usually the father or a brother of the wife, but sometimes her son or even another woman.[296] The husband might also be represented by a *wakīl*,[297] and sometimes all the proceedings involved in divorce by agreement (renunciation, compensation and even divorce itself) were conducted by proxies of the parties without the latter meeting at all.[298] The spouses might agree on a "renunciation divorce" or "compensation divorce" in the course of a proceeding before a civil court and afterward resort to the *sharīʿa* court for implementation of the agreement.[299] It would seem that the timing of the divorce was of secondary importance compared with the terms of the agreement. Yet, under certain circumstances, the time factor was so material as to become part of the terms. Thus, in one case, it was agreed between the parties that if the husband divorced the wife within 40 days the matrimonial maintenance should be regarded as including maintenance for the waiting-period, but if he divorced her later, he should have to pay maintenance for the waiting-period in addition to the matrimonial maintenance.[300]

In many dozens of instances, there is express evidence that the initiative for dissolution by agreement came from the wife.[301] More than two-thirds of all divorces by agreement involved renunciation by the wife of certain rights, or compensation to the husband. In most of these cases, especially where compensation was paid to the husband, the initiative probably came from the wife.[302] But it is not impossible that even under such circumstances it came from the husband.[303] Moreover, initiative by the wife may be doubted in dozens of cases of exchange marriage.[304]

Dissolution along with the wife's renunciation of rights or the payment of compensation to the husband was practised mainly in towns, and in mixed towns—where women's social liberation had made most progress—more than in Arab towns. The rate of such divorces in mixed towns was three times as high as in villages and Arab towns: 0.9–1.0 per mille as against 0.3 per mille (in 1967).[305] Such divorces also occurred among the Beduin, especially those in Galilee, who were at an advanced stage of sedentarization. They were more frequent in exogamous than in endogamous marriages: in exogamous marriages, the wife who wanted a divorce was free from pressures arising out of blood-relationship. It seems, however, that the type of settlement was more important in this connection than the type of marriage. The wife's education had not yet had significant bearing on the measure of her initiative in bringing about a divorce. Only in a few cases did the wife sign her name to the divorce agreement or divorce judgment.[306] As a rule, her fingermark (*baṣma*) appeared on these documents.

2. JUDICIAL DISSOLUTION

In theory, the most important mode of effecting a divorce on the wife's initiative is by judicial proceedings on grounds recognized by law, without need of the husband's consent. Dissolution by the court is alien to the Ḥanafī school, which is stricter in this respect than the three other Sunnī schools.[307] The two Sulṭānic decrees of 1915 provided to the wife a limited number of grounds for judicial dissolution. These grounds were considerably widened by the Ottoman Family Rights Law of 1917. Most of the Ottoman amendments were based on orthodox schools of law other than the Ḥanafī.

As appears from Table III below, judicial dissolution was not very common.

TABLE III: JUDICIAL DISSOLUTION AND ANNULMENT ACCORDING TO GROUNDS AND COURTS[a]

Court	Total	Defect or Illness of Husband	Non-Payment of Maintenance by Absent Husband	Discord and Incompatibility	Irregular and Void Marriages
Jaffa	43	—	26	14	3
Ṭayyiba	1	—	—	1	—
Nazareth	21	2	7	11	1
Acre	15	1	9	2	3
Total	80	3	42	28	7

a) The data relate only to actions which ended in dissolution.

a. Option of Puberty

According to the prevailing view in the Ḥanafī school, the option of puberty (*khiyār al-bulūgh*), i.e., the right of a minor girl to terminate her marriage on reaching sexual maturity, exists only where the guardian is not the father or paternal grandfather.[308] The author came across only one case where a wife asked to terminate her marriage in reliance on this option. Her husband having crossed to the West Bank before the 1948 War without the marriage having been consummated, she declared: "I have opted for myself" as soon as she had her first menstruation.[309] The infrequency of this plea had several causes: the great majority of marriages were arranged by the father or grandfather; the wife was not aware of her right, which lapsed on consummation of the marriage[310]; and the age of marriage of Muslim women in Israel had risen.[311]

b. Dissolution by Mutual Imprecation

An unproved charge of adultery (*zinā*) against the wife is liable to be a ground for judicial dissolution on her initiative. This is an archaic type of dissolution, which belongs to the domain of criminal law; it is connected with the mechanism of denial of paternity,[312] and involves mutual curses (*liʿān*). *Liʿān* dissolutions were not customary in Israeli Muslim society. There was not a single dissolution of this kind, although several cases involving *liʿān* were dealt with by the courts, a few of them on the wife's initiative.[313] The wife was not inclined to use this mechanism to obtain her freedom, probably out of concern for her good name, and sought other ways to effect dissolution.[314] Nor did the husband readily resort to this device when he denied paternity; he preferred more scientific methods, such as examination of the child's blood-type.[315]

c. Defects and Diseases of the Husband

A defect (*ʿayb*) of the husband preventing intercourse is a ground for judicial dissolution on the wife's initiative under the Ottoman Family Rights Law (articles 119–121). If the defect is incurable, the court dissolves the marriage there and then; if it is transitory, the husband is given one year's respite, and if it persists, the marriage is dissolved. The acceptability of this ground is subject to several conditions: that the wife has not herself a defect preventing intercourse; that the application is not made after intercourse has taken place; that the wife did not know of the defect before the marriage (unless it be impotence, in which case she may demand dissolution even if she did); and that she did not accept the defect after the marriage. The scope of this ground is much wider under the Family Rights Law than it was prior to the latter's enactment.[316] A new more radical ground under that law (article 122) is an infectious disease of the husband not permitting continuation of the marriage without injury (*ḍarar*) to the wife. In this case, too, the husband is given a year's respite if there is hope that the disease will pass; if there is no hope, the marriage is dissolved there and then. If the wife knew of the husband's ailment at the time of the marriage or agreed to continue the marriage after she became aware of his condition, her right lapses. A further ground for dissolution (article 123) is mental illness of the husband discovered after the marriage. Here also, the husband is given a year's respite, and if he is not cured in the meantime, the court dissolves the marriage at the wife's request.

These grounds were not often invoked. The judgments indicate that the defects and diseases caused agony, humiliation and injury to the wife and might even lead to her being beaten by the husband.[317] She usually waited several years before applying to the court for dissolution.[318] In fact, marriages were dissolved on one of the said grounds in only three cases.[319] In some of the cases in which the application was dismissed, the suspicion arises that the wife had invented the ground in order to obtain her freedom. Thus, in one instance, she alleged that the husband was impotent and mentally defective and that she was still a virgin, but afterward she admitted that she had received medical treatment to enable her to become pregnant and that she was no longer a virgin; she added that she did not love her husband and would not have him "even if he were 'Antar ibn Shaddād or were capable of taking four virgins in one night"—all she wanted was an irrevocable divorce.[320] The rarity of reliance on these grounds for dissolution may be due to several causes: the infrequency of the defects and diseases in question; the fact that the disclosure of unpleasant intimate matters is involved; and the wife's ignorance of the new grounds made available to her by the Ottoman legislator. Moreover, the proof of contentions as to a defect or disease of the husband involves wearying errands and various proceedings, such as medical examinations, with which the wife finds it difficult to cope.

d. Dissolution of Marriage to an Absent Husband

The Ottoman legislator provided two grounds for dissolution of the marriage to an absent husband: his absence and the impossibility of collecting maintenance from him; the marriage is dissolved after the necessary inquiries as to the husband's whereabouts have been made (article 126); and, if the husband has left property from which maintenance can be collected (*māl min jins al-nafaqa*), the marriage is dissolved four years after hope is given up of finding out his whereabouts or whether he is alive or dead; if he disappeared in an enemy country as a result of war, the marriage is dissolved one year after the fighting forces and prisoners have returned home (article 127). These two new grounds are based on elements from different schools, the teachings of which are more liberal from the point of view of the status of women. By contrast, according to the Ḥanafī school, a marriage to an absent husband cannot be dissolved.[321]

Many dozens of cases of wives of absent husbands have been dealt with by the courts. In most of them, the husbands had gone to Arab countries under circumstances connected with the 1948 War. The gravity of the problem was greatly relieved by the family reunion scheme proclaimed by the Government of Israel after the armistice agreements with the Arab countries, by frontier rectifications in the Little Triangle area, and especially by the legitimation of infiltrators who had returned to Israel after the war. Still, the problem had not yet found its complete solution. Moreover, the political tension between Israel and the Arab countries, even without actual war, encouraged men who, for various reasons, wished to leave their wives and families.[322] In most cases, the wife knew nothing of the husband's whereabouts except that he had gone to an Arab country, nor whether he was alive or dead; she sometimes waited for him for years before she gave up and sought relief in court.[323] There were cases in which the wife was deserted before the marriage had been consummated.[324] In some instances, it is evident that the husband meant to harm the wife: he stole her jewels or his departure was prompted by a desire for revenge.[325]

The most frequent ground for dissolution under these circumstances was non-provision of maintenance to the wife. One stereotyped formula was that the husband "left her without maintenance and did not instruct anyone to support her and has no money deposited with anyone and no debt due to him from anyone and no house and no land and no-one from whom she might borrow and who might collect the debt from him [the husband]."[326] The wife might ask assistance from her family (her father's house), but it was not always possible to obtain it; her relatives might be old, poor or ailing. One wife started to work away from home, but could not continue because she had no-one to look after her young children. The wife might find herself in "a desperate plight" or her position could become "grievous owing to lack of food and clothing."[327] In many cases, the wife had definite knowledge of the husband's whereabouts, and sometimes she even succeeded in contacting him. Thus, in one instance, she claimed maintenance from him and when he refused she applied to the court to dissolve her marriage. The wife might face the husband with the alternative of returning to Israel and supporting her or dissolving the marriage.[328]

Another ground for the application of the wife of an absent husband for dissolution is connected with the protection of the reputation and chastity of women in traditional society.[329] Remarriage is a structural solution to this problem, especially in the case of a young woman. In several instances, the wife stated that she wished to dissolve her marriage so that she might marry someone who would protect her reputation and chastity and at the same time support her.[330] A further ground was the injury (*ḍarar*) caused to the wife by the husband's absence and failure to provide maintenance.[331] In one instance, the plea of injury arose out of the husband's imprisonment. The wife insisted that her marriage to a prisoner was causing her injury and that this alone was a sufficient ground for dissolution even if he had left property from which maintenance might be obtained.[332] Injury and the husband's imprisonment are not grounds for dissolution under the Ottoman Family Rights Law, but they are recognized by modern legislation in Arab countries.[333]

The wife might be ready to join the husband at his place of residence outside Israel if only he would ask her to do so.[334] On the other hand, there are cases where the impression is received that the wife invoked non-provision of maintenance as a ground for dissolution although she had an opportunity to be reunited with the husband. In several instances, she learnt of his whereabouts but when contact had been established between them and she could have joined him abroad, she hastened to reject this chance on the formal ground that she was not bound to follow him because the distance between them exceeded the specified maximum (*masāfat al-qaṣr*).[335] In these cases, the husbands had migrated from Jaffa no further than the Gaza Strip or Khān Yūnis in the south or Sidon in the north.[336]

The author came across no case in which the wife asked for dissolution merely by reason of the husband's being absent, under article 127 (opening passage), i.e., because, although he had left maintenance, she despaired of ever hearing of him again, having waited four years in vain for his return. On the other hand, the author did encounter one case in which the wife asked for the application of the closing passage of article 127. She pleaded, in addition to non-provision of maintenance, that more than a year had elapsed since the signing of the armistice agreement, i.e., more than the period within which, in her case, the fighting forces and prisoners could have been expected to return home.[337]

In some cases, the wife of an absent husband did not ask at all for her marriage to be dissolved. Instead, she asked to be awarded maintenance and to be certified as a *mahjūra* (a woman whose husband has deserted her and disappeared).[338] There may have been several motives behind this course of action: the wife might not yet have despaired of the husband's return to Israel; she might have considered the provision of maintenance more essential in her circumstance than divorce; thus, in several cases, wives asked that their husband's pay maintenance and that only if they failed to do so should they divorce them or the court dissolve the marriages.[339] The question of marital status is immaterial to an elderly wife who does not expect to remarry or to a wife who for some reason does not wish to remarry. Moreover, in this situation, the wife has several advantages: she continues to live in the husband's house; she receives maintenance from him or collects it from his property; she is independent, not taking orders from anyone; she has a share in the family property; and as a married woman, she is largely immune to family pressures and social sanctions to make her remarry. These advantages are particularly apparent in the nuclear family, in which the wife becomes the family head. In other words, being tied to an absent husband may sometimes be a structural solution convenient to the wife.[340] It does not prevent her from drawing a pension from the National Insurance Institute like a widowed or divorced woman. Shaykh Amīn Qāsim Mudlij and Shaykh Muḥammad Ḥubayshī said that women applied to the court for confirmation as *mahjūra*s in order to obtain such pensions.

e. Discord and Incompatibility

Another ground for dissolution of the marriage on the initiative of both spouses is "discord and incompatibility" (*nizāʿ washiqāq*) between them (article 130 of the Family Rights Law). According to the relevant provision, the *qāḍī* is to appoint two arbitrators (*ḥakam*), if possible from the families of the spouses, and they, also referred to as "the family council" (*al-majlis al-ᶜāʾilī*), are to try to the best of their ability to bring about a reconciliation. If they fail through the husband's fault, they are to decide on dissolution of the marriage[341]; if through the wife's fault, she is to be divorced by *khulᶜ* (a form of repudiation by which the wife releases herself from the marriage for a consideration) while losing the right to the whole or part of the dower. If the arbitrators fail to reach agreement between themselves, the *qāḍī* is to appoint other arbitrators from the families of the spouses or a third arbitrator from neither family. The arbitrators' award is final and non-appealable. Dissolution by arbitrators on this pattern, which is based on the teachings of the Mālikī school, constitutes a far-reaching reform in the status of women. According to the Ḥanafī school, arbitrators are not competent to dissolve a marriage unless the spouses have authorized them in advance to do so; if they have not, the arbitrator's task is confined to reconciliation.[342]

Arbitration was indeed the most effective means available to the wife to obtain her freedom in legal proceedings when the husband ill-treated her and yet was unwilling to divorce her. A study of the circumstances in which the wife sought to apply article 130 reveals a tendency to widen the meaning of the term "discord and incompatibility" as much as possible, far beyond the sphere of matrimonial rights.

The most frequent ground adduced was cruelty and the infliction of injury. The husband's cruelty consisted in acts causing physical or mental harm: severe beatings and aggravated assault, to the extent of endangering the wife's life[343]; locking up the wife in the house, forcing her to work away from home and hand her earnings over to him[344]; accusing the wife of adultery (*zinā*) and disclaiming paternity of her child.[345]

In cases of non-provision of maintenance, a court judgment requiring the husband to pay was not always an effective remedy although it was theoretically enforeable by execution. According to the testimony of Shaykh Amīn Qāsim Mudlij, there were husbands who preferred prison to paying maintenance, and the wife could not always obtain a loan for her upkeep.[346] Under these circumstances, there were wives who sought dissolution by arbitrators.[347] Cruelty, injury and non-provision of maintenance are recognized by modern legislation in several Arab countries as grounds for judicial dissolution.[348]

It sometimes appears that the wife used the mechanism of arbitration as an expedient or device to obtain her freedom where she had no *sharʿī* ground for dissolution. This was particularly so in cases where she was prepared in advance to be found guilty by the arbitrators, to bear responsibility for the dissolution and to renounce various rights, such as dower, maintenance during the waiting-period and custody of the children.[349] In fact, in most of the cases in which the marriage was dissolved under article 130, the arbitrators found that the wife was to blame for the dissolution and was obliged to renounce various matrimonial rights. They might require the wife to pay the husband compensation "for her deliverance" (*badal mukhālaʿatihā*) or "for her divorce" (*muqābil taṭlīqihā*).[350] This compensation was sometimes the equivalent of the whole or part of the dower, the amount of the expenses incurred by the husband on contraction of the marriage and consideration for the right to stay and live in his house and to use his household equipment.[351] In addition, the wife might be required to return to the husband jewelry, gifts, clothes, a bedroom suite, and so forth, which she had received from him. She might also pay compensation for not having let the husband exercise his conjugal rights.[352]

Sometimes the arbitrators found both parties guilty and determined the legal effects accordingly, having regard to the circumstances of the case. Thus, in one instance, the husband was ordered to pay the wife a part only of the deferred dower, and in another, mutual renunciation of rights was enjoined.[353] On one occasion, the arbitrators reached the conclusion that both parties wanted the divorce but that neither wanted to disclose his or her position "so as not to incur the consequences this would entail."[354]

Arbitration was not often resorted to. It was mainly practised in the towns. It seems that townswomen know their legal rights, including the possibilities of dissolving their marriages, better than countrywomen. Some actions for dissolution by arbitrators were brought by Beduin. The custom of arbitration, established in Beduin society, has received *sharʿī* legitimation and become institutionalized in family law. The arbitrators are shaykhs and heads of subtribes of Beduin in the Negev and *mukhtār*s of Beduin in advanced stages of sedentarization in Galilee[355] and are therefore experienced in the settling of disputes by traditional methods, which they apply also to matrimonial matters. Arbitration was thus practised especially in the most Westernized and the most traditional society, which accounts for its rarity.

In dozens of cases, the wife demanded in court that the husband divorce her or that the court direct or compel him to do so[356] although this type of dissolution is not recognized in Islamic law. These cases did not involve *sharʿī* grounds for judicial dissolution but circumstances connected with the husband's behavior, for instance, his ill-treatment of the wife, or expulsion of her from the house, or simply her desire to live away from him, and detestation of him, etc.[357] In some of these cases, the husband refused the wife's demand for a divorce, but, significantly enough, found it necessary to justify his refusal, declaring that he loved her, wanted her and was utterly unwilling to part from her.[358] In other cases, he agreed to divorce her, but only because she had taken the initiative and the terms of the divorce that had thereby been formulated were favorable to him.[359]

f. Dissolution of the Marriage of a Girl Under 17

The Knesset did not content itself with imposing a sanction on a person found guilty of marrying, performing the marriage of, or giving in marriage, a girl under 17, but wished to remedy the position also with regard to such a girl already married, and therefore created an additional, secular ground for judicial dissolution: the Age of Marriage Law provides that the fact of the wife having been married under the age of 17 is a ground for an action for dissolution by the religious court. An action for dissolution on this ground may be brought by the wife (before she attains the age of 19) or by either of her parents or her guardian or a welfare officer (before she attains the age of 18). The said law also provides that if the husband dissolves the marriage at the wife's request or complies with a judgment requiring him to dissolve it, the court shall take this into account as a mitigating factor. However, the Knesset added the proviso that the dissolution shall be carried out "in accordance with the provisions of the law applicable to matters of personal status of the parties."[360] This addition blurs the distinction between the substantive and the technical-procedural character of the new ground.[361] Despite its similarity to *khiyār al-bulūgh* in several respects, the new ground has no basis in the Islamic legal heritage. It is the legislative act of a secular, non-Muslim parliament guided by norms totally different from those of the *sharīʿa*.[362] Islamic law does not recognize the wife's having been under 17 at the time of the marriage as a ground for dissolution and this ground is not valid in a *sharīʿa* court.[363]

The *sijills* do not record a single instance of the wife, her parents or guardian or a welfare officer seeking to avail themselves of the new ground created by the Knesset in order to dissolve the marriage of a girl under 17. It seems that it is not to be expected that the girl, who does not know her legal rights, should take the initiative for dissolution, let alone her parents or guardian, who are responsible for her early marriage. The main reason for this situation is a basically social one, deriving legitimation from the *sharīʿa*.

g. Termination of an Irregular or Void Marriage

Another method of having her marriage terminated is open to the wife where there is a defect or flaw in it which makes it irregular (*fāsid*) or void (*bāṭil*). Such a marriage is illicit, and if the spouses do not themselves effect a separation, the court will do so. There are material differences between an irregular and a void marriage as regards the legal status of the children and the rights of the partners.[364] The Ottoman legislator, guided by a liberal outlook, and especially by the interest of the children, confined voidness to marriages between a Muslim woman and a non-Muslim man. Other marriages defective from a *sharʿī* point of view were classified as irregular.[365]

Only in isolated cases were marriages terminated on such grounds. Thus, a wife contended that her husband maintained sexual relations with her germane sister and had a child by her and that this created a prohibited situation necessitating termination of their marriage; the court accepted her contention: although it had not been contended that the husband was married to both sisters, it treated his sexual relations with the plantiff's sister as a marriage.[366] In some cases, the court ordered termination of the "marriage" of an already married woman to a man other than her husband, or of the remarriage of a divorced woman before the expiration of the waiting-period.[367]

Marriages between a Muslim woman and a non-Muslim man are considered void, also according to the Family Rights Law.[368] In one case, a marriage was annulled on this ground: a Jewess married to a Jew had adopted Islam and immediately afterward applied to the *sharīʿa* court for annulment of her marriage on the ground of difference of religion (*ikhtilāf al-dīn*); the *qāḍī* allowed her suit and directed her to apply to the appropriate authorities for an annulment judgment in accordance with the *sharīʿa*.[369]

IV. EFFECTS OF DIVORCE

1. IRREVOCABLE AND REVOCABLE DIVORCE; TRIPLE REPUDIATION

An irrevocable (*bāʾin*) divorce becomes operative immediately with all the legal effects attendant on the dissolution of a marriage with regard to matrimonial and financial rights. After divorcing the wife for the first and the second time, the husband may take her back by means of a new marriage and a new dower. A revocable (*rajʿī*) divorce becomes operative only after the expiration of the waiting-period; within that period, the husband may take the wife back without her consent and without a new marriage, by express declaration or significant conduct, provided the marriage had been consummated; he may take her back in this way after the first and the second divorce. If the husband does not take the wife back within the waiting-period, the divorce becomes irrevocable, and if he subsequently wishes to take her back, it has to be by means of a new marriage and a new dower. After the third divorce, the wife is not permitted to return to the husband either during the waiting-period or by means of a new marriage until she has been married to another man, the new marriage has been consummated and she has been divorced by the other man in good faith. The purpose of this harsh provision, the *taḥlīl* introduced by Muḥammad, is to prevent ill-usage of the wife by unlimited alternate divorce and reinstatement (without a new marriage), in other words, to deter the husband from such a divorce by creating a formidable obstacle to his taking back the wife after she has been divorced for the third time. This provision was stultified by all the orthodox schools, which permit divorcing one's wife in one session by the use of an expression known as triple repudiation, which has the effect of three separate divorces, although they deprecate this form of divorce as *ṭalāq al-bidʿa* (in contrast to the various forms of *ṭalāq al-sunna*, recommended by them).[370] Muḥammad's provision thus did not achieve its purpose and may even have aggravated the position from the point of view of both spouses.

The various kinds of divorce take effect through explicit (*ṣarīḥ*) or metaphorical (*kināya*) *ṭalāq* expressions and differ from one another as to the formula, the degree of finality and the element of the husband's intent (*niyya*). The Ottoman legislator, although recognizing both explicitly and metaphorically pronounced divorces, laid down that the meaning of the expression used must be known and clear; if it is not, the divorce is valid only after the husband's intention to divorce the wife has been proven.[371]

The *sijill*s contain a variety of triple repudiation formulas, including some combining triple repudiation with archaic expressions, such as *īlāʾ* and *ẓihār*.[372] About 90% of *ṭalāq* divorces were single, irrevocable ones.[373] In fewer than 10% of divorces other than by judicial proceedings, the wife was divorced three times. This was almost always done in one session by triple repudiation; only rarely was the wife divorced by three separate acts.[374] Almost three-quarters of the triple repudiations were *ṭalāq* divorces performed unilaterally by the husband, as against about one-quarter which were by mutual agreement. Triple repudiations constitute about one-quarter of *ṭalāq* divorces other than by agreement. Triple repudiation was particularly frequent under the following circumstances: a fit of anger, or provocation by the wife[375]; an affront to the husband's honor, disgraceful misconduct of the wife, such as adultery[376]; serious disputes between the spouses or their families[377]; suspended repudiation intended to make the wife obey the husband by the threat of the ultimate sanction, or a vow of divorce intended to demonstrate serious intention or firm belief regarding a matter not necessarily connected with the wife (more than one-third of suspended repudiations were by triple repudiation[378]); in the case of exchange marriages, triple repudiation of one of the wives, which leads to triple repudiation of the other[379]; in the case of childlessness or a cousin marriage, where the spouses wish to demonstrate that they do not intend to restore their marriage in the future[380]; the husband's wish to grant the wife maximum freedom in return for renunciation of matrimonial rights[381]; and the intention to take another wife in place of the divorced one.[382]

The *sijill*s do not to a significant extent reflect the grave human problems likely to arise from the desire of the spouses to restore their marriage legally after a triple divorce. The author came across only one instance of an intermediate marriage, and this was undoubtedly a fictitious marriage contracted specifically *biqaṣd al-taḥlīl*, in order that the wife might again be permitted to return to her first husband, in express contradiction to the *sharīʿa* (as propounded by some schools of law). The second "husband" told the court ingenuously that he had contracted the marriage as a *muḥallil min al-ṭalāq*, one who causes the wife to be again permitted to her first husband, from whom she has been separated by triple repudiation. He swore that he had consummated the marriage. Thereupon the wife was divorced, at her request, on agreed terms of renunciation; the *qāḍī* confirmed the divorce and instructed her to observe the *ʿidda* before remarrying. The ease with which this divorce was performed and confirmed may indicate that this was a customary way of circumventing the intermediate-marriage provision.[383] Another method was referred to in a case in which the wife alleged that the husband had divorced her some years previously by triple repudiation and had remarried her a year later without her having been married to another man.[384] There can be no doubt that such things actually happened, and if they are not reflected in the *sijill*s, it is because neither of the spouses was anxious to raise problems.[385] The author came across only a limited number of cases in which the wife denied or objected to a triple repudiation,[386] and not one case in which she tried to soften the blow by claiming there had only been a single repudiation. Moreover, in a not inconsiderable number of cases, the wife applied to the court on her own initiative for registration of a triple repudiation,[387] and sometimes she demanded that the husband perform such a repudiation in return for her renouncing various matrimonial rights or paying him compensation.[388]

Revocable divorce was not widely practised: according to the *sijill*s, it represents about 3% of all divorces other than judicial. The real figure is probably higher because there is evidence that the husband who divorced his wife and then took her back during the waiting-period sometimes did not trouble to register the divorce.[389] This can also be inferred from the fact that the *qāḍī*, when called on to confirm the divorce and the wife's reinstatement, sometimes asked the parties to declare any divorce that might have preceded the divorce in question or decided that the husband might take back or remarry the wife if the quota of three divorces had not been filled.[390] In other words, the courts had no way of keeping track of the matter.

It seems that revocable divorce achieved its original purpose in the sense that the husband, regretting his rash act, took back the wife before the end of the waiting-period. He sometimes did so at the very time the divorce was registered,[391] and sometimes he used go-betweens, *ahl al-khayr*, for the purpose.[392] He might ask the court to regard the divorce as revocable so that he could take the wife back; this request was occasionally backed up by the plea that the divorce was pronounced in a fit of anger.[393] Sometimes in the case of an irrevocable divorce a husband asked a religious functionary or *qāḍī* for a legal opinion (*fatwā*) enabling him to take the wife back without a new marriage.[394] In a few cases the wife was not taken back during the waiting-period and the divorce became irrevocable.[395]

Revocable divorce might be combined with suspended repudiation. This combination was apparently intended to ensure the wife's obedience by deterrence while giving her two chances before the final dissolution of the marriage. If she failed to obey and the condition was thus fulfilled, she became revocably divorced, but if she persisted in her disobedience during the waiting-period, the husband might not take her back and the divorce would then become irrevocable. Also, in this manner, the husband reserved to himself the option to preserve the marriage and take the wife back during the waiting-period.[396] Moreover, on reinstatement of the wife during the waiting-period, the question of divorce against the wife's will was no longer of real concern although the divorce was still counted as one of the three permitted by the *sharīʿa*. At the same time, there is evidence that the question of the wife's consent arose also in the case of revocable divorce.[397] In several cases in which a suspended repudiation was to give added weight to some pronouncement of the husband totally unconnected with the wife, the husband asked that the divorce be regarded as revocable when the pronouncement had proved wrong.[398] In other cases, the wife was revocably divorced under an agreement between the parties according to which she renounced various matrimonial rights.[399] It seems that the husband wished to retain an option to take the wife back while restoring the rights she had renounced.[400]

From the wife's point of view, revocable divorce was advantageous or disadvantageous according to the circumstances of the case: where she did not want a divorce, she hoped that the husband would exercise his right to take her back during the waiting-period; where she wanted a divorce, she feared that he would exercise this right. Both cases involved an intermediate state of uncertainty and insecurity for the wife: she might be for many months in a limbo between marriage and divorce.[401] This situation is perhaps the most unpleasant manifestation of the freedom of *ṭalāq* vested in the husband by Islamic law. The author came across some cases in which the husband divorced his wife, took her back, divorced her again, took her back again and then divorced her a third time.[402] The outrage was still greater in the case of an exchange marriage, where the alternate divorce and reinstatement of one wife automatically entailed a similar treatment of her *badīla*.[403] On the other hand, where the wife was not interested in the marriage, she might claim that she had been revocably divorced, that the waiting-period had passed without her being reinstated and that the divorce had thus become irrevocable; or she might contend that she had been irrevocably or triply divorced in the first place whereas the husband might deny having divorced her at all or admit only to a revocable divorce or ask that the divorce be regarded as revocable.[404] In one case, the wife said that the husband had taken her back against her will by having intercourse with her by force and threats, and that she still did not want ever to be his wife again.[405] In sum, it may be said that Muslims are not strict with regard to *ṭalāq al-sunna* and *ṭalāq al-bidʿa*. Revocable divorce, which is the type most recommended by all the schools, was rather rare, while divorce by triple repudiation, which is the most frowned on, was rather frequent.

2. MAINTENANCE DURING THE WAITING-PERIOD

A divorced woman is entitled to maintenance during the waiting-period (*ʿidda*), provided she is not rebellious. The waiting-period is usually three menstruations if the marriage has been consummated or *khalwa* (privacy of husband and wife) has taken place.[406] If the divorced woman is pregnant, she is entitled to maintenance until delivery.[407] The rate of maintenance is fixed by mutual agreement or, in the absence of agreement, by experts (*mukhbirūn*). The *sijill*s show fewer than 50 claims for maintenance during the *ʿidda* although about 1,900 divorces of all kinds were confirmed and registered by the courts. There are several reasons for the small number of maintenance claims: about three-quarters of the different kinds of *ṭalāq* divorces are, as stated, by agreement between the parties, and such divorces usually involve renunciation of maintenance during the *ʿidda*; the spouses may on divorce determine the wife's rights by agreement, so that the wife need not file a claim for maintenance; if maintenance is not claimed within the waiting-period, the right to it lapses.[408] Only in one case did the husband agree to pay maintenance although the waiting-period had expired.[409] Rebelliousness of the wife at the time of the divorce was a (rare) ground for loss of the right to maintenance.[410]

From the evidence, it appears that the wife did not usually enjoy her right to maintenance during the ʿ*idda*, just as she did not enjoy her right to deferred dower—this, too, because she renounced the right on divorce by agreement. On the other hand, as set out above, a revolutionary change in the matter of ensuring the divorced woman's subsistence was the practice of paying her maintenance beyond the waiting-period: for life, until remarriage, or until she became entitled to a National Insurance pension.

V. DECLINE OF THE DIVORCE RATE

The divorce rate in Israeli Muslim society has considerably declined since the end of the Mandate. It dropped sharply until the middle 1960s and stabilized only by the late 1960s: it was 1.7 per thousand persons in 1946, 1.2 in 1953, 0.6 in 1960 and 0.4 in 1965 and 1968.[411] In other words, since the middle 1960s the rate has been about one-quarter of what it was at the end of the Mandate. These data should be treated with some caution for a number of reasons: official statistics, based on divorce certificates issued by the *sharīʿa* courts,[412] are underestimates because in Muslim society, for reasons extensively discussed above,[413] the registration of divorces is not complete. This is true especially for divorces followed by reinstatement of the wife before the end of the ʿ*idda* and for arbitrary *ṭalāq* divorces. Moreover, a divorce is sometimes registered many years after the event. The data of the Central Bureau of Statistics reflect the dates of registration and not the dates of the divorces themselves. Legal statistics of divorces[414] have similar defects and thus do not reflect the divorce rate accurately. Besides, the subject-matter of the claim is not necessarily identical with the final judicial award. Thus, for instance, many claims for maintenance, obedience and so forth ended in divorce, and on the other hand, many actions for the confirmation of divorces were dismissed. These shortcomings existed also during the Mandate, but in Israel, although data collection procedures in vital statistics have greatly improved, there is a further motive for abstention from registration of divorces, viz., the wish to conceal infringements of the ban on divorce against the wife's will.

It can therefore safely be assumed that the real divorce rate was higher than that reflected in official statistics. At the same time, it seems that this does not basically affect the conclusion that the divorce rate in Israeli Muslim society was low.[415] A Muslim did not hasten to exercise his right of *ṭalāq* despite the ease of divorce in Islam. The divorce rate has dropped significantly since the time of the Mandate. The traditional factors likely to deter from divorce are the prospect of having to discharge the attendant obligations, especially to pay the deferred dower; the possible deterioration of relations with the wife's family or *ḥamūla*; the expenditure involved in taking another wife (prompt dower, celebration of the marriage, gifts) etc.[416] The importance of some of the traditional factors seems to have increased in Israel, and some new ones have been added. The respective weight of the different factors cannot be ascertained, but they can be divided into two groups: factors accounting for the decline of the divorce rate compared with the closing period of the Mandate and factors likely to account for its decline in Israel. Within the latter group, one may distinguish between those operative in the early years of the State and those operative at a later period.

One of the chief factors in the decline of the divorce rate as against the Mandate period has been the decline in the Muslim urban population. The divorce rate in towns is higher than in rural areas.[417] There is a striking difference in Israel between the respective rates of Muslim divorces in mixed towns and in Arab villages and towns: 0.9–1.0 as against 0.3 (1967), respectively; among the Beduin, the rate is 0.4–0.5.[418] The high rates in mixed towns are certainly due to the influence of norms prevailing in Israeli society. Some villages, especially in the Little Triangle, are not inferior in economic, social and cultural respects to Nazareth or Shafā ʿAmr. The data on Beduin should be treated with caution, although it is usually assumed that divorce is frequent among them.[419]

Another factor involved was the youthful age-structure of the Muslim population in Israel compared with that during the Mandate. Also of account in considering the declining divorce rate was the solution during the early years of the State, either by divorce or reunion, of the problem of families separated as a result of the 1948 War. The enormous increase in the amount of dower from the late 1950s, and the necessity to pay compensation, or provide maintenance (including a dwelling) for life or until remarriage in return for the wife's consent to the divorce, also mitigated against divorce. As stated, this custom, sometimes involving an outlay of thousands of pounds, was prevalent in the prosperous Little Triangle villages yet rare elsewhere. The increased expenditure involved in a new marriage as a result of a rise in economic expectations, the standard of housing and the standard of living, must also have had an effect.

It is difficult to assess to what extent the decline of the divorce rate is attributable to the Knesset's ban on divorce against the wife's will. Although there are signs of a deterrent effect of the penal sanction, the main result of the ban, as stated, may simply have been avoidance of registration. Moreover, divorce against the wife's will was still frequent and the ban was circumvented by various devices. As stated above, the divorce rate also decreased in the Jewish sector of the population from 2.6 per thousand persons in 1946 to 1.8 in 1951 and 0.9 in 1968,[420] i.e., to one-third of the figure at the end of the Mandate, although the ban on divorce against the wife's will was almost without significance for this sector.[421] The decline of the divorce rate must therefore be mainly attributed to other factors: demographic, social and economic, rather than to Knesset legislation—as is also the case with the rise in the age of marriage.[422] In fact, Israeli legislation has, in another way, led to an increase of the divorce rate. As has been shown, the Knesset's ban on polygamy was one of the most frequent causes of divorce.[423] If the increase in the divorce rate from this cause is not reflected in statistics, this is, apparently, because it was offset by other factors making for a decline.

VI. THE *QĀḌĪ*S AND DIVORCE

1. ESTABLISHMENT OF PEACE BETWEEN THE PARTIES

The *qāḍī*s held that the primary task of the *sharīᶜa* courts is to establish peace between the spouses and to preserve the marriage intact. Thus, Shaykh Ḥasan Amīn al-Ḥabash suggested that the courts should make it standard practice not to register a divorce before its efforts to reconcile the estranged spouses had failed,[424] and Shaykh Ḥusnī al-Zuᶜbī considered that even where there was a legal ground for dissolution the *qāḍī* should not dissolve the marriage before all avenues to the restoration of domestic peace had been exhausted.[425] The comparison of the *qāḍī* to a family doctor was very frequent and is of special significance in this context.[426] The *sijill*s contain many instances of *qāḍī*s using their judicial and personal authority in order to smooth out differences between spouses with a view to preventing dissolution. The judgment frequently notes that the *qāḍī* "strove with all his might" for a reconciliation and compromise settlement[427]; he sometimes adjourned the case in the hope that meanwhile tempers would cool and peace be restored[428]; occasionally he used intermediaries (*ahl al-khayr, ahl al-wāsiṭa*), who were to try to bring the parties closer again[429]; or he might dismiss one party's action for dissolution and direct the other to adopt a conciliatory attitude.[430] But in almost all cases, "the court's efforts were in vain": it was not able to avoid dissolution of the marriage.[431]

As has previously been mentioned, the conciliatory role of the *qāḍī*s is in keeping with a basic attitude long observed in them, viz., a desire to avoid, as far as possible, the rendering of judgment and the application of the *sharīʿa*, for fear of perverting the latter, and a striving to get the spouses to settle their dispute by agreement.[432] An institutionalized manifestation of this attitude is the "family council" of arbitrators with the meaning of article 130 of the Family Rights Law. All the *qāḍī*s believed that the main function of the arbitrators is to effect a compromise and reconciliation between the spouses or, as Shaykh Tawfīq ʿAsaliyya put it, "to save the marriage from dissolution."[433] Some *qāḍī*s, especially Shaykh Ṭāhir Ḥamād and Shaykh Ḥusnī al-Zuʿbī, appointed arbitrators on their own initiative.[434]

2. DIVORCE ON THE HUSBAND'S INITIATIVE

a. The Freedom of *Ṭalāq*

The *qāḍī*s condemned arbitrary *ṭalāq*, stressing, in accordance with the orthodox Islamic view expressed in a saying attributed to the Prophet, that "of all permitted things, the most hateful to God is *ṭalāq*" (*abghaḍ al-ḥalāl ilā Allāh al-ṭalāq*). At the same time, different nuances can be discerned in their attitudes. Shaykh Ḥasan Amīn al-Ḥabash said that "*ṭalāq* is an institution of Islamic law resorted to when necessary, when the marriage cannot be preserved," that *ṭalāq* "is a necessity making the forbidden permissible" (*al ḍarūrāt tubīḥ al-maḥẓūrāt*) and that "the *qāḍī* only orders a divorce for a compelling reason," whence the legal distinction between *ṭalāq al-sunna*, which is recommended and *ṭalāq al-bidʿa*, which is deprecated. Although marriage in Islam is not a religious act but a civil contract, he called it a "sacred union" (*ʿaqd* *muqaddas*) and stressed that Islam had "sanctified woman." But beyond the religious argumentation, a progressive social philosophy is recognizable in Shaykh Ḥasan. According to him, divorce, even if based on *sharʿī* grounds, destroys the family and harms especially the wife and the young children. He saw a great danger to society in the high divorce rate prevailing in the Little Triangle villages.[435]

Shaykh Tawfīq ʿAsaliyya likewise combined religious with social arguments. He condemned *ṭalāq* as hateful to Allāh and stressed the importance of the happiness of the family, as the basic social cell, to the welfare of the *umma* and civilization. Since "women are the natural source of the *umma*'s existence," Islam shows great solicitude for them; it enjoins men to provide for their subsistence and to treat them gently so as to enable them to "fulfil their destination in the best and most perfect manner," for the "supreme goal of marriage is offspring." But marriage, like every other human relationship, sometimes runs into difficulties that make life unbearable, so that there is no way out but dissolution (which in itself is "a crime against the children"); for this purpose, Islam has devised the different forms of *ṭalāq*.[436]

Shaykh Ḥusnī al-Zuʿbī stressed that the *sharīʿa* advocates the stability of marriage, an institution "vital to the survival of the human race." Divorce without reason or necessity is foolish and impious as well as injurious to the wife and children.[437] Shaykh Amīn Qāsim Mudlij said that the exercise of the right of *ṭalāq* in an unjust and aggressive manner, without a legal ground, was the most hateful way of using a permission granted. Shaykh Ṭāhir Ḥamād treated *ṭalāq* as a necessary evil which had to be endured. "Divorce in Islamic law is not a custom (*ʿāda*) but is [unavoidable] on accumulation of tension between the spouses."[438]

Despite the condemnation of *ṭalāq* by all the *qāḍī*s, they hardly ever challenged the actual system which grants the husband a unilateral right of divorce. They accepted the inequality of the sexes and sometimes even found justification for it in nature. Shaykh Ḥusnī al-Zuʿbī thought that *ṭalāq* was given to the husband because there were natural differences in the qualities of men and women: "God has entrusted *ṭalāq* to the husband because patience, determination, foresight and the faculty of soberly weighing up benefit and damage are usually male qualities, and He has not entrusted *ṭalāq* to the woman because she is quick-tempered, excitable, impressionable and emotional. Dissolution of the marriage [even] on her initiative is entrusted solely to the husband, who may effect it at will, or to the *qāḍī*." On the other hand, the financial consequences of divorce are borne by the husband.[439]

The motif of the natural inequality between the sexes is found also with other *qāḍī*s. Shaykh Tawfīq ᶜAsaliyya said that the *sharīᶜa* was designed to regulate what he called the "natural relationship" of the spouses while preserving the equilibrium between the rights and duties of each party in accordance with his or her natural status.[440] Shaykh Amīn Qāsim Mudlij said that Allāh had given the husband a "natural right" to dissolve the marriage unilaterally and that he might exercise this right at any time and place.[441] Shaykh Ṭāhir al-Ṭabarī and Shaykh Mūsā al-Ṭabarī stressed time and again when confirming divorces that according to the *sharīᶜa ṭalāq* is the husband's exclusive right.[442]

Shaykh Ḥasan Amīn al-Ḥabash indeed maintained that according to the *sharīᶜa* there is full equality between man and woman, but he probably meant equality in the religious sense, equality before the Creator, for immediately afterward he said that there were material differences between them originating in nature. Thus, woman's task was to bear and bring up children, whereas man's task was to provide the family's living.[443] At the same time, he was undoubtedly unique among the *qāḍī*s in his professed attitude toward *ṭalāq* as a legal and social problem, although he was fettered by inhibitions originating in adherence to the Ḥanafī school. In his opinion, the husband's right of *ṭalāq* ought to be restricted, though he dared not actually restrict it in view of an express provision of the *sharīᶜa* in this matter. "*Ṭalāq* of any kind pronounced by the crowds in coffee-houses, alleyways, etc., is vanity and vexation of spirit; it carries no more weight than the gossip they utter most, if not all, of their lives; and *sharᶜī* law must not be applied to such a divorce [!]." The children of the couple, Shaykh Ḥasan said, were likely to be abandoned; the wife's and her family's honor would be defiled though she had had no part in bringing about the divorce; and her home would be in ruins. *Ṭalāq* was valid, he thought, where the spouses, or the husband alone, appeared in court, explained the reasons which led to the divorce and convinced the court of their justness; but only when the court had failed to effect a reconciliation should the divorce be officially registered. This is no other than a bold attempt to turn *ṭalāq* into a judicial divorce. But Shaykh Ḥasan added regretfully that this reform had no basis in the *sharīᶜa*, which recognizes even a divorce pronounced by a man in jest (*hāzil*), thus lacking the element of intent. He wished that the *qāḍī*s and *ʿulamāʾ* might find elements in the rich Islamic legal heritage that would allow a compromise between the orthodox point of view and the requirements of society.[444] He said so even before the Knesset's ban on divorce against the wife's will. In fact, he tried, by means of a religious-legal device, to achieve the same object as the Knesset had set itself, viz., to compel the husband to have recourse to the court and give the *qāḍī* wide discretion to examine in each case whether, under the circumstances, a divorce was justified.

b. Suspended Repudiation

The declared position of some *qāḍī*s as to suspended repudiation is represented by their comments on the Egyptian Personal Status Bill of 1966, which, if enacted, would have lain down that deferred divorce and suspended repudiation were invalid. According to the majority of the *qāḍī*s the proposed reform was contrary to the provisions of the *sharīʿa*, to the position of all the orthodox schools and to the Ottoman Family Rights Law, and according to Shaykh Ṭāhir Ḥamād, it was contrary also to customary practice (*al-istiʿmāl al-ʿurfī*). Shaykh Tawfīq ʿAsaliyya feared that the reform might lead to infringements of prohibitions and, in consequence, to acts of apostasy. Shaykh Ḥusnī al-Zuʿbī opposed the reform, but conceded that its adoption would have solved many problems. Only Shaykh Amīn Qāsim Mudlij agreed to the reform; he said that his decisions were conceived in the same reformist spirit, in reliance on the teachings of the Ḥanafī school.[445]

Until the early 1960s, the general attitude of the *qāḍī*s to suspended repudiation was formalistic and rigid. No account was taken of the intention (*niyya*) of the husband who resorted to this mechanism,[446] of the contents of the condition or of the circumstances under which it was fulfilled. When the fulfilment of the condition had been proven, the *qāḍī* immediately decided that the divorce was effective. Thus, in the case of a man who had sworn to divorce his wife although he "had not intended to forbid her to himself but only to humor his father," Shaykh Ṭāhir Ḥamād said: "Since our faith is based on linguistic expressions (*alfāẓ*) and constructions (*mabān*) and not on intentions (*maqāṣid*) and meanings (*maʿān*) . . . he must be judged according to his oath and admission, and no importance attaches to his intention (*walā ʿibra liniyyatihi*) that his wife should not be under prohibition (*taḥrīm*) [to him]"; and he decided that the divorce was effective.[447]

A surprising change in the position of the *qāḍī*s as to this question became apparent at their 1963 conference. This conference resolved, *inter alia*, that whenever a divorce due to the wife's fulfilment of a condition was referred to the court, the *qāḍī* should examine the circumstances of the fulfilment, and if he reached the conclusion that it had been unavoidable, compelled by circumstances (*iḍṭirāriyya*), he should decide that the divorce was not effective.[448] This resolution, the legal basis of which was not indicated, gives the *qāḍī* wide discretion to rely on social considerations. In other words, what is involved here is an application of the principle of *ḍarūra* (necessity), which is a form of *maṣlaḥa* (public interest).[449] The resolution curtails the husband's unilateral right of *ṭalāq*.

The *qāḍī*s' resolution was put into practice shortly afterward. A husband had made the divorce of his wife conditional on her leaving the house without his permission. The wife contended that she had been compelled to fulfil the condition by most vital necessity (*ḍarūra*) in that the husband had deserted her and she had had to go to the courthouse to claim maintenance for herself and her starving children, and that the divorce was therefore not effective. The wife's attorney, Advocate S. Darwish, sought support for this contention in Muḥammad Zayd al-Abayānī's modern commentary, which states that a suspended repudiation becomes an effective divorce if the wife is not under compulsion (*muḍṭarra*), for example, in danger of being burned or drowned.[450] The wife's going to the courthouse to claim maintenance for her children was, he argued, immeasurably more a matter of compulsion than escaping death by fire or water. Shaykh Ḥusnī al-Zuᶜbī accepted this contention and decided that the divorce was not effective. The husband resorted to the *Sharīᶜa* Court of Appeal, whose members were divided on the issue. Shaykh Amīn Qāsim Mudlij accepted the plea that fulfilment of the condition under compulsion did not count, relying on the view of the three orthodox Sunnī schools, as against that of the Ḥanafī school, that "a sin is not imputed to him who is forced to transgress"; he also stressed the social aspect: divorce was a very serious matter, hurting the whole family, and especially the innocent children. Shaykh Ḥasan Amīn al-Ḥabash, a staunch adherent of the Ḥanafī school, allowed the appeal, stating that the plea that the condition had been fulfilled under compulsion was not one of the *sharᶜī* grounds on which the effectiveness of the divorce might be denied.[451]

c. Divorce Pronounced in a State of Intoxication

It seems that the *qāḍī*s accepted the Ottoman legislator's precept that a divorce pronounced in a state of intoxication shall not be valid. In one case, Shaykh Ṭāhir Ḥamād set aside a judgment for divorce after the husband had proved that the wife had extorted a *ṭalāq* from him by provocation when he was drunk, and Shaykh Mūsā al-Ṭabarī dismissed a husband's application to set aside a judgment for divorce because his witnesses did not confirm his plea that he had been drunk at the time of the divorce.[452] Shaykh Tawfīq ᶜAsaliyya, Shaykh Amīn Qāsim Mudlij and Shaykh Ḥusnī al-Zuᶜbī agreed to a provision in the Egyptian Personal Status Bill of 1966 invalidating divorce pronounced in a state of intoxication on the ground that it was in conformity with the Ottoman Family Rights Law,[453] which deviates from the Ḥanafī school in this matter.

3. THE BAN ON DIVORCE AGAINST THE WIFE'S WILL

a. The Knesset's Restriction on the Freedom of *Ṭalāq*

The declared position of the *qāḍī*s was, with immaterial differences in wording and style, that they did not object to the Knesset's intervention as far as it was of a penal or procedural character; on the other hand, they objected most vigorously to reforms derogating from substantive provisions of Islamic law even if enacted by the parliaments of Arab states. Shaykh Ṭāhir Ḥamād said that Israeli legislation in the matter of divorce against the wife's will and other matters not only did not abolish religious law but heightened its effectiveness by means of the criminal sanction. Islam, too, condemns the practices in question, but its ethical sanctions (*al-ᶜiqāb al-ukhrawiyy*) are not effective deterrents. At the same time, Shaykh Ṭāhir was at pains to emphasize that "the [secular] law is designed to preserve the existing rightful order" and that "Qurʾānic legislation fits every time and place."[454]

Shaykh Ḥasan Amīn al-Ḥabash not only did not oppose secular legislation on divorce but welcomed further reforms of a procedural or penal character, as will be seen below. Shaykh Tawfīq ᶜAsaliyya condemned the ban on divorce against the wife's will and other enactments of the Knesset, but was careful to note that they were introduced "whilst preserving the validity of religious law."[455] Most of the *qāḍī*s who commented on the Egyptian Personal Status Bill of 1966 strongly opposed any curtailment of the husband's right of *ṭalāq*.[456]

b. The Wife's Consent to the Divorce

The question of consent in cases where the wife was unilaterally divorced did not usually concern the *qāḍī*s, and even where it was referred to it is not always certain that this was done under the influence of Israeli legislation, for the subject was known even before the enactment of the Women's Equal Rights Law and the wife's consent usually related to the settlement of matrimonial rights. A clear indication of such influence exists only in cases where the *qāḍī* took the trouble to ascertain, himself or through an agent, whether the wife had agreed to the divorce.[457]

A more meaningful conception of the *qāḍī*s' stand on the ban on divorce against the wife's will may be obtained from those cases in which the wife contested the divorce. Here can be distinguished two diametrically opposed approaches. One, which was common to Shaykhs Ṭāhir al-Ṭabarī, Ḥasan Amīn al-Ḥabash, Tawfīq ᶜAsaliyya and Ḥusnī al-Zuᶜbī, conformed with the Knesset's intention. In dozens of judgments given by them, it was found, with differences in wording and style, that the *qāḍī* warned the husband not to divorce the wife against her will and drew his attention to the penal sanction; when the wife had been divorced against her will, the *qāḍī* confirmed the divorce, sometimes explaining that it was valid according to religious law, registered it and, if the wife was not in court, directed that she be notified[458]; occasionally he noted that the wife did not consent to the divorce or, if she was absent, that it was not known whether she consented or objected to it[459]; he might also add that the court had not given permission for the divorce, as required in the absence of the wife's consent.[460] In some cases, the judgment notes that if the competent authority found that an offense had been committed the husband should be punished in accordance with law.[461] Moreover, in most cases, the *qāḍī*s stepped outside their own province by stating expressly that the husband had violated the secular law.[462] Shaykh Ḥasan went so far as to draw the wife's attention to the fact that she could file a criminal charge with the competent authority,[463] and Shaykh Tawfīq directed that those of his decisions which indicated that the wife had been divorced against her will and without the husband having obtained in advance permission of the court for divorce, be communicated to the Attorney-General or the Ministry of Religious affairs for appropriate action against the husband.[464]

The second approach is marked by indifference to the significance of divorce against the wife's will from the point of view of secular law. The emphasis is on its significance from the point of view of religious law. The chief exponent of this approach was Shaykh Ṭāhir Ḥamād. In his judgments, he pointed out that the wife's consent was not essential to the validity of the divorce and that it was the duty of the court to confirm it even if it was against the wife's will because the validity of *ṭalāq* was recognized by secular law. The wife's consent was only required as a defense against the penal sanction. But Shaykh Ṭāhir himself did not trouble in his *ṭalāq* judgments to refer to the criminality of divorce against the wife's will. Only in one case did he note that the wife had the right to bring a criminal action in a civil court because she had been divorced under these circumstances, but in this case he apparently made an exception because the wife had threatened to have him (and the husband) jailed if he confirmed the divorce.[465] Shaykh Mūsā al-Ṭabarī and Shaykh Amīn Qāsim Mudlij also did not refer in their judgments to infringements of the ban on divorce against the wife's will, although there must have been some in their areas of jurisdiction. This may in part be due to their attitude regarding permission for divorce.[466] Shaykh Tawfīq ᶜAsaliyya was not strict about the wife's consent in the case of divorces performed in East Jerusalem.[467]

The question of the wife's consent to the divorce and the criminality of divorce against the wife's will did not concern the *qāḍī*s in the case of revocable divorce, barring exceptional instances. This was probably because in most cases revocable divorce ended in reinstatement of the wife and there was no reason, as far as the *qāḍī* was concerned, to raise problems likely to exacerbate relations between the spouses. A particularly striking example is the attitude of Shaykh Ḥasan Amīn al-Ḥabash. In all the cases in which the divorce ended in reinstatement of the wife, he completely ignored the question of her consent, whereas in the only case in which the divorce became irrevocable because the wife had not been reinstated during the ᶜ*idda* he decided that the divorce was valid and, as was his wont, advised her to take legal steps against the husband.[468]

c. Suspended Repudiation as a Means to Circumvent the Penal Sanction

It has been shown that suspended repudiation served as a device to circumvent the ban on divorce against the wife's will.[469] The *qāḍīs* were divided as to the criminality of this mode of dissolution. Shaykh Ḥasan Amīn al-Ḥabash said that a suspended repudiation was like an ordinary divorce from the point of view of the general law: a husband who pronounced it against the wife's will before obtaining the permission of the court did commit a criminal offense; although the divorce was valid according to religious law and the husband was exercising a *sharʿī* right, it was forbidden by secular law. Shaykh Ḥasan, therefore, confirmed and registered such a divorce rather reluctantly,[470] and if he was satisfied that the wife opposed the divorce, he advised her to apply to the appropriate authorities for prosecution of the husband.[471] Moreover, it seems that he spared no effort to place procedural and other difficulties in the way of husbands wishing to dissolve their marriages by suspended repudiation.[472] Out of concern for the preservation of the marriage, he dismissed applications for the confirmation of divorces by husbands trying to use suspended repudiation as a means to evade the penal sanction. He also dismissed such applications by wives seeking to avail themselves of that mechanism in order to obtain their freedom.[473] In one case, Shaykh Tawfīq Maḥmūd ʿAsaliyya decided that the wife's admission of the fulfilment of the condition "makes it necessary to declare that the divorce is valid according to *sharʿī* law"; but he added that since it had not been definitely proven that the wife consented to the divorce, or rather, since the wife had clearly stated that she did not consent, he left the matter to be decided by the "competent agencies."[474]

A different approach to the question can be found with other *qāḍīs*, especially with Shaykh Ṭāhir Ḥamād. He was not only unwilling to admit any restriction on the husband's unilateral right of *ṭalāq* as being without foundation in religious law, but helped, directly and indirectly, to turn suspended repudiation into an efficient means to circumvent the penal sanction. In one case, a husband wished to have the divorce of his wife confirmed because she had fulfilled one of the stipulated conditions, and contended that she had "divorced herself voluntarily and by her own choice." The wife's representative, on the other hand, contended that the divorce had been against her will; he told the *qāḍī* that the court's duty was not to help the husband to commit a criminal offense, but "to help the law and censure him who broke it." The *qāḍī* replied that the husband's action was not contrary to section 181A of the Criminal Code Ordinance because "the wife was not divorced against her will; the husband did not divorce her but made the divorce conditional on a certain occurrence . . . and left the matter in her hands" (*fajaᶜala al-amr biyadihā*).[475] This latter expression is, as stated, typical of the phraseology of delegated repudiation (*tafwīḍ al-ṭalāq*) and its use and that of similar expressions permits the assumption that in this case there was a conscious, systematic attempt to circumvent the ban on divorce against the wife's will without becoming guilty of a criminal offense. Shaykh Ṭāhir admitted to Advocate S. Darwish that he had been in the habit of advising husbands who wished to divorce their wives without becoming guilty of a criminal offense to use the mechanism of suspended repudiation. Moreover, in one of these cases, the *qāḍī* himself had been called by the husband to testify in court that suspended repudiation had been pronounced and that he, the *qāḍī*, had seen the wife leaving the house and thus fulfilling its condition. The husband declared in court that she "had opted for *ṭalāq* for herself."[476] The attempt to treat suspended repudiation as similar to or even identical with delegated repudiation is, of course, unwarranted and misleading. Although the two mechanisms are similar in that it is the wife who fixes the time at which the divorce becomes complete and effective, there is a fundamental, undeniable difference: while the power to divorce herself is delegated to the wife and used by her at her discretion, suspended repudiation is forced on her arbitrarily by the husband.

Shaykh Ḥusnī al-Zuᶜbī and Shaykh Amīn Qāsim Mudlij also considered that suspended repudiation did not involve a criminal offense. Referring to the wife's contention that the divorce was contrary to law, they decided, as members of a Court of Appeal (under the chairmanship of Shaykh Ṭāhir Ḥamād), that "the court does not think so and holds that there is nothing contrary to law in this pronouncement [of suspended repudiation] because of the wife's opting for *ṭalāq* for herself by leaving the house."[477] Shaykh Ṭāhir al-Ṭabarī confirmed a suspended repudiation in several cases under circumstances raising a suspicion of a circumvention of the penal sanction without touching at all on the question of the wife's consent[478]; in the cases in which the question of the criminality of suspended repudiation came up, it was not the *qāḍī* but one of the parties who raised it.[479]

d. Confirmation and Registration of Divorce

As stated, the ban on divorce against the wife's will without permission from the court does not invalidate unilateral divorce as far as it is valid according to the *sharīʿa*. Most *qāḍī*s were alive to the fact that the Knesset's intervention was of no substantive significance. They explained to the parties on several occasions that non-registration of the divorce did not affect its validity.[480] The registration of divorces is not a *sharʿī* but a civil obligation, and most *qāḍī*s regarded it as a requirement of good order which should be fulfilled in the public interest; they usually did not connect it with the question of the ban. Thus, for instance, Shaykh Ṭāhir Ḥamād, even before the enactment of the Women's Equal Rights Law, suggested that divorces should be registered "for fear of disavowal" of the divorce by the husband. After the prohibition of divorce against the wife's will by the Knesset, he said that secular law recognized *ṭalāq* divorces, whether they had been pronounced with or without the wife's consent, in her presence or in her absence in or out of court, but that the infringer of the ban was liable to a penal sanction; in his opinion, it was the *qāḍī*'s duty to register the divorce although it was contrary to secular law, and then hand over the offender to the competent authority for punishment.[481] Shaykh Mūsā al-Ṭabarī, in 1950, directed all *maʾdhūn*s and *imām*s in his area of jurisdiction to prepare an exact record of every divorce in the village and have it signed by the witnesses who heard the divorce; thereafter the husband was to be summoned to the court for the divorce to be registered and the marriage to be dissolved in accordance with law. Shaykh Mūsā believed that the requirement of registration was likely to prevent hasty divorces.[482]

Shaykh Ḥasan Amīn al-Ḥabash was an exception among the *qāḍī*s as regards his attitude toward the confirmation and registration of divorces. Before the enactment of the Women's Equal Rights Law, there was, in his opinion, no choice but to confirm arbitrarily *ṭalāq* divorces. After the prohibition of divorce against the wife's will, and especially since the amendment of that prohibition in 1959, he considered that the *qāḍī* was not doing justice to all parties if the divorce of a wife who did not consent to it was registered automatically, before the husband had obtained a judgment permitting it. The husband's punishment was no remedy to the wife's position, for "what benefit," he asked, "does a murdered man, who has breathed his last, derive from the punishment of the murderer?" In his opinion, it was pointless to explain to the divorced wife that she was entitled to bring a criminal action against the husband. Such advice was belated. Since the wife did not know her rights and was unfamiliar with legal proceedings, the filing of a criminal action against the husband involved costs and advocate's fees. Under these circumstances, the wife would forgo the action and the husband would escape the penal sanction provided for by law. The solution at first suggested by Shaykh Ḥasan was that the court should refrain from registering the divorce. He said that he, for one, did not automatically confirm every divorce brought before him; if he did not use his discretion he would be turning the court into "a dwelling-place of lovers of *ṭalāq*"; in many cases, stratagems (*ḥiyal*) were applied to circumvent the provisions of both the *sharīʿa* and secular law.

Shaykh Ḥasan thought that in this way he was carrying out the Knesset's intention as to divorce against the wife's will. He ingenuously believed for some time that the court should refrain from registering a divorce when it had been performed in contravention of the criminal law; a conflict thus seemed to have arisen in his mind between secular law and the *sharīʿa*, which latter requires the confirmation of valid divorces. He declared, though not with a light heart, that in the event of such a conflict the *qāḍī* must follow the secular law. "What is the court to do under such circumstances?" he asked rhetorically. Is it to register the divorce and ignore the law which forbids divorce without permission from the court, especially the amended version of 1959? His reply was that the *sharīʿa* courts were integrated in the State and duty-bound to apply its laws. He also maintained that there was no express provision in either Islamic or secular law requiring the court to register a divorce, whether lawfully performed or not.[483] He did not, he asserted, by taking the said attitude, permit anything Allāh forbade or forbid anything He permitted. He found support for this view in the sources: God "deters [from transgression] through the ruler what He has not deterred through the Qurʾān." But he soon realized that this remedy was illusory—that the *qāḍī* had no choice but to register the divorce if its validity according to the *sharīʿa* had been proven. He then suggested reframing the section concerning divorce against the wife's will so as to make it more procedural and technical: a man who divorced his wife out of court or before obtaining permission from the court should be liable to heavy punishment. He also suggested that the divorce should only be registered by the court after the offender had been punished.[484] In one case, he refrained from registering a divorce on the ground that an action had first to be filed with the court and the wife summoned to the hearing. The husband refused, submitted there and then a letter to the effect that the wife had already been divorced, and asked that the divorce be registered. The *qāḍī* decided that the divorce was valid "only after the requirements of the existing law had been fulfilled."[485]

In fact, as far as appears from the *sijill*s, the *qāḍī*'s function in *ṭalāq* divorces was essentially technical and hardly ever involved discretion. He was seldom asked to permit the divorce when the wife opposed it. He was usually confronted with an accomplished fact: the divorce was performed and completed out of court or in his presence without his being able to prevent it. For, the *ṭalāq* is *a unilateral act of the husband, the court having no standing in it*, and therefore nothing remained for him but to confirm it as far as its validity had been proven to his satisfaction, and to register it.[486] The husband's admission (*iqrār*, *iᶜtirāf*) that he had divorced the wife was usually sufficient to satisfy the *qāḍī*.[487] If the wife denied the divorce, the testimony of two persons who were present was required, but the *qāḍī*s were not always very strict on this point. Thus, Shaykh Tawfīq ᶜAsaliyya confirmed a divorce in a case where the witnesses, as usual among Beduin, did not know the wife and were unable to give her name.[488] Where a doubt arose as to the divorce, the husband sometimes repeated it in the presence of the *qāḍī* "to make sure" (*ziyāda fī al-taʾakkud, al-istithāq*).[489]

The *qāḍī*s' main concern was that the divorcing husband should be in fit condition for divorce: deliberate, calm (not angry), in control of his nerves and mental faculties, not insane, not drunk, not bewildered (*madhūsh*), not disconcerted, clear-headed, and whatever else is required for the divorce to be valid.[490] In one case, Shaykh Tawfīq ᶜAsaliyya set aside a judgment for divorce (triple repudiation) on the basis of the husband's plea that he had pronounced the divorce in a fit of anger without understanding the meaning of his act. The *qāḍī* explained his decision by arguing that *ṭalāq* was "conditional on intactness of the mental powers."[491]

In many cases, the husband divorced the wife in her absence, but the *qāḍī* confirmed the divorce without hesitation.[492] The question of the wife's presence at the divorce did not trouble the *qāḍī*s; it was not relevant to the validity of the divorce. The same is true of the question of where it was performed—whether in or out of court. These remarks apply especially to Shaykh Ṭāhir Ḥamād. He felt no concern about criminal offenses being committed by divorces against the wife's will. He confirmed almost mechanically every divorce brought before him, whether the wife was present in court or not, whether the divorce was performed out of court or in court in the presence of the *qāḍī* and also when the wife had not been asked to consent to the divorce or had expressly opposed it. In one case, a man was unable to prove that he had divorced his wife by suspended repudiation. When the wife had left the court, relieved that her husband's design had failed, the husband declared before the *qāḍī* that he was under no circumstances willing to accept "that this one should be my wife" and divorced her in the *qāḍī*'s presence, and the *qāḍī* confirmed the divorce there and then in the wife's absence, in the certain knowledge that she did not want the divorce and had not consented to it; and he did not trouble to point out to the husband that he had committed a criminal offense. In another case, a husband wanted to divorce his wife outside Shaykh Ṭāhir Ḥamād's house, and the *qāḍī* advised him to do so in court[493]; he held that if the divorce was valid on the sole admission of the husband, it was the more so if pronounced in court.[494]

Under these circumstances, it is not surprising that a civil court should have expressed the view that such an interpretation of the ban on divorce against the wife's will made a mockery of the law. It suggested that the legislator reformulate the relevant section so as to make it more rigorous in procedure. It also expressed the wish that Israeli *qāḍī*s might follow reformist *ʿulamāʾ* and jurists who advocated a renewed *ijtihād* ("effort," the use of individual reasoning) to adapt Islamic law to the requirements of modern life.[495] In one case, the Supreme Court reduced the sentence of a man who had divorced his wife without her consent in view of the fact that he had followed the instructions of Shaykh Ṭāhir Ḥamād, who had advised him, because of the wife's opposition to the divorce, to divorce her first and then to obtain confirmation from him that she was divorced. In another case, that *qāḍī* was convicted and fined by the district court for drawing up a divorce agreement fraudulently. The wife had not consented to the divorce and had not been present in court when it was pronounced, and her signature to the record had been forged with the knowledge of the *qāḍī*.[496] Other *qāḍī*s, too, confirmed and registered almost blindly every *ṭalāq* divorce brought before them, though the author did not get the impression that they treated the retroactive confirmation of divorce as a device for circumventing the ban on divorce against the wife's will. They proceeded in this matter as the *sharīʿa* courts had done before the enactment of the Women's Equal Rights Law.

e. Permission for Divorce Granted by the Court

How did the *qāḍī*s exercise the wide discretion granted them by the Knesset in dealing with husbands' applications for permission to divorce their wives? Most of them were aware of the need for such permission where the wife did not agree to the divorce, but some did not interpret this need correctly. Thus, in some cases, Shaykh Mūsā al-Ṭabarī and Shaykh Amīn Qāsim Mudlij granted permission only when the wife had consented to the divorce,[497] and thereby restricted the husband's right of *ṭalāq* to an unprecedented degree. Still, barring a few exceptions, the *qāḍī*s granted permission because they thought that the circumstances afforded legitimate grounds for divorce according to the customary and *sharʿī* norms. Such grounds were the wife's absence, departure from Israel, barrenness, or inability to fulfil her domestic duties toward her husband and family by reason of illness or age. The principal arguments in all these cases were that the husband needed another wife to look after the children and the household and that "the legal purpose of marriage is the production of offspring and the continuance of the family line."[498] Shaykh Ḥasan Amīn al-Ḥabash permitted a man to divorce his barren wife after 25 years of marriage in order to take another wife, and Shaykh Mūsā al-Ṭabarī granted permission to divorce an incurably insane wife on the ground that she was "unfit for marital life."[499] Sometimes the impression is given that permission was granted solely because the wife, though summoned, had not appeared at the hearing of the court and not for any substantive reason.[500] In fact, for some decisions no reason at all was given, so that it seems—and this goes especially for the judgments of Shaykh Ṭāhir Ḥamād and Shaykh Mūsā al-Ṭabarī—that the response to the application for dissolution was automatic or, in other words, that this was no more than an *ex post facto* confirmation and registration of a *ṭalāq* divorce.[501]

Perhaps more significant in this context is the question of the extent to which the *qāḍī*s refused to permit a divorce where in their opinion there was no justification for it. In only one or two cases did a *qāḍī* expressly refuse permission. In one case, the husband applied for permission on the ground that the wife had borne him no children after 15 years of marriage and that "he lived with her compulsorily." The wife opposed the divorce vehemently, declaring that she preferred death. Shaykh Ḥasan Amīn al-Ḥabash dismissed the application.[502] He was probably influenced by the wife's desperate resistance, for, as has been seen, he, too, regarded barrenness as a ground for dissolution. At any rate, the dismissal of the application in this case was, in the author's opinion, the boldest instance of the exercise of discretion by a *qāḍī* in Israel in accordance with a norm set by the Knesset and not rooted in Islamic law. At the 1963 *qāḍī*s' conference, this *qāḍī* stated that he knew from judicial experience that not every man applying for permission for divorce was an aggrieved person deserving legal relief; in fact, it was mostly the other way round, so that, in the words of a popular saying, it was a case of "he hits, and then cries and goes to complain."[503] Yūsuf Dasūqī, Secretary of the *Sharīʿa* Court of Ṭayyiba, attested that it was very difficult to obtain permission for divorce from Shaykh Ḥasan.[504]

In another case, Shaykh Amīn Qāsim Mudlij refused to permit a wife to be divorced on the ground that she was mentally ill. More exactly, the husband applied for the marriage to be dissolved under article 123 of the Family Rights Law. The *qāḍī* declared that even if *ṭalāq* were intended he would dismiss the application because, in his opinion, *ṭalāq* required the consent of both spouses (and the wife was unable to consent owing to her mental condition).[505] In other words, permission was withheld not because the *qāḍī* did not think the wife's illness a ground for divorcing her against her will but owing to an incorrect interpretation of the law.

It is true that in several cases there are indications that Shaykh Ṭāhir Ḥamād opposed the divorce and tried to dissuade the husband from performing it. In one decision such an attitude is suggested by the statement that the husband "insisted" on divorcing the wife and in fact carried out his intention and that the *qāḍī* had no choice but to confirm and register the divorce.[506] But in other cases it appears that this *qāḍī*'s intervention under such circumstances was not guided by the Knesset's legislation but by the court's custom of seeking to reconcile the spouses.[507] Moreover, when despairing of his efforts to restore domestic peace, he sometimes decided on divorce even though no initiative for it had come from the parties themselves.[508] This enforcement of divorce on the spouses is, of course, another form of interference with the husband's freedom of *ṭalāq* (although it was he, the husband, who actually performed the divorce).

4. DISSOLUTION ON THE WIFE'S INITIATIVE

a. *Talāq* Divorces

It has been shown that the wife sometimes played an active part in the dissolution of the marriage and that she pursued this object in various ways. To what extent did the *qāḍīs* assist her efforts to obtain her freedom? The matter hardly troubled them with regard to *ṭalāq* divorces because in their view the wife was a passive party to them. In some cases, they dismissed the wife's demand that the husband should divorce her or that the court should compel him to do so on the formal ground that the court could not force a divorce on the husband or dissolve the marriage judicially in the absence of a legal ground.[509] The *qāḍīs* confirmed the different kinds of *ṭalāq* divorces on the wife's application as far as their validity had been proven to their satisfaction. The question of initiative or of the exploitation of weak spots in the *ṭalāq* mechanism by the wife, as in the case of suspended divorces, did not trouble them.

i. Delegated Repudiation

As regards delegated repudiation (*tafwīḍ al-ṭalāq*), which, as stated, is the most striking manifestation of the wife's freedom of divorce, the *qāḍīs* did not depart from the formal conception that this sophisticated type of divorce is a form of *ṭalāq* not impairing the husband's sovereignty. They seemed to think that it was a legitimate device and that all that was required of the wife in order for her to obtain her freedom by it was to prove that she had indeed been delegated the power to divorce herself, either in the marriage contract or in a special agreement subsequent to the marriage, that the husband had fulfilled the condition of the conditional delegation (and thereby given her the right to divorce herself), and lastly, that she had divorced herself in the manner required by law.

Shaykh Ṭāhir Ḥamād sometimes encouraged the estranged spouses to use the mechanism of delegated repudiation, probably as a last resort short of actual divorce.[510] At the same time, the author did not encounter an instance of a *qāḍī* encouraging the wife, through the *maʾdhūn* or otherwise, to assure herself freedom of divorce by a stipulation in the marriage contract.

ii. "Renunciation Divorces" and "Compensation Divorces"

It seems that dissolution by agreement between the parties was the type of divorce most acceptable and convenient to the *qāḍī*s. *Ṭalāq* under these circumstances was not arbitrary; it did not involve any infringement of the ban on divorce against the wife's will and thus did not embarrass the *qāḍī* by a conflict between the religious-legal and the secular-legal norms; it did not require him to exercise his discretion as to whether to permit or prohibit the divorce. All that was really required of him was to give an official stamp in the shape of a judgment to the agreement reached by the parties or to certify that the divorce was operative when the agreed condition of suspended repudiation had been fulfilled.[511] As regards the mechanism, it is little more than a kind of agreement for arbitration concerning the dissolution of the marriage. This mechanism was very much to the liking of the *qāḍī*s, who refrained as far as possible from applying the law. The *qāḍī*s' influence on the contents of the agreement seems to have been limited. The spouses usually came to court after agreeing on the terms; they sometimes brought a text properly drawn up and signed. In one case, it was agreed between the parties that the wife, after marrying another man, should compensate the former husband. Although this was a departure from the *sharʿī khulʿ*, Shaykh Tawfīq ʿAsaliyya held that "mutual agreement is stronger than the *qāḍī*" (*al-tarāḍī yaghlib al-qāḍī*).[512]

b. Judicial Dissolution

Only in judicial dissolutions did the *qāḍī*s refer to the question of dissolution on the wife's initiative. Considerable importance attaches to the manner in which they interpreted the grounds (widely or narrowly), and different attitudes were indeed adopted by them as to some of the new grounds provided by the Ottoman legislator (but not as to Knesset legislation). Their attitudes in this matter were determined by religious-legal reasoning, school affiliation, and by social factors.

i. Defects and Diseases of the Husband

The main difficulty in applying grounds of disease or defect in the husband seems to lie in the fact that they are based on provisions not emanating from the Ḥanafī school. Shaykh Ḥasan Amīn al-Ḥabash dismissed, for various reasons, all suits women filed with him for dissolution of their marriages on these grounds.[513] These dismissals were probably due to opposition in principle. The *Sharīʿa* Court of Appeal intervened several times in Shaykh Ḥasan's decisions concerning the application of the aforesaid grounds. Thus, in one case, it pointed out to him that he should have applied article 123 of the Family Rights Law, which deals expressly with mental illness, and not article 120, which deals with defects in a general way. It is difficult to assume that the *qāḍī* had overlooked article 123. It seems more likely that he applied article 120 because its provisions conform with the view of the Ḥanafī school, which does not count the husband's mental illness among the grounds for dissolution.[514]

Shaykh Mūsā al-Ṭabarī was willing to consider the wife's suit for dissolution on one of the said grounds, but he frequently proceeded in accordance with the teachings of the Ḥanafī school. Thus, for instance, he did not trouble to examine beforehand, as required by article 121, whether the husband's impotence was temporary, curable, or permanent. In all cases of this kind that were brought before him he gave the husband a year's respite in the hope that the defect would disappear.[515] On the other hand, as regards mental illness, he strictly followed the provisions of article 123.[516]

Shaykh Ḥusnī al-Zuʿbī carefully observed the provisions of the Family Rights Law, uninhibited by the teachings of any school.[517] In one case, he indeed deviated from the provisions of article 121, but not for any religious-legal reason. The wife had charged the husband with impotence after she had borne him one child; the husband was given respite three times at his request. The *qāḍī* gave effect to an agreement reached between the parties on the intervention of village notables that the wife should return to the husband's home "for the last time" for three months, and if there was no improvement in his performance during that period the marriage should be dissolved by the court. A medical institution found that his condition was incurable, and the *qāḍī* dissolved the marriage.[518] This deviation from the provisions of article 121 is another indication that the *sharīʿa* courts were disinclined to apply the full force of the law when the dispute could be settled by agreement between the parties.

Shaykh Ḥusnī al-Zuᶜbī and also Shaykhs Amīn Qāsim Mudlij and Tawfīq Maḥmūd ᶜAsaliyya recognized the husband's mental illness as a ground for dissolution, as provided in article 123 of the Family Rights Law.[519] Shaykh Amīn expressly recognized the wife's right to dissolve the marriage where the husband suffered from an illness likely to cause injury (*ḍarar*) to her; he probably had in mind article 122. He took the trouble to add that this right was granted her by the *sharīᶜa*, quoting the modern legal commentator al-Abayānī in evidence. The same *qāḍī* dismissed a husband's application for dissolution on the ground of mental illness of the wife with the argument that the grounds provided by the Family Rights Law were intended for the protection of the wife only, since the husband was able to protect himself by *ṭalāq*.[520]

ii. Dissolution of Marriage to an Absent Husband

The *qāḍī*s were divided as to the dissolution of the marriage of the wife of an absent husband. Some were loath to apply articles 126 and 127 for religious-legal, technical-procedural and other reasons, some applied them unhesitatingly and some even stretched the grounds provided by them far beyond their original meaning. The question of the wives of absent husbands was discussed as early on as the first *qāḍī*s' conference in 1950, when it was decided to adjourn the discussion until the Muslim Division of the Ministry of Religious Affairs had clarified how information as to the whereabouts of the husbands might be obtained from Arab governments.[521] The *qāḍī*s again discussed the matter on July 18, 1951, when it was decided that the court should dissolve the marriage of a wife left without maintenance after the following procedure: the court, through the Muslim Division, should forward a notice of the wife's application for dissolution to the Red Cross, which should see that it was transmitted to the husband; and if within three months from the delivery of the notice to the Red Cross the husband did not provide maintenance to the wife—himself or through another—the court would regard this as evidence of "inability to obtain maintenance from him . . . after making the necessary inquiries," within the meaning of article 126 of the Family Rights Law.[522] This decision was liberal from the point of view of the wife. It emphasized non-provision of maintenance in the spirit of the Ottoman reform.

The arrangement with the Red Cross did not work. An attempt to transmit the notices to the husbands via the mixed armistice commissions also failed. Except for isolated cases, the members of the Arab delegations refused to cooperate.[523] The problem soon arose again, this time in all its poignancy. The reason was seemingly a technical-procedural one, but behind it were fundamental differences between the *qāḍī*s. On the strength of a custom dating from the Ottoman period (the legal basis for which had lapsed since the establishment of the *Sharīʿa* Court of Appeal during the Mandate), the head of the *Sharīʿa* Court of Appeal, Shaykh Ṭāhir al-Ṭabarī, directed that every judgment for divorce under article 126 of the Family Rights Law should be referred to the *Sharīʿa* Court in Jerusalem for confirmation prior to execution. This direction was issued following a series of such judgments by the *Sharīʿa* Court of Jaffa. The *Sharīʿa* Court of Appeal set aside one of those judgments and declared that article 126 required the court to conduct the necessary inquiries about the absent husband itself and not to content itself with the publication of a notice of the legal proceedings in the Israeli press, because, under existing circumstances, while the country was at war, the husband was unable to appear in court and answer the wife's contentions. Shaykh Ṭāhir al-Ṭabarī held that article 126 of the Family Rights Law was applicable only during a period of peace and voluntary absence of the husband, but not during a period of war, armistice or forced absence, when it was impossible to make the necessary inquiries as to the husband's whereabouts. As for the absent man's wife, he suggested that she earn her own living or ask assistance from welfare institutions.[524]

Shaykh Ḥasan Amīn al-Ḥabash also opposed application of articles 126 and 127. Although he was a party to the abovementioned *qāḍī*s' decision of July 18, 1951, he somehow always dismissed applications for dissolution on formal or technical grounds, such as inability to give notice (*tablīgh*) to the husband in an Arab country.[525] In one case, a woman whose husband had been absent for many years asked for dissolution in reliance on the closing passage of article 127. She contended that more than a year had passed since the signing of the armistice agreement and that the fighters and prisoners of war were supposed to have returned home. The *qāḍī* dismissed the suit on the ground that "the Arabs of Palestine, in addition to the Arab countries, are still fighting both in practice and theory and have not returned to their homeland, which is under Israeli rule, and peace has not been concluded, an armistice not being peace . . ." and in reliance on the aforesaid judgment of the *Sharīʿa* Court of Appeal.[526] It seems that all the technical reasons for the dismissal of the suits were merely intended to cover up opposition in principle to the application of provisions contrary to the view of the Ḥanafī school. As for the wife, Shaykh Ḥasan suggested that she join the husband or ask for his admission to Israel under the family reunion scheme.[527]

Shaykh Mūsā al-Ṭabarī at first held that articles 126 and 127 could not be applied because of the state of war between Israel and its neighbors, and in any case he believed that there were no laws in Israel allowing the dissolution of the marriage of a deserted wife. Referring to Shaykh Ṭāhir Ḥamād's dissolution decisions, he complained that the laws of the *sharīʿa* were transgressed and that some of the women added sin to transgression by living maritally with men other than their husbands (i.e., remarried after the first marriage had been dissolved), whereas chaste women "expect early salvation from God. . . ."[528] In one case, he decided that if the absent husband was found he would have to divorce the wife at her request, and in another case he held that the husband would have to pay maintenance to the wife, and if he was unable to do so, divorce her.[529] On the other hand, in judgments rendered a few years later, this *qāḍī* did not hesitate to dissolve the marriage of the wives of absent husbands.[530]

Shaykh Ṭāhir Ḥamād and Shaykh Ḥusnī al-Zuʿbī showed exceptional liberalism toward the wife in that they were inclined to widen the ground for dissolution under article 126 by the inclusion of new elements. Shaykh Ṭāhir held that the court should grant full relief to the wife. He said that although the article was contrary to the teaching of the Ḥanafī school, the court should apply it because it was in the nature of a Sulṭānic decree, which must be obeyed by order of the *fuqahāʾ* (specialists in the science of the *sharīʿa*).[531] The wife, he thought, was not required to join the husband because there was more than *masāfat al-qaṣr* between them, and moreover, if she did so she would be liable to hardship and humiliation. He also dismissed the contention that article 126 was inapplicable in wartime because the *tablīgh* could not be effected then. He said that the principal element in that article was non-provision of maintenance and that the wife could not be expected to support herself or to ask assistance from welfare institutions. The distinction between peacetime and voluntary absence on the one hand and war, armistice or forced absence on the other was irrelevant.

Lastly, Shaykh Ṭahīr rejected as without legal foundation the practice of referring the dissolution of marriages of deserted wives to the *Sharīᶜa* Court of Appeal for confirmation.[532] This liberal attitude was also reflected in his judgments.[533] In fact, he recognized non-provision of maintenance as a ground for dissolution even when the husband had been located and negotiations had been conducted with him but it had been proven to the *qāḍī*'s satisfaction that he had no property in Israel. The reasons Shaykh Ṭahīr gave for this decision were that maintenance judgments of Israeli courts were unenforceable in Arab countries and that the state of war between Israel and its neighbors did not permit the husband either to come to Israel to pay maintenance or to legally send maintenance payments to Israel.[534]

For some time, Shaykh Ṭahīr followed the directives contained in the *qāḍī*s' resolution of July 18, 1951, whereby, in his opinion, he was fulfilling his obligation to "carry out the necessary inquiries" within the meaning of article 126.[535] He said that the Government had done all it could in the matter; he put the blame on the Arab members of the armistice commissions, who had refused to cooperate.[536] But he soon ceased trying to send notices to the husbands through these bodies and contended himself with publishing notices in the local press; and when the husband did not appear in court within 30 days to answer the claim, he pronounced the dissolution of the marriage.[537] At a later period, he did not even publish a notice but contented himself with the wife's statement on oath and confirming testimonies that the husband had gone abroad without leaving her maintenance.[538] It is probably no accident that more than half of the judgments of *sharīᶜa* courts dissolving the marriages of wives of absent husbands were given by Shaykh Ṭahīr. It seems that he acquired a reputation for leniency in this domain as against the more severe attitude of other *qāḍī*s; in fact, women from the areas of jurisdiction of other *sharīᶜa* courts would apply to him in such matters.[539] Not a single application to him for dissolution of a marriage to an absent husband was refused.

Shaykh Ḥusnī al-Zuᶜbī also granted almost every application of this kind. He was not punctilious as to the "necessary inquiries" concerning the husband's whereabouts, and performed this obligation by publishing a notice in the local press. Although he was usually careful to note in his judgments that it had proven impossible to collect maintenance from the husband, he seemed to think that the injury (*ḍarar*) caused to the wife by the husband's absence was a more, or at any rate not less, important element of the ground for dissolution under article 126 than non-provision of maintenance.[540] In one case, the allegation of injury arose in connection with the husband's imprisonment. After dissolution under article 126, it suddenly appeared that the husband was in prison in Israel, and the *qāḍī* rescinded the dissolution at his request. The wife again applied for dissolution, this time on the grounds of non-provision of maintenance and injury caused during the husband's absence in an Arab country and during his imprisonment. Shaykh Ḥusnī granted the application, holding that the husband's imprisonment was tantamount to absence without providing maintenance within the meaning of article 126. The wife was also, in his opinion, entitled to dissolution if the husband had been absent for over a year even if he had left property for her upkeep, because the wife's being alone for such a long time was contrary to human nature and intolerable.[541] In sum, Shaykh Ṭāhir Ḥamād and Shaykh Ḥusnī al-Zuᶜbī, by their liberal interpretations, gave a wider meaning to the ground for dissolution under article 126. Whereas the Ottoman legislator had meant only non-provision of maintenance to the wife of an absent husband, they had included new elements: non-provision of maintenance in cases where the husband had been traced and contacted in another country, and injury caused to the wife by the husband's absence and imprisonment. These elements are unknown to the Ḥanafī school, but are each recognized as an independent ground for dissolution in the modern legislation of several Muslim states.[542]

Shaykh Tawfīq ᶜAsaliyya and Shaykh Amīn Qāsim Mudlij applied article 126 without any inhibitions, religious-legal or other, though not in quite the same way. The former insisted on fulfilment of all the conditions imposed by that article,[543] while the latter did not exert himself unduly making inquiries about the husband's whereabouts; he generally contented himself with the wife's testimony and the oaths of witnesses as proof of the husband's absence and of the non-provision of maintenance.[544] It is true that in more recent years, Shaykh Amīn was accustomed to certify to the wife that she was a *mahjūra* (deserted wife) and that this status did not involve a dissolution of her marriage, but he did so at the wife's request.

The differences between the *qāḍī*s as to the interpretation and application of article 126 remained unsettled. The opposition of some *qāḍī*s to its application was probably due to their zealous adherence to the Ḥanafī school. In the absence of a supreme *sharᶜī* authority in

Israel there was no-one who might have been asked to decide the matter. Following the setting aside by the *Sharīʿa* Court of Appeal of a judgment of Shaykh Ṭāhir Ḥamād dissolving a marriage to an absent husband, there were several inquiries to the President of the Jordanian *Sharīʿa* Court of Appeal, *inter alia*, as to whether there was a legal basis for the direction forbidding *sharīʿa* courts to apply article 126 on the ground that it was impossible to make the "necessary inquiries" in wartime; whether the criterion of dissolution was the making of the necessary inquiries (as asserted by the *Sharīʿa* Court of Appeal) or the impossibility of obtaining maintenance (as held by Shaykh Ṭāhir Ḥamād); and what was the procedure in Jordan concerning the dissolution of a marriage to an absent husband on the ground of impossibility of obtaining maintenance. Shaykh Mūsā al-Ṭabarī asked that the Jordanian Law of Family Rights be adopted so that *sharīʿa* courts in Israel might apply it in regard to wives of absent husbands. No reply to those and other questions has yet been received from Jordan.[545]

The *Sharīʿa* Court of Appeal had another opportunity to deal with the issue in 1958. Shaykh Ḥasan Amīn al-Ḥabash dismissed the wife's action for dissolution in reliance on previous decisions of the Court of Appeal, while Shaykh Ṭāhir Ḥamād held that there was no legal obligation at all to refer the judgment to the Court of Appeal for confirmation.[546] The question was thus not decided. Since then, the *qāḍī*s practically ceased to refer their judgments in matters of marriages to absent husbands to the Court of Appeal. Every *qāḍī* dealt with the matter in accordance with his social and religious philosophy, and, as has been seen, the legal consequences of the case depended on the venue.

A problem also arose over the divorce of wives who had gone to an Arab country and could not be served with the notice (*tablīgh*) of divorce. This question occupied the *qāḍī*s especially in the early years of the state. Shaykh Ḥasan Amīn al-Ḥabash held that *tablīgh* was essential to the completeness of the divorce.[547] Shaykh Ṭāhir Ḥamād and Shaykh Mūsā al-Ṭabarī decided that the divorce should be registered whether or not *tablīgh* was possible; a circular to this effect was issued by the Muslim Division, ordering that the certificate of divorce be kept by the court "until required"; the *qāḍī*s acted accordingly.[548]

iii. Discord and Incompatibilty

As to the application of article 130 of the Family Rights Law, the *qāḍī*s were at variance on two basic points: the power of the arbitrators to dissolve the marriage and the circumstances under which a family council might be established. Some *qāḍī*s were unwilling to apply the article properly, apparently because of their adherence to the Ḥanafī school, whereas others applied it unhesitatingly in accordance with the conception of the Mālikī school. Shaykh Ṭāhir al-Ṭabarī and Shaykh Ḥasan Amīn al-Ḥabash confirmed dissolution by arbitrators only if effected in the way determined by the Ḥanafī school, i.e., if the spouses had empowered the arbitrators in advance to perform it.[549] Shaykh Ḥasan held that article 130 was not applied by the *sharīʿa* courts during the Mandate and that its application by the courts in Israel was unwarranted. In one case, he stopped arbitration proceedings because, in his opinion, the arbitrators had strayed "from the ancient path," and ordered obedience, probably for fear that they might decide on dissolution.[550] In another case, the *Sharīʿa* Court of Appeal set aside his judgment dismissing the wife's demand for arbitration.[551]

Shaykh Amīn Qāsim Mudlij expressly declared that a condition for dissolution by arbitrators was that the husband empower the arbitrator serving on his behalf to pronounce *ṭalāq* or *khulʿ* if efforts at reconciliation should fail and that the wife empower the arbitrator serving on her behalf to pay the husband monetary compensation in that event. In one case, he ordered obedience because the wife refused to appoint a family council "for purposes of reconciliation." On another occasion, he expressed the view that where reconciliation was impossible the Ḥanafī school saw no need to appoint arbitrators because the *qāḍī*s themselves acted in that capacity before giving judgment.[552] Shaykh Mūsā al-Ṭabarī changed his attitude in this matter in the course of time. He at first adopted the mechanism devised by the Ḥanafī school and afterward applied article 130 properly.[553] But other *qāḍī*s were not inhibited by adherence to a particular school of law from applying article 130. Most noteworthy in this respect was Shaykh Ṭāhir Ḥamād. He considered that in cases of discord and incompatibility the provisions of this article should be followed and not those of article 210 of Qadrī's collection, which is based on the Ḥanafī school. He argued that "the Sulṭān of the Muslims chose and confirmed it [the article] because it agrees with one of the four schools, and directed that judgment should be given in accordance with it; and obedience to his command is a *sharʿī* duty, as explained by Ibn ʿĀbidīn; and judgments in accordance with other provisions, prescribed by other schools, are contrary to *sharʿī* duty." In one judgment, he remarked incidentally in this connection that "the [Ottoman] legislator did not transgress the bounds of the Muslim *sharīʿa*."[554] In other words, he suggested that the four orthodox schools had equal standing and that inter-school mobility of the *qāḍī* was permitted and even required by virtue of the *siyāsa* (policy) principle.

Shaykh Ḥusnī al-Zuʿbī also did not shrink from resorting to the mechanism of arbitration created by article 130. He was accustomed to confirm the arbitrators' awards, whether the result was *tafrīq* or something else[555]; when sitting in appeals, he did not hesitate to set aside judgments of other *qāḍī*s which deviated from the provisions of article 130 or to dismiss appeals against *tafrīq* judgments validly given.[556] Nor did the judgments of Shaykh Tawfīq ʿAsaliyya suggest in any way that dissolution required advanced authorization by the parties. He instructed the arbitrators to settle the dispute between the parties "peacefully or by *tafrīq*."[557] The circumstances of "discord and incompatibility" (*nizāʿ washiqāq*) in which arbitration may be applied tended to be defined by most of the *qāḍī*s within the limited framework of the matrimonial obligations and rights of the spouses. Thus, Shaykh Amīn Qāsim Mudlij held that where the spouses fulfilled their mutual matrimonial duties there was no basis at all for arbitration. Where the wife refused without just cause to live with the husband she not only could not invoke article 130 but was considered rebellious; she could not contend that the husband had quarreled with her since he was not a party to the dispute; the husband, on other hand, might demand a judgment for obedience. Again, Shaykh Amīn said that where the wife fulfilled all her matrimonial duties toward the husband, his demand for application of article 130 was disregarded and he was considered a rebel against her rights and ordered to pay maintenance. In Shaykh Amīn's opinion, article 130 could only be applied where the wife refused to comply with an order for obedience and might be declared rebellious, or where the husband refused to comply with an order for maintenance and the wife was in danger of incurring injury (*ḍarar*).[558] The restriction of the possibility of dissolution to cases in which the defendant did not fulfill his or her obligations to the plaintiff and the orthodox legal remedies had been exhausted, had no basis in article 130.

Shaykh Ḥasan Amīn al-Ḥabash decided in an appeal that there had been no basis for appointing arbitrators and that the matter before the court of first instance had not been a dispute between the parties but a question of maintenance. He set aside the judgment for dissolution and returned the case to the lower court for further consideration of the maintenance claim although that court had held that there was a serious dispute between the spouses which required arbitration.[559]

Shaykh Ḥusnī al-Zuᶜbī and Shaykh Tawfīq ᶜAsaliyya also tended to interpret the term "discord" in the limited context of matrimonial rights.[560] At the same time, the former sometimes departed from this line when he was convinced that there was no point in preserving the marriage. Thus, in one case, when the wife sued for maintenance and the husband for obedience, he reached the conclusion that the rift between the spouses was fundamental and could not be healed, and appointed a family council on his own initiative. In another case, when the wife sued for maintenance and the husband rejected the claim and applied for the appointment of a council of arbitrators, he granted the husband's application.[561]

Shaykh Ṭāhir Ḥamād was the only *qāḍī* who gave a wide interpretation of the circumstances under which the mechanism of arbitration might be applied. He held that "discord" was not necessarily a *mutual* action or attitude of the spouses. In his opinion, a hostile attitude of one spouse toward the other was sufficient to warrant resort to arbitration, and the attempt to interpret "discord" within the narrow context of matrimonial rights contradicted the general meaning of the term. Moreover, he held that article 130 gave the *qāḍī* absolute discretion to appoint arbitrators even where only one of the spouses wished it.[562] This approach was reflected in many judgments for dissolution in reliance on article 130.[563] In almost all cases, Shaykh Ṭāhir appointed arbitrators when his attempts at reconciliation had failed.[564] He sometimes appointed arbitrators on his own initiative.[565] In appeals, he would set aside judgments of courts of first instance which deviated in the matter of arbitration from the provisions of article 130 as he interpreted them.[566] By this attitude, he consciously or unconsciously helped to turn arbitration into a refined instrument of dissolution by the wife in cases of cruelty and injury to her, non-provision of maintenance to her and the children, disputes in consequence of exchange marriages, social or cultural incompatibility between the spouses, and so forth.

As stated, some of these achievements were recently recognized by parliamentary legislation of several Arab countries as new grounds for judicial dissolution.

iv. Dissolution of the Marriage of a Girl under 17

It seems that the *qāḍīs*, contrary to the expectations of the Knesset, were unwilling to recognize the bride's being under 17 as a ground for dissolution, seeing that it was not so recognized by Islamic law. On the other hand, they did not oppose the application of the penal sanction attached to contraventions of the Age of Marriage Law. The first *qaḍīs*' conference in 1950 resolved unanimously that dissolution by the court must be based on "express religious-legal law laid down by the Ḥanafī school save in so far as it conflicts with [secular] law." Shaykh Ṭahīr Ḥamād expressed the opinion that a marriage must not be dissolved on this ground because this was contrary to Islamic law and also because it was likely to cause damage. He suggested upholding the validity of the marriage and replacing dissolution with the imposition of blood-money (*diya*) or a substitute payment (*badal*); this would leave both the marriage and the law intact. Shaykh Tawfīq Maḥmūd ʿAsaliyya declared that he tried as hard as he could to avoid dissolving marriages of girls under 17 "with a view to protecting the offspring." In doing so, he acted, in his opinion, in accordance with the spirit of both the *sharīʿa* and the secular legislator, since the parties were liable to the penal sanction prescribed by law.[567] The attitude of the *qāḍīs* is not reflected in judgments, which means that the matter was of no practical concern to them.[568]

v. Termination of Irregular or Void Marriage

The *qāḍīs* were not always alive to the reforms introduced by the Family Rights Law in the classification of irregular and void marriages and continued to follow the rigorous precepts of the Ḥanafī school in this matter. Thus, in one case, Shaykh Ṭāhir Ḥamād decided that the "marriage" of a woman already married to another man was void, although according to the Ottoman legislator it was merely irregular.[569] Such deviations are, of course, significant as to the legal consequences for the woman and her children.

5. EFFECTS OF DIVORCE

a. Triple Repudiation and Revocable Divorce

The declared position of the *qāḍīs* as to triple repudiation is indicated by their attitude toward the Egyptian Personal Status Bill of 1966, which would have provided that successive repudiation, i.e., repudiation pronounced in one session with the force of two or three separate repudiations, should be considered a single repudiation. Shaykh Ṭāhir Ḥamād and Shaykh Tawfīq ᶜAsaliyya opposed the suggested reform in reliance on the various sources of religious law. Shaykh Ḥusnī al-Zuᶜbī and Shaykh Amīn Qāsim Mudlij welcomed it and found support for it in the teachings of non-Ḥanafī schools and in other sources.[570] Anyhow, the *qāḍīs*' attitude in this matter as displayed in practice was generally orthodox traditional. They blindly confirmed every triple repudiation that came their way.[571] They did not refer in any manner to the damage likely to be caused by this kind of divorce to the wife, the family and even the husband. They admitted no normative difference between three repudiations pronounced separately and a triple repudiation, pronounced on a single occasion. Their distinction between these two was purely technical: in the case of separate repudiations they counted the times that the wife had already been repudiated and noted how many repudiations the husband still had left, and when three had been performed, they noted this fact and drew the couple's attention to the requirement of an intermediate marriage.[572] They did not try to influence the definition of the type of divorce or to mitigate the legal consequences.

Only once did one of the *qāḍīs*, Shaykh Tawfīq ᶜAsaliyya, make an exception in order to accommodate a couple who asked for a triple repudiation to be annulled on the plea that it had been performed in a fit of anger. He granted the application, *inter alia*, on the ground that "*ṭalāq* requires soundness of the mental faculties, and the continuance of married life is better than its discontinuance . . . and the *ṭalāq* was performed at a single session, contrary to what should be the practice according to the *sharīᶜa*, and there is someone who says that three repudiations performed at one and the same time have the effect of a single repudiation. . . ."[573] In other words, the *qāḍī*'s decision was based on legal and social grounds. This was, in fact, a bold attempt to rely on the opinion of an individual Islamic jurist who, contrary to the orthodox schools, did not recognize the validity of triple repudiation.

The *qāḍī*s' indifference to triple repudiation is particularly surprising in view of the pains they sometimes took to prevent ordinary divorce. They possibly did not treat triple repudiation very severely because the requirement of an intermediate marriage was usually circumvented by a fictitious marriage or some other device. In fact, at least Shaykh Mūsā al-Ṭabarī lent his hand to such a circumvention. The case has been described of a fictitious intermediate marriage obviously designed to permit the woman to her first husband; surprisingly enough, this *qāḍī* did not reject outright the woman's attempt to get round the legal requirement although the stratagem was quite transparent. He confirmed dissolution of the intermediate marriage, acquiescing in the ruse.[574] In other words, an important contribution of the *qāḍī*s in the matter of triple repudiation may consist, not in their having denied its validity or mitigated its legal consequences, but in having helped to circumvent the requirement of an intermediate marriage through conscious or unconscious disregard of the fiction involved.

Revocable divorce did not often occupy the *qāḍī*s, and its handling did not as a rule deviate from orthodox doctrine.[575] Still, their attitude was less formal to it than to triple repudiation; they sometimes made an effort to mitigate the consequences of the divorce and to help the couple to rebuild their marriage, provided the husband regretted his hasty action. This is seen especially in cases where the husband contended that he had divorced the wife in a fit of anger.[576] In one case, the husband had used a formula particularly expressive of finality: "You are divorced; no Ḥanafī, no Shāfiʿī, no Mālikī and no Ḥanbalī, no demon and no devil shall bring you back." He claimed that he had said this in a very angry mood, and Shaykh Ṭāhir Ḥamād decided that the wife was revocably divorced; he added that that formula was "foolishness, not to be taken seriously from a *sharʿī* point of view."[577]

In many cases in which a marriage to an absent husband was dissolved by reason of non-provision of maintenance, the *qāḍī*s, and especially Shaykh Ṭāhir Ḥamād, decided that the dissolution was equivalent to a revocable divorce.[578] This was in deviance from the provisions of article 131 of the Family Rights Law, which provides that judicial dissolution is to be treated as irrevocable divorce. The Mālikī school recognizes non-provision of maintenance as a ground for dissolution equivalent to revocable divorce: the husband may have the wife back if during the *ʿidda* he proves to the satisfaction of the court that he is able and willing to support her.[579]

b. Maintenance during the Waiting-Period and Compensation to Divorced Women

The *sharʿī* law of maintenance is adapted to the structure of the patriarchal family, in which a woman is completely exempt from the care for her own maintenance. After a divorce, she returns to her father's or brother's house or remarries as soon as possible, so that the responsibility for her livelihood passes to other men.[580] Maintenance during the waiting-period (*ʿidda*) is without functional significance; unlike, for instance, deferred dower, it is not designed to afford economic security to the divorced wife or to act as a deterrent to divorce. The waiting-period has two purposes: to provide certainty as to the identity of the natural father in the event of pregnancy and to enable the revocably divorced wife to be reinstated without need for the contraction of a new marriage, the payment of dower, etc.; and as the wife remains in the husband's house during the waiting-period, he meanwhile continues in any case to be responsible for her maintenance. But in view of the changes in the structure of the family and the social status of women in recent times, when a divorced wife does not necessarily return to her father's house or remarry and her upkeep becomes more and more her own affair, maintenance begins to be appreciated in economic terms: it now has functional significance as a means to secure her economic position. It follows that maintenance for three months, which is generally the waiting-period of a non-pregnant woman, does not ensure a decent living to a divorced wife who wishes to be independent or who has no relatives required or able to provide for her.

To what extent were the *qāḍī*s alive to this problem and did they give their minds to improving the position of divorced women? The attitude of Shaykh Ḥasan Amīn al-Ḥabash and Shaykh Ḥusnī al-Zuʿbī in this matter was radical to the point of explicit deviation from religious law. As against this, the other *qāḍī*s did not deviate from the traditional religious-legal conception. At a *qāḍī*s' conference in 1963, measures were discussed to ensure the position and rights of the divorced woman. Shaykh Ḥasan Amīn al-Ḥabash expressed the view that it was the court's "most sacred duty" to protect her rights. In his opinion, the problem was not her right to maintenance during the waiting-period but how to ensure to her "a decent life until her death or until God prescribed a way for her," i.e., until she remarried.[581] He recently expressed the belief that the problem required a radical solution by

Knesset legislation: a man who divorced his wife should not only be liable to the penal sanction but should be *ordered* to compensate her rather than left to do so voluntarily. He did not regard compensation to a divorced wife as conflicting with religious law since in his opinion there was no express provision in the *sharīʿa* forbidding it. He considered that the provision prescribing compensation should be treated as based on the doctrine of *siyāsa* (policy), as a provision of state law intended to supplement the *sharīʿa*.[582] Shaykh Ḥusnī al-Zuʿbī suggested specifically that a provision should be enacted, by an amendment to section 7 of the Penal Law Amendment (Bigamy) Law, 5719–1959, or to the Criminal Code Ordinance to the effect that a man must compensate his divorced wife in accordance with the circumstances of the case or until she remarries.[583]

Shaykh Ṭāhir Ḥamād and Shaykh Amīn Qāsim Mudlij, on the other hand, were strongly opposed to any deviation from the duty of maintenance imposed on the husband by Islamic law. They rejected the proposal to require him to pay the wife maintenance until she remarried on the ground that it was contrary to the *sharīʿa*. Shaykh Ṭāhir held that Islamic law "has left nothing, great or small, without an express provision (*naṣṣ*) for it in the law books." There was no need, in his opinion, to change the law of maintenance because "Qurʾānic legislation is suitable for every time and place." He saw only one way to increase the amount of maintenance to a divorced woman, viz., by agreement between the parties. Moreover, he insisted that if the wife neglected to file a claim for maintenance before the expiration of the waiting-period she would lose her right to it, as prescribed by Islamic law.

Shaykh Amīn Qāsim Mudlij's attitude to the question of the maintenance of a divorced woman was rooted in the traditional view that there is a close connection between maintenance and the existence of the marriage. On the expiration of the waiting-period, the wife leaves the husband's *ʿisma* completely and there is no longer any reason to require him to pay maintenance. He saw this view confirmed by the absence of maintenance out of the estate in Islamic law, that is to say, in the fact that a widow is not entitled to obtain maintenance out of the husband's estate. Another argument advanced by him was that "by the nature of things, when her *ʿidda* is over, she passes to another husband, who will provide her maintenance." On the other hand, a man should not, in Shaykh Amīn's opinion, be ordered to pay maintenance to his divorced wife until she remarries because this may take 20 years and he may thus suffer damage. He suggested referring the question of the divorced woman's maintenance to the court, which was to proceed in accordance with the principles of dissolution by arbitration, that is to say, the rights of the parties were to be determined by distinguishing between the party responsible for the dissolution and the injured party. He said that the courts were accustomed to settle the question of maintenance before deciding on divorce and to delay judgment until the parties had reached agreement as to the amount of maintenance or the latter had been fixed by experts. At a *qaḍi*s' conference in 1963, it was in fact decided that on giving a judgment for *ṭalāq* the court might adjudicate the rights of the divorced woman in accordance with an agreement between the parties or [in the absence of such an agreement] "at the court's discretion in accordance with the circumstances of the case," and that the court should remind the *maʾdhūn*s to clearly indicate in the marriage contract the stipulations ensuring the wife's rights, such as compensation (*taʿwīḍ*) on divorce in accordance with the circumstances of the case or as fixed by the court.[584] Wide discretion of the *qāḍī* as to the divorced woman's rights permits him to award maintenance or fix compensation over and above maintenance for the waiting-period, and he is in fact guided in this matter, consciously or unconsciously, by his social philosophy.

From the evidence of the *qāḍī*s it is doubtful whether, in introducing such a radical reform, the *sharʿī* basis of which is slight, in the status of women, the *qāḍī*s actually drew encouragement from the fact that a similar reform had been introduced in several Arab countries by way of secular legislation.[585] Their decision was probably intended to confirm a social custom established in several areas, especially in the Little Triangle villages, of compensating a divorced woman. Shaykh Ḥusnī al-Zuʿbī explained that the idea was that the court should be competent, when confirming a divorce, to adjudicate the rights of the woman and that the rate of maintenance should, in the absence of agreement between the parties, be fixed by experts "having regard to the interest of the woman and to every other right arising out of the divorce in the circumstances of the case (in accordance with my basic proposal)," with a view to doing justice to the woman.[586] He did not make it clear to what "basic proposal" he was referring, but, as stated above, he was credited with two proposals in this connection: compensation to the woman by the enactment of a binding provision of secular law and assurance of maintenance to her until her remarriage. Both proposals deviate from the religious law of maintenance. Shaykh Ḥasan Amīn al-Ḥabash gave to understand that the decision was intended to enable the *qāḍī*, in the absence of agreement between the parties, to pronounce on the wife's rights when confirming the divorce, whereas until then the wife had in this case been compelled to file a separate claim for her rights.[587] At a *qāḍī*s' conference in 1966, it was decided to make provision, when drawing up the marriage contract, for deferred dower in addition to prompt dower so that it might serve as security to the wife in the event of divorce or widowhood and as a deterrent to hasty divorce by the husband.[588]

A *qāḍī*s' conference is not a statutory institution competent to decide questions of the material law applicable to *sharīʿa* courts or to enact religious-legal provisions. Nor have its decisions the effect of religious-legal opinions in the orthodox sense of this term, and if the *qāḍī*s took it on themselves to act in accordance with them, they did so voluntarily. In fact, these decisions are meaningful to the extent that they were applied in judgments. Moreover, the decisions concerning the rights of divorced women left wide discretion to the *qāḍī*s to adjudicate "in accordance with the circumstances of the case" as each of them understood them. In other words, each *qāḍī* was guided by his religious-legal and social philosophies.

The *sijill*s indeed reveal two diametrically opposed attitudes in this matter, one conservative-formalistic, the other liberal-reformist. The exponents of the former, who were the majority of the *qāḍī*s, insisted on the wife's right to maintenance during the *ʿidda*, but not beyond it, in strict adherence to religious law. For this very reason, it may be assumed, Shaykh Ṭāhir Ḥamād ordered a man to pay maintenance to his divorced wife although she admitted having been the principal supporter of the family, including her jobless husband.[589] Moreover, they did not shrink from denying a divorced woman's right to maintenance during the *ʿidda* on some technical *sharʿī* ground. Thus, for example, Shaykh Ṭāhir al-Ṭabarī and Shaykh Ṭāhir Ḥamād in some cases dismissed a divorced woman's application for such maintenance for the sole reason that it had been filed after the expiration of the waiting-period, and Shaykh Ṭāhir Ḥamād denied a divorced woman's right because she had left the *bayt al-ʿidda* and refused to return there.[590] It might happen that a woman at the time of her divorce renounced her right to maintenance for her children and undertook to support them "with her own money," but after a time found herself unable to do so and asked the court to order the father of the children to pay maintenance for them. In all the cases brought before Shaykh Ṭāhir Ḥamād and Shaykh Mūsā al-Ṭabarī, the wife's application was dismissed although she pleaded that she was in distress or had become impoverished after her divorce.[591]

As mentioned, the number of cases when maintenance was awarded to a divorced woman beyond the waiting-period—for life, until remarriage, etc.—was rather limited. It is characteristic that the *qāḍī*s were careful to point out in these circumstances that the husband undertook to pay such maintenance "of his own free will," so as to make it clear that the court did not impose a maintenance arrangement deviating from religious law. This scrupulous observance of the *sharīʿa* is particularly noticeable in the judgments of Shaykh Ṭāhir Ḥamād, Shaykh Mūsā al-Ṭabarī and Shaykh Amīn Qāsim Mudlij.[592]

The radical views of Shaykh Ḥasan Amīn al-Ḥabash and Shaykh Ḥusnī al-Zuʿbī as to safeguarding the subsistence of divorced women are apparent also in their judgments, although they showed some embarrassment when they awarded benefits beyond those due under religious law. They usually sought to get around this difficulty by various means: in many cases, they represented compensation as a substitute (*badal*) for maintenance for the waiting-period, "whatever its amount may be"; sometimes they added the words "and the other rights connected with the marriage" which were vested in the wife in advance "in a final manner."[593] They might add that the amounts of money to be paid to the wife were "in accordance with our position and that of those like us."[594] This formula is customary in fixing maintenance and denotes that it benefits the economic position of the spouses. But the attempt to equate compensation with maintenance for the waiting-period is out of place since there was often a wide gap between the amount of the latter, which was at most a few hundred Israeli pounds, and that of the former, which sometimes ran to several thousands; the same is the case where property given as compensation included several dunams of land, buildings and the like, the value of which exceeded the usual amount of maintenance.[595] Moreover, compensation was occasionally equated with maintenance for the waiting-period even where the wife was not entitled to the latter, as where the marriage had not been consummated.[596] The *qāḍī*s seemed to feel uncomfortable when representing compensation as maintenance for the waiting-period, and this is probably why they often made a point of noting that those large amounts were paid "of my own volition and at my own free choice."[597] It indeed seems that in all the cases when a woman received compensation or was assured maintenance beyond the waiting-period this was by mutual agreement without the intervention of the *qāḍī*, who only gave the arrangement the force of a judgment.[598] At the same time, there can be no doubt that the *qāḍī*s were aware of the difference between maintenance for the waiting-period and compensation. They sometimes said that the husband had to pay two amounts: one as maintenance for the waiting-period and the other, larger one, for another purpose, which was really compensation[599] and which now and then they did not hesitate to call by this name without attempting to disguise it.[600] Under these circumstances, compensation was frequently explained as redress for the injury (*ḍarar*) caused to the wife by the divorce.[601] Although the relevant utterances were in the first person, there can be no doubt that Shaykh Ḥasan Amīn al-Ḥabash had a hand in formulating them, and they may represent an attempt to provide a *sharᶜī* legitimation for a social practice increasingly adopted in the Little Triangle villages.

From this it is clear that the decisions of the *qāḍī*s' conference of 1963 were implemented only in part and only by some of the *qāḍī*s. The author found no confirmation in the *sijill*s of Shaykh Amīn Qāsim Mudlij's assertion that the *sharīᶜa* courts pronounced on the rights of the divorced woman at the same time as they gave judgment concerning the divorce itself. On the contrary, in one case, when the wife claimed various rights at the time the judgment for divorce was given, that *qāḍī* directed her to file a separate action for these rights.[602] The interpretation of the 1963 decision as meaning that the *qāḍī*'s discretion is not confined to the wife's *sharᶜī* rights was applied to a considerable extent by Shaykh Ḥasan Amīn al-Ḥabash only and only in part by other *qāḍī*s and found its expression in compensation to the wife and maintenance beyond the waiting-period. Shaykh Ḥusnī al-Zuᶜbī declared that compensation and maintenance beyond the waiting-period were assured in advance by stipulations in the marriage contract,[603] but there is no evidence of this in either the *sijill*s or in the registers of marriage contracts of the years 1962 and 1968.

NOTES

1. See Rosenfeld, *Peasants,* pp.39–40, 64, 127, 129–31, 136, 150; Baer, pp.34, 37; Marx, *Social Structure,* p.6; Granqvist, vol.2, p.283 n.2.
2. *JfQ2,* p.330:no.518–f.72/58; *AcṬ3,* p.10:f.5/57; *ṬbḤ2,* p.238:no.15, and p. 231:no.5, respectively. Cases of this kind were numerous. See, e.g., *JfQ2,* p.579:no.600–f.16/63; *JfQ3,* p.103:no.159–f.49/64; *ṬbI1,* p.112:no.1–f. 42/57, p.139:no.1–f.58/59; *NzḤ21,* p.139:no.2/69–f.110/61; *AcṬ2,* p.94; *AcṬ3,* p.137:f.33/59.
3. References to childlessness do not necessarily indicate barrenness of the wife. Thus, in one case, the ground for divorce is said to be that the couple "now has no living child," *JfQ4,* p.53:no.49–f.153/67.
4. Cf. Woodsmall, p.124.
5. *AcṬ2,* p.106; *AcṬ3,* p.104:f.3/59, p.236:f.13/62; *ṬbḤ2,* p.157:no.38 (nine daughters).
6. *AcṬ3,* p.58:f.46/57; *AcṬ4,* p.33:f.23/65.
7. See e.g., *JfQ3,* p.170:no.278–f.40/65, p.205:no.338–f.25/66 (after 23 years of a childless marriage, they decided to separate in the hope "that God will cause something to happen afterward," i.e., that the husband would have children by another wife); *ṬbḤ2,* p.63:no.29 (the wife consented to the divorce "because she has borne no children and no sons"); *ṬbḤ3,* p.22:no. 28 (the wife consented to the divorce "in order that he may be able to take another wife; perhaps He will bless him with children").
8. Shaykh Ḥusnī al-Zu^c^bī confirmed that barrenness of the wife was a frequent cause of divorce by mutual agreement; the wife consented to the divorce in order that the husband might marry another woman and produce offspring (the *qāḍī*'s letter to the author of January 2, 1971).
9. See Rosenfeld, *Peasants,* p.127; Baer, p.37. For a more extensive discussion see the chapter "Polygamy," p.78.
10. *ṬbI1,* p.86:no.5–f.8/56. See also *ṬbI1,* p.185:no.6–f.9/61; *ṬbḤ4,* p.177: no.44.
11. See, e.g., *ṬbI1,* p.100:no.8–f.28/57 (after 50 years of marriage); *NzḤ16,* p.26:no.44/245.
12. Another possible reason for divorce was referred to by Shaykh Ḥusnī al-Zu^c^bī. He said that divorce "was in many cases aimed at obtaining a pension from [National] Insurance" (*AI,* vol.11 (1968), Nos.1–2, p.7; see also English Summary, *ibid.,* p.1). In other words, this kind of divorce is intended solely to entitle the wife to an increased old-age pension of several tens of pounds a month (a married woman was entitled to about half the amount due to a single woman). There was no confirmation of this point in the *sijill*s.
13. See, e.g., *JfQ1,* p.180:no.296–f.38/55 (the wife "has reached the age of

despair (*sinn al-ya's*)"); *JfQ4*, p.142:no.169–f.2/69; *AcṬ3*, p.197:f.1/61, p. 224:f.2/62; *Ṭb11*, p.147:no.10–f.17/59.

14. See, e.g., *JfQ1*, p.97:no.156–f.30/53; *JfQ3*, p.313:no.452–f.4/67.
15. *AI*, vol.9(1964), Nos.1–2, p.5.
16. *Ṭb11*, p.242:no.30–f.34/63, and p.116:no.5–f.2/58, respectively. Cf. Cohen, p.76; Anderson, *Islamic Law*, pp.52–3. Professor Z. Falk told the author that divorce upon sudden enrichment for the purpose of marrying a young woman appropriate to the changed circumstances had been observed by him among Jews who had received compensation from Germany.
17. To such an extent that Shaykh Ḥasan Amīn al-Ḥabash believed the divorce rate in his area of jurisdiction to be several times higher than the marriage rate. *AI*, vol.8(1962), Nos.1–2, p.37. Cf. Baer, p.38. See above, sec.V. "The Decline of the Divorce Rate," pp.178 *seq.*
18. Cf. Anderson, *Patriarchal Family*, p.231. The problem in his opinion was no longer polygamy but divorce for the purpose of another marriage or, as he called it, successive polygamy. See also Meron, p.530.
19. *NzḤ24*, p.29:no.7/77–f.134/66; *AcṬ2*, p.151; *AcṬ3*, p.199:f.3/61.
20. See, e.g., *JfQ3*, p.341:no.481–f.50/67(22 years); *AcṬ3*, p.106:f.5/59 (16 years); *NzḤ22*, p.1:no.8/50–f.73/62 (ten years).
21. See, e.g., *NzḤ24*, p.29:no.7/77–f.134/63 (husband aged 77; were married for a week).
22. See, e.g., *JfQ1*, p.37:no.65–f.71/52 (the wife was unwilling to move into the husband's house in Jaffa because "it was unbefitting her status and such a one as she was"), p.275:no.423–f.31/57; *JfQ2*, p.465:no.482–fs.69/60, 75/60, 22/61. See also the chapter "Maintenance and Obedience," pp.95 *seq.*
23. See, e.g., *NzḤ24*, p.225:no.3/39–f.91/69. Cf. Baer, p.37.
24. See, e.g., *JfQ3*, p.285:no.425–f.116/66.
25. See, e.g., *JfQ1*, p.79:no.123–f.98/52; *JfQ3*, p.29:no.49–f.115/63; *NzI4*, p. 46:no.1/1–f.1/49 and p.49:no.6/8–f.13/49; *AcI1*, p.4:f.4/48, p.56:f.3/50.
26. *JfQ4*, p.57:no.53–f.150/67. See also *AcI3*, p.14:no.17/55–f.55/55; *NzI4*, p.235:no.2/34–f.42/63, p.237:no.1/4–f.4/64, p.239:no.2/5–f.21/64, p.247: no.2/20–f.83/64, p.256:no.8/37–f.151/64. Cf. Coulson, *History*, p.173.
27. See, e.g., *JfQ1*, p.97:no.155–f.28/53; *AcI1*, p.72:f.41/50, p.74:f.42/50; *AcI2*, p.11:no.9–f.14/51.
28. See, e.g., *JfQ2*, p.235:no.508–f.56/58, p.542:no.536–f.33/62.
29. *JfQ4*, p.85:no.84–f.22/68; see also *Ṭb11*, p.157:no.21–f.23/59 (the wife delayed the filing of the claim for 11 years).
30. See, e.g., *JfQ1*, p.144:no.243–f.50/54; *JfQ2*, p.317:no.496–f.39/58; *JfQ3*, p.294:no.434–f.131/66; *Ṭb11*, p.78:no.18–f.30/55; *AcṬ2*, p.11. Cf. Granqvist, vol.2, p.260.
31. See, e.g., *Ṭb11*, p.220:no.15–f.13/63 (schoolteacher); *NzI4*, p.227:no.1/19–f.60/63 (laborer).

32. See, e.g., *JfQ1,* p.55:no.85–f.58/52 (claim for obedience dismissed) and p. 55:no.86–f.21/52 (divorce); *JfQ4,* p.88:no.87–f.3/68 and p.102:no.114–f. 70/68; *Ṭbl1,* p.129:no.17–f.9/58 and p.131:no.20–f.26/58.
33. See, e.g., *JfQ4,* p.183:no.235–f.70/69 and p.184:no.237–f.87/69 (judgment for obedience and divorce); *Ṭbl1,* p.179:no.19–f.37/60, p.183:no.4–f.11/61 and p.184:no.5–f.12/61, *NzI4,* p.345:no.1/1–f.177/67 and p.369:no.6/36–f.72/68; *AcI2,* p.54:f.119/53 and p.56:f.127/53.
34. See, e.g., *JfQ1,* p.162:no.268–f.3/55.
35. Cf. Fāris Fallāh, *AD,* vol.3(1966) Nos.1–2, p.10.
36. *JfQ1,* p.26:no.43, p.133:no.224–f.33/54; *JfQ2,* p.380:no.533–f.18/59; *Ṭbl1,* p.60:no.13–f.25/54, p.61:no.15–f.27/54, p.116:no.5–f.2/58.
37. *Ṭbl1,* p.119:no.8–f.10/58 and p.124:no.12–f.18/58 (rumors had reached the husband that the wife's way of life prior to the marriage had been free and easy; he divorced her and left the village). Cf. Rosenfeld, *Peasants,* p.130; E. Hareʾuveni, *Maʿariv*, July 3, 1966.
38. *Ṭbl1,* p.53:no.2–f.3/54, p.149:no.11–f.22/59 (the marriage had not been consummated during the three years of its existence).
39. *Ṭbl1,* p.120:no.9–f.13/58; *JfQ3,* p.329:no.470–f.30/67.
40. *Ṭbl1,* p.44: no.4–f.11/53 (the wife, who was pregnant, had told the husband that she wished to marry another man); *NzḤ19,* p.17:no.4/12; *NzḤ24,* p. 166:no.9/67–f.133/68. Cf. Granqvist, vol.2, p.260; Rosenfeld, *Peasants,* pp.120, 130.
41. *NzḤ20,* p.72:no.1/63 ("she abducted my brother" and they went to live in another village); *JfQ5,* p.98:no.84–f.191/69; *AcṬ2,* p.95. Cf. Granqvist, vol.2, p.267.
42. See, e.g., *AcṬ4,* p.80:f.18/67, p.142:f.32/68; *ṬbḤ1,* p.108:no.1/78.
43. *AcṬ4,* p.117:f.5/68. Cf. Granqvist, vol.2, pp.259–60.
44. *Ṭbl2,* p.82:no.50/55, p.83:no.51; *JfQ4,* p.153:no.185–f.18/69. Cf. Granqvist, vol.2, pp.191, 263–5; Rosenfeld, *Peasants*, p.129.
45. See the chapter "Maintenance and Obedience," p.100–1.
46. See, e.g., *JfQ4,* p.165:no.203–f.49/69 (no children) and p.166:no.204–f. 50/69 (two children); *NzḤ24,* p.148:no.6/46–f.83/68 (no children) and p. 149:no.7/47–f.84/68 (two children); *AcṬ4,* p.53:f.21/66 (a son) and p.54: f.22/66 (a daughter). Cf. Granqvist, vol.2, p.258; Rosenfeld, *Peasants*, p.129.
47. *AcṬ4,* p.7:f.13/64.
48. See, e.g., *JfQ3,* p.294:no.434–f.131/66 and p.295:no.435–f.132/66; *JfQ4,* p.183:no.235–f.70/69 and p.183:no.236–f.71/69.
49. *AcṬ3,* p.172:f.15/60.
50. *AI,* vol.11(1968), Nos.1–2, p.4.
51. See, e.g., *JfQ3,* p.294:no.434–f.131/66 and p.295:no.435–f.132/66; *ṬbḤ4,* p.286:no.19–f.34/67 and p.287:no.20–f.35/67; *NzḤ23,* p.158:no.11/15–f.20/66 and p.159:no.12/16–f.21/66.

52. See, e.g., *NzḤ15,* p.15:no.19/34 and p.16:no.20/35; *NzḤ18,* p.212:no.9/34 and p.212:no.10/35; *NzḤ22,* p.109:no.5/5–f.8/64 and p.110:no.6/6–f.9/64.
53. Cf. Marx, *Bedouin,* pp.121, 160.
54. See Baer, p.66.
55. *ṬbḤ3,* p.104:no.12.
56. See, e.g., *ṬbḤ1,* p.114:no.87; *NzḤ19,* p.42:no.5/40; *AcṬ3,* p.159:f.3/60, p.180:f.22/60, p.190:f.33/60; *AcṬ4,* p.19:f.1/65, p.21:f.5/65.
57. See, e.g., *AcṬ2,* p.112; *ṬbḤ2,* p.166:no.49.
58. See, e.g., *JfQ1,* p.247:no.384–f.17/56; *JfQ4,* p.12:no.12–f.108/67, p.17: no.17–f.67/67; *ṬbḤ4,* p.259:no.30–f.53/66; *ṬbI1,* p.108:no.15–f.31/57, p.131:no.20–f.26/58. Cf. Granqvist, vol.2, p.258.
59. See, e.g., *ṬbḤ2,* p.227:no.136; *NzḤ18,* p.232:no.8/60; *JfQ5,* p.67:f.227/69; *AcṬ2,* p.86.
60. See above, in sec.III, 2. "Judicial Dissolution," pp.164–5.
61. *NzḤ20,* p.124:no.3/50; *NzḤ22,* p.129:no.5/24; *AcṬ4,* p.41:f.6/66.
62. *NzI4*, p.301:no.2/28–f.188/65.
63. See, e.g., *JfQ1,* p.157:no.261–f.63/54, p.167:no.276–f.13/55, p.199:no. 321–f.67/55, p.237:no.366–f.21/56, p.252:no.391–f.45/56; *JfQ2,* p.333:no. 521–f.74/58, p.544:no.541–f.81/62; *JfQ3,* p.182:no.299–f.85/65; *AcṬ2,* pp.32, 82, 87, 132, 136; *NzḤ18,* p.257:no.5/91.
64. See, e.g., *JfQ1,* p.167:no.275–f.10/55; *JfQ2,* p.237:no.512–f.65/58, p.399: no.559–f.47/59, p.544:no.544–f.81/62; *JfQ5,* p.69:no.118–f.230/69; *ṬbḤ1,* p.139:no.37; *ṬbḤ2,* p.129:no.1, p.272:no.63; *ṬbI1,* p.53:no.1–f.28/53, p.54:no.4–f.5/54; *AcṬ1,* p.24. Cf. Cohen, p.77; Rosenfeld, *Peasants,* p.130.
65. See, e.g., *JfQ1,* p.167:no.276–f.13/55; *ṬbI1,* p.51:no.12–f.25/53; *AcṬ2,* pp.32, 66, 132.
66. *NzḤ18,* p.257:no.6/92; *AcṬ4,* p.77:f.15/67; *ṬbḤ1,* p.157:no.4/4.
67. *JfQ2,* p.308:no.476–f.20/58, p.327:no.2/5–f.65/58, p.537:no.526–f.65/62; *ṬbḤ2,* p.60:no.25; *ṬbḤ3,* p.28:no.37. Cf. Cohen, p.72.
68. See, e.g., *ṬbI1,* p.51:no.12–f.25/53; *AcṬ4,* p.2:f.3/64, p.2:f.4/64; *NzḤ22,* p.47:no.11/36–f.55/63.
69. *NzḤ18,* p.176:no.3/286; *AcṬ3,* p.19:f.12/57; *ṬbḤ1,* p.182: no.11.
70. For more detail, and source references, see above, in the discussion of the various forms of divorce, pp.163 *seq.*
71. See, e.g., *JfQ1,* p.37:no.65–f.71/52; *JfQ2,* p.430:no.415–f.58/59; *NzḤ20,* p.128:no.2/56; *AcṬ3,* p.83:f.17/58.
72. See, e.g., *ṬbI1,* p.249:no.5–f.8/64; *AcI1,* p.76:f.47/50. Cf. Granqvist, vol.2, p.286.
73. See, e.g., *NzḤ20,* p.98:no.13/13; *AcṬ3,* p.57:f.45/57; *ṬbI1,* p.238:no.26–f. 28/63 (the wife wished to stipulate that if the husband did not pay her the monthly maintenance or fell one week behind with the payments he should have to divorce her).

74. See, e.g., *AcṬ2,* pp.152–4. Cf. Rosenfeld, *Peasants,* p.130.
75. *JfQ1,* p.56:no.87–f.71/52; *NzḤ20,* p.5:no.8/99; *AcṬ4,* p.136:f.25/68.
76. See, e.g., *JfQ2,* p.296:no.460–f.70/57; *JfQ3,* p.46:no.76–f.122/63; *JfQ4,* p.146:no.175–f.111/68; *JfQ5,* p.105:no.176–f.296/69; *Ṭb11,* p.198:no.20–f.24/62.
77. Cf. Granqvist, vol.2, p.260.
78. See, e.g., *JfQ2,* p.300:no.464–f.5/58.
79. See, e.g., *JfQ3,* p.47:no.77–f.152/63, p.359:no.501–f.31/67. Cf. Baer, p.37.
80. See, e.g., *JfQ5,* p.105:no.176–f.296/69.
81. See, e.g., *ṬbḤ2,* p.14:no.33, p.226:no.135; *AcṬ3,* p.235:f.12/62; *AcI1,* p. 85:f.59/50; *JfQ5,* p.117:no.198–f.322/69; *NzḤ23,* p.143:no.2/2–f.3/66. Cf. Granqvist, vol.2, pp.259, 266–7, 286; Rosenfeld, *Peasants,* p.129.
82. See, e.g., *AcI1,* p.83:f.56/50 (the husband "drinks wine, smokes hashish and has no occupation but stealing").
83. See Qadrī, art.217. Cf. Baer, pp.35–7; Anderson, *Islamic Law,* pp.51–2; Hinchcliffe, *Divorce,* p.14.
84. *FRL,* arts. 104–7, 109. See *ENFRL*; Qadrī, art.218; Anderson, *Dissolution,* pp.273–6; Goitein and Ben-Shemesh, pp.225–6; Fyzee, pp.148–9.
85. *FRL* art.110. See Goitein and Ben-Shemesh, p.138.
86. Cf. Anderson, *Islamic Law,* pp.51–2; el-Naqeb, p.165.
87. Women's Equal Rights Law, sec.8(b) (addition of sec.181A to Criminal Code Ordinance). See Explanatory Note to Women's Equal Rights Bill, p.192.
88. Cf. Silberg, pp.428–9; Zadok, pp.76–7; Goitein and Ben-Shemesh, pp. 241–2.
89. See Silberg, pp.429 *seq.*; Zadok, p.77.
90. Penal Law Amendment (Bigamy) Law, sec.7.
91. See Explanatory Note to Penal Law Amendment (Bigamy) Bill, 5717–1957; Glasner, p.276; remarks by the Minister of Justice in the Knesset on the first reading of the bill, *KP,* vol.23, p.266 col.2.
92. The ban on divorce against the wife's will is patterned on the Jewish norm of divorce. See Eisenman, p.375; Schereschewsky, pp.298–300; Silberg, pp. 429 sec.
93. This form of restriction of the freedom of divorce has no parallel in Islamic legal reformism in the Arab Middle East.
94. Dower (Prohibition) Bill, 5726–1966 (Private Member's Bill No.26), sec.8. See *KP,* 74th meeting of June 22, 1966.
95. Rosenfeld, too, on the basis of his research, reached the conclusion that 70–80% of divorces were by mutual agreement of the spouses (interview with him).
96. Marriages and Divorces (Registration) Ordinance, 1919.
97. See, e.g., *JfQ1,* p.67:no.106–f.3/52.

98. See, e.g., *JfQ4*, p.157:no.191–f.33/69 (the couple was at first divorced in the *Sharīʿa* Court of East Jerusalem and the divorce was then confirmed by the *Sharīʿa* Court of Jaffa to give it effect *vis-à-vis* the civil authorities); *JfQ5*, p.138:no.229–f.6/70.
99. *AcṬ2*, pp.82, 97.
100. See, e.g., *NzI4*, p.215:no.1/3–f.56/62; *ṬbḤ3*, p.33:no.45; *AcI3*, p.95:no. 125–f.113/58.
101. See, e.g., *JfQ4*, p.142:no.169–f.2/69; *NzI4*, p.215:no.1/3–f.56/62; *AcṬ4*, p.1:f.1/64; *ṬbḤ4*, p.33:no.45.
102. See, e.g., *NzḤ14*, p.18:no.71; *NzḤ18*, p.176:no.3/286; *JfQ1*, p.101:no. 163–f.63/52, p.193:no.4/3–f.55/55; *JfQ3*, p.218:no.357–f.14/66, p.273: no.413–f.97/66; *JfQ4*, p.149:no.178–f.19/69, p.162:no.198–f.41/69, p.153: no.185–f.18/69.
103. Cf. Shaykh Ḥusnī al-Zuʿbī, *AI*, vol.11 (1968), Nos.1–2, p.7.
104. See, e.g., *JfQ3*, p.230:no.369–f.50/66.
105. See, e.g., *JfQ1*, p.85:no.133–f.114/52, p.114:no.193–f.63/53; *ṬbI1*, p.33: no.1–f.10/52, p.36:no.5–f.15/52; *NzI4*, p.159:no.1/6–f.13/54.
106. For more detail see above, in sec.II,3,a "The Wife's Consent to the Divorce," pp.143 *seq.* See Ghālib Shibl, *AI*, vol.1(1950), No.8, p.7.
107. *FRL*, art.105; for a more extensive discussion see Qadrī, arts.251–9.
108. See Schacht, pp.117, 119.
109. *ṬbI1*, p.136:no.24–f.21/58, p.138:no.26–f.32/58; and *NzḤ20*, p.115: no. 3/39, respectively. See also *NzI4*, p.12:no.29–f.56/46 ("during the day"), p. 83:no.1/39–f.93/50 ("tonight"), p.147:no.2/13–f.39/53 ("tonight"); *JfQ3*, p.149:no.240–f.180–63 ("within ten days"); *JfQ4*, p.147:no.176–f.118/68 ("now").
110. *ṬbI1*, p.14:no.1/16–f.34/50, p.94:no.2–f.43/56, p.111:no.17–f.40/57, p. 146:no.9–f.16/59, p.218:no.13–f.10/62, p.242:no.29–f.28/62, p.242:no. 30–f.34/63, p.275:no.23–f.36/64; *NzḤ18*, p.182:no.11/294; *NzḤ19*, p.1: no.5/115; *NzḤ4*, p.125:no.2/22–f.95/52, p.237:no.1/4–f.4/64; *JfQ1*, p.30: no.50–f.8/52; *JfQ2*, p.486:no.522–f.71/61.
111. *JfQ3*, p.273:no.412–f.94/66; *NzI4*, p.31:no.45–f.87/47, p.58:no.3/24–f. 40/49.
112. *HzḤ14*, p.18:no.17; *NzḤ18*, p.180:no.8/8; *NzḤ19*, p.2:no.7/117.
113. *ṬbI1*, p.220:no.15–f.13/63 (her teaching job entailed absence from home for five days a week; on these days, she stayed at her mother's house); *NzI4*, p.227:no.1/19–f.60/63.
114. *ṬbI1*, p.87:no.6–f.15/56.
115. *ṬbI1*, p.130:no.18–f.14/58, p.177:no.18–f.32/60; *NzḤ20*, p.7:no.10/101.
116. *NzḤ15*, p.114:no.11/116.
117. *JfQ2*, p.426:no.413–f.79/59.
118. *AcI1*, p.1:no.1 (the husband contended in court that the wife had become

a human being and that the divorce thus had not become effective).

119. *AcṬ4,* p.7:f.13/64. See also *AcQ5,* p.6:f.5/63; *AcṬ4,* p.34:f.25/65.
120. *JfQ1,* p.2:no.4–fs.3/51, 4/51.
121. *JfQ1,* p.112:no.190–f.52/53.
122. *NzI4,* p.31:no.45–f.87/47; *JfQ1,* p.53:no.82–f.54/52.
123. *AcI1,* p.85:f.59/50.
124. *NzḤ16,* p.23:no.41/242; *ṬbḤ2,* p.101:no.11; *ṬbḤ1,* p.184:no.15; and *NzI4,* p.23:no.37–f.44/47, respectively. Cf. Granqvist, vol.2, pp.273–4.
125. See, e.g., *AcṬ3,* p.58:f.19/57, p.261:f.22/63; *AcṬ4,* p.14:f.27/64.
126. See, e.g., *JfQ3,* p.306:no.446–f.44/66, p.309:no.470–f.30/67, p.350, no. 492–f.59/67.
127. Cf. Anderson, *Islamic Law,* pp.52–3; *idem, Africa,* pp.54, 209.
128. See, e.g., *JfQ3,* p.285:no.425–f.116/66; *JfQ5,* p.60:no.102–f.211/69.
129. *NzḤ17,* p.139:no.293, p.146:no.7/245; *NzI4,* p.179:no.1/7–f.5/57.
130. *NzḤ20,* p.70:no.72/61.
131. *JfQ3,* p.122:no.192–f.61/64.
132. Cf. Granqvist, vol.2, p.272.
133. See, e.g., *JfQ3,* p.294:no.434–f.131/66 and p.295:no.435–f.132/66.
134. See, e.g., *JfS6a,* no.323; *JfS7,* p.3:no.20, p.33a: no.258, p.56:no.460; *JfS88,* p.9:no.180. Cf. Granqvist, vol.2, pp.272–4; Fyzee, p.152 and the sources indicated there.
135. *ṬbI1,* p.116:no.5–f.2/58, p.120:no.9–f.13/58, p.131:no.20–f.26/58, p.146: no.9–f.16/59, p.218:no.13–f.10/62; *NzḤ18,* p.253:no.6/18, p.257:no.5/91, p.257:no.6/92; *NzḤ19,* p.6:no.4/121, p.171:no.7/62; *NzḤ20,* p.72:no. 1/63; *NzI4,* p.156:no.1/3–f.8/54, p.115:no.3/39; *JfQ3,* p.313:no.452–f. 4/67; *JfQ4,* p.126:no.146–f.119/68.
136. *ṬbI1,* p.63:no.17–f.35/54, and p.116:no.5–f.2/85, respectively.
137. See *ha-Aretz,* November 14, 1968.
138. For more detail see above, sec.II,3,a "The Wife's Consent to the Divorce," pp.143 *seq.*
139. *JfQ1,* p.436:no.421–f.18/60. See Criminal File 340/60—Attorney-General *vs.* Shaykh Ṭāhir Ḥamād. The author was told of this device by S. Nawi.
140. For more detail see above, sec.VI. "The *Qāḍī*s and Divorce," pp.180 *seq.*
141. *AcṬ3,* p.2.
142. *JfQ2,* p.426:no.413–f.79/59 ("of her own choice" (*biʾkhtiyārihā*)); *JfQ4,* p.147:no.176–f.118/68 (since the wife had refused to return to her husband, it was she who "had effected the divorce (*awqaʿat al-ṭalāq*) . . . and she consents to the *ṭalāq* . . ."); *ṬbI1,* p.136:no.24–f.21/58, p.220:no.15–f.13/63, p.242:no.29–f.28/62, p.242:no.30–f.34/63; *NzḤ20,* p.7:no.70/101; *NzI4,* p.227:no.1/19–f.60/63, p.237:no.1/4–f.4/64.
143. *JfQ2,* p.426:no.413–f.79/59. See above, sec.III,1,a "Delegated Repudiation," pp.153 *seq.*

144. *ṬbI1,* p.220:no.15–f.13/63 (in his opinion, suspended repudiation did not require permission by the court).
145. *ṬbI1,* p.218:no.13–f.10/62, p.266:no.17–f.22/64; *NzḤ19,* p.1:no.5/115; *NzḤ20,* p.115:no.3/39; *JfQ3,* p.149:no.240–f.180/63.
146. *ṬbI1,* p.242:no.30–f.34/63.
147. Cf. Schacht, pp.59, 164.
148. *Yediᶜoth Aḥaronoth,* December 29, 1959.
149. See, e.g., *JfQ1,* p.6:no.11; *NzḤ14,* p.45:no.1, p.85:no.14/30; *AcṬ1,* p.3: no.4, pp.18, 23–4, 48, 54.
150. In 170 cases, i.e., about 10% of *talāq* divorces, the marriage had not been consummated. See. e.g., *NzḤ18,* p.155:no.18/256.
151. See, e.g., *NzḤ16,* p.53:no.5/283; *NzḤ22,* p.36:no.13/23–f.38/63; *JfQ4,* p.65:no.61–f.12/68; *JfQ5,* p.78:no.132–f.245/69; *AcṬ3,* p.8:f.3/57.
152. See, e.g., *JfQ3,* p.174:no.285–f.48/65; *NzḤ22,* p.18:no.1/1–f.6/63; *AcṬ4,* p.23:f.9/65.
153. See, e.g., *AcṬ3,* p.164:f.7/60.
154. See, e.g., *ṬbḤ1,* p.114:no.87; *ṬbḤ2,* p.114:no.32 and p.114:no.33; *JfQ1,* p.80:no.126–f.104/52.
155. Qadrī, art.281.
156. See, e.g., *JfQ1,* p.196:no.318–f.60/55; *JfQ2,* p.591:no.626–f.46/63; *NzḤ17,* p.116:no.9/260; *NzḤ19,* p.63:no.6/65; *AcṬ3,* p.130:f.27/59, p.191:f.34/60.
157. See, e.g., *JfQ1,* p.96:no.152–f.26/53; *JfQ2,* p.415:no.583–f.80/59; *NzḤ19,* p.160:no.5/52; *NzḤ20,* p.79:no.4/73; *AcṬ3,* p.202:f.6/61.
158. See, e.g., *JfQ3,* p.351:no.493–f.15/67 (the husband will withdraw an application to the district court to restrain the wife from leaving the country).
159. *AcṬ3,* p.99:f.30/58, p.267:f.36/63.
160. In many cases, compensation in the Little Triangle reached IL 5,000, in some cases IL 6,000 or more. See, e.g., *ṬbḤ3,* p.103; no.11, p.131:no.47; *ṬbḤ4,* p.12:no.45, p.116:no.92, p.138:no.1; *TbI1,* p.192:no. 12–f.20/61.
161. Interview with Shaykh Ḥasan Amīn al-Ḥabash. No confirmation in the *sijill*s.
162. See, e.g., *ṬbḤ1,* p.115:no.1/1; *ṬbḤ2,* p.255:no.37; *ṬbḤ4,* p.198:no.26, p.306:no.14.
163. See, e.g., *ṬbḤ4,* p.58:no.19, p.115:no.91, p.116:no.92, p.127:no.103; *ṬbI1,* p.73:no.13–f.19/55, p.140:no.3–f.3/59.
164. See, e.g., *ṬbḤ1,* p.119:no.1/5; *ṬbḤ2,* p.59:no.24, p.142:no.20, p.166:no. 49, p.237:no.14; *ṬbḤ4,* p.127:no.103; *ṬbI1,* p.100:no.8–f.28/57, p.112: no.1–f.42/57, p.113:no.2–f.37/57, p.140:no.3–f.3/59, p.161:no.2–f.6/60; *NzḤ20,* p.119:no.2/43; *NzḤ22,* p.13:no.2/66–f.93/62; *NzḤ23,* p.9:no.9/ 86–f.145/64; *NzḤ24,* p.183:no.25/94–f.169/68, p.265:no.3/6–f.13/70; *AcṬ4,* p.52:f.20/66; *JfQ3,* p.159:no.256–f.5/65, p.246:no.385–f.73/66; *JfQ4,* p.101:no.112–f.66/68, p.103:no.116–f.69/68, p.170:no.212–f.61/69.
165. See, e.g., *ṬbḤ2,* p.57:no.22 (a sale agreement was attached to the judg-

ment); *AcṬ3,* p.120:f.18/59. Shaykh Ḥusnī al-Zuʿbī notes that compensation in land was usual in villages; his letter to the author dated November 22, 1970.

166. See, e.g., *ṬbḤ2,* p.3:no.20, p.63:no.28; *ṬbḤ4,* p.56:no.15, p.191:no.19; *JfQ4,* p.101:no.112–f.66/68 (a house and a cow were to be the property of the wife).
167. See, e.g., *AcI3,* p.133:f.30/59, p.177:f.20/60; *AcT2,* pp.31, 46, 126–7; *AcṬ3,* p.56:f.44/57 (a fine of IL 2,000), p.132; f.29/59, p.171:f.14/60; *AcṬ4,* p.112:f.50/67.
168. *AcṬ3,* p.142:f.38/59.
169. *JfQ1,* p.219:no.343–f.2/56; *JfQ3,* p.97:no.153:f.32/64; *JfQ4,* p.130:no. 153–f.132/68; *ṬbḤ2,* p.157:no.38 (annual amounts of maintenance were fixed); *ṬbḤ4,* p.218:no.50; *ṬbI1,* p.100:no.8–f.28/57; *AcṬ2,* p.86, 126–7; *AcṬ4,* p.59:f.29/66.
170. *JfQ2,* p.590:no.624–f.45/63; *NzḤ23,* p.10:no.1/87–f.148/64.
171. *AcṬ3,* p.206:f.10/61; *AcṬ4,* p.133:f.22/68.
172. See, e.g., *JfQ1,* p.219:no.343–f.2/56; *ṬbḤ4,* p.218:no.50; *AcṬ2,* pp.126–7.
173. See, e.g., *ṬbI1,* p.100:no.8–f.28/58.
174. Shaykh Ḥasan Amīn al-Ḥabash's letter to the author, No.2/2 244 of November 19, 1970.
175. Shaykh Tawfīq ʿAsaliyya's letter to the author dated December 13, 1970. See also *JfQ1,* p.219:no.343–f.2/56 (the husband "tried to induce the wife to consent [to a divorce]" by showing readiness to support her for life).
176. See, e.g., *JfQ3,* p.246:no.385–f.73/66; *NzḤ23,* p.10:no.1/87–f.148/64; *ṬbI1,* p.100:f.28/57.
177. Use is made of conditional particles and the words *muqābil, liqāʾ* and *badal* which have the connotation of "in return for." See, e.g., *ṬbḤ2,* p.82: no.50/55; *ṬbḤ3,* p.38:no.50, p.41:no.55, p.64:no.26; *ṬbI1,* p.100:no.8–f. 28/57, p.112:no.1–f.42/57; *NzḤ18,* p.232:no.8/60; *NzḤ22,* p.17:no.101/ 62, p.123:no.4/19–f.36/64; *NzḤ23,* p.43:no.4/24–f.48/65; *NzḤ24,* p.265: no.3/6–f.13/70; *JfQ3,* p.246:no.385–f.73/66; *JfQ5,* p.8:no.14–f.103/69.
178. *ṬbI1,* p.73:no.13–f.19/55.
179. The earliest cases of payment of compensation to divorced women were in the Little Triangle at the end of 1951 and the beginning of 1952. See *ṬbḤ1,* p.116:no.90, p.119:no.1/5.
180. See Granqvist, vol.2, p.283 n.2 and the sources indicated there. Cf. Anderson, *Africa,* p.268.
181. See, e.g., *ṬbI1,* p.192:no.12–f.20/61; *ṬbḤ3,* p.51:no.12, p.73:no.39, p.91: no.65; *ṬbḤ4,* p.53:no.12.
182. See, e.g., *ṬbI1,* p.82:no.1–f.34/55; *ṬbḤ2,* p.237:no.14.
183. See, e.g., *ṬbI1,* p.73:no.13–f.9/55, p.161:no.2–f.6/60, p.165:no.6–f.14/60.
184. Shaykh Ḥusnī al-Zuʿbī's letter to the author dated November 22, 1970.

185. *AI,* vol.9(1964), Nos.1–2, p.11. For a more extensive discussion see above, pp.212 *seq.*
186. Interview with Shaykh Ḥasan Amīn al-Ḥabash.
187. Cf. Granqvist, vol.2, pp.282–5; Rosenfeld, *Peasants,* pp.127, 131, 150. See the chapter "Polygamy," p.78.
188. Interview with Rosenfeld.
189. *ṬbḤ2,* p.157:no.38; *ṬbḤ3,* p.165:no.12; *NzḤ22,* p.13:no.2/66–f.93/62; *AcṬ4,* p.26:f.13/65, p.110:f.48/67. See *ha-Aretz* of November 14, 1968.
190. *JfQ1,* p.96:no.152–f.26/53; *AcṬ2,* pp. 126–7. Cf. Granqvist, vol. 2, pp.265–6, 268; Anderson, *Africa,* p.260.
191. See, e.g., *ṬbḤ3,* p.218:no.50.
192. See the chapter "Polygamy," pp.76–7.
193. See, e.g., *JfQ2,* p.511:no.476–f.4/62.
194. See, e.g., *JfQ3,* p.215:no.352–f.21/66; *AcṬ3,* p.97:f.28/58.
195. *ṬbI1,* p.116:no.5–f.2/58.
196. Shaykh Ḥasan Amīn al-Ḥabash's letter to the author, No.2/2 244/of November 9, 1970.
197. There were women in the Little Triangle who regarded compensation as "a *sharᶜī* right." See, e.g., *ṬbI1,* p.82:no.1–f.34/55.
198. Shaykh Tawfīq ᶜAsaliyya's letter to the author dated December 13, 1970.
199. See, e.g., *JfQ2,* p.292:no.457–f.3/58; *JfQ3,* p.201:no.331–f.11/66.
200. See, e.g., *JfQ2,* p.496:no.453–f.94/61; *JfQ3,* p.285:no.425–f.116/66; *JfQ4,* p.95:no.99–f.85/68; *AcṬ4,* p.8:f.16/64.
201. See, e.g., *AcṬ3,* p.56:f.44/57, p.120:f.18/59; *ṬbḤ4,* p.229:no.60.
202. See, e.g., *ṬbḤ1,* p.116:no.90; *ṬbI1,* p.100:no.8–f.28/57; *AcṬ2,* p.163.
203. See, e.g., *ṬbḤ1,* p.159:no.3/7, p.166:no.18; *ṬbḤ2,* p.61:no.26, p.63:no.29, p.83:no.51; *ṬbI1,* p.47:no.7–f.18/53, p.52:no.13–f.29/53, p.73:no.13–f.19/55.
204. See, e.g., *ṬbḤ2,* p.59:no.24, p.63:no.28, p.63:no.29, p.227:no.136, p.231:no.5; *NzḤ19,* p.127:no.7/19; *NzḤ20,* p.2:no.4/95; *NzḤ23,* p.10:no.1/87–f.148/64; *JfQ3,* p.205:no.338–f.25/66, p.217:no.355–f.40/66; *JfQ4,* p.163:no.200–f.44/69; *JfQ5,* p.3:no.5–f.95/69, p.8:no.14–f.103/69; *AcṬ2,* pp.94, 106, 124 (the wife: "There are no children and I have therefore agreed with him on *ṭalāq*"), p.86; *AcṬ3,* p.22:f.15/57, p.224:f.2/62.
205. Shaykh Ḥusnī al-Zuᶜbī's letter to the author dated January 2, 1971.
206. See, e.g., *ṬbḤ2,* p.82:no.50/55, p.83:no.51.
207. See, e.g., *ṬbḤ2,* p.134:no.10 and p.135:no.11, p.141:no.18 and p.141:no.19; *NzḤ19,* p.227:no.2/38 and p.228:no.3/39; *NzḤ21,* p.23:no.3/46 and p.24:no.4/47; *AcṬ2,* pp.84–5, 166–7; *AcṬ3,* p.50:f.38/57 and p.51:f.39/57; *JfQ5,* p.26:no.46–f.144/69 and p.27:no.47–f.145/69.
208. See, e.g., *JfQ4,* p.174:no.219–f.90/68.
209. See, e.g., *JfQ3,* p.64:no.98–f.206/63; *ṬbḤ2,* p.53:no.19; *ṬbḤ3,* p.21:

no.26; *NzḤ19,* p.143:no.6/36; *NzḤ24,* p.108:no.21/90–f.161/68; *AcṬ2,* p.66.

210. See, e.g., *NzḤ16,* p.82:no.34/16; *AcṬ3,* p.35:no.25, p.129:f.26/59, p.265: f.31/63; *AcṬ4,* p.15:f.29/64, p.109:f.47/67, p.134:f.23/68.

211. *JfQ2,* p.523:no.500–f.37/62; *JfQ3,* p.338:no.478–f.44/67; *JfQ4,* p.138: no.165–f.126/68; *JfQ5,* p.55:no.92–f.150/69, p.102:no.171–f.258/69.

212. *JfQ2,* p.583:no.608–f.35/63 (a document was submitted indicating that the wife had been divorced with her consent; the *qāḍī* noted that the wife had confirmed her consent in court), p.591:no.626–f.46/63 (the wife maintained that her signature had been forged and that she had not consented to the divorce); *JfQ4,* p.48:no.48–f.89/66 (the wife's attorney maintained that it had been proven in the District Court of Tel Aviv (Criminal File 822/64) and the High Court of Justice (26/66) that the wife's signature had been forged in the presence of the *qāḍī* and asked that the judgment for divorce be set aside).

213. See, e.g., *JfQ5,* p.93:no.156–f.248/69, p.106:no.178–f.259/69; *NzI4,* p. 189:no.1/9–f.30/58.

214. See, e.g., *JfQ1,* p.123:no.208–f.15/54; *JfQ3,* p.230:no.369–f.50/66 (the wife had heard from someone that she had been divorced "and I consented to what I had heard"); *AcQ6,* p.1:no.1/63–f.111/62.

215. See, e.g., *JfQ3,* p.11:no.19–f.77/63; *JfQ4,* p.58:no.54–f.155/67, p.172: no.215–f.63/69; *ṬbḤ2,* p.53:no.19; *NzḤ18,* p.20:no.21/84; *NzḤ19,* p. 179:no.4/71; *NzI4,* p.156:no.1/3–f.8/54; *AcI3,* p.85: no.18–f.?/58.

216. *ṬbI1,* p.108:no.15–f.31/57, p.124:f.18/58, p.131:no.9–f.13/58.

217. *JfQ3,* p.5:no.9–f.88/63.

218. *JfQ5,* p.49:no.85–f.89/69; *ṬbI1,* p.131:no.9–f.13/58.

219. *JfQ5,* p.35:no.58–f.30/69, and p.93:no.156–f.248/69, respectively.

220. In one case, the husband contended that the divorce was not valid because the wife had not consented to it. See *JfQ3,* p.13:no.22–f.81/63.

221. See, e.g., *NzḤ19,* p.179:no.4/71.

222. See, e.g., *AcI1,* p.48:no.41–f.30/49, p.52:no.45–f.40/49, p.57:f.4/50; *AcI2,* p.17:no.14, p.19:no.16; *AcṬ1,* pp.18, 23; *AcṬ2,* pp.30, 32, 64–6, 79, 81; *AcQ5,* p.35:no.35–f.125/61 (the husband asked the court to "hear" the divorce); *JfQ1,* p.148:no.249–f.60/54, p.158:no.263–f.63/54.

223. See, e.g., *JfQ2,* p.308:no.476–f.20/58; *AcṬ2,* p.136; *ṬbI1,* hearing of May 26, 1971.

224. See, e.g., *AcṬ2,* pp.2, 4; *AcṬ4,* p.117:f.5/68.

225. See, *JfQ1,* p.74:no.117–f.74/52 (it was contended that the husband had divorced the wife after receiving a legal opinion *(fatwā sharʿiyya)* from the court for the divorce).

226. *JfQ2,* p.330:no.518–f.72/58, and p.380:no.533–f.18/59, respectively.

227. *ṬbI1,* p.185:no.6–f.9/61 and *Ap1,* p.198:no.19–f.21/62.

228. See, e.g., *Ṭb11,* p.108:no.15–f.31/57.
229. *AcD8,* p.99:no.16/70–f.139/68.
230. See, e.g., *JfQ5,* p.35:no.58–f.30/69 (the arbitrators decided that the husband had wished the marriage to continue and had therefore applied for the establishment of a family council; but they were unable to mediate between the parties and dissolved the marriage, fixing responsibility on the wife for refusing to obey the husband); *NzI4,* p.369:no.9/36–f.72/68; *AcD8,* p. 107:no.24/70–f.9/70; *NzI4,* p.301:no.2/28–f.188/65.
231. *NzI4,* p.237:no.1/4–f.4/64, p.256:no.8/37–f.151/64. See also *NzI4,* p.264: no.4/12–f.7/65; *JfQ4,* p.172:no.215–f.63/69.
232. See Fyzee, p.151.
233. See Qadrī, art.260.
234. See *ibid.,* art.222. This was so in many cases. In one instance, a man from Sidon empowered his father to divorce his wife in Israel in his name. See *NzḤ17,* p.80:no.35/215.
235. The registers of marriage contracts from 1968 onwards record but one such case. *JfMC68,* no.9515.
236. Qadrī, arts.261 *seq.*
237. See Coulson, *History,* p. 207.
238. See *JfQ1,* p.105:no.167–f.43/53, p.166:no.273–f.5/55; *JfQ2,* p.394:no. 552–f.42/59; *NzḤ20,* p.121:no.6/47; *AcI2,* p.36:f.91/51. Cf. Schacht, p.164.
239. *JfQ1,* p.11:no.20; *JfMC68,* no.9515; *AcQ5,* p.31:f.63/63.
240. *JfQ1,* p.266:no.415–f.13/57.
241. *JfQ3,* p.145:no.230–f.108/64, and p.209:no.344–f.10/66, respectively.
242. *JfQ1,* p.166:no.273–f.5/55, *JfQ2,* p.394:no.552–f.42/59; and *AcI2,* p.36:f. 91/51, respectively.
243. *NzḤ20,* p.121:no.6/47.
244. *JfQ1,* p.11:no.21.
245. *JfQ1,* p.266:no.415–f.13/57. See also *JfQ1,* p.105:no.127–f.43/53.
246. *JfQ1,* p.11:no.21.
247. *AcI3,* p.43:no.4–f.9/57.
248. This form of divorce is rare also in Egypt and Iraq. See el-Hamamsy, p.593; el-Naqeb, pp.121–3. Cf., on the other hand, Fyzee, pp.151–2, 466–8.
249. *NzḤ20,* p.121:no.6/47.
250. *JfQ3,* p.145:no.230–f.108/64.
251. *Ṭb11,* p.111:no.17–f.40/57. See also *NzI4,* p.97:no.2/7–f.14/51.
252. *JfQ3,* p.149:no.240–f.180/63.
253. *JfQ1,* p.74:no.117–f.74/52.
254. *JfQ1,* p.112:no.190–f.52/53. Advocate S. Darwish told the author of this case, as reported to him by Shaykh Ṭāhir Ḥamād. The husband contended that the food he had eaten had not been cooked by the wife but was tinned meat which the wife had merely heated. The *Sharīʿa* Court of Appeal

accepted this contention and set aside the judgment for dissolution. *Ap1*, p.8: no.7.

255. *Ṭb11*, p.226: no.17–f.22/64; and *Nz14*, p.58: no.3/24–f.40/49, respectively.
256. *NzḤ16*, p.23: no.41/242.
257. See, e.g., *Ac12*, p.39: f.132/51; *AcQ5*, p.7: no.7/63–f.153/62; *JfQ1*, p.2: no. 4–fs.3/51, 4/51.
258. *Nz14*, p.12: no.29–f.56/46 (their testimony was disqualified on the ground that they were "sinners"), p.83: no.1/39–f.93/50 (the witnesses were found incompetent and their testimony was contradictory), p.215: no.2/22–f.95/52.
259. *AcMC68*, no.3441. Cf. Woodsmall, p.127; Granqvist, vol.2, p.274 n.1. On the other hand, this device was fairly common in various places in Africa. See Anderson, *Africa*, pp.25–6, 29, 72.
260. See, e.g., *Nz14*, p.292: no.2/19–f.30/66.
261. *AcQ4*, p.46–f.105/95; *Nz14*, p.156: no.2/2–f.4/54, p.186: no.2/4–f.16/58.
262. *Nz14*, p.207: no.4/7, p.369: no.6/36–f.72/68.
263. Qadrī, art.218; *FRL*, art.104; *ENFRL;* see Eisenman, p.124.
264. *JfQ2*, p.539: no.529–f.64/62. See also *JfQ1*, p.66: no.105–f.4/52, p.112: no.190–f.52/53; *Ac12*, p.30 [40]–f.134/51. Cf. Fyzee, pp.148–9.
265. See, e.g., *JfQ2*, p.312: no.484–f.24/58, p.460: no.475–f.35/61; *Nz14*, p.54: no.3/18–f.29/49 (the wife: "There was no one present at the divorce but I, he, God, and his second wife . . ."), p.206: no.1/3–f.9/61; *Ac12*, p.41: f.189/52 (she has no witnesses and she does not wish to put her husband on his oath because he "does not fear God and does not heed the oath and does not know to what punishment he who perjures himself is liable"), p.42: f.192/52.
266. See, e.g., *JfQ1*, p.133: no.224–f.33/54, p.247: no.384–f.17/56.
267. See, e.g., *Nz14*, p.52: no.2/14–f.23/49, p.285: no.1/8–f.8/66; *Ṭb11*, p.271: no.20–f.5/64.
268. See, e.g., *JfQ1*, p.181: no.299–f.39/55.
269. The former kind of divorce is called *ibrāʾ* or *mubāraʾa*, the latter *khulʿ*, in legal literature. See Schacht, p.164; Coulson, *Conflicts*, pp.53–4; *idem*, *Succession*, p.19; Fyzee, pp.155–8; Hinchcliffe, *Divorce*, pp.15–16; Goitein and Ben-Shemesh, pp.126, 138–9, 227–8. Qadrī's collection of personal status laws blurs the distinction between these two concepts (see Qadrī, arts. 273–97). For simplicity's sake, these two kinds of divorce are hereinafter referred to as renunciation divorce and compensation divorce.
270. See, e.g., *AcṬ3*, p.89: f.21/58; *JfQ1*, p.77: no.120–f.90/52, p.265: no.4/4–f.22/57; *ṬbḤ1*, p.64: no.60/108, p.174: no.31; *NzḤ23*, p.25: no.2/7–f.18/65.
271. See, e.g., *JfQ5*, p.9: no.16–f.105/69; *Ṭb11*, p.274: no.22–f.32/64; *AcṬ4*, p.4: f.7/64, See the chapter "Dower," p.46.
272. See, e.g., *JfQ1*, p.161: no.267–f.2/55; *JfQ2*, p.570: no.585–f.1/63; *JfQ4*,

p.97:no.104–f.60/68; *ṬbḤ1,* p.174:no.31; *NzḤ15,* p.127:no.5/181; *AcI1,* p.37:no.31–f.21/49; *AcṬ2,* p.19; *AcṬ3,* p.196:f.39/60, p.267:f.36/63.

273. *AcṬ2,* p.96; *AcṬ1,* p.15; and *JfQ1,* p.77:no.120–f.90/52, respectively.

274. See, e.g., *NzḤ24,* p.114:no.3/3–f.4/68; *AcṬ3,* p.111:f.9/59; *JfQ3,* p.210: no.347–f. 34/66.

275. For a more extensive discussion see the chapter "Custody," pp.247 *seq.*

276. See, e.g., *JfQ2,* p.569:no.582–f.132/62; *JfQ4,* p.60:no.102–f.211/69; *AcI1,* p.54:no.48–f.36/49; *AcṬ2,* p.129; *AcṬ3,* p.38:f.28/57; *NzḤ18,* p.1:no.27/ 57; *ṬbḤ1,* p.141:no.41.

277. See, e.g., *JfQ1,* p.275:no.424–f.29/57; *JfQ3,* p.210:no.347–f.34/66, p.351: no. 493–f.15/67 (it was agreed to close a file relating to the divorce and the wife declared that she consented to it); *NzḤ21,* p.2:no.4/19; *NzḤ24,* p.190: no.9/103–f.187/68; *AcṬ3,* p.111:f.9/59.

278. In several cases, it was said that the wife "had redeemed herself" *(fadat nafsahā)* with a certain sum of money. See, e.g., *AcṬ2,* pp.151, 152–4, 161. See also *ṬbḤ2,* p.255:no.37.

279. Cf. Qadrī, art.277

280. *JfQ3,* p.357:no.499–f.70/67; *JfQ4,* p.17:no.17–f.67/67.

281. See, e.g., *AcṬ2,* p.19; *ṬbḤ4,* p.243:no.12.

282. See, e.g., *ṬbḤ1,* p.175:no.32; *ṬbḤ2,* p.14:no.33, p.177:no.61; *NzḤ23,* p. 163:no.2/22–f.32/66; *NzḤ24,* p.6:no.6/51–f.58/66; *AcṬ3,* p.12:f.7/57; *AcṬ4,* p.6:f.12/64. Cf. Granqvist, vol.2, pp.285–7; see Anderson, *Africa,* pp.54, 111, 140, 209, 292, 296; Coulson, *History*, pp.137–8.

283. See, e.g., *ṬbḤ1,* p.175:no.32; *AcṬ3,* p.48:f.36/57, p.49:f.37/57; *AcṬ4,* p. 103:f.41/67; *NzḤ23,* p.163:no.3/22–f.32/66; *NzḤ24,* p.202:no.4/11–f.29/ 69.

284. Cf. Granqvist, vol.2, p.282.

285. *NzI4,* p.234:no.2/30–f.65/63 and p.249:no.2/26–f.127/64 (the man appeared in court a year after divorcing his wife, claiming that she had remarried and demanding the consideration for the *ṭalāq*); *NzḤ22,* p.95:no.10/ 89–f.147/63; *NzI4,* p.291:no.1/18–f.128/65; *JfQ4,* p.41:no.40–f.137/67.

286. *JfQ3,* p.6:no.11–f.129/62.

287. Interview with Shaykh Muḥammad Ḥubayshī.

288. Shaykh Tawfīq ʿAsaliyya's letter to the author dated December 13, 1970. Cf. al-ʿĀrif, pp.133–4; Anderson, *Africa,* pp.320–1; Coulson, *History,* p.136.

289. See, e.g., *JfQ1,* p.275:no.424–f.29/57; *JfQ4,* p.102:no.114–f.70/68; *NzI4,* p.71:no.1/20–f.51/50; *NzḤ14,* p.85:no.14/30; *NzḤ18,* p.29:no.11/96; *NzḤ24,* p.29:no.7/77–f.134/66; *AcṬ3,* p.28:f.19/57.

290. *AcṬ2,* pp.36, 120.

291. See, e.g., *JfQ1,* p.121:no.267–f.2/55; *JfQ4,* p.101:no.112–f.66/68; *ṬbḤ2,* p.57:no.22; *ṬbI1,* p.112:no.421/57; *NzḤ23,* p.37:no.4/18–f.39/65; *NzḤ24,*

p.187:no.6/100–f.184/68; *AcṬ2,* p.147; *AcṬ3,* p.56:f.44/57; *AcṬ4,* p.83: f.22/67.

292. A usual formula of renunciation divorce is " . . . I renounce every one of my matrimonial rights, both prior and subsequent to the *ṭalāq,* in your favor . . . in return for my divorce from you . . ."; the husband then replies at once at the session of the court: "And I, in return for this, divorce you." See, e.g., *ṬbḤ1,* p.1:no.1/2.
293. See, e.g., *AcI1,* p.31:no.25–f.14/49; *AcṬ3,* p.172:f.15/60 and p.173:f.16/60, p.236:f.13/62.
294. See, e.g., *NzḤ19,* p.135:no.9/28; *NzḤ20,* p.5:no.8/99; *NzḤ23,* p.110:n. 9/87–f.138/65.
295. See, e.g., *JfQ3,* p.357:no.499–f.70/67; *NzḤ21,* p.49:no.11/18–f.23/60; *AcṬ4,* p.15:f.29/64.
296. See, e.g., *NzḤ19,* p.41:no.4/39; *AcṬ4,* p.40:f.5/66, p.43:f.10/66, p.52:f. 20/66.
297. See, e.g., *NzḤ17,* p.80:no.35/215; *AcṬ2,* pp.152–4; *AcṬ3,* p.126:f.23/59.
298. See, e.g., *AcṬ4,* p.134:f.23/66.
299. See, e.g., *ṬbI1,* p.155:no.19–f.33/59.
300. *NzI4,* p.162:no.1/10–f.34/54.
301. See, e.g., *JfQ4,* p.130:no.153–f.132/68; *JfQ5,* p.59:no.100–f.207/69, p.105: no.176–f.296/69.
302. Cf. Rosenfeld, *Peasants,* p.129; Granqvist, vol.2, pp.266–7; Dirks, p.89; Anderson, *Africa,* p.209.
303. See, e.g., *JfQ3,* p.192:no.316–f.103/65 (the wife said that her relations with the husband had worsened to an intolerable degree). Cf. Anderson, *Islamic Law,* pp.52–3.
304. See, e.g., *JfQ4,* p.165:no.203–f.49/69 and p.166:no.204–f.50/69, p.184: no.237–f.87/69 and p.184:no.238–f.88/69; *ṬbḤ1,* p.103:no.2/70 and p.103: no.3/71, p.164:no.15 and p.165:no.16.
305. *SAI,* 1969, No.20, p.64.
306. See, e.g., *ṬbḤ3,* p.103:no.11; *ṬbḤ4,* p.53:no.12, p.135:no.114; *NzḤ20,* p.128:no.2/56; *NzḤ22,* p.21:no.4/4–f.9/63; *NzḤ24,* p.2:no.5/45–f.70/66, p.15:no.10/60–f.95/66, p.35:no.4/84–f.147/66.
307. See Anderson, *Dissolution,* pp.271, 273; Coulson, *Succession,* p.19.
308. Qadrī, arts. 44–50; Anderson, *Islamic Law,* pp.44, 47; Schacht, pp.161–2; Goitein and Ben-Shemesh, pp.131–2.
309. *ṬbI1,* p.46:no.6–f.5/53 and p.68:no.5–f.28/54 (her application was dismissed on a formal ground).
310. *JfQ2,* p.528:no.510–f.93/61; *JfQ3,* p.137:no.215–f.10/64; *NzḤ20,* p.149: no.11/88.
311. See the chapter "Age of Marriage," Table II, p. 22.
312. Qadrī, arts. 344–40. See Goitein and Ben-Shemesh, p.139; Fyzee, pp.159–60; Schacht, p.165; Levy, pp.120, 136.

313. *JfQ1,* p.275:no.424–f.29/57; *JfQ2,* p.383:no.537–f.58/58; *NzI4,* p.109: no.1/21–f.86/51 and p.118:no.1/14–f.50/52.
314. But cf. Anderson, *Africa,* p.168.
315. *JfQ2,* p.434:no.421–f.27/55.
316. Qadrī, arts.298–302. See Anderson, *Dissolution,* pp.277–9; Fyzee, pp.165–6.
317. See, e.g., *Ṭbl1,* p.58:no.10–f.14/54, p.145:no.7–f.9/59; *NzI4,* p.362:no.3/26–f.70/68.
318. *Ṭbl1,* p.145:no.7–f.9/59, p.58:no.10–f.14/54; *NzI4,* p.222:no.3/8–f.88/62; *AcI1,* p.75:f.43/50.
319. *NzI4,* p.257:no.9/38–f.42/64, p.362:no.3/26–f.70/68; *AcI2,* p.36 [46]:f.110/52.
320. *Ṭbl1,* p.145:f.7/59. See also *Ṭbl1,* p.66:no.4–f.14/54; *NzI4,* p.47:no.2/4–f.6/49.
321. Qadrī, arts.190, 575–8; *ENFRL;* Anderson, *Dissolution,* pp.279–83; Coulson, *Succession,* pp.19–20, 196–8; Goitein and Ben-Shemesh, pp.229–30.
322. *JfQ2,* p.333:no.525–f.3/59, p.378:no.530–f.14/59; *NzI4,* p.276:no.3/34–f.99/65, p.344:no.9/46–f.123/67, p.347:no.3/3–f.150/67, p.361:no.1/24–f.36/68; *AcD7,* p.62:f.22/67.
323. See, e.g., *JfQ5,* p.52:no.86–f.161/69 (wife asked for dissolution of the marriage 21 years after the husband's disappearance); *AcD6,* p.27:no.27–f.60/64 (16 years); *NzI4,* p.282:no.3/3–f.156/65 (18 years).
324. See, e.g., *JfQ1,* p.148:no.250–f.9/54; *Ṭbl1,* p.46:no.6–f.5/53, p.71:no.10–f.13/55; *NzI4,* p.282:no.4/4–f.177/65; *AcQ5*:p.12–f.13/62.
325. *NzI4,* p.347:no.3/3–f.150/67; *AcI3,* p.78:no.10/58–f.60/57.
326. See, e.g., *JfQ1,* p.43:no.71–f.38/51, p.44:no.72–f.46/51.
327. *NzI4,* p.344:no.9/46–f.123/67, p.185:no.1/3–f.12/58, p.276:no.3/34–f.99/56, p.184:no.1/14–f.32/57; *Ṭbl1,* p.98:no.6–f.10/57; *AcD7,* p.62:f.22/67.
328. *JfQ1,* p.189:no.308–f.10/54, and p.46:no.74–f.32/52, respectively.
329. This is a ground for dissolution under the Sudanese Judicial Circular No. 17 of 1916. See Anderson, *Dissolution,* p.285.
330. *Ṭbl1,* p.46:no.6–f.5/53, p.71:no.10–f.13/55, p.98:no.6–f.10/57.
331. See, e.g., *NzI4,* p.244:no.5/15–f.50/64, p.282:no.3/3–f.156/65.
332. *NzI4,* p.344:no.9/46–f.123/67, p.351:no.7/10–f.123/67 and p.361:no.1/24–f.36/68.
333. See Anderson, *Dissolution,* pp.284–5. For a more extensive discussion see below, sec.VI. "The *Qāḍis* and Divorce," pp.180 *seq.*
334. See, e.g., *JfQ1,* p.117:no.199–f.21/52.
335. A three days' journey on camelback. Qadrī, art.208.
336. *JfQ1,* p.44:no.72–f.46/51, p.106:no.170–f.86/52, p.111:no.178–f.41/53.
337. *Ṭbl1,* p.98:no.6–f.10/57.

338. See, e.g., *AcQ4*, p.10:f.?/62; *AcQ5*, p.63:f.164/63; *AcD6*, p.51:f.139/65. Cf. Granqvist, vol.2, p.202.
339. See, e.g., *JfQ1*, p.46:no.74–f.32/52; *NzI4*, p.184:no.1/14–f.32/57.
340. Cf. Rosenfeld, *Peasants*, pp.41–2, 153.
341. According to *ENFRL*, dissolution under these circumstances does not involve the payment of a consideration (*badal*) to the husband.
342. Qadrī, art.210; *ENFRL*. See Anderson, *Dissolution*, p.285; *idem*, *Islamic Law*, pp.54–5; Coulson, *History*, pp.186–7; Hinchcliffe, *Divorce*, pp.16–17; Goitein and Ben-Shemesh, p.140.
343. See, e.g., *JfQ2*, p.296:no.460–f.70/57; *JfQ4*, p.146:no.175–f.111/68; *JfQ5*, p.4:no.7–f.12/69.
344. See, e.g., *JfQ2*, p.300:no.464–f.5/58; *JfQ3*, p.46:no.76–f.122/63.
345. *JfQ2*, p.434:no.421–f.27/59.
346. *AI*, vol.9 (1964), Nos.3–4, p.4.
347. *JfQ2*, p.296:no.460–f.70/57; *NzI4*, p.179:no.1/7–f.5/57.
348. Anderson, *Islamic Law*, pp.54–5; *idem*, *Dissolution*, p.279; Coulson, *History*, pp.186–8. See also Fyzee, p.166.
349. See, e.g., *JfQ3*, p.63:no.97–f.177/63, p.559:no.501–f.31/67; *Ṭb11*, p.249: no.5–f.8/64.
350. See, e.g., *NzI4*, p.369:no.6/36–f.72/68; *AcD8*, p.107:no.24/70–f.9/70.
351. See, e.g., *JfQ2*, p.434:no.421–f.27/59; *JfQ3*, p.6:no.11–f.129/62, p.70: no.109–f.100/63, p.559:no.501–f.31/67.
352. See, e.g., *Ṭb11*, p.284:no.4–f.8/64; *AcQ5*, p.21:no.21/63–f.151/62.
353. *NzI4*, p.301:no.2/28–f.188/65, p.316:no.5/6–f.6/67.
354. *NzI4*, p.322:no.3/16–f.15/67.
355. See, e.g., *JfQ2*, p.417:no.586–f.57/59; *NzI4*, p.369:no.6/36–f.72/68.
356. See, e.g., *JfQ2*, p.527:no.508–f.62/61; *AcṬ2*, pp.12, 68; *AcI1*, p.79:f.49/50.
357. See, e.g., *JfQ1*, p.60:no.95–f.42/51; *Ṭb11*, p.246:no.2–f.4/64 (she would not live in his house "even if it were a palace in Paradise"); *AcD7*, p.8:f.37/66; *NzI4*, p.374:no.5–f.102/68.
358. *AcṬ2*, p.13; *AcI1*, p.5:no.43–f.34/49 (the husband: "I will not divorce her at any price"); p.76:f.47/50; *AcD7*, p.4:f.20/66; *NzI4*, p.124:no.1/21–f.90/52; *JfQ4*, p.102:no.113–f.50/68.
359. See, e.g., *NzI4*, p.207:no.4/7–f.98/60; *NzḤ23*, p.163:no.2/22–f.32/66; *AcṬ4*, p.34:f.25/65 (the wife was divorced at her request), p.39:f.4/66.
360. Age of Marriage Law, secs. 3–4. See *KP*, vol.5, p.1703 col. 2, p.1733 col.2.
361. See Silberg, p.429; Dykan, p.437; *KP*, vol.5, p.1727 col.2, p.1728 col.2.
362. Cf. Fyzee, pp.91–2.
363. But cf. the attitude of the Chief Rabbinate. *KP*, vol.5, p.1728 col.2; Eilon, p.164.
364. *FRL*, arts.75–7. See Schacht, p.163.
365. *FRL*, arts.13–19, 52–8, *ENFRL*; see Goitein and Ben-Shemesh, pp.220–1.

366. *NzI4,* p.232:no.7/27–f.128/63. See *FRL,* arts.16, 19.
367. *FRL,* arts.13, 54. See *JfQ2,* p.290:no.451–f.63/57; *AcD6,* p.48:f.124/64, p.50:no.51–f.119/64. See also *AcI2,* p.27:f.38/51; *NzI4,* p.49:no.1/9–f.14/49.
368. *FRL,* arts.58, 77; Qadrī, art.126.
369. *JfQ2,* p.501:no.461–f.99/61. See also *JfQ3,* p.154:no.248–f.151/64.
370. See Linant de Bellefonds, pp.321 *seq*; Amīn, pp.149 *seq.*
371. *FRL,* arts. 109, 111–18; *ENFRL*; Qadrī, arts.226–50, 263. See Linant de Bellefonds, pp.365 *seq.*, 395 *seq.*; Schacht, pp.163–4; Anderson, *Islamic Law,* p.42; Coulson, *History,* pp.111–12; Levy, p.121; Goitein and Ben-Shemesh, pp.136–8, 227–8; Fyzee, pp.143–51.
372. E.g., "you are thrice divorced from me according to all the schools; neither a shāfiᶜī nor a Ḥanafī nor another shall bring you back to me"; "*ᶜalayya al-ṭalāq* from you threefold; whenever a Shaykh permits you, a Shaykh shall prohibit you"; "be divorced sixty- and seventyfold"; "be divorced; whenever you are permitted, you shall be prohibited like my sister, according to the four schools of the Muslims"; "you shall never be permitted to me by any school and shall be like my mother and my sister"; "you shall be to me, absolutely, like my mother's back . . ."; "*ᶜalayya al-ḥarām* . . .". See, e.g., *JfQ1,* p.30:no.50–f.8/52, p.53:no.82–f.54/52; p.99:no.159–f.35/53, p.112:no.190–f.52/53, p.247:no.384–f.17/56; *JfQ3,* p.5:no.9–f.88/63, p.206:no.339–f.27/66; *JfQ4,* p.58:no.54–f.155/67; *ṬbI1,* p.14:no.1/16–f.34/50, p.116:no.5–f.2/58, p.131:no.20–f.26/58, p.220:no.15–f.13/63; *NzḤ15,* p.114:no.11/166; *NzḤ20,* p.7:no.10/101; *NzI4,* p.51:no.4/14–f.20/49, p.156:no.1/3–f.8/54; *AcṬ2,* p.68; *AcṬ4,* p.39:f.4/66. Cf. Granqvist, vol.2, pp.273, 275, 279; al-ᶜĀrif, p.133. See Ibn ᶜĀbidīn, p.600; Schacht, pp.164–5; Fyzee, pp.154–5.
373. Judicial dissolution has the effect of one irrevocable divorce. See *FRL,* art. 131.
374. See, e.g., *NzI4,* p.156:no.1/3–f.8/54; *AcI2,* p.17:no.14.
375. See, e.g., *JfQ1,* p.97:no.155–f.28/53; *JfQ2,* p.412:no.579–f.53/59; *ṬbḤ1,* p.102:no.1/61; *NzḤ17,* p.215:no.16/396; *NzI4,* p.207:no.4/7–f.98/60; *AcṬ3,* p.237:f.?/62.
376. *JfQ1,* p.275:no.424–f.29/57; *JfQ2,* p.399:no.559–f.47/59; *NzḤ20,* p.72:no.1/63.
377. See, e.g., *JfQ1,* p.144:no.243–f.50/54; *ṬbI1,* p.108:no.15–f.31/57; *NzḤ18,* p.253:no.6/86; *NzI4,* p.51:no.4/14–f.20/49, p.156:no.1/3–f.8/54.
378. See, e.g., *JfQ2,* p.426:no.413–f.79/59; *JfQ4,* p.147:no.176–f.118/68; *ṬbI1,* p.14:no.1/16–f.34/50, p.87:no.6–f.15/56, p.275:no.23–f.36/64; *NzḤ18,* p.182:no.11/294, p.190:no.8/8; *AcI1,* p.1:no.1; *AcṬ4,* p.34:f.25/65.
379. See, e.g., *JfQ4,* p.165:no.203–f.49/69; *JfQ5,* p.102:no.171–f.258/69; *AcṬ2,* p.43.

380. See, e.g., *JfQ2,* p.323:no.505–f.53/58 (the spouses, "not content with a single divorce, wanted a triple repudiation"); *JfQ3,* p.306:no.446–f.144/66, p.343:no.480–f.51/67; *AcṬ3,* p.204:f.8/61; *ṬbḤ2,* p.53: no.19; *ṬbI1,* p.14: no.1/16–f.34/50.

381. See, e.g., *JfQ2,* p.527:no.508–f.62/61; *AcṬ2,* p.253:f.15/63.

382. *ṬbI1,* p.116:no.5–f.2/58.

383. *AcṬ1,* pp.27–8. There were probably more such cases, which, however, the author was unable to discern because the motive for the divorce (or marriage) was not indicated as it was in this particular case. Cf. Goitein and Ben-Shemesh, p.137; Granqvist, vol.2, pp.281–2; Anderson, *Islamic Law,* pp.42–3.

384. *NzI4,* p.54:no.3/18–f.29/49.

385. Cf. Granqvist, vol.2, p.276, and the sources indicated there; Anderson, *Africa,* pp.167, 213–14, 232, 260, 272, 292.

386. See, e.g., *ṬbI1,* p.108:no.15–f.31/57, p.116:no.5–f.2/58; *JfQ3,* p.5:no.9–f.88/63, p.11:no.19–f.77/63; *JfQ4,* p.67:no.63–f.17/68 (the couple applied for the triple repudiation to be annulled); *NzḤ18,* p.20:no.21/84; *NzI4,* p.156:no.1/3–f.8/54.

387. See, e.g., *JfQ1,* p.133:no.224–f.33/54, p.134:no.225–f.37/54, p.247:no. 384–f.17/56, p.275:no.424–f.29/57; *NzI4,* p.52:no.2/14–f.23/49, p.125:no. 2/22–f.95/52, p.147:no.2/13–f.39/53; *AcṬ4,* p.1:f.1/64, p.13:f.26/64, p.39: f.4/66.

388. See, e.g., *JfQ4,* p.17:no.17–f.67/67; *NzḤ21,* p.173:no.2/44–f.63/62.

389. See, e.g., *NzḤ14,* p.18:no.71; *NzI4,* p.48:no.4/6–f.8/49. Cf. Rosenfeld, *Peasants,* p.129; Anderson, *Africa,* p.244.

390. See, e.g., *NzḤ15,* p.127:no.5/181; *NzḤ20,* p.24:no.11/125.

391. *ṬbḤ1,* p.184:no.15; *ṬbI1,* p.130:no.18–f.14/58.

392. See, e.g., *JfQ3,* p.358:no.500–f.71/67; *JfQ5,* p.96:no.161–f.246/69.

393. See, e.g., *JfQ1,* p.18:no.30, p.54:no.84–f.62/52; *ṬbḤ4,* p.259:no.30–f. 55/66; *ṬbI1,* p.130:no.18–f.14/58.

394. *ṬbI1,* p.11:no.2/12–f.26/50; *NzḤ14,* p.18:no.71; *NzI4,* p.58:no.3/24–f. 40/49; *AcṬ2,* pp.156, 159. Cf. Rosenfeld, *Peasants,* p.129; Granqvist, vol.2, p.266.

395. See, e.g., *JfQ4,* p.142:no.170–f.4/69; *JfQ5,* p.49:no.85–f.89/69; *ṬbI1,* p.218:no.13–f.10/62; *NzḤ19,* p.2:no.7/117, p.5:no.3/120; *AcI2,* p.28:f.41/ 51; *AcṬ3,* p.267:f.35/63.

396. See, e.g., *ṬbI1,* p.130:no.18–f.14/54, p.177:no.18–f.32/60, p.178:no.26–f. 32/58.

397. See, e.g., *AcṬ3,* p.254:f.15/63.

398. *ṬbḤ1,* p.184:no.15; *ṬbḤ2,* p.101:no.11; *NzI4,* p.23:no.37–f.44/47.

399. *JfQ2,* p.445:no.463–f.65/60; *JfQ3,* p.350:no.492–f.59/67.

400. *JfQ1,* p.104:no.165–f.26/53.

401. *JfQ5,* p.49:no.85–f.89/69 (the waiting-period was seven months because the woman was "perplexed as to her menstruation"), p.96:no.161–f.246/69.
402. *Ṭbl1,* p.177:no.18–f.22/60 and p.181:no.2–f.8/61; *NzḤ17,* p.108:no.17/251; *NzḤ20,* p.44:no.1/26 (the second divorce was irrevocable).
403. See, e.g., *Ṭbl1,* p.31:no.16–f.38/51.
404. *NzI4,* p.23:no.37–f.44/47, p.36:no.52–f.108/47, p.285:no.1/8–f.8/66; *Ṭbl1,* p.14:no.1/16–f.34/50; *AcI3,* p.100:no.130–f.116/58.
405. *NzI4,* p.101:no.1/13–f.40/51.
406. *FRL,* arts.139–47, 150–1; Qadrī, arts.315, 324–8. See Eisenman, p.127.
407. *FRL,* art.144. See, e.g., *JfQ1,* p.101:no.163–fs.63/52, 12/53; *JfQ4,* p.162:no.199–f.25/69; *AcI2,* p.32:f.77/51.
408. See, e.g., *JfQ1,* p.64:no.102–f.16/52; *NzI4,* p.90:no.1/1–f.2/51.
409. *Ṭbl1,* p.64:no.1–f.37/54.
410. *JfQ4,* p.162:no.199–f.25/69; *JfQ1,* p.116:no.198–f.62/53. See Qadrī, art. 326.
411. *GMBCS,* 1948, p.82; *SAI,* 1969, No.20, p.60; *Society,* 1960, p.60.
412. *SAI,* 1969, No.20, p.53.
413. See above, pp.135–6.
414. Legal statistics of personal status matters dealt with by the *sharīᶜa* courts are regularly published in *AI.* Those for 1969 appeared in vol.12 (1970), Nos.1–2, p.53.
415. See Rosenfeld, *Peasants,* pp.128–9. Granqvist, vol.2, pp.268, 284–5.
416. See Rosenfeld, *Peasants,* pp.130–1; Baer, p.36; Shaykh Ḥusnī al-Zuᶜbī, *AI,* vol.8 (1963), Nos.3–4, p.4.
417. Cf. Baer, pp.36–7.
418. *SAI,* 1969, No.20, p.64.
419. Marx, *Social Structure,* p.5. Cf. al-ᶜĀrif, p.133.
420. *GMBCS,* 1948, p.82; *SAI,* 1969, No.20, p.58.
421. Owing to Rabbenu Gershom's Ban. See Schereschewsky, pp.298–300.
422. See the chapter "Age of Marriage," pp.22 *seq.* But cf. Ben Amram, p.15.
423. Rosenfeld, too, believed that the divorce rate was rising in consequence of the ban on polygamy (interview with him).
424. *AI,* vol.1 (1950), No.8, pp.7–8. He stressed the *qāḍī*'s function in establishing domestic peace between the spouses (at interviews).
425. *AI,* vol.8 (1963), Nos.3–4, p.4; *AI,* vol.9 (1964), Nos.1–2, p.6.
426. See Layish, *Qāḍīs,* p.304.
427. See, e.g., *JfQ1,* p.79:no.124–f.100/52; *JfQ2,* p.410:no.576–f.70/59 (Shaykh Ṭāhir Ḥamād); *JfQ4,* p.53:no.49–f.153/67 (Shaykh Tawfīq ᶜAsaliyya), p.104:no.117–f.75/68(the same *qāḍī* tried "to give the matter a different turn acceptable to Allāh"); *Ṭbl1,* p.120:no.9–f.13/58 (Shaykh Ḥasan Amīn al-Ḥabash).

428. See, e.g., *AcṬ3,* p.261 :f.22/63 (Shaykh Amīn Qāsim Mudlij); *JfQ2,* p.430: no.415–f.58/59 (Shaykh Ṭāhir Ḥamād), p.542:no.536–f.33/62.
429. See, e.g., *JfQ3,* p.70:no.109–f.100/63 (Shaykh Ṭāhir Ḥamād), p.294:no. 434–f.131/66 (Shaykh Tawfīq ᶜAsaliyya); *NzI4,* p.362:no.3/26–f.70/68 (Shaykh Ḥusnī al-Zuᶜbī).
430. See, e.g., *NzI4,* p.206:no.9/61 (Shaykh Mūsā al-Ṭabarī).
431. See, e.g., *JfQ1,* p.79:no.124–f.100/52; *JfQ2,* p.410:no.576–f.70/59, p.492: no.445–f.80/61; *AcṬ3,* p.237:f.14/62.
432. See Goitein and Ben-Shemesh, pp.39–40. See also the chapter "Maintenance and Obedience," p.106.
433. *AI,* vol.5(1957), No.4, pp.19–21. See also Shaykh Amīn Qāsim Mudlij, *AI,* vol.9 (1964), Nos.3–4, p.5.
434. See, e.g., *JfQ2,* p.417:no.586–f.57/59; *JfQ3,* p.63:no.97–f.177/63; *NzI4,* p.301:no.2/28–f.188/65.
435. *AI,* vol.8 (1962), Nos.1–2, p.37; *AI,* vol.9 (1964), Nos.1–2, pp.3–4. Interview with Shaykh Ḥasan Amīn al-Ḥabash. See Coulson, *Conflicts,* pp.84, 92; Schacht, p.161; Fyzee, pp.144–7.
436. *AI,* vol.5 (1957), No.4, pp.19–21.
437. *AI,* vol.8 (1963), Nos.3–4, pp.2–3; *AI,* vol.9 (1964), Nos.1–2, p.6.
438. *AI,* vol.10 (1967), Nos.3–4, p.10; *AI,* vol.9 (1964), Nos.1–2, p.9.
439. *AI,* vol.8 (1963), Nos.3–4, pp.2–4; *AI,* vol.9 (1964), Nos.1–2, p.6.
440. *AI,* vol.10 (1967), Nos.3–4, pp.1, 16–18. See also *AI,* vol.5 (1957), No.4, p.19; *JfQ3,* p.338:no.478–f.44/67; *JfQ4,* p.5:no.5–f.98/67; *JfQ5,* p.55:no. 92–f. 150/69.
441. *AI,* vol.10 (1967), Nos.3–4, p.20.
442. See, e.g., *NzḤ18,* p.253:no.6/86, p.257:no.5/91, p.257:no.6/92; *NzḤ19,* p.200:no.8/8; *NzḤ21,* p.50:no.13/20–f.25/60, p.58:no.1/32–f.48/60.
443. Interview with Shaykh Ḥasan Amīn al-Ḥabash. He also spoke in terms of the natural inequality of the sexes.
444. *AI,* vol.1 (1950), No.8, pp.7–8.
445. *AI,* vol.10 (1967), Nos.3–4, pp.5, 14, 18–20, 22.
446. Modern legislation in Arab countries confines the validity of suspended repudiation to cases in which the husband *intends* to divorce the wife. For more particulars see Layish, *Qāḍīs,* pp.295–6, 298, and the sources indicated there.
447. *JfQ1,* p.53:no.82–f.54/52. See also *NzḤ15,* p.114:no.11/166; *NzḤ16,* p.23: no.41/242; *NzḤ18,* p.199:no.8/8; *NzI4,* p.31:no.45–f.87/47.
448. *AI,* vol.9 (1964), Nos.1–2, p.11.
449. See Linant de Bellefonds, pp.389–90; Kerr, p.90 *seq.*
450. al-Abayānī, p.260.
451. *NzI4,* p.237:no.1/4–f.4/64; *Ap1,* pp.71–2:f.23/64. See also *ṬbI1,* p.242:no. 30–f.34/63.

452. *JfQ2*, p.539:no.529–f.64/62; and *AcI2*, p.30 [40]:f.134/51, respectively.
453. *AI*, vol.10 (1967), Nos.3–4, pp.8, 15, and 19, respectively.
454. *AI*, vol.1 (1950), No.8, p.7; *AI*, vol.8 (1963), Nos.1–2, pp.1–2; *AI*, vol.9 (1964), Nos.1–2, p.9.
455. *AI*, vol.9 (1964), Nos.1–2, pp.4–5; and *AI*, vol.11 (1968), Nos.1–2, pp.10–12, respectively.
456. *AI*, vol.10 (1967), Nos.3–4, pp.1, 5, 8, 10, 15–20.
457. See, e.g., *JfQ4*, p.142:no.169–f.2/69, p.230:no.369–f.50/66; *NzḤ19*, p.179:no.4/71; *AcṬ2*, p.48; *AcṬ3*, p.91:f.23/58; *AcṬ4*, p.1:f.2/64, p.13:f.26/64. At a court session in the Little Triangle on May 26, 1971 (attended by the author), Shaykh Ḥasan Amīn al-Ḥabash asked the wife whether she consented to the divorce and whether she had not been pressed by her father (who was present) or others to consent.
458. See, e.g., *JfQ3*, p.313:no.452–f.4/67, p.338:no.478–f.44/67; *JfQ4*, p.11:no.11–f.109/67, p.12:no.12–f.108/67, p.58:no.54–f.155/67; *NzḤ18*, p.257:no.5/91; *NzḤ19*, p.200:no.8/8.
459. See, e.g., *JfQ4*, p.57:no.53–f.150/67; *JfQ5*, p.55:no.92–f.150/69 (the husband submitted the wife's written consent to the divorce, but Shaykh Tawfīq ʿAsaliyya left it to the competent authority to determine whether she had in fact consented because the consent had not been given in court), p.98:no.84–f.191/69.
460. See, e.g., *ṬbI1*, p.131:no.20–f.26/58.
461. See, e.g., *JfQ4*, p.11:f.109/67, p.12:f.108/67; *JfQ5*, p.69:no.118–f.230/69; *NzḤ18*, p.253:no.6/86.
462. *JfQ4*, p.126:no.146–f.119/68 (Shaykh Tawfīq ʿAsaliyya noted that the divorce "is in conformity with the *sharīʿa* but contrary to secular law . . ."), p.172:no.215–f.63/69; *NzḤ19*, p.17:no.4/12, p.27:no.2/23; *NzḤ18*, p.20:no.21/84; *NzḤ19*, p.200:no.8/8; *NzḤ22*, p.47:no.11/36–f.55/63.
463. *ṬbI1*, p.108:no.15–f.31/57, p.116:no.5–f.2/58, p.120:no.9–f.13/58, p.124:no.12–f.18/58, p.131:no.20–f.26/58.
464. *JfQ4*, p.126:no.146–f.119/68; *JfQ5*, p.98:no.84–f.191/69.
465. *JfQ3*, p.5:no.9–f.88/63, p.13:no.22–f.81/63.
466. See p.195. The fact that Shaykh Ḥusnī al-Zuʿbī referred in only one judgment to the question of the criminality of divorce against the wife's will was due to the almost complete absence of such divorces during his tenure.
467. *JfQ4*, p.142:no.170–f.4/69.
468. *ṬbI1*, p.218:no.13–f.10/62.
469. See above, pp.141–2.
470. *AI*, vol.8 (1962), nos.1–2, pp.37–8; *AI*, vol.9 (1964), Nos.1–2, p.10; *ṬbI1*, p.218:no.13–f.10/62, p.220:no.15–f.13/63.
471. *ṬbI1*, p.146:no.9–f.16/59, p.218:no.13–f.10/62, p.220:no.15–f.13/63.

472. See, e.g., *Ṭbl1,* p.242:no.29–f.28/62, p.263:no.16–f.28/62, p.242:no.30–f. 34/63; *Ap1,* f.81/64; *Ṭbl1,* p.268:no.18–f.34/63.
473. *NzI4,* p.58:no.3/24–f.40/49.
474. *JfQ4,* p.147:no.176–f.118/68.
475. *JfQ2,* p.426:no.413–f.79/59.
476. *NzI4,* p.237:no.1/4–f.4/64.
477. *Ap1,* p.50:f.72/63.
478. See, e.g., *NzḤ19,* p.1:no.5/115; *NzḤ20,* p.7:no.10/101.
479. *NzḤ18,* p.182:no.11/294: *NzḤ20,* p.115:no.3/39.
480. See, e.g., *NzḤ18,* p.176:no.3/286; *JfQ5,* p.49:no.85–f.89/69.
481. *AI,* vol.1(1950), No.8, p.7; *AI,* vol.8(1962), Nos.1–2, pp.38–9.
482. *AI,* vol.1(1950), No.8, p.7; *Yediᶜon,* vol.1(1950), No.8, p.4.
483. He did not refer to art.110 of the *FRL,* which requires the husband to notify the *qāḍī* of the divorce, or to the Marriages and Divorces (Registration) Ordinance, 1919, which prescribes, *inter alia,* the procedure for the registration of divorces.
484. *AI,* vol.8 (1962), Nos.1–2, pp.37–8; *AI,* vol.9 (1964), Nos.1–2, pp.4–6. On registration as a procedural device for the introduction of reforms in matrimonial matters used in modern legislation of Arab lands see Coulson, *History,* pp.172 *seq.*
485. *ṬbḤ2,* p.106:no.21.
486. The *qāḍī* sometimes stated expressly that the registration of the divorce was inevitable. See, e.g., *JfQ3,* p.129:no.204–f.100/64, p.209:no.345–f.32/66; *JfQ4,* p.97:no.104–f.160/68, p.107:no.121–f.80/68.
487. See, e.g., *JfQ1,* p.99:no.159–f.35/53, p.111:no.179–f.57/53; *Ṭbl1,* p.77:no. 17–f.25/57, p.108:no.15–f.31/57; *NzḤ19,* p.10:no.3/3, p.200:no.8/8.
488. *JfQ4,* p.17:no.17–f.67/67. See also *JfQ3,* p.230:no.369–f.50/66.
489. See, e.g., *JfQ3,* p.184:no.303–f.77/65, p.206:no.339–f.339/66; *JfQ4,* p.5: no.5–f.98/67, p.157:no.191–f.33/69; *ṬbḤ2,* p.60:no.25; *Ṭbl1,* p.120:no. 9–f.13/58.
490. See, e.g., *JfQ1,* p.14:no.24–f.27/51, p.70:no.125–f.103/52, p.92:no.147–f.23/53; *Ṭbl1,* p.61:no.15–f.27/54.
491. *JfQ4,* p.67:no.63–f.17/68.
492. See, e.g., *JfQ1,* p.114:no.193–f.63/53; *JfQ2,* p.399:no.559–f.47/59; *Ṭbl1,* p.33:no.1–f.10/52, p.35:no.4–f.14/52; *NzḤ19,* p.5:f.3/120; *NzI4,* p.159: no.1/6–f.13/54; *AcṬ2,* p.62.
493. *JfQ3,* p.148:no.237–f.140/64; and *JfQ2,* p.312:no.484–f.24/58, respectively.
494. *AI,* vol.8 (1962), Nos.1–2, p.39.
495. Criminal File, Tel Aviv 376/59–Attorney-General *vs.* ᶜAbd al-Raḥīm Maḥmūd ᶜIrāqī. See also Criminal File, Tel Aviv 616/58, *PM,* vol.22, p.158. Cf. Goitein and Ben-Shemesh, pp.132–3; *ha-Tzofeh* of January 7, 1962.

496. *Ha-Yom* and *Lamerhav* of February 15, 1966; *ha-Aretz* of January 3, 1966.
497. *AcṬ2,* p.48; *AcṬ4,* p.81:f.19/67; *AcD8,* p.99:no.16/70–f.139/68 (the *qāḍī* refused to permit *ṭalāq* because its permissibility "depends according to law on agreement between the spouses").
498. *JfQ2,* p.327:no.512–f.65/58, p.330:no.518–f.72/58. See also *JfQ1,* p.114: no.191–f.58/53; *ṬbI1,* p.51:no.12–f.25/53.
499. *ṬbI1,* p.86:no.5–f.8/56; *AcṬ3,* p.84:f.18/58. See also *AcṬ2,* pp.97, 132; *AcṬ4,* p.117:f.5/68, p.142:f.32/68, p.80–f.18/67; *AcṬ4,* p.5:f.10/64; *AcQ5,* p.35:no.35–f.125/61.
500. See, e.g., *ṬbI1,* p.61:no.15–f.27/54; *AcṬ4,* p.41:f.6/66.
501. See, e.g., *JfQ1,* p.114:no.191–f.58/53; *AcṬ2,* pp.97, 132; *AcṬ4,* p.77:f.15/67. An essentially similar situation has been found to exist in Iraq. According to modern Iraqi legislation, *ṭalāq* must be performed in court. If the husband insists on exercising his right, he is not debarred from doing so, and he is not required to assign reasons for the divorce. The legislator intended to allow the husband time to think again as well as to give the *qāḍī* an opportunity to prevent a divorce where, in his opinion, it is unjustified for other than *sharᶜi* reasons. In other words, the legislator expected to bring about reforms in divorce by judicial means; but the *qāḍī*s did not come up to his expectations: divorce proceedings in court are no more than routine, without the *qāḍī*s trying to influence them. See el-Naqeb, pp. 128-9, 159–64.
502. *ṬbI1,* p.185:no.6–f.9/61 (the wife said: "Even though I be strangled or slaughtered [I shall not mind] so long as my husband does not divorce me; I prefer death to divorce").
503. *AI,* vol.9 (1964), Nos.1–2, p.5.
504. Interview with Yūsuf Dasūqī.
505. *AcD8,* p.99:no.16/70–f.139/68.
506. See, e.g., *JfQ1,* p.158:no.263–f.64/54; *JfQ2,* p.380:no.533–f.18/59.
507. See, e.g., *AcṬ3,* p.243:f.5/63 (the spouses expressed the wish that their marriage be dissolved and "persisted in this wish," and the court granted it), p.244:f.6/63.
508. See, e.g., *JfQ2,* p.430:no.415–f.58/59, p.436:no.421–f.18/60.
509. See, e.g., *NzI4,* p.87:no.5/46–f.115/50; *JfQ1,* p.60:no.95–f.42/51; *Ap1,* p.63:f.13/64.
510. *JfQ3,* p.145:no.230–f.108/64, and p.209:no.344–f.10/66, respectively.
511. See, e.g., *JfQ1,* p.275:no.424–f.29/57; *JfQ2,* p.527:no.508–f.62/61; *JfQ3,* p.329:no.470–f.30/67; *AcṬ3,* p.31:f.22[58]; *AcṬ4,* p.8:f.16/64; *NzḤ18,* p.146:f.7/245.
512. Shaykh Tawfīq ᶜAsaliyya's letter to the author dated December 13, 1970.
513. *ṬbI1,* p.145:no.7–f.9/59; *NzI4,* p.47:no.2/4–f.6/49.
514. *ṬbI1,* pp.58, 66:no.10–f.14/54; *Ap1,* p.12:no.11, p.87:f.1/66, p.20:no.25.

515. *AcI1,* p.75:f.43/50; *AcI2,* p.34:f.26/52; *NzI4,* p.202:no.1/8–f.21/59.
516. *AcI2,* p.36[46]:f.110/52.
517. See, e.g., *NzI4,* p.222:no.3/8–f.88/62 and p.257:no.9/38–f.42/64.
518. *NzI4,* p.362:no.3/26–f.70/68.
519. *Ap1,* p.87:f.1/66.
520. *AcD8,* p.99:no.16/70–f.139/68.
521. *Yediᶜon,* vol.1(1950), No.7, p.3.
522. *JfQ1,* p.43:no.71–f.38/51, p.44:no.72–f.46/51 (the text of the decision of the *qāḍī*s' conference is quoted in these judgments).
523. *AI,* vol.7(1959), No.1, Hebrew Summary, p.2; *JfQ1,* p.106:no.170–f.86/52, p.111:no.178–f.41/53, p.117:no.199–f.21/52, p.140:no.235–f.94/54, p.145:no.246–f.6/53; *Ṭb I1,* p.68:no.5–f.28/54.
524. *Ap1,* p.18:no.21; *AI,* vol.7 (1959), no.1, pp.29, 31.
525. *ṬbI1,* p.71:no.10–f.13/55. See also *Ap1,* p.13:no.13.
526. *ṬbI1,* p.98:no.6–f.10/57.
527. *AI,* vol.7(1959), No.1, p.29.
528. *Ap1,* p.18:no.21; *AI,* vol.7 (1959), No.1, pp.29–30.
529. *AcI2,* p.33:f.83/51, p.60:f.152/53.
530. *AcI2,* p.78:no.10/58–f.60/57 (the judgment was sent to the *Sharīᶜa* Court of Appeal for confirmation and the wife was meanwhile forbidden to remarry); *AcQ5,* p.12:f.13/62; *NzI4,* p.216:no.1/7–f.64/62.
531. A hint of the *siyāsa* doctrine. See Schacht, p.54; Coulson, *Succession,* p.137.
532. *AI,* vol.7 (1959), No.1, pp.29–30; *Ap1,* p.23:no.30.
533. See, e.g., *JfQ1,* p.87:no.137–f.34/52; *JfQ3,* p.49:no.79–f.186/63; *JfQ5,* p.26:no.26–f.134/62.
534. *JfQ1,* p.111:no.178–f.41/53, p.189:no.308–f.10/54, p.48:no.77–f.37/51.
535. See, e.g., *JfQ1,* p.43:no.71–f.38/51, p.106:no.170–f.86/52.
536. *JfQ1,* p.117:no.199–f.21/52.
537. See, e.g., *JfQ1,* p.175:no.289–f.19/55, p.193:no.312–f.47/55.
538. See, e.g., *JfQ2,* p.334: no.525–f.3/59; *JfQ5,* p.34:no.34–f.58/63; *Ap1,* p.18: no.21.
539. *JfQ1,* p.189:no.308–f.10/54[66/55]; *Ap1,* p.19:no.22.
540. See, e.g., *NzI4,* p.244:no.5/15–f.50/64, p.282:no.3/3–f.156/65.
541. *NzI4,* p.344:no.9/46–f.123/67, p.351:no.7/10–f.123/67 and p.361:no.1/24–f.36/68.
542. See Anderson, *Dissolution,* pp.284–5; Coulson, *History,* pp.186, 188–9; Fyzee, pp.163–4, 463. See also the Egyptian Personal Status Bill of 1966, published in *al-Ahrām* of August 27, 1966, and reprinted in *AI,* vol.10 (1967), Nos.3–4, pp.3–4.
543. *JfQ3,* p.161:no.197–f.3/69; see also *JfQ5,* p.52:no.86–f.161/69.
544. See, e.g., *AcD6,* p.27:f.60/64; *AcD8,* p.67:f.17/69.

545. *AI,* vol.7 (1959), No.1, pp.30–2.
546. *Apl,* p.23:no.30.
547. See, e.g., *ṬbḤ1,* p.170:no.24, p.182:no.11; *ṬbI1,* p.51:no.12–f.25/53.
548. *ṬbḤ2,* p.56:no.21, p.58:no23, p.129:no.1, p.272:no.63; *ṬbḤ3,* p.28:no.37; *JfQ1,* p.157:no.261–f.63/54.
549. *NzI4,* p.179:no.1/7–f.5/57; *ṬbI1,* p.249:no.5–f.8/64; *Apl,* p.67:f.19/64; *ṬbI1,* p.284:no.4–f.8/64.
550. *Apl,* p.47:no.69; *ṬbI1,* p.56:no.7–f.31/53.
551. *Apl,* p.63:f.13/64. See also *Apl,* p.83:f.10/65.
552. *AcD8,* p.59:f.120/68; and *AI,* vol.9 (1964), Nos.3–4, pp.3–5, respectively.
553. *AcI2,* p.39:no.140/52; *NzI4,* p.214:no.1/1–f.50/61.
554. *AI,* vol.9(1964), Nos.3–4, pp.6–7; and *JfQ2,* p.296:no.460–f.70/67, respectively.
555. See, e.g., *NzI4,* p.315:no.4/5–f.2/67, p.316:no.5/6–f.6/67, p.330:no.1/27–f.110/67, p.332:no.3/29–f.86/67.
556. *Apl,* p.47:no.69, p.54:f.3/64, p.55:f.4/64, p.63:f.13/64.
557. See, e.g., *JfQ5,* p.35:no.58–f.30/69.
558. *AI,* vol.9(1964), Nos.3–4, pp.2–5.
559. *Apl,* p.47:no.69.
560. See, e.g., *NzI4,* p.256:no.8/37–f.151/64, p.264:no.4/12–f.7/68, p.281:no.2/2–f.151/64, p.292:no.2/19–f.30/66, p.315:no.4/5–f.2/67, p.369:no.6/36–f.72/68; *JfQ5,* p.35:no.58–f.30/69. See also *JfQ3,* p.359:no.501–f.31/67.
561. *NzI4,* p.322:no.3/16–f.15/67, and p.301:no.2/28–f.188/65, respectively.
562. *AI,* vol.9 (1964), Nos.3–4, pp.6–7.
563. See, e.g., *JfQ2,* p.434:no.421–f.27/59 (the husband denied paternity of the son, and the *qāḍī,* regarding this as a cause of discord between the spouses, appointed arbitrators).
564. See, e.g., *JfQ2,* p.417:no.586–f.57/59; *JfQ3,* p.63:no.97–f.117/63.
565. See, e.g., *AcQ5,* p.21:no.21/63–f.151/62.
566. See, e.g., *Apl,* p.63:f.13/64, p.67:f.19/64.
567. *AI,* vol.1 (1950), No.7, p.4; *AI,* vol.11 (1968), Nos.1–2, p.12.
568. S. Nawi told the author that Shaykh Ṭāhir Ḥamād had refused to dissolve the marriages of three minor girls (up to the age of 13) who were brought before him.
569. *JfQ2,* p.290:no.451–f.63/57. Shaykh Amīn Qāsim Mudlij, on the other hand, decided that the marriage was irregular and acknowledged the husband's paternity of the children. See *AcD6,* p.48:no.49–f.124/64.
570. *AI,* vol.10 (1967), Nos.3–4, pp.5, 8–9, 15, 19, 22; *AI,* vol.8 (1963), Nos.3–4, p.3.
571. See, e.g., *JfQ1,* p.126:no.213–f.20/54; *JfQ5,* p.29:no.50–f.48/69; *ṬbḤ1,* p.105:no.1/73; *NzḤ18,* p.20:no.21/84; *NzI4,* p.231:no.4/24–f.123/63; *AcṬ2,* p.143; *AcṬ4,* p.40[1]–f.40/68.

572. See, e.g., *NzḤ15,* p.109:no.5/160; *NzḤ17,* p.108:no.17/251; *NzḤ20,* p.44:no.1/26.
573. *JfQ4,* p.57:no.53–f.150/67, p.58:no.54–f.155/67 and p.67:no.63–f.17/68.
574. *AcṬ1,* pp.27–8.
575. See, e.g., *Ṭb11,* p.77:no.17–f.25/55; *JfQ1,* p.266:no.415–f.13/57; *JfQ5,* p.49:no.85–f.89/69; *NzḤ19,* p.5:no.3/120; *AcI1,* p.56:f.3/50; *AcṬ3,* p. 267:f.35/63.
576. *ṬbḤ4,* p.259:no.30–f.55/66; *JfQ1,* p.54:no.84–f.62/52; *NzI4,* p.36:no.52–f.108/47.
577. *JfQ1,* p.18:no.30. See also *AcI1,* p.56:f.3/50. Cf. Granqvist, vol.2, p.261.
578. See, e.g., *JfQ1,* p.148:no.250–f.9/54; *JfQ3,* p.161:no.197–f.3/69; *AcQ5,* p.34:f.58/63.
579. See Coulson, *Succession,* pp.19–20.
580. See Shaykh Amīn Qāsim Mudlij, *AI,* vol.9 (1964), Nos.1–2, p.2.
581. *AI,* vol.9(1964), Nos.1–2, pp.10–11.
582. Remarks taken down at an interview. See also *Maʿariv* of June 12, 1970.
583. *AI,* vol.9 (1964), Nos.1–2, pp.6–10. The idea of a statutory obligation of the husband to pay compensation to the wife is repeated in Shaykh Ḥusnī's letter to the author of November 22, 1970. See also a suggestion by Advocate Maḥmūd al-Māḍī that "everything should be permitted [by secular legislation] that is not expressly forbidden in the sources of Islamic law." *AI,* vol.9 (1964), Nos.1–2, pp.7–8.
584. *AI,* vol.9 (1964), Nos.1–2, pp.2–3, 11.
585. See Anderson, *Islamic Law,* pp.56–7; *idem, Tunis,* pp.271–2; Coulson, *History,* pp.209–12; *idem, Conflicts,* pp.47–8; Schacht, p.167. These reforms were not mentioned by the *qāḍīs*. See *AI,* vol.9 (1964), Nos.1–2, p.7.
586. Shaykh Ḥusnī al-Zuʿbī's letter to the author dated November 22, 1970.
587. Shaykh Ḥasan Amīn al-Ḥabash's letter to the author, no.2/2 244 of November 19, 1970.
588. *AI,* vol.10(1966), Nos.1–2, p.83.
589. *JfQ2,* p.432:no.418–f.12/60. See also *Ṭb11,* p.97:no.5–f.8/57.
590. See, e.g., *NzI4,* p.90:no.1/1–f.2/51; *JfQ1,* p.64:no.102–f.16/52, p.116:no. 198–f.62/53.
591. See, e.g., *JfQ3,* p.63:no.97–f.177/63 and p.103:no.160–f.24/64; *AcI3,* p.35:fs.29/56, 96/56.
592. See, e.g., *JfQ1,* p.219:no.343–f.2/56; *JfQ2,* p.590:no.624–f.45/63; *AcṬ2,* p.86; *AcT3,* p.206:f.10/61; *AcṬ4,* p.59:f.29/66, p.133:f.22/68.
593. See, e.g., *ṬbḤ2,* p.233:no.8, p.265:no.52; *Ṭb11,* p.192:no.12–f.20/61; *NzḤ22,* p.16:no.5/69–f.97/62, p.97:no.1/96–f.149/63, p.123:no.4/19–f.36/64.
594. See, e.g., *ṬbḤ3,* p.58:no.19.
595. See, e.g., *ṬbḤ2,* p.3:no.20; *Ṭb11,* p.161:no.2–f.6/60.

596. See, e.g., *ṬbḤ4,* p.12:no.45.
597. See, e.g., *ṬbḤ2,* p.166:no.49, p.227:no.136; *NzḤ23,* p.162:no.16/20–f.27/66.
598. *ṬbḤ2,* p.157:no.38; *ṬbI1,* p.100:no.8–f.28/57. In one divorce under such circumstances, which the author witnessed in court, the husband produced a sum of money previously agreed on with the wife and handed it to her in return for her consent. After the session, Shaykh Ḥasan Amīn al-Ḥabash explained that he did not interfere in the matter of compensation in any way (session of May 26, 1971).
599. See, e.g., *ṬbḤ4,* p.127:no.103; *NzḤ23,* p.43:no.4/24–f.48/65, p.183:no.25/94–f.169/68.
600. See, e.g., *AcṬ3,* p.91:f.23/58; *ṬbḤ2,* p.57:no.22, p.59:no.24.
601. See, e.g., *ṬbḤ1,* p.116:no.90; *ṬbI1,* p.73:no.13–f.9/55.
602. *AcṬ4,* p.39:f.4/66.
603. Shaykh Ḥusnī al-Zuʿbī's letter to the author dated November 22, 1970.

Chapter Seven
CUSTODY

I. LEGAL BACKGROUND

Islamic law distinguishes between guardianship (*wilāya*) and the custody of minor children (*ḥaḥāna*). Having regard to the interest of the minor, who needs the proximity of a woman, it lays down that the mother has the best title to *ḥaḍāna*, provided that she meets the conditions of eligibility to this task, viz., that she is adult, of sound mind, honest, responsible and capable of seeing to the minor's education and well-being and is not an apostate (*murtadda*). The mother's right is independent of the legal relationship between the parents; it does not lapse on her divorce. But if after her divorce she marries a stranger, i.e., a man not a *maḥram* (a kinsman of the child within the forbidden degrees), she is denied the right to *ḥaḍāna* so long as the marriage exists. Where there is not a mother or where the mother is denied the right to *ḥaḍāna* for any reason, that right passes to the maternal grandmother and to other female cognative relatives in the order of degrees of kinship and then to female agnative relatives in the same order; only in the absence of eligible women does the right pass to the father and then to male agnatic relatives (*ʿaṣabāt*) entitled to succession, again in the order of degrees of kinship. The period of *ḥaḍāna* ends when the child is seven in the case of a son or nine in the case of a daughter, whereupon the child passes into the charge of the father. The custody of the children in no way affects the father's natural guardianship over their persons. He owes them maintenance during the *ḥaḍāna* period.[1]

The Women's Equal Rights Law, which grants the mother the status of a natural guardian of the children, does not refer expressly to custody,[2] but although section 1 provides that "a man and a woman shall have equal status with regard to any legal act," the mother's precedence over the father in the matter of custody remains unimpaired owing to section

6, which provides that "this law shall not derogate from any provision of law protecting women as women."[3] The Capacity and Guardianship Law, 5722–1962 expressly includes the right to the custody of the children in the guardianship of the parents (section 15); but again, equality in this sphere between father and mother does not do away with the mother's precedence as to custody, although it introduces certain deviations from *sharʿī* law. The law provides that where the parents of a minor live separately for any reason they may, with the approval of the court, agree between themselves which of them is to have custody of the minor, and in the absence of such an agreement or if the agreement is not carried out, the court may determine matters of custody at its discretion, having regard to the interest of the minor, "provided that children up to the age of six shall be with their mother unless there are special reasons for directing otherwise" (section 25). In other words, the *ḥaḍāna* period has been shortened and like treatment has been prescribed for sons and daughters.

II. THE EXERCISE OF THE RIGHT TO CUSTODY BY THE MOTHER

As a rule, a mother enjoyed her right to custody of her minor children. She did not need confirmation of this right from the court unless someone challenged it. The *sijill*s thus reflect only those cases in which the mother wished to exercise this right or someone wished to deny it to her. The questions of custody naturally arose where the parents did not live together. It especially did so where they were divorced and sometimes where the mother was widowed, but it might also concern a married woman who for some reason had left her husband's house or whose husband had deserted her. There is ample evidence of women of different marital status demanding that the court confirm their right to custody of their children, reject attempts from various quarters to deprive them of this right, or direct that children who were taken from them against their, the women's, will be returned to them.[4] A woman sometimes stressed that her right to custody of her children was based on both religious and secular law,[5] and she might enlist the help of the execution office or the welfare officer to realize it.[6]

In dozens of cases of divorce by agreement it was expressly indicated that the children were to remain in the custody of the mother and that the father was to pay maintenance for them or custody money to the mother.[7] In one case, the father undertook to transfer some land and a house to the children.[8] If the divorce agreement does not indicate that the wife renounced her right to custody—and most divorce agreements do not—it means that she continued to have custody. Moreover, a mother sometimes had custody of her children even after the expiration of the *ḥaḍāna* period. This appears from cases in which a relative demanded to take charge of them on the *sharʿī* ground that the period had expired. Several years sometimes passed under these circumstances before application was made to the court for relief against a woman who seemed to be unwilling to give up her children.[9] It may be assumed that retention of the children beyond the *ḥaḍāna* period was more frequent than would appear from the *sijill*s. It was especially likely to occur in cases where the mother brought them up and provided for all their needs by her own efforts or at any rate did not claim maintenance from the father.[10]

In many dozens of cases, the wife at the time of the divorce renounced the custody money or maintenance for the children, provided that they remained in her custody, and she might undertake to keep them at her own expense even after the expiration of the *ḥaḍāna* period; sometimes it was stipulated that if she went back on this undertaking she would have to pay monetary compensation to the husband,[11] and occasionally she renounced everything due to her by virtue of a *sharʿī* right, i.e., maintenance for the children, accumulated maintenance for herself, dower and maintenance for the waiting-period, provided the children remained with her. Renunciation as aforesaid was particularly frequent where the wife's right to custody had lapsed for any reason.[12]

In many cases, the mother concluded an agreement with the father as to the custody of the child. Most of these agreements were made incidentally to divorce. The agreement might relate to the realization of the wife's *sharʿī* right. Thus, for instance, a wife might reserve to herself the choice between keeping the child until he no longer needed her or until the expiration of the *ḥaḍāna* period.[13] The agreement might provide that the wife should keep the child even after that period; usually it imposed certain conditions, such as a limitation of the period of custody,[14] the provision of education during the period of custody,[15] permission for the father to see the children from time to time,[16] careful protection of the children and abstention of the mother from remarrying,[17] and prohibition of the mother (and the child) from living outside the father's place of residence without his consent.[18] A frequent arrangement between the parents was the division (*tawzīʿ* or *taqsīm*) of the children between them: the girls might be handed over to the mother and the boys to the father,[19] but the opposite might also occur.[20] The mode of division seems to have depended on the circumstances of the case; anyhow, there was a tendency to give young children to the mother.[21] Sometimes the child, on reaching puberty, was allowed to choose the parent with whom he would live.[22] A woman might on divorce undertake to assume custody of her husband's children by another wife in addition to her own children and even to pay compensation if she infringed the undertaking. These conditions were probably forced on the woman, who strove to her utmost to attain her release, in return for the husband's consent to divorce her.[23]

The proportion of endogamous wives enjoying the right to *ḥaḍāna* was particularly high in rural society, but it is doubtful whether there was a causal connection between endogamy and the exercise of this right. In fact, if endogamy indeed had any effect here it should have been in the opposite direction, for blood-relationship between the spouses restricts the wife's freedom of action as compared with the position in exogamous marriages. The main factor here was the woman's economic and social position, which was especially significant in the case of divorced and widowed women. A certain measure of economic independence, freedom of movement and social contact is essential to a woman's ability to bring up her children. In traditional society, the structural solution of such problems is the divorced or widowed woman's return to her father's or brother's house, where she stays until—as soon as possible—she marries again (although she loses her right to *ḥaḍāna* if she marries a stranger); this solution is to be understood in terms of kinship and property relations.[24] But in recent years, widows and divorced women have shown an increasing tendency not to return to their fathers' or brothers' houses. Rosenfeld discerned this tendency in the Galilean villages he studied. He notes that widows of all ages were then permitted to keep their children without remarrying. He attributes this to the rapid transition from the extended to the nuclear family.[25] The economic and social position of women varied according to their type of settlement: in the towns, especially the mixed towns, they enjoyed greater economic independence and freedom of social contact than in other types of settlement, a fact which is reflected in the *sijill*s.

III. DEPRIVATION OF WOMEN'S RIGHT TO CUSTODY

Besides the cases where women enjoyed their right to *ḥaḍāna* and even retained their children beyond the *sharʿī* period, there were many cases in which they were deprived of this right for *sharʿī* and other reasons. The most frequent reasons were termination of the *ḥaḍāna* period[26] and marriage to someone not of a forbidden degree of kinship to the children; such a marriage was regarded as an orthodox *sharʿī* ground for deprivation of *ḥaḍāna*, and its validity was usually not disputed even by the mother.[27] Moreover, the mother might on her own initiative deliver the children into the custody of relatives in the order of their entitlement to *ḥaḍāna*, either because she was unable to support them or because she could not devote herself to them owing to her duties toward her new husband and her children by him or because the new husband objected to the presence of children not his own.[28] Occasionally the spouses agreed at the time of the divorce that the children should remain in their mother's custody until she remarried, when they were to pass into the charge of their father.[29] As stated, the dissolution of the mother's marriage to a stranger removes the ground for the denial of her right to *ḥaḍāna*, and there were in fact cases in which she wished to reassert it under these circumstances.[30]

The qualifications for *ḥaḍāna* were framed in accordance with the norms of a traditional society in which the inferiority of women is a basic feature. On the other hand, Muslim women in Israel—in the towns, and also in the large, developed villages—enjoyed a greater measure of economic independence and social contact than they ever had before. Their behavior and habits did not conform to orthodox concepts and gave rise to demands that *ḥaḍāna* be denied to them on various grounds: moral flaws in their conduct and the pursuit of disreputable occupations[31]; frequent absence from home for various purposes,[32] especially work, causing the children to run wild[33]; exploitation of the child for heavy work in the employ of strangers or non-Muslims,[34] disobedience and being declared rebellious (*nāshiza*),[35] etc.

A woman might not accept the removal of her children from her custody and might try to frustrate it in various ways. To an attempt to disqualify her from *ḥaḍāna* on the ground that she would leave the house and thereby neglect her children, one woman reacted by declaring through her lawyer that such an argument was "untenable and invalid from a *sharʿī,* a secular-legal and a modern social point of view," since it was intolerable that a woman should be imprisoned in her house and not be allowed to go out on housekeeping errands.[36] In another case, the wife admitted that her *sharʿī* right to *ḥaḍāna* had lapsed and passed to the paternal grandmother, but her devotion to her little daughter deeply touched the grandmother, and with the latter's consent it was decided that the little girl should divide her time between the two women.[37] A woman might try to disqualify others from *ḥaḍāna* in order to assure it to herself. Thus, in one case, a divorced woman contended that her former husband had their children live together with his second wife and that they were "like orphans" at his house.[38] In another case, a woman asked that her daughter's father be disqualified from *ḥaḍāna* because she had brought up the girl by her own efforts, without assistance from him; he had abandoned them at their gravest hour (during the evacuation of Jaffa in 1948); he had no house where he might bring up the girl properly, in fact, no fixed abode at all; he wished to smuggle the daughter out to an Arab country and give her into the custody of his sister; and in addition, "she will lose her legal right to be a national of this country and to be heir to her mother"; a previous smuggling attempt had ended with the killing of a person; the man was a drunkard and had broken a promise he had made in court during the Mandate to give up drinking; he was "sinful (*fāsiq*), unreliable and could not be entrusted with an educational task, with the protection of honor and its preservation from decay . . . he had already violated the honor of a virgin."[39]

In dozens of cases, a woman renounced her right to *ḥaḍāna.* It seems that only in a few cases did she do so of her own free will—because she wished to join her new husband abroad, because she had married a stranger or for other reasons.[40] It may be assumed that a woman was generally not inclined to give up that right. In most cases, the renunciation was made on divorce, or more exactly, was the condition or one of the conditions for the husband's consent to divorce his wife. In some cases, the judgment states expressly that the wife waived her right to *ḥaḍāna* on condition that the husband divorce her or "in return for" (*muqābil*) a divorce,[41] i.e., as a last resort to obtain her freedom. In one case, the wife opposed a divorce for fear that she might have to give up her two-year-old son.[42] In some cases, a woman was divorced during pregnancy and compelled to renounce her unborn child.[43] Lest the wife were to withdraw her renunciation, the husband frequently stipulated that she would have to forgo future claims in respect of her children and that if she changed her mind and wished to exercise her *sharʿī* right she would have to maintain the children at her own expense or even pay compensation to him as a fine (*gharāma*) for infringing the agreement.[44]

A woman might set a series of conditions to allay as far as possible the bitterness of her renunciation of the right to *ḥaḍāna*. In the case of a very young or unborn child she might stipulate that before he was handed over to his father he should be in her custody for one or several years[45]; that she be enabled to see the child from time to time and to buy him presents and clothes; that the child, if a girl, be allowed to stay the night at her house[46]; and lastly, that if any of these conditions was infringed or the father neglected or caused injury (*ḍarar*) to the child, she should be entitled to claim her right to *ḥaḍāna* and the child should return to her.[47] But these conditions were not routine; as a rule, the wife renounced her right to *ḥaḍāna* on divorce without any conditions. In fact, the divorce agreement sometimes states expressly that the renunciation was made "unconditionally and unreservedly" in return for her freedom.[48]

Only in a few cases—all involving women from urban types of settlement—did the *ḥaḍāna*, when the mother was debarred from exercising it, pass to the maternal grandmother.[49] Usually under these circumstances it passed to the paternal grandmother[50] or to another of the agnatic relatives (*ᶜaṣabāt*), especially to an uncle,[51] the grandfather,[52] or a brother.[53] The custody of the children is a very important matter. Where questions of succession were involved, in addition to kinship relations, considerations relating to the estate would also occur.[54] In traditional society, not only do men take precedence over women, but also agnatic relatives over cognatives ones, and this finds its expression in the sphere of the custody of children.

IV. THE *QĀḌĪ*S AND CUSTODY

The *qāḍī*s were not inclined to apply the provisions of the *sharīᶜa* where an agreement existed between the parties concerning custody of the children, even if this agreement was in flagrant contradiction of the religious-legal norm. Thus, for instance Shaykh Ḥasan Amīn al-Ḥabash and Shaykh Mūsā al-Ṭabarī confirmed agreements leaving the children in the mother's *ḥaḍāna* although she was married to a stranger.[55] The *qāḍī*s almost blindly confirmed divorce agreements in which the wife renounced the custody of her young children.[56] The will of the parties, as manifested in an agreement, was thus stronger than religious-legal provisions, and it might happen that a *qāḍī* would not permit the parties to exercise their *sharʿī* rights once the agreement was in force. In one case, the parents agreed that their son should be in the mother's *ḥaḍāna* until he was 19; a few years later, the father changed his mind, but Shaykh Ṭāhir al-Ṭabarī decided that the question of the implementation of the agreement was not within his competence and referred the parties to a civil court.[57] The contents of the agreement were determined in accordance with local custom, and the *qāḍī* did not interfere as to its details. In fact, he sometimes used arbitration to solve disputes in matters of *ḥaḍāna* without resort to *sharʿī* sanctions. Thus, in one case, a woman claimed that her husband—both belonged to the al-Huzayyil tribe—had taken her daughters from her by force. Shaykh Ṭāhir Ḥamād succeeded in ending the dispute "thanks to Allāh" on certain conditions, including restoration of the daughters to the mother, and appointed a famous shaykh and chief of the al-Huzayyil tribe, who had probably taken part in the arbitration, to serve as a supervisor (*murāqib*) whose decision was to be binding in the event of any difference of opinion between the spouses. In another case, the same *qāḍī* adjourned the hearing in the hope that the couple would reach a settlement, and in doing so suggested solving the dispute in one of the following ways: the daughter should be in the custody of her father, who would provide for her upkeep, but should spend her nights at her mother's house, or she should be sent to a boarding-school.[58]

In the absence of agreement between the parties, the *qāḍī*s had no choice but to apply the religious law. If there was not a clear *sharʿī* ground disqualifying the mother from *ḥaḍāna,* they all took care that she was not deprived of this right: that her children were under her control and that the agnatic relatives paid the children's maintenance and the *ḥaḍāna* money. All the *qāḍī*s stressed, with some differences in wording and style, that *ḥaḍāna* was the mother's right and that she took precedence in this regard over the father and every member of her or his family.[59] Moreover, some *qāḍī*s held that a mother's right to *ḥaḍāna* never lapsed and that if she had renounced it she might cancel her renunciation.[60]

The same degree of strictness was shown by the *qāḍī*s in upholding the right to *ḥaḍāna* of women other than the mother, in the order prescribed by Islamic law. Thus, for instance, Shaykh Ḥasan Amīn al-Ḥabash and Shaykh Mūsā al-Ṭabarī repeatedly decided that the maternal grandmother's right was prior to that of the paternal grandmother.[61]

Where relatives were unwilling to exercise *ḥaḍāna*, the *qāḍī*s compelled them to do so, again in strict adherence to the prescribed legal order.[62] The *qāḍī*s required the relatives to pay maintenance to the minors in accordance with their share in the latters' inheritance.[63]

Although this attitude of the *qāḍī*s was very advantageous to the mother, it seems that its motive was not, as a rule, her best interest or that of the child, but the wish to apply the provisions of the *sharīʿa* unswervingly. This is suggested by their frequent references to Qadrī's collection of laws of personal status, and to Ibn ʿĀbidīn's interpretations.[64] The same motive underlay Shaykh Ṭāhir Ḥamād's opposition to giving a Muslim baby girl of unknown paternity into the custody of a Christian family. He decided that handing the girl over to a non-Muslim for guardianship or adoption was forbidden because it was "contrary to the Muslim *sharīʿa*." On another occasion, he opposed a Jewish family's having the custody of a 15-year-old Muslim girl because "Jewish tutelage is contrary to the *sharīʿa*."[65]

The most significant test of a *qāḍī*'s attitude regarding a woman's rights to *ḥaḍāna* occurred where a bid was made to disqualify her on one of the *sharʿī* grounds. These grounds, are, as stated, based on the norms of traditional society, and a difficulty arose when it was to be determined whether the habits and behavior of a woman in contemporary society were consistent with the conditions of eligibility to *ḥaḍāna* or whether she was disqualified.[66] None of the *qāḍī*s called into question the fact that a woman's right to custody of her children lapses on the termination of the *ḥaḍāna* period. Shaykh Ḥusnī al-Zuʿbī in one case dismissed the plea of a woman that her child was still of tender age and in need of maternal care and female attendance. In another case, he decided that a girl should be returned to her father because after the *ḥaḍāna* period he was entitled more than anyone else to have custody of her."[67] The same attitude was usually taken where a woman was legally disqualified by reason of her marriage to a man not of one of the forbidden degrees of relationship to the children.[68] In one case, a man asked that his former wife be declared disqualified because she had married a stranger. While the case was pending, the woman was divorced by her second husband, and Shaykh Ṭāhir Ḥamād thereupon declared her again eligible for *ḥaḍāna* because "she was now free to attend to her children."[69]

The position is different with regard to the appraisal of a woman's personal qualifications, which are vaguely defined by the *sharīʿa* and whose interpretation is by the nature of things subjective, dependent on each *qāḍī*'s philosophy. Two diametrically opposed attitudes may here be distinguished, an orthodox-conservative one and a liberal one.

Shaykh Ṭāhir Ḥamād was the most typical representative of the orthodox school. He measured a woman's eligibility for *ḥaḍāna* in terms of traditional society, in which women are confined to their homes, debarred from social contacts and outside employment. It therefore did not appear difficult to convince him that a woman who regularly left the house, especially for work, and had close contacts with strangers and non-Muslims, was not fit to have custody of her children.[70]

On the other hand, there were *qāḍī*s whose attitude to a woman's eligibility for *ḥaḍāna* was liberal in that they did not regard her social liberation and freedom of movement as grounds for disqualification. This attitude found its main expression in the judgments of Shaykh Ḥasan Amīn al-Ḥabash. Thus, in one case, this *qāḍī* dismissed a man's action to disqualify his divorced wife from *ḥaḍāna* on the ground that she frequently left the house, abandoning her little girls in the street. He accepted the wife's argument that this demand was unfounded in religious-legal, secular-legal and social respects and that it was intolerable that in this modern age a woman should be confined to her home and not allowed to go out on housekeeping errands. The ex-husband appealed to the *Sharīᶜa* Court of Appeal, which set aside the judgment, declaring that the court below had dismissed the action without entering on the substance of the case and that it should have enabled the man to prove that the girls were neglected as a result of their mother's leaving the house. Shaykh Ḥasan Amīn al-Ḥabash appealed against the setting aside of his judgment, but his appeal was dismissed.[71] The difference in attitude between the two levels of jurisdiction was not confined to the procedural aspect, but expressed different social philosophies.

Shaykh Ḥasan Amīn al-Ḥabash and Shaykh Ḥusnī al-Zuᶜbī did not regard a wife's disobedience or having been declared rebellious a sufficient ground to disqualify her from *ḥaḍāna*.[72] They did not regard it as unlawful if a woman who fled from her husband's house to her premarital abode took her children with her. Shaykh Ḥasan decided in one case that *ḥaḍāna* was "bound up with the *ḥāḍina* herself and not with her place of residence," but that the latter could not, in any event, be a ground for disqualification if it was her own parents' house.[73] This attitude, which is not contrary to the *sharīᶜa*, corresponds to the liberal social outlook of the two *qāḍī*s.

There were definite deviations from the religious-legal norm under the influence of Israeli legislation. Signs of this influence were the application of the principle of the best interest of the child, which is alien to Islamic law,[74] and resort to the welfare officer. Thus, in one case, Shaykh Amīn Qāsim Mudlij rejected an attempt to disqualify a mother from *ḥaḍāna* because she had married a stranger on the ground that under the Women's Equal Rights Law both parents are the natural guardians of their children and that section 25 of the Capacity and Guardianship Law enables the court to deal with the question of custody in accordance with the best interest of the children; since in that case this interest required that they be with their mother, the *qāḍī* refused to take them from her.[75] Shaykh Ṭāhir Ḥamād in one case disqualified a woman from *ḥaḍāna* because of unchaste behavior and decided that the best interest of the child required that he be handed over to his father, and in another case he decided that it was best for the daughter if she was left in the *ḥaḍāna* of the mother.[76] He and Shaykh Ḥasan Amīn al-Ḥabash, sitting as a Court of Appeal, decided, in reliance on the Women's Equal Rights Law, that a daughter's best interest required, in the circumstances of the case, that she remain with her mother or with both her parents so long as they remained husband and wife.[77]

A welfare officer's task is to examine the circumstances of each case involving a minor and to recommend to the court the most desirable solution. He is guided by the principle of the child's best interest. His status and mode of operation are regulated by the Welfare (Procedure in Matters of Minors, Mentally Sick Persons and Absent Persons) Law, 5715–1955.[78] The *qāḍī*s availed themselves a great deal of the services of this official, who attended the hearings of the court and prepared a memorandum (*taqrīr*) recommending a suitable candidate for *ḥaḍāna*. Shaykh Ḥusnī al-Zuᶜbī noted that the *qāḍīs* regularly relied on this memorandum in deciding which of the parents was eligible for *ḥaḍāna*[79]; he, at any rate, frequently had recourse to the welfare officer and always accepted his recommendations. Thus, in one case, it had been contended that a woman's work as a teacher led to neglect of her daughter and that she should therefore be disqualified from *ḥaḍāna*. The welfare officer declared that the daughter should be left with the mother and the *qāḍī* decided accordingly. In anoter case, the welfare officer declared that although the children loved their mother, who was very devoted to them, and did not want to join their father, who had neglected them until then, their interest required that they be handed over to the father because they needed education and a trade, which only he was able and willing to provide. The *qāḍī* decided in accordance with the welfare officer's recommendation. He had asked his opinion although he, the *qāḍī,* had already found that the mother's marriage to a stranger disqualified her from *ḥaḍāna* according to *sharᶜī* law.[80] This case shows that the welfare officer's intervention was not necessarily in favor of the woman if he determined the best interest of the child in accordance with traditional concepts. A similar attitude toward the welfare officer has been taken by other *qāḍī*s in recent years.[81]

An ambivalent attitude is discernible where the *qāḍī* applied substantive elements of the two systems, the secular and the religious, at one and the same time. This was particularly so in the case of Shaykh Ḥusnī al-Zuᶜbī. In one instance, he decided that the best interest of the children required that they should be with their grandfather and not with their mother, who had remarried and had a small child to look after, and then he went on to declare that the grandfather was their *sharᶜī* guardian. In another case, he said that "the court must exercise its discretion, having regard to the best interest of the minor, in accordance with the power vested in it by the Women's Equal Rights Law of 1951 and the Capacity and Guardianship Law of 1962," and added that the mother was the child's natural guardian according to the [secular] law and the holder of the right to *ḥaḍāna* according to the *sharīᶜa.*[82] In yet another case, he declared that the spouses had not yet reached agreement as to *ḥaḍāna* in accordance with section 24 of the Capacity and Guardianship Law, that the mother had the strongest title to the office under article 380 of Qadrī's collection and the strongest claim to custody of the children up to the age of six under section 25 of the Capacity and Guardianship Law, that the court had considered the matter with reference to the best interest of the minors, that no-one had sought to disqualify the mother from *ḥaḍāna* and that she was therefore eligible under article 382 of Qadrī; and "in reliance on the *sharᶜī* provisions and the Capacity and Guardianship Law" he decided that the minors should be given to the mother. He also referred to Goitein and Ben-Shemesh and to al-Abayānī.[83] A similarly ambivalent attitude was adopted by Shaykh Amīn Qāsim Mudlij and Shaykh Tawfīq ᶜAsaliyya.[84] Such an attitude was also reflected in the stand taken by the *qāḍī*s concerning the Egyptian Personal Status Bill of 1966, which, *inter alia,* proposed raising the age of *ḥaḍāna* to 11 years for boys and 13 years for girls.[85]

NOTES

1. Qadrī, secs.380–94, 420. See also Fyzee, pp.189–92; Schacht, p.167; Levy, pp.140–3; Abu Zahra, pp.154–6.
2. The Legal Adviser to the Ministry of Social Welfare, interviewee M. Horvitz, was of the opinion that the custody of children is included in guardianship.
3. See Schereschewsky, pp.203–5; Silberg, pp.420–1.
4. See, e.g., *JfQ2*, p.528:no.579–f.108/62 (a divorced woman asked that her children, whom their imprisoned father had entrusted to a stranger, be handed over to her); *JfQ3*, p.144:no.229–f.123/64 (the wife alleged that the husband had taken her two daughters from her by force), p.272:no.411–f.93/66; *Ṭbl1*, p.29:no.14–f.34/51, p.65:no.2–f.1/55, p.99:no.7–f.23/57 (a widow asked that the court order her husband's children by another woman to return her daughter to her), p.215:no.10–f.6/63; *AcQ4*, p.91:f.106/60; *NzI4*, p.251:no.5/29–f.133/64, p.279:no.3/38–f.159/65.
5. See, e.g., *JfQ2*, p.502:no.462–f.90/61; *Ṭbl1*, p.237:no.25–f.21/63; *AcQ5*, p.54:f.88/63 (the wife said that custody was "her natural right according to religious and secular law").
6. See, e.g., *NzI4*, p.311:no.6/40–f.149/66, p.298:no.1/25–f.29/66, p.309:no.4/39–f.115/66, p.362:no.2/25–f.115/66, p.376:no.8/45–f.68/68.
7. See, e.g., *JfQ5*, p.29:no.50–f.198/69, p.67:no.115–f.227/69; *Ṭbl1*, p.35:no.4–f.14/52; *NzḤ23*, p.37:no.4/18–f.39/65; *AcṬ3*, p.42:f.32/57; *AcṬ4*, p.110:f.48/67.
8. *NzḤ24*, p.257:no.7/81–f.155/69.
9. See, e.g., *JfQ1*, p.41:no.70–f.39/51 (daughter, aged 12 at the time of the hearing), p.108:no.173–f.49/53 (son, over ten years of age); *Ṭbl1*, p.20:no.2/3–f.7/50, p.90:no.11–f.36/56.
10. See, e.g., *Ṭbl1*, p.141:no.4–f.4/59 and p.143:no.6–f.7/59, p.90:no.11–f.36/56; *NzI4*, p.130:no.3/29–f.115/52, p.259:no.2/2–f.111/64.
11. See, e.g., *JfQ1*, p.229:no.254–f.18/56; *JfQ3*, p.157:no.254–f.130/64; *JfQ5*, p.60:no.102–f.211/69 (the wife undertook to support her daughter "voluntarily, for the sake of Heaven" and renounced the daughter's maintenance on condition that she was left in her charge so long as she was in need of protection, "even if she [the mother] should remarry"); *NzḤ17*, p.272:no.19/49; *NzḤ18*, p.212:no.9/34; *NzḤ22*, p.48:no.13/38–f.58/63; *AcṬ2*, p.3:f.?/50, p.74 (the wife, who was pregnant at the time of the divorce, undertook that if she gave birth to a live child she would suckle him, bring him up and support him with her own money for seven years), p.159 (if she went back on her undertaking to support her son gratuitously she would pay his father IL 500); *AcṬ4*, p.8:f.16/64 (the wife undertook to bring up the children at her expense "for life"). The practice has also been observed in Iraq. See el-Naqeb, pp.161–2.

12. See, e.g., *AcI2*, p.7:f.6/51 (the woman had married a stranger); *AcṬ4*, p.23:f.8/65.
13. *AcṬ3*, p.76:f.11/58. See also *AcṬ3*, p.14:f.8/57. The father also sometimes reserved such a choice to himself. See, e.g., *AcṬ2*, p.44; *NzI4*, p.173:no.3/8–f.28/65.
14. See, e.g., *NzI4*, p.145:no.1/12–f.25/53 (the parents had made an agreement that the mother should have custody of the son until he was 19 and that if the father infringed the agreement by claiming the son he should pay a fine of IL 500), p.378:no.1/46–f.128/68.
15. *NzI4*, p.362:no.2/25–f.115/66.
16. See, e.g., *AcI3*, p.31:no.22–f.62/56, p.34:no.27–f.81/56.
17. *AcD8*, p.110:no.27–f.90/70. See also *AcD7*, p.66:f.26/67.
18. *AcṬ3*, p.44:f.34/57.
19. See, e.g., *JfQ3*, p.329:no.470–f.30/67; *AcṬ3*, p.148:f.43/59, p.195:f.38/60.
20. See, e.g., *AcṬ4*, p.82:f.21/67, p.85:f.24/67.
21. See, e.g., *AcṬ4*, p.139:f.29/68.
22. *JfQ3*, p.329:no.470–f.30/67.
23. *AcṬ2*, pp.25, 78.
24. See, Rosenfeld, *Peasants*, pp.40, 132, 152; Baer, p.59.
25. Rosenfeld, *Peasants*, pp.41–2. See also *ibid.*, pp.152–3.
26. See, e.g., *JfQ2*, p.315:no.491–f.38/58; *JfQ3*, p.30:no.50–f.144/63, p.133:no.208–f.95/64; *ṬbI1*, p.20:no.2/3–f.7/50; *NzḤ18*, p.154:no.17/255; *NzI4*, p.130:no.3/29–f.115/52, p.259:no.2/2–f.111/64.
27. See, e.g., *JfQ1*, p.3:no.5–f.5/51, p.95:no.151–f.22/53; *NzI4*, p.178:no.1/6–f.21/57; *AcI2*, p.48:f.57/53; *ṬbI1*, p.95:no.11–f.36/56 (the woman contended that she had married an agnatic (ʿ*aṣabi*) relative of her daughters and that her right to custody had therefore not lapsed).
28. See, e.g., *ṬbI1*, p.19:no.6–f.14/51, p.163:no.4–f.10/60; *JfQ5*, p.84:no.144–f.264/69. See also *NzI4*, p.302:no.1/29–f.97/66.
29. See, e.g., *JfQ5*, p.58:no.99–f.204/69; *JfQ4*, p.128:no.149–f.122/68; *AcṬ4*, p.53:f.21/66 and p.54:f.22/66, p.91:f.29/67, p.110:f.48/67.
30. See, e.g., *JfQ1*, p.262:no.409–f.3/57.
31. See, e.g., *JfQ1*, p.196:no.317–f.61/55 (the wife had fled from the husband's house, lived with a strange man "and joined a nest of corruption"); *JfQ2*, p.383:no.537–f.58/58 (the magistrates' court had convicted the wife of a civil offense); *ṬbI1*, p.29:no.14–f.34/51 (the wife had subsisted by begging).
32. See, e.g., *JfQ1*, p.157:no.262–f.49/54; *ṬbI1*, p.237:no.25–f.21/63 (the wife went out on household errands).
33. See, e.g., *JfQ1*, p.196:no.317–f.61/55; (the wife frequently left the house for the purpose of supporting the husband); *JfQ2*, p.502:nos.462/3–f.90/61; *JfQ3*, p.9:no.15–f.74/63 (it was contended that the wife took employment with Jews), p.327:no.468–f.16/67 (the husband contended that the wife

worked "from morning to four o'clock in the afternoon and that he did not know where she was at midday"); *ṬbI1*, p.215: no.10–f.6/63; *NzI4*, p.298: no.1/25–f.29/66 (the husband alleged that because of her teaching job the wife neglected their daughter and deprived her of "natural suckling").

34. See, e.g., *JfQ2*, p.467: no.488–f.13/61; *ṬbI1*, p.20: no.2/3–f.7/50.
35. *NzI4*, p.349: no.3/6–f.162/67; *ṬbI1*, p.215: no.10–f.6/63, p.228: no.19–f.20/63.
36. *ṬbI1*, p.237: no.25–f.21/63.
37. *AcI1*, p.67: f.34/50.
38. *JfQ1*, p.262: no.409–f.3/57. See also *NzI4*, p.145: no.1/12–f.25/53.
39. *JfQ1*, p.41: no.70–f.39/51. See also *JfQ1*, p.108: no.173–f.49/53.
40. *NzḤ19*, p.15: no.1/9; and *NzḤ18*, p.154: no.17/255, respectively. See also *NzḤ20*, p.158: no.1/100; *JfQ3*, p.238: no.276–f.66/66; *AcQ5*, p.7: no.7/63–f.153/62.
41. See, e.g., *JfQ3*, p.252: no.391–f.77/66; *AcṬ3*, p.236: f.13/62, p.261: f.22/63. For the same practice in Iraq see el-Naqeb, p.161.
42. *ṬbI1*, p.108: no.15–f.31/57 and p.109: no.16–f.24/57.
43. See, e.g., *NzḤ20*, p.113: no.10/36; *NzḤ21*, p.29: no.3/53.
44. See, e.g., *NzḤ20*, p.63: no.3/52; *NzḤ24*, p.149: no.7/47–f.84/68, p.187: no. 6/100–f.184/68; *JfQ3*, p.124: no.194–f.16/64; *AcṬ2*, pp.88, 91.
45. See, e.g., *AcṬ2*, pp.111, 174; *AcṬ3*, p.39: f.29/57; *AcṬ4*, p.123: f.11/68; *JfQ2*, p.557: no.560–f.104/62; *JfQ3*, p.295: no.435–f.132/66.
46. See, e.g., *AcṬ2*, p.91; *AcṬ4*, p.23: f.9/65, p.58: f.28/66, p.121: f.9/68 (the wife might visit her children but not at their father's house, and the children might visit her at her house once a week "from sunrise to sunset"), p.123: f.11/68; *JfQ4*, p.178: no.226–f.68/69; *JfQ5*, p.38: no.63–f.159/69.
47. See, e.g., *AcṬ3*, p.37: f.27/?, p.80: f.15/58; *AcṬ4*, p.47: f.14/66, p.121: f.9/68.
48. See, e.g., *AcṬ3*, p.80: f.15/58.
49. See, e.g., *JfQ5*, p.115: no.194–f.289/69); *NzI4*, p.76: no.2/28–f.72/50. See also *NzI4*, p.265: no.3/15–f.41/65 (the mother entrusted the daughter to her brother for temporary custody during her rebelliousness and absence from her husband's house, and the brother kept her for six years and eventually handed her over to the girl's cousins; the father feared that the 15-year-old girl's chastity would be impaired; the cousins were willing to return her to her father on condition that he first reimburse them for her maintenance and the expenses incurred by them in bringing her up).
50. See, e.g., *ṬbḤ2*, p.133: no.8, p.253: no.35; *NzI4*, p.162: no.1/11–f.46/54, p.254: no.4/33–f.147/64; *AcṬ4*, p.136: f.25/68.
51. See, e.g., *JfQ3*, p.147: no.234–f.128/69; *ṬbI1*, p.90: no.11–f.36/56; *ṬbḤ4*, p.121: no.98.
52. See, e.g., *NzI4*, p.302: no.1/29–f.97/66; *AcD6*, p.52: f.135/64.

53. See, e.g., *Ṭbl1*, p.20: no.2/3–f.7/50; *Nzl4*, p.314: no.2/3–f.14/67.
54. See chapter "Guardianship," pp.265–6.
55. *Ṭbl1*, p.90: no.11–f.36/56; and *AcI2*, p.7: f.7/51, respectively.
56. See, e.g., *AcD6*, p.13: f.22/64; *Nzl4*, p.254: no.4/33–f.147/64; *JfQ4*, p.178: no.226–f.68/69.
57. *Nzl4*, p.145: no.1/12–f.25/53. See also *Nzl4*, p.378: no.1/46–f.68/68.
58. *JfQ3*, p.144: no.229–f.123/64; and *JfQ2*, p.467: no.488–f.13/61, respectively. See also *AcQ4*, p.54: f.199/59.
59. See, e.g., *JfQ2*, p.411: no.578–f.71/59; *JfQ3*, p.9: no.15–f.74/63; *Ṭbl1*, p.115: no.4–f.39/57; *AcI3*, p.37: no.33–f.115/56, p.72: no.48–f.112/57; *Nzl4*, p.197: no.4/8–f.17/59, p.295: no.6/23–f.24/66, p.312: no.1/1–f.163/66.
60. See, e.g., *JfQ2*, p.536: no.534–f.56/62; *Ṭbl1*, p.40: no.10–f.26/52.
61. See, e.g., *Nzl4*, p.76: no.2/28–f.72/50; and *AcQ4*, p.93: f.105/60, respectively.
62. See, e.g., *JfQ3*, p.243: no.381–f.62/66; *Ṭbl1*, p.19: no.6–f.14/51.
63. See, e.g., *JfQ1*, p.62: no.100–f.59/51.
64. See, e.g., *JfQ3*, p.158: no.255–f.124/64; *Ṭbl1*, p.40: no.10–f.26/52, p.99: no.7–f.123/57; *AcQ5*, p.60: f.143/63.
65. *JfQ1*, p.15: no.26, and p.16: no.27/8–f.33/51, respectively.
66. Cf. Fyzee, p.190.
67. *Nzl4*, p.259: no.2/2–f.11/64, and p.265: no.13/15–f.41/65, respectively. A similar attitude is reflected in decisions of Shaykh Mūsā al-Ṭabarī and Shaykh Amīn Qāsim Mudlij. See e.g, *AcI2*, p.48: f.57/53; *AcQ5*, p.15: f.59/61; *AcD6*, p.63: f.175/64.
68. See, e.g., *JfQ1*, p.1: no.5; *JfQ3*, p.30: no.50–f.144/63 (Shaykh Ṭāhir Ḥamād); *Ṭbl1*, p.163: no.4–f.10/60 (Shaykh Ḥasan Amīn al-Ḥabash); *Nzl4*, p.309: no.4/39–f.115/66, p.314: no.2/3–f.14/67, p.314: no.2/3–f.14/67 (Shaykh Ḥusnī al-Zuᶜbī).
69. *JfQ1*, p.262: no.409–f.3/57.
70. See, e.g., *JfQ1*, p.196: no.317–f.61/55; *JfQ2*, p.467: no.488–f.13/61, p.502: no.462–f.90/61, p.502: no.463–f.91/61.
71. *Ṭbl1*, p.237: no.25–f.21/63; *Ap1*, p.56: f.6/64, p.59: f.9/64. See also *Ap1*, p.5: no.4, p.29: no.37. A *sharīᶜa* court in Iraq once disqualified a mother from custody, on the application of her husband, on the ground that she was a Communist; the court of appeal disqualified also the maternal grandmother on the ground that she lent support to her daughter. See el-Naqeb, pp.192–3.
72. *Ṭbl1*, p.215: no.10–f.6/63; *Nzl4*, p.349: no.3/6–f.162/67.
73. *Ṭbl1*, p.228: no.19–f.20/63. See also *Nzl4*, p.376: no.8/45–f.68/68.
74. See Anderson, *Patriarchal Family*, p.232.
75. *JfQ3*, p.157: no.254–f.130/64.
76. *JfQ1*, p.196: no.317–f.61/55. See also *JfQ1*, p.261: no.408–f.11/57.
77. *Ap1*, p.31: no.41. See also *AcQ5*, p.30: f.116/61 and p.8: f.21/63. Modern

Iraqi legislation likewise adopted the principle of "the best interest of the child" in matters of custody, but to no effect because the *qāḍī*s did not apply it; they continued to adhere to Ḥanafī principles as regards the Sunnites and to Jaᶜfarī principles as regards the Shiᶜites. See el-Naqeb, p.200.

78. The welfare officer within the meaning of this law has no standing in the *sharīᶜa* court unless summoned by the *qāḍī* (sec.2); the *qāḍī* may summon him, but is not required to do so. The Attorney-General, on the other hand, may intervene in proceedings of the *sharīᶜa* court whenever he wishes to do so by virtue of his powers under the said Welfare Law or under the Capacity and Guardianship Law (sec.8). The Attorney-General has delegated his powers under these two laws to the District Welfare Officer of the Ministry of Social Welfare (as intimated by the Legal Adviser of that Ministry, M. Horvitz). See Schereschewsky, p.380. For simplicity's sake, the various functionaries of the Ministry of Social Welfare are hereinafter described by the term "welfare officer."
79. *AI*, vol.10(1967), Nos.3–4, p.9.
80. *NzI4*, p.298:no.1/25–f.29/66, and p.309:no.4/39–f.115/66, respectively. See also *NzI4*, p.280:no.1/1–f.111/64, p.311:no.6/40–f.149/66, p.353:no. 3/13–f.145/67, p.362:no.2/25–f.115/66, p.376:no.8/45–f.68/68. Advocate Darwish told the author of a case in which he persuaded the *Sharīᶜa* Court of Nazareth to leave a child with his mother, having regard to his best interest, although he was past the age of *ḥāḍāna*; the *qāḍī* decided accordingly in the light of an opinion of the welfare officer.
81. See, e.g., *AcṬ4*, p.136:f.25/68; *JfQ3*, p.244:no.382–f.50/66.
82. *NzI4*, p.302:no.1/29, and p.335:no.8/34–f.93/67, respectively.
83. *NzI4,* p.376:no.8/45–f.68/68 (al-Abayānī, pt.2, p.85).
84. See, e.g., *AcD7*, p.26:f.92/66; *JfQ5*, p.84:no.144–f.264/69.
85. *AI*, vol.10(1967), Nos.3–4, pp.5, 15, 9–10, and 19, respectively.

Chapter Eight
GUARDIANSHIP

I. LEGAL BACKGROUND

Islamic law distinguishes between guardianship over the person (*wilāya al-nafs*) and guardianship over property (*wilāya al-māl*). Guardianship over property concerns especially administration of the inheritances of minor heirs (*wiṣāya*). The inequality between men and women is apparent in this sphere as well. The father alone is the natural guardian of his children, and this status corresponds to the patriarchal concept, which regards him as the head of the family. Although a woman is not disqualified from guardianship, she does not serve in this capacity by virtue of blood-relationship; the power is vested in her by appointment only, either by the legal guardian, in which case she is an "elected guardian" (*waṣī mukhtār*), or by the *sharīʿa* court. Article 974 of the *Mejelle* prescribes a combined series of legal guardians and appointed guardians. The status of legal guardian is given only to the father and the agnatic ancestors in ascending order (grandfather, great-grandfather, and so forth). A woman is also discriminated against as to the power to deal with property under her guardianship. Guardianship terminates when the minor reaches puberty. According to the *Mejelle* (section 986), pubescence begins at the age of 12 in the case of a boy and nine in the case of a girl, and is completed in both cases by the age of 15.[1]

The Women's Equal Rights Law, 5711–1951, enabled a woman to be a natural guardian of her children and abolished the discrimination against her embodied in article 974 of the *Mejelle* and in other provisions of religious law. Section 3(a) of the Women's Equal Rights Law provides: "Both parents are the natural guardians of their children; where one parent dies, the survivor shall be the natural guardian." At the same time, the court is competent to deal with matters of guardianship, both over the person and the property,[2] "with the interest of the children as the sole consideration" (section 3(b)).[3] Section 1 of the law, which prescribes equal status for a man and a woman with regard to any legal act, abolished the restrictions imposed by religious law on a woman's capacity to deal with the property of minors under her guardianship. Apart from the new rules expressly laid down in the law, matters of guardianship are still to be dealt with in accordance with religious precepts.[4] The religious court is to follow the new rules unless all the parties are 18 years of age or over and have agreed before the court, of their own free will, to litigate in accordance with the law of their community (section 7).

The Capacity and Guardianship Law, 5722–1962, supplements and develops the principles established by the Women's Equal Rights Law. It distinguishes between natural guardians and guardians appointed by the religious court. Natural guardianship is based on complete equality of the parents as to their duties and rights with regard to their children: they are the natural guardians of the children (section 14); they are to act in agreement and cooperation (section 18); on the death of one of them, the guardianship of the minor is vested in the other (section 28). The principle of equality finds expression also in the status of the children: the same age (18 years) is fixed for daughters and sons for the termination of guardianship (section 3). The law does not distinguish between the person and the property of the minor; both come within the scope of the duties of parents toward their children (section 15), which implies the mother's equal entitlement with the father to deal with the property of the minor children.[5] Under certain circumstances, the court may appoint a guardian for the minor alongside one or both of the parents (sections 17–29 and 33). There is nothing to prevent the appointment of a woman as guardian of a child not her own. The court acts at its discretion in this matter, with the interest of the ward as its sole consideration (section 35); it is not tied to the rigid order of agnates or their testamentary appointees,[6] and even if the appointment of a testamentary guardian is confirmed, this does not affect the natural guardianship of the surviving parent (section 64).

The Capacity and Guardianship Law gives civil authorities standing in matters of minors. The Attorney-General and the welfare officer are authorized to intervene in certain ways (including the institution of legal proceedings) if, in their opinion, it is appropriate to do so in order to protect the minor (sections 68–70).[7] There is some doubt as to the applicability of this law in *sharīʿa* courts. Some think that the provisions relating to guardianship are intended also for religious courts and supercede the religious law. Others say that since this law does not contain an express provision in the matter, as is customary in some other laws, the religious law continues to apply.[8]

II. WOMEN AS GUARDIANS OF THEIR CHILDREN

Women were guardians in about half the approximately 500 cases in which guardianship orders were issued by *sharīʿa* courts. In most instances, they were guardians of their own children. Usually the woman was the sole guardian, but in several dozen cases a *nāẓir,* or additional guardian, was appointed, who was either the father, or an agnatic relative of the minor, or a stranger. The *nāẓir*'s task is to supervise the guardian's activities, lest the children or their property suffer damage.[9] In some cases, a divorced woman became the guardian of her children after some time; in others the spouses agreed to this at the time of the divorce.[10] In dozens of cases, women were appointed guardians over children not their own; such women were either blood-relations of various degrees or strangers. A woman is not disqualified from guardianship under these circumstances even according to the *sharīʿa,* and Israeli legislation is of no significance in this context. In most cases, the woman was an agnatic relative: a germane sister (*shaqīqa*),[11] a paternal aunt (*ʿamma*)[12] and especially the paternal grandmother,[13] but in some instances the maternal grandmother was appointed[14] or even a non-blood-relation, as when a woman became guardian of her husband's children by another wife or of a girl of unknown parentage.[15] The common feature of most of these latter appointments is that the mother and the agnatic relatives had died or were found ineligible for one reason or another.

The majority of guardianship orders deal with the property accrued to minors by way of inheritance.[16] The principle motive for seeking appointment as guardian was thus the property aspect. In many dozens of cases, the woman, very soon after the issue of the guardianship order, applied to the *qāḍī* for permission (*idhn*) to carry out various transactions in respect of property of the minor: to sell it, to exchange it for other property, to consolidate rights scattered over several properties in a single property, to receive compensation for expropriation, and so on.[17] In dozens of cases, a woman applied for a succession order for the estate of her late husband on the very day she was appointed guardian over the property of her children.[18] A woman's appointment as guardian is thus the clearest possible indication of her capacity to hold and dispose of property.

As a matter of fact, such an appointment was nothing new. A sample from the *sijill*s of Jaffa and Nazareth of the Ottoman era reveals that women, of different degrees of relationship to the minor, were appointed in about one-quarter of the cases in which guardianship orders were issued by the courts. Evidence of such appointments is found also in the *sijill*s of Jaffa and Nazareth of the Mandate era,[19] but it seems that they were less frequent then than in Israel.

The *sijill*s contain evidence that Israeli Muslim women were alive to their status as natural guardians of their children and claimed their rights as such, sometimes with express reference to the relevant legislation.[20] In some cases, a distinction (unknown in secular law) was made between guardianship over the person of the minor, in respect of which the woman sought confirmation (*tathbit*) of her status, and guardianship over the property of the minor, in respect of which she sought appointment (*naṣb*).[21] In one case, a woman asked that the uncle of a minor girl be removed from the office of guardian and that she be appointed in his stead, being her mother and the natural guardian of her person and property, as the general law required; in another case, a woman contended that the Knesset had empowered her to handle the affairs of her minor children and that there was no need for the appointment of a guardian by the court; and in yet another case, a woman applied to the High Court of Justice when it seemed to her that the *sharīʿa* court was about to deprive her of her status as a natural guardian of her children.[22] In several cases, both parents were appointed guardians of their children, sometimes with express reference to secular legislation or with the remark that "the parents are the natural guardians,"[23] in open contradiction of the *sharʿī* concept.

It may thus safely be affirmed that Israeli legislation has materially affected the position of women as guardians. But it seems that it is not the only or principle factor, for in most of the cases in which a woman was appointed guardian of her children the appointment was made not by virtue of her legal status but either because there was no natural guardian (in the *sharʿī* sense) or person elected by such a guardian,[24] or because the natural guardian was disqualified by old age, illness or the like,[25] or the office had fallen vacant owing to dismissal, resignation or death of the agnatic guardian.[26] The *maḍbaṭa* (petition) frequently notes the mother was worthy of the office because of her outstanding qualities, "that there is no-one in the land worthier of the *wiṣāya* than the mother,"[27] that her appointment was in the best interest (*maṣlaḥa*) of the minor, or the like.[28] But in all these cases, the mother's appointment was made *ex gratia* and not as of right, or as a provisional measure pending the availability of a natural guardian. Thus, in a case in which the mother had taken the place of the paternal grandfather owing to his inability to serve, the *maḍbaṭa* stated that the grandfather had permitted (*ajāza*) the mother to be a legal guardian (*waṣī sharʿī*) of the minors, and in another case, in which the mother replaced the absent father for seven years, the *maḍbaṭa* stated that "a guardian was required for the duration of the father's absence."[29] Where a woman was appointed guardian of her children on her own initiative, she was frequently careful to point out that there was no natural or elected guardian and that she was capable of carrying out the task.[30] The appointment was usually initiated by the signatories to the *maḍbaṭa,* who were close to the family and could be relied on to know the situation, while the woman agreed to serve, sometimes without material reward.[31] In some cases, the father of the minor appointed the mother, his wife, to be *waṣī mukhtār* on his behalf after his death, and she accepted the appointment.[32]

Urban women provided twice as many guardians as corresponded to the proportion of urban Muslims among the total Muslim population. They enjoyed a better economic and social position than their sisters in other types of settlement, which was also reflected in their ability to handle property matters connected with the office of guardian.[33] Isolated instances of women being appointed guardians occurred in Beduin society, mostly among the Galilean Beduin, who were at a more advanced stage of sedenterization than those of the Negev.

On the other hand, there seems to have been no causal connection between female guardianship and the type of marriage (endogamy or exogamy). The orders are almost equally divided between the two types. It may thus be concluded that blood-relationship between the spouses was not a serious obstacle to the wife's seeking to exercise her right.

Nor did education, at any rate at that time, affect the position of women as guardians. The *Sharīʿa* Courts of Ṭayyiba and of Nazareth had the guardian sign the order of appointment. The *sijill*s of these courts record only a few cases in which a woman actually signed the order with her name (as distinct from her fingermark (*baṣma*) in other cases).[34] There can be no doubt that education will leave its imprint when the generation of girls who grew up in Israel reaches the stage at which the question of guardianship becomes relevant to it.

III. DEPRIVATION OF WOMEN'S RIGHT TO GUARDIANSHIP

In half the cases of orders issued by the courts, women were not appointed guardians of their children. One must of course take into account the fact that some of these orders were issued when the mother was no longer alive or before the enactment of the Women's Equal Rights Law. At the same time, it may be assumed that in other cases the question of guardianship did not arise while the father was alive because as a natural guardian under religious law he did not require appointment or recognition of his status.[35] It thus appears that in a large proportion of cases women did not serve as guardians of their own children. It might happen that they refused the office from the outset or resigned from it on various grounds.[36] In many dozens of cases, they renounced their right to guardianship and consented, ostensibly of their own free will, to the appointment of various agnatic relatives. In somes cases, the renunciation was in favor of other women, especially the maternal grandmother and other cognative relatives.[37] Women might make their renunciation dependent on certain conditions, such as a specific mode of distribution of the estate among the heirs,[38] or withdraw their renunciation on various grounds.[39]

There appear to be various causes of a woman's renunciation of her right to guardianship of her children or of her deprivation of that right. It seems that the woman who renounced was usually not aware of her legal right and accepted the rigid *sharʿī* order of agnatic guardians and their appointees (article 974 of the *Mejelle*). Thus, in one case, a woman said: "I cannot perform the functions of a *waṣī* and have no *sharʿī* right to this guardianship unless the court so wishes . . .," and later she added (apparently after her legal right had been explained to her): "It is all the same to me whether I am a legal or an illegal *waṣī*—I renounce my right to this guardianship and shall content myself with being the *ḥāḍina* of my children . . . and let the court select whom it sees fit to be *sharʿī* guardian. . . ."[40] In many cases, a woman agreed to or acquiesced in the appointment of the paternal grandfather as the guardian of her children or even resigned the office in his favor in the belief that he preceded her in the order of priority.[41] Also significant in this context is the fact that there was not a single case of a woman being appointed sole guardian while the children's paternal grandfather was alive, unless he had renounced his *sharʿī* right for some reason, such as old age or inability to perform the task.[42]

A woman might be disqualified from guardianship (frequently even in her own view) because she was unfit by *sharʿī* and traditional standards or incapable of fulfilling the task properly. Justifications for this were marriage—after being widowed or divorced—to a stranger, i.e., a man not within the forbidden degrees of kinship to the minor[43] (this was the principal ground); neglect of the children[44]; immoral conduct[45]; inexperience and inability in matters of property, especially as regards dealing with the authorities[46]; illness[47]; and various other circumstances.[48]

Pressure within the family over questions of property might force renunciation. Where the renunciation was in favor of the paternal grandfather or uncle, it is very doubtful that it was voluntary. Both had strong reasons for wishing to prevent the fragmentation of the family property after the death of the children's father, and this was comparatively easy to achieve as guardian of their property. In fact, as regards the grandfather, this is the institutionalized method which has received *sharʿī* sanction by his recognition as a natural guardian. In one case in which the mother wished to oust the grandfather from the guardianship on the ground that he was incapable of looking after the children's property owing to weakness of mind, he said that he was a *sharʿī* guardian by the grace of God: "It is God, praise be to Him, who appointed me over him [the minor] and no-one but He is authorized to dismiss me from this *wilāya*."[49] The institutionalized method by which the paternal uncle (*ʿamm*) prevents fragmentation of the family property is to marry his sons to the minor girls or to gain control over the property through guardianship. Thus, in one case in which a woman renounced her guardianship over her daughter in favor of the daughter's uncle, the daughter was the wife of that uncle's son.[50] In another case, the uncle and guardian "was always trying to marry his sons to his brother's minor daughters in spite of the latter's minority and against their will. He also tried to gain control of the property of the minors . . . and in fact gained such control."[51] The Jaffa *sijill* describes a long drawn out, complicated dispute between the brother and the uncle of some minor girls over the management of the girl's share in the estate of their grandfather, who had been a wealthy Jaffa resident. They were alternately appointed guardians of the property of the girls and dismissed for dereliction of duty, and the girls were not free of them until they reached puberty.[52]

Paradoxically, the welfare officer, a creation of the Knesset, contributed to the curtailment of women's rights as guardians of their children. As stated, he is guided in his considerations by the child's best interest, which does not always coincide with the best interest of the mother. The welfare officer translated this principle into terms accepted in traditional Muslim society, in which a woman's ability to provide for the subsistence and education of children is inferior to a man's and in which the kinship factor is still of importance. As a matter of fact, he did not propose candidates for guardianship but weighed up the candidates proposed in the *maḍbaṭa*, and these were generally selected on traditional considerations. He relied chiefly on the opinions of local welfare workers, who were familiar with social realities and supplied him with the relevant facts. He might recommend in principle the appointment of a guardian in addition to the one proposed in the *maḍbaṭa* but leave the choice of the person to the *sharīʿa* court or to the local council on the assumption that they would know how to find a candidate suitable from the point of view of the child's best interest.[53] There was not a single instance of the welfare officer disqualifying someone proposed for the office. In almost none of the cases in which the mother was appointed was it on his initiative.[54]

The appointment of a guardian alongside the mother, which in several cases was requested by her because she found it difficult to manage the affairs of the minor,[55] was not an innovation but had undoubtedly been given considerable encouragement in Israel by the intervention of the welfare officer. The Legal Adviser to the Ministry of Social Welfare explained that his ministry encouraged the appointment of two or more guardians with a view to preventing collusion and embezzlement of the property of the minor.[56] The addition of a guardian beside the mother ostensibly confirmed her right to the natural guardianship of her children without prejudice to the best interest of the child by traditional standards. The appointment of an agnatic relative, especially the paternal grandfather, who is a natural guardian under religious law, alongside the mother is a compromise between the norm of secular law and the social custom supported by the *sharīʿa*. In several cases, the mother and the grandfather demanded to be guardians—by virtue of secular and religious law respectively—and both were appointed.[57] The appointment of the husband's brother or son beside his widow maintained some equilibrium between the interests of the wife and those of the husband's family.[58] In one case, the welfare officer suggested appointing a guardian from the wife's family in addition to the guardian from the husband's family proposed by the *maḍbaṭa*.[59]

In other cases, the welfare officer's intervention to the detriment of the mother was more explicit. Thus, on one occasion, he deprived her of her right to guardianship on the traditional ground that she had married a stranger, and joined the signatories of the *maḍbaṭa* in proposing that the minor's sister be appointed in her stead.[60] In another case, he supported a proposal to appoint an agnatic relative as guardian in addition to the mother, who had married a stranger, and in this connection remarked that the mother's natural guardianship was confined to the persons of the children whereas the agnatic relative was fully entitled to control the management of the entire property, although the distinction between guardianship over the person and over the property does not exist in Israeli legislation.[61] In other cases, the officer accepted the mother's renunciation of the guardianship and agreed to the appointment of an uncle or other agnatic relative even though it was not certain that the renunciation had been of her own free will.[62] In this way, the welfare officer, perhaps unwittingly, sanctioned the restriction of women's rights to guardianship by the court, and even their total deprivation of that right, since his intervention was based on the principle of the best interest of the child, by virtue of which the court may deviate from the provisions of section 3(a) of the Women's Equal Rights Law. This sanction shields the *qāḍī* from a plea of *ultra vires* on a question of material law.[63]

IV. THE *QĀḌĪS* AND GUARDIANSHIP

Most *qāḍī*s were alive to the status of women as natural guardians of their children, although some discovered it rather late.[64] They sometimes noted expressly in the order that the appointment of the mother or of both parents was made in reliance on Israeli legislation.[65] They might even point out to the woman or indicate in the order that as the mother she had the status of a natural guardian.[66] In several cases in which a guardian other than the mother was appointed, such as the paternal grandfather, who, as stated, is a natural guardian according to the *sharīʿa*, this was only done after the mother had renounced her right or agreed to the appointment.[67] Such a renunciation or agreement is not required by religious law, and the author has not encountered it prior to the enactment of the Women's Equal Rights Law.

As stated, the Knesset gave wide discretion to the court to appoint someone other than the natural guardian "with the interest of the children as the sole consideration." In several cases, this principle was consciously applied by Shaykh Ṭāhir Ḥamād and Shaykh Ḥusnī al-Zuʿbī when appointing someone other than the mother.[68] Shaykh Tawfīq ʿAsaliyya also sometimes applied it, though not with reference to Israeli legislation.[69] He and Shaykh Ḥasan Amīn al-Ḥabash made a point of inviting the welfare officer to the hearings of the court, asking his opinion as to the appointment of a guardian and acting in accordance with it, and if the welfare officer was absent from the hearing, he was reserved the right to oppose the appointment.[70] The alertness of the *qāḍī*s to the status of women as natural guardians should probably be attributed in no small measure to the presence of the welfare officer in court.[71]

At the same time, in all cases in which the mother served as guardian, including also cases in which the *qāḍī*s treated her as a natural guardian, she was *appointed* by the court, as had been usual before the enactment of the Women's Equal Rights Law and as in the case of a woman's guardianship of children not her own.[72] This is, of course, a distorted interpretation of the law since a natural guardian does not require appointment.[73] The distinction between natural guardianship and guardianship by court appointment exists also in Islamic law and was thus not strange to the *qāḍī*s; Shaykh Ṭāhir Ḥamād mentioned it in one case in connection with Israeli legislation.[74] Shaykh Ḥasan Amīn al-Ḥabash explained to the author that the court did not really appoint a natural guardian, because he was appointed by Allāh, but only supplied him with a formal certification of his guardianship for the purposes of his contacts with the authorities.[75] In fact, in some cases, Shaykh Ṭāhir al-Ṭabarī gave a certificate of guardianship (*tathbīt wilāya*) to natural guardians within the meaning of the religious law, and Shaykh Ḥusnī al-Zuʿbī, on several occasions, issued such documents to women as natural guardians within the meaning of the general law, although he restricted their powers to the persons of the children and officially *appointed* other guardians for their property. Similarly, other *qāḍī*s issued certificates to natural guardians—within the meaning of the religious law—of the persons of minors and at the same time *appointed* them guardians of the property.[76] It thus seems that some *qāḍī*s tended to limit the mother's natural guardianship to the person of the minor; an express indication of such a tendency is contained in a decision of Shaykh Ḥasan Amīn al-Ḥabash. Shaykh Ṭāhir Ḥamād declared in one case that the guardianship of the persons of the children was indeed vested in both parents by law but that, since the mother had not asked to share the guardianship of the property with the father, he assigned this function to the father alone.[77]

On the other hand, there were cases in which the *qāḍī*s applied religious law to matters of guardianship and adhered to the order of guardians prescribed by article 974 of the *Mejelle* as if nothing had happened. Shaykh Mūsā al-Ṭabarī and Shaykh Amīn Qāsim Mudlij regarded the father (but not the mother) and the paternal grandfather as natural guardians.[78] Most *qāḍī*s were in the habit of confirming an elected guardian (*waṣī mukhtār*) appointed by a *sharᶜī* natural guardian.[79] Shaykh Mūsā al-Ṭabarī himself appointed his wife to be *waṣī mukhtār* of his children after his death,[80] and in another case a woman contended in the High Court of Justice that this *qāḍī* had meant to deprive her of the guardianship through the children's aunt, who had been elected to the office by their father.[81] In most of the cases in which the mother was appointed it was after it had been found that "there is no real grandfather and no elected guardian on his behalf" or after the *sharᶜī* natural guardian had renounced his position for some reason not relevant to the status of women as natural guardians[82]; under such circumstances, the *qāḍī*s did not, when the mother was alive, necessarily appoint her.[83] They continued, in accordance with the *sharᶜī* norm, to disqualify a woman from the guardianship of her children on the ground that, after being widowed or divorced, she had married a stranger.[84] Since the father's remarriage did not disqualify him under religious law from the natural guardianship of his children, this practice of the *qāḍī*s constituted discrimination against women and was thus quite out of keeping with section 1 of the Women's Equal Rights Law.[85] Shaykh Ṭāhir Ḥamād in one case appointed a 16-year-old girl guardian of her brother on the ground that she was physically mature, adding that her maturity was not conditional on her having reached the age of 18, the appointment thus being made in conscious disregard of the general law.[86]

The *qāḍī*s sometimes sought support for the appointment of a guardian, at one and the same time, in substantive elements of both legal systems, the religious and secular, though based on utterly different philosophies. Thus, Shaykh Mūsā al-Ṭabarī in some cases gave as reasons for the appointment of the mother as guardian of the children that she was a natural guardian within the meaning of Israeli law and that the father had left neither a legal guardian nor an elected guardian behind him.[87] Shaykh Amīn Qāsim Mudlij in one case appointed the mother in reliance on her consent, on section 1 of the Women's Equal Rights Law and on the *sharīʿa*[88]; and Shaykh Tawfīq ʿAsaliyya on one occasion based the appointment of the father on his being "the one among the guardians and agnatic relatives (*aṣaba*) who is nearest to the children, and on section 14 of the Capacity and Guardianship Law."[89]

The only way to circumvent the provisions of the Women's Equal Rights Law relating to guardianship (and its other substantive provisions) is, as has been noted, by the parties agreeing to litigate in accordance with the law of their community. But in none of the orders appointing someone other than the mother guardian of her children, sometimes in express contradiction to her wishes, did the author find that the mother had in fact been asked or had agreed to apply religious law to matters of guardianship. It does not seem that the *qāḍī*s were alive to this question; at any rate, the author found no evidence to this effect in the *sijill*s.

NOTES

1. See Qadrī, arts.420 *seq.*, 435 *seq.*; Fyzee, pp.188, 193–4, 198; Abu Zahra, pp.156–7; Levy, p.143–4; Silberg, pp.407–8, 410; Schereschewsky, pp.375–6; Vitta, p.183; Zadok, pp.66–7, 70; Eisenman, pp.365–6. *KP*, vol.9, p.2004 col.1, p.2005 col.2 (remarks by the Minister of Justice in the Knesset).
2. In the opinion of the Ministry of Justice, the two kinds of guardianship were mentioned "not in order to differentiate between them but to combine them." See *IFB,* Explanatory Note, p.149.
3. See Silberg, pp.414 *seq.*; Women's Equal Rights Bill, 5711–1951, p.191.
4. E.g., the distinction between sons and daughters as to the expiration of the period of guardianship remains in force. See Silberg, pp.412–3.
5. On the other hand, parental control over the person and property of the child is curtailed with a view to equating parents as far as possible to appointed guardians, but there is no discrimination between the parents in this respect (see sec.22).
6. The enactments repealed by this law include, *inter alia*, arts.941–7, 957–97 of the *Mejelle* (sec.82).
7. See *IFB,* Explanatory Note, pp.133–4, 148–61, 172–89; Explanatory Note

to Capacity and Guardianship Bill; *KP*, vol.32, p.45 col.2, p.47 col. 2, p.49 col.2 (remarks by the Minister of Justice on the first reading of the bill), p.3077 col.1–p.3080 col. 1 (remarks by the chairman of the Constitution, Legislation and Juridical Committee concerning this bill).

8. See Shaki, p.266; *KP*, vol.34, p.3095. At any rate, sec.3 of the Women's Equal Rights Law, which deals with matters of guardianship, was not repealed by the law under reference.
9. See, e.g., *JfQ2*, p.379:no.532–f.17/59 (the guardian required the supervisor (*nāẓir*) to consent to any act of transfer in respect of the property); *AcD6*, p.43:f.106/65.
10. See, e.g., *JfQ1*, p.144:no.244–f.51/54; *JfQ4*, p.101:no.112–f.66/68; *AcD8*, p.74:f.91/69.
11. See, e.g., *JfQ3*, p.245:no.383–f.16/66; *AcQ5*, p.36:f.71/63.
12. *NzḤ24*, p.267:no.6/9–f.17/70.
13. See, e.g., *JfQ3*, p.206:no.340–f.46/65; *ṬbḤ2*, p.133:no.8; *NzḤ24*, p.22: no.4/68–f.11/66.
14. See, e.g., *JfQ1*, p.242:no.375–f.30/56; *NzḤ14*, p.116:no.8/76.
15. *JfQ1*, p.90:no.144–f.3/53, and p.15:no.26, respectively. See also *NzḤ24*, p.57:no.11/22–f.41/67 (appointment of paternal uncle's wife), p.192:no. 3/106–f.191/68 (stepmother, who was also a blood-relation of the children).
16. Only in two cases was guardianship over the persons and not over the property of the minors referred to. In both, Negev Beduin sought to use the mechanism of execution to recover a minor girl who had been abducted or fled from their house; their suit was allowed. See *JfQ2*, p.553:no.554–f.97/62, p.582:no.606–f.32/63.
17. See, e.g., *AcQ4*, p.7:no.7/59–f.49/59; *JfQ3*, p.216:no.353–f.36/66, p.348: no.490–f.58/67; *ṬbḤ2*, p.54:no.20; *NzḤ23*, p.153:no.8/12–f.7/66.
18. See, e.g., *JfQ4*, p.70:no.66–f.4/68 and p.71:no.67–f.19/68; *ṬbḤ2*, p.222: no.130 and p.223:no.131; *NzḤ23*, p.84:no.5/63–f.107/65 and p.85:no.6/46–f.108/65; *AcIr3*, p.146:no.41–f.65/52 and p.147:no.42–f.106/52.
19. See, e.g., *JfḤ19*, p.47:no.310, p.104:no.416; *NzḤ14*, p.16:no.68, p.20: no.72.
20. *JfQ2*, p.388:no.543–f.30/59; *JfQ3*, p.25:no.40–f.128/63; *ṬbḤ2*, p.246: no.26; *ṬbḤ3*, p.31:no.42; *AcD6*, p.26:f.59/64; *AcD7*, p.15:f.65/66; *NzḤ24*, p.144:no.2/42–f.75/68.
21. See, e.g., *NzḤ24*, p.86:no.2/56–f.120/67, p.224:no.1/37–f.85/69. This matter is discussed above, pp.272–3.
22. *NzI4*, p.329:no.5/29–f.100/67; *JfQ3*, p.224:no.364–f.58/65; High Court of Justice 187/54—Ḥalīma Sulaymān Barriyya *vs.* *Qāḍī* of the *Sharīʿa* Court of Acre *PD*, vol.9, p.1193. Parts of the judgment are quoted by Goitein and Ben-Shemesh, pp.242–5.
23. See, e.g., *JfQ2*, p.553:no.554–f.97/62; *ṬbḤ3*, p.36:no.48.

24. The *maḍbaṭa* usually notes that "there is not a paternal grandfather or *waṣī mukhtār*." See, e.g., *JfQ3*, p.304 : no.444–f.138/66; *NzḤ19*, p.14 : no. 8/8; *AcI2*, p.55 : f.124/53; *AcQ4*, p.28 : f.119/59.
25. See, e.g., *NzḤ21*, p.176 : no.5/47–f.70/62.
26. See, e.g., *NzḤ20*, p.3 : no.5/96; *AcQ4*, p.7 : no.7/59–f.49/59; *AcD6*, p.66 : f. 192/64; *AcD8*, p.52 : f.141/68.
27. *JfQ1*, p.146 : no.247–f.56/54. See also *NzḤ22*, p.57 : no.9/47–f.73/63.
28. See, e.g., *JfQ3*, p.309 : no.448–f.143/66; *NzḤ23*, p.171 : no.3/30–f.42/66.
29. *NzḤ20*, p.40 : no.3/20, and p.13 : no.9/110, respectively.
30. See, e.g., *AcI2*, p.55 : f.124/53.
31. See, e.g., *JfQ4*, p.71 : no.67–f.19/68; *ṬbḤ4*, p.25 : no.64; *NzḤ21*, p.5 : no. 8/23; *AcD6*, p.64 : f.157/65.
32. *JfQ1*, p.168 : no.277–f.14/55; *ṬbḤ2*, p.72 : no.39; *NzḤ19*, p.76 : no.3/76; *AcI2*, p.62 : f.16/54; *AcIr3*, p.67 : no.64/56–f.87/56.
33. In several cases, it was noted that a townswoman managed her husband's property even during his lifetime. See, e.g., *JfQ1*, p.90 : no.144–f.3/53, p.168; no.277–f.14/55.
34. See, e.g., *ṬbḤ2*, p.232 : no.6; *NzḤ24*, p.213 : no.8/25–f.58/69.
35. See, e.g., *NzḤ24*, p.121 : no.1/12–f.21/68.
36. See, e.g., *NzḤ19*, p.182 : no.7/74; *NzḤ21*, p.132 : no.4/60–f.95/61; *AcIr2*, p.145 : no.40–f.129/52; *AcD8*, p.68 : f.49/69.
37. See, e.g., *JfQ3*, p.326 : no.467–f.25/67; *AcD6*, p.37 : f.75/65; *NzḤ17*, p.201 : no.28/278; *ṬbḤ2*, p.235 : no.12.
38. See, e.g., *JfQ2*, p.379 : no.532–f.17/59; *JfQ3*, p.165 : no.267–f.6/65.
39. *JfQ2*, p.534 : no.520–f.54/62 (the woman at first consented to the appointment of the children's uncle as *waṣī* for their property; later she contended that her renunciation had been made while she was very ill with grief at her husband's death and that now she had recovered she had reassumed control of the children; the uncle resigned and the mother was appointed in his stead).
40. *NzḤ17*, p.172 : no.21/337.
41. See, e.g., *NzḤ21*, p.133 : no.5/61–f.96/61; *NzḤ23*, p.14 : no.5/91–f.156/64.
42. See, e.g., *NzḤ23*, p.14 : no.5/91–f.156/64 (when the grandfather recovered from sickness, the mother was dismissed and the grandfather reappointed).
43. See, e.g., *JfQ3*, p.30 : no.51–f.147/63; *ṬbḤ2*, p.133 : no.8; *NzḤ24*, p.192 : no. 3/106–f.191/68; *AcD6*, p.37 : f.75/65.
44. See, e.g., *JfQ3*, p.245 : no.383–f.16/66; *NzḤ21*, p.156 : no.2/21–f.27/62.
45. See, e.g., *NzḤ23*, p.141 : no.18/122–f.185/65; *AcIr3*, p.118 : no.38/57–f.152/57.
46. See, e.g., *JfQ3*, p.270 : no.409–f.100/66, p.328 : no.469–f.27/67; *NzḤ17*, p.201 : no.28/278; *NzḤ19*, p.36 : no.3/33; *ṬbḤ1*, p.122–f.6/10.

47. See, e.g., *NzḤ24,* p.78:no.4/46–f.101/67; *JfQ3,* p.279:no.418–f.102/66.
48. See, e.g., *NzḤ21,* p.43:no.1/8–f.11/60.
49. *NzI4,* p.52:no.3/15–f.26/49.
50. *NzḤ19,* p.178:no.3/70. See also *AcIr3,* p.164:no.3–f.29/58 (a man was appointed guardian of his female cousin).
51. *NzḤ20,* p.3:no.5/96. Cf. Rosenfeld, *Peasants,* p.145.
52. See *JfQ2,* p.318:no.497–f.42/58, p.337:no.529–f.13/59, p.442:no.434–f.9/60, p.476:no.500–f.52/61 (another guardian was appointed for the girls), p.483:no.516–f.61/61 (here, too, the guardian was dismissed by reason of embezzlement of property of the wards), p.551:no.550–f.95/62.
53. See, e.g., *ṬbḤ3,* p.79:no.48; *ṬbḤ4,* p.121:no.98.
54. See, e.g., *ṬbḤ3,* p.88:no. 61; *ṬbḤ4,* p.57:no.16. See also *ṬbḤ3,* p.36:no.48; *ṬbḤ4,* p.93:no.65.
55. See, e.g., *JfQ3,* p.249:no.388–f.75/65; *NzḤ24,* p.144:no.2/42–f.75/68.
56. Interview with M. Horvitz.
57. *NzḤ24,* p.213:no.8/25–f.58/69, p.252:no.1/75–f.145/69. See also *AcD8,* p.57:f.126/68; *ṬbḤ3,* p.49:no.10.
58. See, e.g., *ṬbḤ1,* p.18:no.9/35; *ṬbḤ3,* p.92:no.66; *JfQ3,* p.323:no.463–f.19/67; *AcD7,* p.48:f.30/67; *NzḤ19,* p.66:no.9/68.
59. *ṬbḤ3,* p.107:no.16.
60. *JfQ3,* p.245:no.385:f.16/66.
61. *ṬbḤ4,* p.300:no.6–f.13/68.
62. See, e.g., *AcI3,* p.105:no.135–f.158/58; *NzḤ24,* p.111:no.6/83–f.175/67.
63. See High Court of Justice 187/54. Quoted by Goitein and Ben-Shemesh, p.244.
64. See *ṬbḤ2,* p.244:no.22; *ṬbḤ4,* p.279:no.10–f.15/67; *JfQ2,* p.587:no.542–f.29/59; *AcD6,* p.26:f.59/64.
65. See, e.g., *JfQ2,* p.553:no.554–f.97/62; *JfQ3,* p.348:no.490–f.58/67, p.364:no.508–f.82/67; *AcD6,* p.26:f.59/64.
66. See, e.g., *JfQ2,* p.534:no.520–f.54/62; *JfQ3,* p.216:no.353–f.36/66; *ṬbḤ2,* p.244:no.23; *AcD6,* p.16:f.55/65.
67. See, e.g., *JfQ1,* p.141:no.237–f.31/54; *JfQ4,* p.131:no.155–f.137/68; *AcIr3,* p.17:no.15/55–f.42/55; *AcD6,* p.39:f.36/64; *ṬbḤ4,* p.121:no.98.
68. See, e.g., *JfQ2,* p.318:no.497; *NzḤ24,* p.33:no.82/2–f.142/66.
69. See, e.g., *JfQ4,* p.38:no.37–f.140/67. See also *NzḤ24,* p.96:no.12/66–f.140/67.
70. *ṬbḤ2,* p.15:no.19, p.244:no.23; *JfQ3,* p.244:no.382–f.50/66.
71. See, e.g., *ṬbḤ3,* p.5:no.6. This was also the opinion of interviewee Horvitz of the Ministry of Social Welfare.
72. See, e.g., *ṬbḤ1,* p.31:no.10/56; *NzḤ14,* p.71:no.3/12; *JfQ1,* p.15:no.26, p.90:no.144–f.3/53.
73. See Silberg, pp.410–1.

74. *JfQ1,* p.50:no.80–f.48/52 (he distinguished between natural guardianship and "guardianship relying on the *qāḍī*").
75. Interview with Shaykh Ḥasan Amīn al-Ḥabash. Cf. Schereschewsky, p.377.
76. See, e.g., *NzḤ19,* p.123:no.3/15; *NzI4,* p.80:no.8/34–f.83/50, p.329:no.5/29–f.100/67; *NzḤ24,* p.144:no.2/42–f.75/68; *JfQ1,* p.115:no.195–f.1/54; *ṬbḤ1,* p.74:no.1/16; *AcQ4,* p.6:no.6/59–f.47/59; *AcD6,* p.48–f.122/65.
77. *ṬbḤ4,* p.300:no.6–f.13/68; and *JfQ2,* p.582:no.606–f.64/63, respectively.
78. See, e.g., *AcIr3,* p.168:no.7–f.47/58; *AcQ5,* p.79–f.208/63.
79. See, e.g., *NzḤ19,* p.76:no.3/76; *JfQ1,* p.168:no.277–f.14/55. Cf. Schereschewsky, p.377.
80. *AcIr3,* p.67:no.64/56–f.87/56.
81. High Court of Justice 187/54, quoted by Goitein and Ben-Shemesh, pp. 243–4. Advocate S.Darwish told the author that the *qāḍī* "took the hint" of the Supreme Court that he was not to deprive the woman of her status as natural guardian by the application of religious law. He exerted his good offices to reconcile the mother and the aunt so as to avoid rendering a judgment requiring the child to be handed over to the mother.
82. See, e.g., *NzḤ19,* p.45:no.1/43; *NzḤ20,* p.40:no.3/20; *AcIr3,* p.183:no.20–f.64/58; *AcQ4,* p.100:f.175/60; *AcD8,* p.31:f.68/68; *JfQ1,* p.221:no.345–f.6/56.
83. See, e.g., *JfQ1,* p.124:no.210–f.18/54; *AcIr3,* p.33:no.31/55–f.17/55; *NzḤ24,* p.220:no.5/32–f.76/69.
84. See, e.g., *JfQ1,* p.163:no.270–f.4/54; *NzḤ24,* p.200:no.1/8–f.25/69; *AcIr3,* p.168:no.7–f.47/58.
85. See High Court of Justice 187/54. Quoted by Goitein and Ben-Shemesh, pp. 243–4.
86. *AcQ5,* p.24:f.31/63, p.36:f.71/63 (the girl in question was a daughter of Shaykh Mūsā al-Ṭabarī). The appointment was annulled by Shaykh Amīn Qāsim Mudlij as contrary to sec.3 of the Capacity and Guardianship Law. See *AcQ5,* p.57:f.147/63.
87. See, e.g., *AcIr3,* p.68:no.65/56–f.75/56; *AcQ4,* p.10:no.10/59–f.75/59.
88. *AcD7,* p.34:f.184/66. See aslo *NzḤ24,* p.86:no.2/56–f.120/67 (Shaykh Ḥusnī al-Zuᶜbī).
89. *JfQ5,* p.16:no.30–f.123/69. See also *JfQ4,* p.124:no.143–f.113/68.

Chapter Nine
SUCCESSION

I. LEGAL BACKGROUND

The Islamic system of succession is based on the customary law of pre-Islamic Arab tribal society, a law adapted to the structure of the patrilineal, patriarchal family. In that family, only male agnates (*ʿaṣabāt*) inherited; women and cognates were excluded from the succession. Muḥammad did not abrogate the customary law, but sought to naturalize it in Islam by superimposing religious norms on it. He did so by placing the "Qurʾānic heirs" (*dhawū al-farāʾiḍ*) first in line. In other words, he wished to stress the importance of the heirs who belonged to the inner family and to improve the status of woman in this connection. Eight of the 12 members of that group are women of different degrees of kinship to the deceased, both agnates and cognates. Nevertheless, the male agnatic heirs have remained the most important element in the Islamic system of succession. The Qurʾānic female heir usually takes half the share of the male of the same class, degree and strength of the blood-tie to the deceased. Placing the *dhawū al-farāʾiḍ* first in line is designed to assure them of a fixed portion of the estate without affecting the senior status of the male agnatic heirs, who take the lion's share. From the point of view of the status of woman, this system, in spite of the important Islamic amendments, involves discrimination against her in favor of man and against her family in favor of that of her husband.[1]

The Islamic law of wills affords protection, though not complete, to female heirs against deprivation of their shares in the estate at the whim of the deceased. The Sunnite Islamic system is one of the legal systems that do not give the testator absolute freedom to determine the devolution of his property after his death to the exclusion of the legal heirs. Wills are subject to two restrictions: they may not be made in respect of more than one-third of the estate and not in favor of a legal heir. A will disregarding these restrictions is valid only with the consent of the legal heirs (which is only taken into account after the testator's death).[2]

The Ottoman legislator introduced a revolutionary change in the status of women, to the extent of complete equality with men, as regards the transmission by inheritance of *mīrī* property (lands owned by the State, right of possession of which is granted to the individual). The Ottoman Law of Succession of 1913 is a replica of a German law with certain modifications.[3] It does not distinguish between males and females or between agnates and cognates. It only relates to *mīrī* property and certain kinds of *waqf ghayr ṣaḥīḥ* (endowed *mīrī*). It is thus not possible, circumventing its provisions, to deprive women of their rights in the inheritance by creating a *waqf ṣaḥīḥ* (an endowment of property in which the individual has full ownership) or by means of a will.[4] The Mandatory legislator went even further in that he wished to enact a general law of succession. For this purpose, he adopted the Ottoman Law of Succession of 1913, appending it to the Succession Ordinance, 1923, at the Second Schedule. All judicial authorities, including the *sharīʿa* courts, were ordered to have *mīrī* property inherited in accordance with the provisions of the Ottoman law, and their circumvention by will or otherwise was forbidden (section 21). *Mulk* property (in which the individual has full ownership and possession) and movables were indeed distributed, as in the past, in accordance with the provisions of religious law (section 8(1)), but on intestacy the religious court had to distribute them in accordance with the provisions of the Ottoman law if one of the parties so requested (section 8(2)).[5]

The Knesset closed the circle: the Women's Equal Rights Law, 5711–1951, extended the Ottoman Law of Succession to *mulk* property and movables (section 4(a)). This turned that secular law into a general law of succession applicable to all categories of property and all inhabitants of the State—nationals and foreigners, members of recognized religious communities and persons not belonging to any such community. This reform was, however, subject to two reservations: the Ottoman law was not to apply to *mulk* property and movables in the case of testacy (section 4(c)) or where all the parties were over 18 and had, of their own free will, consented before the religious court to litigate in accordance with the law of their religious community (section 7). Barring these reservations, it may be said that a fundamental reform had been achieved: the Islamic law of succession, one of the most characteristic branches of Islamic law, had been superseded by a complete secular law.[6]

The Succession Law, 5725–1965, was a step backward from the point of view of the status of Muslim women in the *sharīʿa* courts, although in substantive respect it maintains the principle of complete equality of men and women and of agnates and cognates of all classes and degrees of relationship to the deceased (sections 12 and 13). The principal innovation is the primacy of the spouse in succession (sections 10–11(a)).[7] This is a deviation from the orthodox concept of inheritance, according to which the latter's main purpose is the linking of the generations.[8] Islamic law and the Ottoman Law of Succession accord decisive precedence to heirs by virtue of blood-relationship. The Israeli Succession Law reaffirms the principle embodied in the Mandatory Succession Ordinance of absolute freedom of testation in quantitative and personal respect (including legal heirs) (sections 40 and 46–7) and, moreover, abrogates in matters of succession the special provisions relating to immovables of the *mīrī* category (section 149), that is to say, lifts the restriction placed on disposal of *mīrī* by will.[9] This removes the protection given legal heirs, including the women, against disinheritance. Along with absolute freedom of testation, the Knesset introduced maintenance out of the estate, intended to serve as a remedy against a will depriving an heir and to give expression to the principle that the needs of the relatives who had been dependent on the deceased must be satisfied first and that only the residue of the estate should be distributed among the heirs. *Inter alia*, there is a tendency to turn the widow's right to maintenance into a permanent and independent right (sections 56–9).[10] Maintenance out of the estate is unknown in Islamic law.[11] To facilitate the concentration of the estate in the hands of the nuclear family after the death of the deceased, the Israeli Succession Law, so long as the estate has not been distributed, does not permit an heir to renounce his share in favor of anyone but the deceased's spouse or children. This provision (section 6), as well as a similar provision relating to beneficiaries under a will (section 50), are mainly designed to benefit the widow, since the family property usually belongs to the husband.[12]

At the same time, the law downgrades the jurisdiction of the *sharīʿa* courts in matters of succession and wills from exclusive to concurrent, i.e., jurisdiction in these matters is transferred to the district court unless all the parties concerned in the matter under the law have consented in writing to the jurisdiction of the religious court (section 151(a) and 155(a)).[13] The provisions of the law apply only if the matter is heard before the district court, while the religious court, after the parties have consented to its jurisdiction, may "follow its religious law" (section 155(b)); consent to the jurisdiction of the religious court is thus sufficient also to allow for the application of religious law not only to *mulk* and movables but also to *mīrī*. In other words, the religious law of succession and wills applies in the religious courts provided that if the parties include a minor (under 18) or a person declared legally incompetent, his rights of succession, either on intestacy or under will, and his rights to maintenance out of the estate are not to be less than they would have been under the Succession Law (section 155). The law has an adverse effect on the status of Muslim women both because their succession rights are generally less under *sharīʿa* than under Ottoman law and because—with the well-known limitations—they may be deprived of their rights in *mīrī* by means of a religious will.

II. THE ISSUE OF A SUCCESSION ORDER ON A WOMAN'S INITIATIVE

From the establishment of the State to the end of the 1960s, the *sharīʿa* courts in Israel granted approximately 2,500 succession orders. Some 30% were issued on the initiative of women,[14] and over 50% of the latter on the initiative of the deceaseds' widows. Rosenfeld found that even in recent times the wife did not succeed the husband and that the property of the family head passed to the sons.[15] However, findings in the *sijill*s reveal that except for some 20 cases where the widow inherited alone or along with other women, she inherited along with the children of the deceased and their descendants, who are first in the line of heirs, as well as with agnates of other classes. The interval between the death of the deceased and the issue of the order was usually short,[16] which strengthens the assumption that the widow was interested in the distribution of the estate and the determination of the rights of succession. Moreover, the widow was in many cases appointed guardian of her minor children at an early date, sometimes on the same day as she initiated the succession order, which indicates that she intended to actually hold their share until they came of age.[17] Occasionally the widow was appointed guardian of her husband's children by another woman and thereupon hastened to initiate a succession order.[18] The aforesaid assumption is confirmed by Rosenfeld's researches in Ṭurʿān village. He found there a number of families consisting of unmarried children and their mother as head of the household after the death of the father.[19]

In 30% of the cases, the woman initiating the order was a daughter of the deceased. In only one-quarter of these cases did the daughter inherit alone or along with women of different degrees of relationship to the deceased; in the latter case, she took the major part of the estate as a Qurʾānic heir. In three-quarters of the cases, the daughter inherited along with a son or several sons, which made her an agnatic heir taking half the share of a brother of hers of the same strength of the blood-tie, and along with other agnates.[20] Rosenfeld and Cohen found that a daughter, like the widow, did not inherit in the presence of a son or sons. They explain this in terms of property and kinship relations.[21]

It may be inferred that a daughter who initiated a succession order was grown up and married. The interval between the death of the deceased and the issue of a succession order on the initiative of the daughter was usually great (sometimes 20 years or more).[22] An unmarried daughter at her father's house, even if she has reached the qualifying age for owning property, does not in fact enjoy this qualification either during her father's lifetime or after his death. At any rate, her dependence on her brothers and her family is greater before her marriage than afterward.[23] A woman is more likely to succeed her husband than her father or brother.[24] Rosenfeld and Cohen, in their researches on Galilean and Little Triangle villages, found that a woman sometimes claimed her share in her father's estate under pressure from her husband.[25] There is no evidence of this in the *sijill*s, except perhaps for a few hints.[26] On the other hand, in some cases, a man initiated a succession order with a view to realizing a woman's right in the estate of her father, husband or other relative; in all these cases, the order was only issued after the woman had died.[27]

In 5% of cases, the woman initiating the order was the deceased's mother. Except for some isolated instances, the order was issued in respect of the estate of a son, and in most cases, the mother inherited along with the children and other relatives of the deceased. In some cases, the mother was appointed guardian of the property of her grandchildren on the day when she initiated the succession order.[28] Only rarely did the mother inherit during the lifetime of the father, i.e., her husband.[29]

In 4% of cases, the woman initiating the order was a sister of the deceased.[30] In 2% of cases, she was his granddaughter.[31] In the rest of the cases, she was a cousin, niece, daughter-in-law[32] or other relative.[33]

It may be surmised that the principal motive inducing women to initiate succession orders was their wish to realize their right in the estate. There is no reason to doubt this where the woman was the sole heir or inherited along with women only. In 13% of the orders issued on the initiative of women, there were no agnatic or other relatives. More than half of these orders were issued on the initiative of a daughter of the deceased,[34] one-fifth on that of the widow[35] and the remainder on that of a germane sister (*shaqiqa*),[36] the mother,[37] a granddaughter[38] or some other relative.[39] The absence of a son removes the main obstacle to a woman's realizing her rights in an estate. Even Rosenfeld and Cohen confirm that the daughter inherits in the absence of a son.[40] In many cases, the woman did not initiate the succession order until all the agnatic relatives had died. Sometimes several years elapsed between the death of the deceased and the death of the agnatic relative, while on the other hand, a short time passed between the death of the latter and the issue of the succession order on the woman's initiative.[41] In many other cases, a woman initiated the succession order while there were agnatic relatives who in the circumstances did not inherit under religious law or the Ottoman Law of Succession owing to the order of priority of heirs or the rules of exclusion[42]; this situation, too, may have been conducive to the woman's initiative.

There may have been a causal connection between the issue of the succession order on a woman's initiative and the fact of the deceased having been a woman. One-tenth of the orders on a woman's initiative were issued for the estates of women of different classes and degrees of relationship: mother,[43] daughter,[44] grandmother,[45] and others.[46] It seems that in families in which a woman, and particularly a divorcee[47] or widow, had property of her own the position of a daughter or other female relative was more favorable than it usually was in families in which the property was in male hands.

Again, one can easily imagine disputes between a woman and other members of the deceased's family arising from structural antagonisms and making her wish to take her share of the estate. Thus, by the side of the widow initiating the order, there often were, at the time of its issue, one or several rival wives,[48] children by another wife,[49] the deceased's parents (i.e., her parents-in-law), his uncles and other agnatic relatives.[50] Similarly, beside the daughter, there were consanguine brothers and sisters (in the case of polygamy or death of the first wife) or uterine brothers and sisters (in the case of the mother's divorce and remarriage). A woman's initiative is particularly understandable in those cases in which she was the daughter of a divorced or deceased wife and the widow and children of the deceased inherited along with her.[51]

The rapid disintegration of the extended family and transition to the nuclear family in Israeli Muslim society encourage women to take their share of the estate. In the nuclear family, the integrity of immovable property and personal security based on kinship protection are, by the nature of things, less important. The issue of a succession order on the initiative of a widow is certainly a manifestation of her aspiration to economic independence and to the termination of her structural dependence on her husband's family with all the tensions it involves (domination by the mother-in-law and the husband's brothers etc.).[52] The issue of a succession order on the initiative of a granddaughter is likewise particularly understandable in the light of changes in the family structure, since the customary law underlying the Islamic system of inheritance is adapted to the structure of the extended family, in which the children of the deceased take precedence over his grandchildren,[53] whereas the principle of representation can be applied in the nuclear family, in which grandchildren take precedence over their uncles.

The proportion of Muslim urban women initiating succession orders was higher than the proportion of city dwellers in the total Muslim population—about a quarter as against one-sixth. This is because urban women enjoyed a greater measure of social freedom and economic independence than women in other types of settlement. The proportion of Beduin women initiating succession orders was considerably lower than the proportion of Beduin in the total Muslim population—6% as against one-sixth. But the very fact that several dozen Beduin women initiated succession orders seems to be a significant indication of changes taking place in Beduin society, especially in Galilee.[54] About 70% of the orders were issued in rural types of settlement, a considerable proportion thereof in large, developed villages in the Little Triangle and near towns (such as Yafīʿa and Furaydīs). These and other villages were undergoing an intensive, all-round process of modernization; in fact, from a social and cultural point of view, the usual ecological division between urban and rural types of settlement was in many respects blurred in Israeli Muslim society. The effects of this modernization are particularly obvious with regard to the change in the structure of the family, i.e., the rapid transition from the extended to the nuclear family, which is extremely significant in the context of inheritance customs.

More than half of the orders issued on the initiative of widows in respect of the estates of their late husbands relate to cases in which no blood-relationship existed between the spouses. Forty-four percent relate to cases in which the spouses belonged to the same clan (*ḥamūla*), and in 20 cases the spouses were first cousins.[55] In cases in which the deceased left two widows, one a blood-relation and the other a stranger, the initiative for the issue of the succession order came sometimes from the blood-relation[56] and sometimes from the stranger.[57] Such a high percentage of endogamous marriages indicates that blood-relationship between the spouses was at any rate no serious obstacle to the wife's wish to realize her right to her husband's estate, although it may be assumed that in this type of marriage she was exposed to pressures from her relatives to avoid fragmenting the family property[58]; in exogamous marriages no such interference could occur, and the wife may even have been encouraged to take her share.

Education does not seem to have been a determining factor in the issue of succession orders on the initiative of women. The *Sharīʿa* Courts of Ṭayyiba and Nazareth (but not those of Jaffa and Acre) had the initiator of the order sign it.[59] Only about 2% of the orders issued on the initiative of women were signed by them; the others were thumbmarked. Most of the signatures were made in very recent years,[60] which may herald a new stage in the development of women's status with regard to inheritance, when the education provided to girls in the State of Israel will find its expression besides other changes in women's economic and social status.

III. WOMEN AND THE LAW APPLICABLE TO INHERITANCE

The question of the law applicable to matters of inheritance is of great significance with regard to the position of women. As stated, the secular law leaves the heirs wide discretion to determine under which law, the religious or the secular, the estate is to be distributed. Consent under the Succession Law, 5725–1965, to the jurisdiction of the *sharīʿa* court determines also the substantive law which is to apply to the succession. Until the coming into force of the Israeli Succession Law, the prevailing practice was for the initiator of the succession order to ask that the estate be distributed in accordance with the *sharīʿa* and the Ottoman law.[61] This meant that *mulk* property and movables were to be distributed under religious law and immovables of the *mīrī* category under the Ottoman Law of Succession.

After the adoption of the Women's Equal Rights Law, there were several cases of women asking the *sharīʿa* court to distribute the estate in accordance with Ottoman law only, which the court was then bound to do in any case. The reason for this request is generally clear and understandable. The widow's share in the estate is greater under Ottoman law than under the *sharīʿa*[62] and, moreover, the widow (like the widower) does not enjoy the *radd*, i.e., the residue of the estate when the Qurʾānic heirs have taken their shares and there are no other heirs. In other words, the maximum the widow can get is one-quarter, and in the absence of heirs in the inner family (all male agnates and Qurʾānic heirs) and outer family (all other heirs), the residue, in accordance with the doctrine of the Ḥanafī school, passes to the *bayt al-māl* (treasury).[63] In fact, there were two cases in which the widow of a deceased who had left no other heirs asked for the estate to be divided solely according to Ottoman law, under which she took everything.[64] Under Ottoman law, a daughter takes a share equal to that of a son and may, in certain circumstances, inherit a much larger share than under the *sharīʿa*[65]; a granddaughter, under Ottoman law, takes the share of the parent through whom she inherits, while the principle of representation is unknown in Sunnite law. Under Qurʾānic law, an agnatic granddaughter, in the absence of sons, takes one-sixth where there is one daughter and is *de facto* excluded from the succession where there are two daughters.[66] In sum, the motive of the women seeking the succession orders seems in those cases to have been the wish to increase their shares.

The most significant test in this context is the extent to which the woman took advantage of the Women's Equal Rights Law, which permanently extends the Ottoman Law of Succession to *mulk* property and movables, save, as stated, where the heirs agree otherwise—in other words, all the woman had to do to increase her share was to avoid giving her consent to the application of religious law. It seems that women, and the public in general, were not alive at all to this reform. When seeking a succession order, the woman would, as in the past, ask for the estate to be distributed according to both the *sharīʿa* and the Ottoman law. The author did not come across a single case in which a woman, either as the initiator of a succession order or as an heir, insisted that the application of religious law required her consent. The question of the consent of all the heirs (and not only of the women among them), their ages, etc., did not arise at all until the adoption of the Israeli Succession Law.

The question of the consent of the parties, under the Women's Equal Rights Law, to the application of the *sharīʿa* to *mulk* and movables arose only in 1969. In 1965, the *Sharīʿa* Court of Acre issued a succession order distributing the estate, as usual, according to both laws. The widow of the deceased, an Acre woman, requested the Land Registry official, through an advocate, to refrain from registering the rights of the heirs according to the *sharīʿa* distribution, as set out in the succession order, on the ground that she had not agreed to litigate in a religious court in accordance with religious law. She also asked that her share in the estate be determined according to the Ottoman Law of Succession alone. She contended that, owing to ignorance of the law, she had not discovered the flaw in the distribution of the estate at the time the order was issued and that only at the land registration stage had she realized that the succession order was contrary to law and therefore void *ab initio*.[67] There was not a single case of recourse to the High Court of Justice regarding excess of authority by the *sharīʿa* court as to consent of the parties to litigate before it in a succession case, although there were such recourses in other matters of personal status.

Why did women not take advantage of the freedom of choice given them by the Women's Equal Rights Law as to the law applicable to succession? The principal reason seems to have been that they did not know of the existence of this right. Land Registry officials would honor succession orders of *sharīʿa* courts without going into the question of the parties' consent to litigate in accordance with religious law,[68] and this practice, too, seems to have contributed to women's inaction. Some people, such as the *mukhtār* of Bayt Ṣāfāfā, said that women did not insist on the estate being distributed in accordance with Ottoman law for the simple reason that such a demand would generally have been without practical significance since most village lands were of the *mīrī* category and officials would in any case register the rights of heirs in such property in accordance with Ottoman law; but as will be seen below, succession orders were seldom registered in the Land Registry. Others, such as Advocate Darwish, said that women dared not oppose the *qāḍī*s' practice of distributing *mulk* and movables according to religious law out of regard for religion and tradition (the borderline between these two was blurred) or for fear of sanctions by their families and social environment.

In some cases, a woman asked for an estate to be distributed in accordance with the *sharīʿa* only although this was not to her advantage.[69] In these cases, and also in cases where the order was sought by a man, the property in question was usually money and movables,[70] and the applicants probably assumed in their ignorance that such property could only be dealt with in accordance with the *sharīʿa*, as before the adoption of the Women's Equal Rights Law. The author found some such cases in records prior to the adoption of that law, and even in the *sijill*s of the late Ottoman and Mandate periods.[71]

To be sure, the question of the consent of women, and of heirs in general, did not arise on a significant scale until after the adoption of the Israeli Succession Law. This law, as stated, provides that the written consent of all the heirs is a condition for the jurisdiction of the religious court, but not for the application of religious law. The relevant provisions were properly applied in only a limited number of cases, in which all the heirs, including the women, in the presence of the *qāḍī*, gave their written consent to the jurisdiction of the religious court, and the estate was distributed in accordance with the *sharīʿa*. This proper application is only reflected in the *sijill*s of Nazareth (for the last few years) and Acre,[72] so that it must probably be attributed to the *qāḍī*s of these courts. Usually the law was given a distorted interpretation: the party interested in the issue of the succession order asked for the estate to be distributed in accordance with the *sharīʿa* and sometimes added a written declaration signed by all the heirs in which they consented to such a distribution. The *sijill*s record dozens of cases in which the law was interpreted in this way, sometimes on the initiative of a woman.[73] In one case a widow asked for the estate of her husband to be distributed in accordance with the *sharīʿa* on the ground that she ought to have the largest share in the estate.[74]

In many cases, a woman asked for or consented to the distribution of the estate in accordance with the *sharīʿa*, or the jurisdiction of the *sharīʿa* court, on behalf also of her minor children by virtue of her being their natural guardian or after being appointed guardian by the *sharīʿa* court.[75] It is doubtful whether in consenting to the distribution in accordance with the *sharīᶜa* the woman was guided by considerations of her interest in the inheritance; on the contrary, distribution according to the *sharīᶜa* is to the detriment of the widow and tantamount to her renunciation of succession rights.[76] It therefore seems reasonable to assume that the woman's request or consent related to the vesting of jurisdiction in the *sharīᶜa* court, which, in turn, distributed the estate in accordance with religious law.

The Muslim public had over the years become used to the idea of the *sharīᶜa* court distributing the estate or certain kinds of estate property in accordance with secular law, but it did not seem to be used to the reduction of the jurisdiction of the *sharīᶜa* court in matters of succession from exclusive to concurrent. It was mostly not aware of this reform at all, and even those who realized its significance preferred the religious to the civil judical authority. At any rate, expert testimony indicates that Muslims, and especially Muslim women, did not in matters of succession resort to any significant extent to the district court and thus did not take advantage of the mechanism placed at their disposal by the Knesset for the application of the Israeli Succession Law to all categories of estate property, without distinction between *mulk* and *mīrī*.[77] There is no trace of any such tendency in the *sijill*s, except, perhaps, for one isolated case.[78]

IV. DISINHERITANCE OF WOMEN

Studies on inheritance customs in Middle Eastern society describe various means of disinheriting women or curtailing their succession rights.[79] In the following, the author will try to evaluate, from *sijill* material, to what extent these and other means were applied to Muslim women in Israel.

i. Renunciation of Succession Rights

Renunciation (*tanāzul*) of rights in the estate was the simplest way of circumventing the succession laws. It was made before the *sharīᶜa* court at the time of the issue of the succession order or at a later stage—by amending the order before the estate had been distributed. Of course, it was stressed from time to time that the renunciation was made "voluntarily," "without coercion or force," or the like,[80] but when a woman renounced in favor of her father or brother, it may be assumed that she did so under pressure and not of her own free will.[81] Although in the *sijill*s the author found only two dozen or so cases of legal heirs renouncing all or part of their rights in favor of other heirs, in reality this phenomenon was undoubtedly much more frequent, despite the lack of formal expression. One of the reasons for formalization, especially after the issue of a succession order, was the wish to carry out transfer operations involving registration in the land register and the provision of other legal safeguards.

In most of the cases, it was a woman who renounced her right in favor of agnatic relatives: the daughter or daughters renounced her or their share in the father's estate in favor of a germane brother (*shaqīq*)[82] or consanguine brother[83]; the daughters renounced their share in the mother's estate in favor of the father[84]; a widow of the deceased renounced in favor of her sons[85] or of another widow and her children[86]; the deceased's mother renounced in favor of his sons (i.e., her grandsons)[87] or of his father (i.e., her husband)[88]; and other combinations.[89] In two-thirds of the cases, the renouncing woman came from a rural, and in one-third of the cases, from an urban type of settlement. The author did not come across a single instance of renunciation among Beduin, but this of course does not warrant the conclusion that the Beduin woman took her share of the inheritance. On the contrary, according to tribal custom she does not inherit at all,[90] but no formal steps are resorted to to deprive her of this right. The possibility that some compensation was received for the renunciation cannot be ruled out.[91]

On the other hand, in some cases, the order states expressly that the woman did not renounce any rights in the estate or that she confined her renunciation to a particular item of property. In two cases, it was indicated that all the daughters except one renounced their shares in favor of the son or sons (their brother(s)), and the one who did not renounce had her right in the estate reaffirmed by an amended succession order. In another case, the daughters renounced in favor of the son—but not the mother, who realized her right.[92] In a case of a different kind, the daughters, who had renounced their right in favor of their brother, asked for the succession order to be amended to the effect that the renunciation was confined to their shares in a certain *ḥākūra*; as to the other estate property, each of them reserved her rights, under religious and secular law, in her father's estate, which right she declared to be "mine and not my brother's."[93] Lastly, in two cases, agnatic relatives renounced their shares in the estate in favor of a woman. In one of these cases, the deceased's brothers and sisters renounced under both laws in favor of their mother on the day when the succession order was issued. In the other, the eldest son renounced his share in his father's estate under the *sharīʿa* and asked for it "to be added" to that of his mother.[94] Both cases occurred in an urban type of settlement. These isolated cases may denote a new development in the status of Muslim women in Israel with regard to succession.

ii. Wills

Wills were not widely resorted to in Israeli Muslim society. There is evidence of about 40 wills made since the establishment of the State—nearly all of it in the *sijill* of Jaffa. Isolated instances were found recorded in Acre and Nazareth, but not a single one in the *sijill* of Ṭayyiba. All but four wills were made in towns.[95] It might seem that one of the causes of the rarity of wills was the dearth of lands of the *mulk* category (especially in non-urban areas), since, as stated, it was not possible to will *mīrī* legally before the adoption of the Israeli Succession Law. But in the towns, too, where a considerable proportion of the property was *mulk*, the absolute number of wills was small, and anyway, there was no legal bar to making a will in respect of movables, money and the like (with the known limitations imposed by the *sharīʿa*). It may indeed be assumed that the number of wills was greater than would appear from the *sijill*s, for according to the Ḥanafī school of law a will need not be made before a *qāḍī* or even in writing. An oral will is valid so long as its contents can be verified by means of ear witnesses who were present at the time of the declaration.[96] There were in fact many instances of wills being made out of court, orally or in writing, and registered in the *sijill* in the testator's lifetime or after his death.[97] But this does not alter the basic finding that wills were not particularly frequent.

An analysis of the wills confirmed by the *sharīʿa* courts does not disclose a distinct and unambiguous tendency to disinherit women *qua* women, although many wills were made in respect of more than one-third of the estate and in favor of a legal heir. There seem to have been only a few cases of women being disinherited or in any way having their rights of succession curtailed—sometimes with their own express consent. In one case, a woman willed all her property to her grandson while her daughter, the grandson's mother, was alive; the daughter, who was the only legal heir, attested in court that she consented to the will. In another case, a man alleged that a relative of his, a member of the al-Huzayyil tribe in the Negev, had willed all his property and rights to him and that the legal heirs had consented to the will; these heirs were the claimant's paternal aunt, his male cousin on the father's side and his uterine sister. All these, except the uterine sister (who was not present in court), attested before the *qāḍī* that they consented to the will.[98] As is known, the consent of all the legal heirs is required to give effect to a will relating to more than one-third of the estate and in favor of a legal heir. The effectiveness of this requirement as a means to prevent circumvention of the law of succession and the exclusion of women from the inheritance depends on the extent of their ability to withstand pressures arising out of a complex of kinship and property relations, and this seems to be the principal weakness of the Islamic system of wills from the point of view of the status of women. In the first-mentioned case, it was probably not difficult to obtain the woman's consent to renounce the whole of the estate in favor of her son, let alone in the other case, where a half-sedentary tribal society was involved and with women of a comparatively distant degree of relationship to the testator. The curtailment of a woman's right of succession, though not her complete disinheritance, occurred in a further case, where a man willed his property to his daughter and her husband in equal shares.[99] But for the will, the daughter would have taken the whole of the estate since there were no other heirs. Other wills disclose no intention of dispossessing a woman *qua* woman.

Moreover, wills were occasionally made for the benefit of women. In some cases, the purpose was probably to prevent rights vested by the *sharīᶜa* in women of various degrees of kinship to the deceased from being frustrated in some way or other.[100] In one case, a man willed his property to his as yet unborn descendants on a basis of equality between males and females, in express deviation from the distribution of the estate under the *sharīᶜa*, which discriminates against females.[101] In two cases, a man willed his property to his wife, who was apparently the only legal heir[102]; as according to the Ḥanafī school spouses do not enjoy the *radd*, he probably wanted to ensure that his wife inherited the whole of the estate. In one of these cases, there was probably still another motive. On the day following the confirmation of the will, the man applied for a certificate that his marriage was valid (*ithbāt zawjiyya*),[103] whence it may perhaps be inferred that at the time of making the will a doubt had arisen as to whether the spouses were legally married. According to the *sharīʿa*, if there is any flaw in the legality of the marital union, the spouses do not inherit one from the other,[104] and this is probably what the man wished to prevent by making the will.[105] In another case, a man willed all his property to a strange woman in recognition of services rendered to him and his blind wife.[106]

About one-half of the wills were made by women. Women enjoyed great freedom of testation: they willed their property to relatives of different degrees and to strangers. True, where the will was in favor of a son, brother or other agnatic relative, doubts might arise as to the measure of the woman's freedom of action. Thus, in one case, two sisters gave their brother a general power of attorney to protect and dispose at will of their property and rights, and a year later they willed that property to him.[107] In another case, a widow made a will in favor of a relative, who subsequently alleged that she had willed to him all her property, including her share in her husband's estate, in return for his having provided for her upkeep.[108] The orders contain nothing to explain the motives of the wills or whether they involved the exclusion of legal heirs, but the beneficiary in each case is known to have been a wealthy Jaffa resident, a shrewd and adroit person, who may have pressured the woman into making the will so as to avoid the family's considerable fortune being fragmented by intestate succession. In yet another case, a woman willed all her property to her son in return for a sum of money she had borrowed from him and been unable to repay; she directed that all the heirs should consent to the will after her death (failing which it would be invalid) and that he who refused to do so should pay her debt [out of his share in the estate] to the beneficiary.[109]

On the other hand, there can be no doubt that the woman's will was freely made in cases where the beneficiaries were her daughters or her son and daughter in equal shares. In one case, the woman did not will her property to her daughters in equal shares within each category of property (lands and houses), as usual on intestacy, but the distribution was by categories, with a view to preserving as complete and economically sound units as possible. In another case, it was provided that the children (of both sexes) entitled under the will might reject or accept the inheritance after the death of the testatrix but must accept it in her lifetime.[110] In some cases, a woman willed her property to the children, of both sexes, of a son or daughter who had predeceased her; in one case, she left it to the children of a daughter still alive at the time and who was thus disinherited.[111] That the will was freely made is certain beyond a doubt in cases where a woman left her property to a stranger. In the absence of legal heirs, the motive was gratitude for services received from the beneficiary.[112] Sometimes a woman willed her property to a stranger with a definite intent to disinherit an agnatic relative. In one case, it was the testatrix's brother[113] and in another a relative of an unspecified degree.[114] The decision to exclude a legal heir, and especially a brother, betokens a great measure of self-confidence and the woman's complete control over her property.

In sum, the abovementioned orders do not leave the impression that wills were used to curtail or nullify womens' rights of succession, though they seem to have been sometimes used to restore a woman's share in her father's property to the family estate, viz., in cases where the will was in favor of near agnatic relatives, and especially of the testatrix's son or brother.[115] Moreover, in many cases, the will indicates that a woman effectively enjoyed the right to own property and was able, with the well-known *sharʿī* limitations, to determine the devolution of her property after her death to the exclusion of legal heirs. The foregoing applies mainly to urban environments. As far as can be judged from the *sijill*s, wills were not frequent in rural society.[116] The author did not come across a single instance of a will disposing of *mīrī* property under the provisions of the Israeli Succession Law.[117] From interviews with experts,[118] the author gained the impression that Muslims did not make use of the complete freedom of testation obtaining in the civil courts.

iii. Gifts

A gift (*hiba*) makes it possible to circumvent the Islamic law of succession without any quantitative or personal limitations. Not being a matter of personal status, within the meaning of article 51 of the Palestine Order in Council, it does not come within the jurisdiction of the *sharīʿa* courts. Nevertheless, some documents are found relating to gifts in the Jaffa *sijill*. The gift might be made in favor of sons only, sometimes with a definite intent to curtail or completely nullify a woman's right of succession. In one case, a man bestowed his property on his wife's son (by another man) as a gift after his death in return for services rendered to him when lying ill and also that he might bury him next to his son and pay all the burial expenses. The gift was revoked a few months later, but for our purposes it is important to note that it was to have deprived the wife and daughter of the donator (*wāhib*) of their shares in the estate. This may be inferred from other transfer operations in respect of the property in question. The man had earlier given it to his wife, but after a time she had given it back to him, and in addition had given him her own property.[119]

In another case, the gift was clearly a means to disinherit women, but also other heirs. A wealthy man gave all his property to his minor sons and none of it to his daughter[120] or to his wife, whom he had appointed guardian on his behalf for his children.[121] He also had sons and daughters by a divorced wife, who were likewise disinherited by the gift. After his death, a grown-up son by the divorced wife contested the gift on the ground that it had been made while his father was mortally ill, and the *qāḍī* indeed invalidated the gift. The *wāhib*'s wife thereupon appealed to the *Sharīʿa* Court of Appeal and the district court.[122] The limited number of the orders does not permit general conclusions to be drawn as to the use of the gifts as means for the disinheritance of women, but a tendency to such use is apparent from the orders reviewed above.[123]

iv. Waqf

The *waqf* (endowment) is one of the principal means of circumventing the Islamic law of succession. Unlike the will, a person may dedicate the whole of his estate, or more exactly, the enjoyment of its proceeds, without any restriction, denying the rights of legal heirs. This denial may take two principal forms: exclusion from the right of enjoyment of the *waqf* and from its administration. The second element is of great importance because the *mutawallī* (*waqf* administrator) is vested with considerable authority, which, in the absence of appropriate supervision, he may exercise to his personal advantage.[124]

It is doubtful, however, whether the *waqf* was used in Israel as a means to disinherit women. For one thing, the inclination of Muslims to dedicate property, considerable in the past, had virtually ceased. There are indeed dozens of judgments and orders relating to endowments—the great majority of them in the *sijill*s of Jaffa and Acre—

but they deal mainly with the appointment or dismissal of *mutawallīs* of existing (mostly family) endowments, permits to sell *waqf* (*istibdāl*), and other similar matters. The author met with only three new endowments, founded after the establishment of the State. Their number may of course be really greater,[125] but this does not basically alter the assumption of a small number of endowments founded in Israel. Some of the main causes—social, religious, economic and cultural[126]—of the strengthening of the *waqf* in the course of centuries seem to have lost their significance and validity in Israeli Muslim society. In addition, the radical reforms introduced by the Knesset probably made a considerable contribution to its decline.[127]

Moreover, the endowments founded in Israel point to no unambiguous tendency to deprive women of rights they would have had in property had it been transmitted by inheritance in the ordinary way. In one case, the man dedicating his property directed in the *waqfiyya* (deed of endowment) that its income should after his death be evenly divided between his daughter on the one hand and charitable, welfare and educational purposes of the Muslims of Jaffa, Ramla and Lod on the other. The daughter's beneficial interest was after her death to pass to her children and be divided "between males and females in equal shares" and thereafter to their descendants until the end of all generations in accordance with the same principle of equal division between the sexes. As his partner in the administration of the endowment (*tawliya*), the dedicator appointed his wife's son by another man, who was not his legal heir. The *waqfiyya* also indicated that the dedicated property had partly been the dedicator's and partly been inherited by him from his son or given him by his wife.[128] The dedication was chiefly injurious to the man's wife (if she was alive at the time of the dedication). The daughter's rights were only partly prejudiced because her Qurʾānic share in the estate (one-half) was assured to her.[129] In the presence of a widow, who would have taken one-eighth, the daughter would have taken seven-eighths, and as sole heir she would have taken everything. The appointment of the stepson as co-administrator also prejudiced the daughter's rights. If she had inherited the property in the ordinary way, she would, at least in theory, have been able to administer it herself.

Another case involved flagrant, unambiguous discrimination in favor of daughters. The dedicator directed that the enjoyment of the proceeds should after his death pass to his daughters and from them to his granddaughters and so on until the end of all generations, and when there were no more daughters, to the holy cities, Mecca and Medina. On the other hand, it is true, the dedicator directed that his (apparently only) son should be the *mutawallī* of the endowment, but he was to be succeeded by female beneficiaries who would be in Jaffa, and only in the absence of such was the *tawliya* to pass to other descendants of the dedicator who would be found worthy, while in the absence of such others the court was to appoint a stranger as *mutawallī*.[130] In a third case, a woman of the Old City of Acre dedicated her property to the Shādhilī Dervish center of worship (*zāwiya*) in Acre and to the local poor.[131]

In two cases, a woman was the administrator of a family *waqf*. One of them concerned the well-known ᶜAlī and ᶜAbdallāh Pasha *waqf* which had property in Haifa, Acre and Mazraᶜa. The woman, probably of the family of the dedicators, acting at her place of residence, Istanbul, empowered her representative in Israel to carry out various transfer operations in respect of the property.[132] In the other case, the *Sharīᶜa* Court of Jaffa appointed an East Jerusalem woman as administrator of the *waqf*—established by her father—after the previous incumbent had left the country during the Six-Day War. She was instructed, *inter alia*, to see that the income was distributed among the beneficiaries in strict adherence to the terms of the endowment.[133] But these cases were exceptional. The persons appointed to be *mutawallī*s were usually men, either of the dedicator's family or strangers.[134]

In sum, the *waqf*, as far as it existed in Israel Muslim society, was not used as a means to deprive women of the family property or to curtail their rights.

v. *Appointment of Estate Administrator*

Another way of circumventing the laws of succession, even after the issue of the succession order and the determination of the shares of the legal heirs, was the appointment of an estate administrator at the stage preceding the registration of the rights in the land register. It was not a widespread phenomenon, and it does not appear to have been specifically used to disinherit women. Its main purpose (apart from the formal purpose of paying the debts of the deceased) was to prevent the fragmentation of the family property. It usually concerned large estates of well-known Jaffa families, the division of which among the heirs was likely to diminish their value. In most cases, the deceased's son was appointed to this office, and he was thus in actual possession of the shares of the women and other heirs. This appointment was frequently made on the initiative of the other heirs, including the women.[135] It cannot, of course, be certain that the women's initiative in these matters was voluntary. The author came across only one case in which the appointment of the son was definitely intended to debar a woman from the actual enjoyment of her inheritance.[136] At the same time, in two cases, women—the deceased's widow and daughter, respectively—were appointed administrators. In the first of these cases, the deceased's children were minors.[137]

vi. Omission from the List of Successors

Another mode of disinheritance was probably the omission of an heir from the list of successors. In several dozen cases, persons applied for a correction of the succession order on the ground that their names or those of other heirs had been omitted from it. The application was mostly made after the issue of the order and not at the stage of publication of the *maḍbaṭa* in the press, the main reason being that the applicant, especially if a woman, could not read and was not able to look out for newspaper advertisements.[138] It may therefore be assumed that the number of cases of omission of the names of heirs from the list of successors was greater than is reflected in the *sijill*s, and it is not impossible that when an omission was detected after a time,[139] the heirs came to some arrangement without going to court.

The omission of the widow was rare; in fact, the author met with only two instances, in which the omission seems to have been due to the fact that a doubt had arisen as to whether the woman had been married to the deceased at the time of his death.[140] In other cases it appeared that the woman had been divorced from the deceased and had cohabited with him without a religious-legal marital bond and was therefore not entitled to succeed him.[141] It has happened that an heir applied for an amendment of the succession order so as to exclude the wife from the list of successors on the ground that she and the deceased had been divorced.[142] The comparatively great frequency of the omission of granddaughters from the list of successors[143] may be due to the fact that only an agnatic granddaughter inherits according to the *sharīʿa*, either as the taker of a Qurʾānic share or as an *ʿaṣaba*.[144] In fact, in one case an heir contended that the omission of the children of his sister, who had predeceased their father, had been in good faith because a daughter's children did not inherit under the *sharīʿa*.[145] In other cases, the initiator of the original order contended that he "had not remembered" that there were any heirs but those indicated in the *maḍbaṭa* or that he had not known that women were entitled to a share in the estate. Such a contention cannot be taken seriously when the omission concerned the deceased's daughter.[146] In several cases it was the woman who disputed the contents of the *maḍbaṭa* or applied for an amendment of the succession order denying her rights.[147]

There is no doubt that the omission was sometimes made in good faith or intended for a purpose other than disinheritance of a woman. Finally, this mode of excluding heirs did not, as far as applied consciously, affect only women. In some cases, men appealed against their non-inclusion among the heirs and asked for the succession order to be amended accordingly, and it has happened that a woman initiating a succession order wronged other heirs by such non-inclusion.

vii. Appointment of a Guardian over the Property of a Minor

Another method of frustrating a woman's right of succession was via guardianship over the property of a minor. The guardian enjoys great freedom of action in managing the property, being allowed to perform various acts in respect thereof, such as a sale, an exchange or consolidation,[148] and it does not seem to have been very difficult to convince the court, on applying for permission to do the act, that it was in the interest of the minor. It is doubtful, moreover, whether the guardian always troubled to apply for permission. The deceased's brother, i.e., the uncle of the minor, was generally more anxious than any other relative to preserve the family property, which accounts for the frequency of his appointment as guardian.[149] Since the children, according to the *sharīʿa* and the Ottoman Law of Succession, take the lion's share of the inheritance, he in fact holds the greater part of the estate. Elsewhere instances have been noted of an uncle's attempts to prevent the partition of the estate between the daughters by marrying them to his sons or by gaining control of their property.[150] In the *sijill*s, there is evidence of daughters considering themselves aggrieved by the way the guardian managed the property. Thus, for instance, a daughter complained that on the uncle's application the estate had been distributed in accordance with the *sharīʿa*; having reached puberty and become free of his tutelage, she asked that the succession order be amended and she be given a share equal to that of her brother, i.e., that the estate be distributed in accordance with the Ottoman Law of Succession.[151]

V. THE EXTENT TO WHICH WOMEN INHERIT IN PRACTICE

The issue of the succession order, even on her initiative, is not proof that a woman actually inherits. The court's function ends with the definition of the rights in the estate under the relevant laws. It has no authority to implement the order. In the areas in which land settlement has been completed, the land registers under the new system of registration are supposed to reflect the position, and any change, with regard to ownership.[152] A right registered in the land registers to a share in an estate (ownership in the case of *mulk*, possession rights (*taṣarruf*) in the case of *mīrī*) is *prima facie* evidence that the heir has realized his right and become the owner in all respects. Inquiries at the land registries in Jerusalem, Netanya and Nazareth[153] showed that only a small proportion of succession orders were registered, and this none too soon after the issue of the order. The *sijill*s and the land registers contain a great deal of evidence that heirs did not hasten to register the succession order in the latter and distribute the estate,[154] which of course might have facilitated the exclusion of heirs.

Moreover, even where the succession order had been registered in the land register, there were still ways of disinheriting a woman. The most notable of them was the transfer defined in the land registers as "sale without consideration." This transfer made it possible to avoid various taxes, such as land appreciation tax and estate duty, and, which is more relevant to our subject, to circumvent the laws of succession. A well-informed source[155] estimated that in the Little Triangle region about 90% of "sales without consideration" registered in the Netanya land register were made within the family. The suspicion of disinheritance of a woman arises in cases where a man transferred property in this way to his son or where women transferred their shares in an estate to their brother.[156] In many other cases, women transferred their property or shares in an estate by "sale without consideration" to men who were apparently their sons.[157] Transfers in these circumstances were generally made under pressure from family members interested in preventing fragmentation of the property. The author was told of several cases where married women who had taken their shares in an estate and registered their rights formally in the land registers transferred those shares years later to their brothers by "sale without consideration" since they were no longer able to withstand family sanctions. Women sometimes received monetary compensation or part of the land in return for renunciation of their shares in the inheritance. The volume of transfers of this kind was greater than is reflected in the land registers because the sale was usually not to be effected until after the seller's death, on the basis of an irrevocable power of attorney. In hundreds of cases, persons renounced their shares in an estate in favor of other heirs in the course of land settlement proceedings (at the stage preceding the publication of the schedule of rights); a strikingly large proportion of these persons were women. It also frequently transpired in settlement proceedings that heirs had sold their shares to relatives, and here, too, there were many "sales without consideration," i.e., renunciations by women in favor of agnatic relatives. Renunciation was usually made by means of an irrevocable power of attorney and sometimes in the presence of the settlement officer.[158]

There can be no doubt that many matters of succession were settled out of court and not in accordance with any law of succession, either secular or religious—in other words, without women inheriting at all. Indirect evidence of this can be found in the *sijills*. Sometimes many years elapsed between the death of the deceased and the issue of the succession order, and in the meantime the property was held and administered in accordance with the local custom of a patriarchal society, a custom usually discriminating against women. A whole generation of heirs might be skipped before the issue of the order.[159] Rosenfeld, Cohen and Marx, who carried out research on Galilean and Little Triangle villages and Negev Beduin, declared that Muslim women did not as a rule inherit; this was said to be due to a desire to prevent the removal of property from the control of the family and clan (*ḥamūla*) and to the system of kinship relations in traditional society, which is so vital to the protection and security of women that they are willing to renounce property rights for its sake. These findings would seem to be confirmed by other research conducted in Palestine and elsewhere in the Middle East.[160]

It nevertheless seems possible to state as a basic fact that Muslim women in Israel did inherit. As mentioned, some 30% of succession orders were issued on the initiative of women, the smaller part in the absence, the greater in the presence of agnatic relatives. Women appealed against their omission from the list of successors or their deprivation at the distribution of the estate and claimed their share according to a system of succession that would assure them of a larger portion. Men appealed against a woman's right to inherit or asked her to pay debts of the deceased out of the estate.[161] Some 400 succession orders for the estates of women, being about one-sixth of the total number, were issued by the *sharīʿa* courts during the period under review. Nearly 60% of them were in favor of the children—sons and daughters[162]—and the remainder in favor of the husband,[163] agnatic brothers and sisters,[164] a brother's children,[165] parents,[166] grandchildren,[167] cousins[168] and other relatives (son-in-law, daughter-in-law, father-in law).[169]

Moreover, the *sijill*s record many dozens of cases in which a woman left property she was to have inherited from the deceased but had not yet received by the time of her death, i.e., she died after the deceased but before the issue of the succession order for his estate, so that she left the share she had taken of his estate to her own heirs.[170] Women willed their property to legal heirs and to strangers, dedicated it as an endowment and bestowed it as a gift. The land registers contain evidence of women leaving their share in an inheritance to their heirs (see below); some wills state expressly that the testatrix had carried out an act of transfer in respect of "what came to her by way of inheritance" (*mā āl ilayhā biṭarīq al-ʾirth*).[171] But the willed property may have come from other sources (dower, purchase and personal efforts). All this evidence, in its cumulative effect, supports the assumption that women realized their right of succession and enjoyed freedom to own and dispose of property.

This conclusion is confirmed by proceedings in other matters dealt with by the *sharīʿa* courts. Women were very active as guardians over the property of minors who had inherited from relatives[172]; in many dozens of cases, a woman asked the *qāḍī*'s permission to carry out a transfer in respect of property administered by her: a sale, an exchange, consolidation or the like. She might, *inter alia*, ask permission to transfer property registered in the land registers in the name of daughters of the deceased or to register rights in the land registers in their names.[173]

From maintenance claims by women against their sons there is evidence that every now and then a woman inherited from her husband or received from him in his lifetime a house, or other property, which was thereupon registered in the land registers in her name.[174] Judgments for divorce and other judgments sometimes show that a woman compensated her husband for her divorce by ceding to him her rights in the estate of her father or agnatic relatives[175] or that a house or dwelling belonged to a woman,[176] and a wife might stipulate in the marriage contract that the house or dwelling should be wholly or partly hers.

The means used for the disinheritance of women, as far as reflected in the *sijill*s, do not always point to a definite tendency to discriminate against women *qua* women. On the contrary, they were sometimes used for women's benefit. The enjoyment of the proceeds of endowments was assigned to them and rights in estates were renounced in their favor. Women occasionally used those means in order to supplant legal heirs, male and female alike. But anyhow, the very resort to means of disinheriting women, and especially to "sales without consideration" or paternal-cousin marriages as far as intended to maintain the integrity of the family property, strengthens the assumption that were it not for them women would have taken their shares of the inheritance.[177]

The fact that only a small proportion of succession orders were registered in the land registers does not prove that women did not realize their rights of succession, at least in cases in which the orders were issued on their initiative. Inquiries the author made revealed that the Land Registry was hardly ever resorted to, except where one of the heirs wished to sell his share and on the occasion of the transfer his rights and those of the other heirs were registered. In all these cases the two acts—the registration of the rights of succession and the transfer on sale—were carried out one immediately after the other on the same day.[178] In other words, the transaction was registered only where the buyer wanted complete legal security; there seem to have been no other incentives. On the contrary, several factors militated against resort to the Land Registry: the wish to avoid expenses involved in carrying out transfers (including the registration of rights of succession) in the land registers; the widespread tendency in the Arab sector to reduce contacts with the various government departments to a minimum for fear of exposing oneself to the grip of taxation authorities and for other reasons; fear of the intervention of the Custodian of Absentees' Property where the deceased or one of the heirs was an absentee. Many thought that actual possession of the property was sufficient guarantee against challenges from whatever quarter and relieved them of the need to establish their rights formally in the land registers. A succession order issued by the *sharīʿa* court affords the members of the family certainty and security as regards the distribution of the estate, and every heir can transfer his share to another person by means of a sale agreement[179] or an irrevocable power of attorney.[180] In fact, most land transactions were effected outside the Land Registry.[181] In this sense, the Land Transfer Ordinance, 1920, did not achieve its objective.[182] Lastly, in many rural and some urban areas, land settlement was not complete and there was no orderly land registration.

On the other hand, land registers faithfully reflect the position as to ownership on the date of completion of land settlement under the Mandatory Ordinance. Here registration was carried out on the initiative of the land settlement officer after the rights in the land had been proven to his satisfaction by means of succession orders and other documents. The particulars of registration permit the certain conclusion that the rights of women in an estate were in many cases registered in accordance with the original distribution indicated in the succession order. In cases in which a plot was registered wholly in a woman's name, it is impossible to tell whether the property came to her by way of inheritance (in the absence of other heirs) or purchase, but in many cases the property was registered in the names of several members of the inner family in accordance with their proportionate shares in the deceased's estate, and since the property was usually *mīrī*, a woman's share was equal to that of a man of the same degree of relationship to the deceased.[183] In most of these cases, the succession order was probably issued on the initiative of the man who maintained contact with the settlement officer. In dozens of cases, a woman carried out an act of transfer—a sale, a purchase or the like—within the family or, which is more important, outside it, an act which from the time land settlement was completed was duly registered in the land registers.[184]

Further confirmation of the assumption that Muslim women inherited may be obtained from the files relating to claims for compensation for land vested in the Development Authority under various laws. The Development Authority does not compensate persons claiming shares in estates acquired by it until the claimants have produced succession orders from the *sharīʿa* court; and compensation is paid on a personal basis, to each claimant according to his share in the estate.

Among the recipients of compensation were women of different degrees of relationship to the deceased. And again, these files clearly reflect women's wide freedom of action in the field of ownership relations: they bought, sold, transmitted and inherited property.[185]

Lastly, on submitting the question under discussion to experts, the author received contradictory answers. Some insisted that women did not inherit at all. Advocate Darwish thought that it was not difficult, in case of need, to persuade a woman to renounce her right in an estate in favor of her agnatic relatives. Shaykh Ḥusnī al-Zuᶜbī believed that women did not take their shares in an inheritance and that the issue of a succession order on a woman's initiative was not proof that she intended to realize her right. At the same time, cases of women inheriting were in his opinion more frequent than they had been in the past.[186] Others declared that women did as a rule inherit. Advocate Fārūq al-Zuᶜbī thought that a woman initiating the issue of a succession order intended to realize her right to the inheritance and regarded the order as a full legal guarantee of the preservation of this right.[187] A person well-versed in land matters in the Jerusalem area believed that the daughters of the deceased actually inherited along with the sons. He knew of cases in which daughters had applied to the civil court in order to realize their right in the estate after an attempt had been made to deny them this right. At any rate, according to him, a daughter seldom renounced her share in the inheritance in favor of her brother; this occurred mainly where she was unmarried, lived at the brother's house and was supported by him. Sometimes she was compensated for the renunciation by a monetary payment or a plot of land. On the other hand, a woman sometimes claimed her share of her father's estate in order to transmit it to her son or her children. It happened that fathers sold land to their sons while representing the sale as a gift so as to secure exemption from land registration fees. They did so when they wished to exclude one of the heirs.[188] The *mukhtār* of Bayt Ṣafāfā, Muṣṭafā ᶜAlayān, likewise confirmed that women actually inherited on frequent occasions. He assumed that women initiated the issue of a succession order in two cases: where the deceased had left no sons and where the sons withheld her share of the estate.[189] Mrs. Suᶜād Qaramān said that women received more than was allotted to them by the *sharīᶜa* and less than was allotted to them by secular law, but that a brother sometimes bought his sister's share,[190] which practically meant that he excluded her from the succession against payment of compensation.

The diversity of opinion on this subject is probably due to the fact that inheritance customs differed from region to region and were constantly changing.[191] One thing seems to be beyond doubt: the phenomenon of Muslim women inheriting was neither marginal nor new, and although no quantitative estimate can be given, the degree of frequency is significant. Of course, this was a transition period, and beside women inheriting (and enjoying considerable freedom in regard to property relations) women were sometimes excluded from the succession (and debarred from owning and disposing of property). A. Granott noted women inheriting during the Mandate. In his opinion, it was one cause of the formation of what he calls the "detached areas of a village," i.e., areas of land belonging to owners in other villages.[192] Nor, as far as can be judged from Mandatory and Ottoman *sijill*s, was the issue of succession orders on the initiative of women an innovation. But it was greatly encouraged in Israel by social, legal and administrative factors, such as the rapid disintegration of the extended family and transition to the nuclear family and, in close connection therewith, manifestations of women's social liberation and economic independence; the speeding-up of land settlement proceedings and the registration of ownership rights in the land registers; changes in the system of land tenure and, especially, the transition from *mushāᶜ* (joint ownership) to individual ownership; a change in the economic role of land and its inclusion in the cycle of economic transactions[193]; and large-scale nationalization of lands along with personal compensation to the owners. All these led to intensified activity in the field of property relations, one of the forms of which is inheritance, and created conditions which enabled the changes in the structure of the family and the status of women to find expression; the weight of these factors was of course different according to region, type of settlement and social stratum. Although some of them already existed in the past, they were never so important, both qualitatively and quantitatively, as in Israel during the period under review.

VI. THE *QĀḌĪ*S AND SUCCESSION

The Women's Equal Rights Law made almost no impression on the *sharīᶜa* courts. The *qāḍī*s went on issuing succession orders under *sharᶜī* and Ottoman law as if nothing had happened.[194] The distribution of the estate under both systems of succession, the religious and the secular, was appropriate before the enactment of the Women's Equal Rights Law.[195] For the court then had to "transfer" *mīrī* property under the provisions of Ottoman law and to apportion the inheritance of *mulk* property and movables under *sharᶜī* law unless one of the heirs asked that they, too, be distributed under Ottoman law. The *sharīᶜa* court was not competent to determine the category of the estate property (*mulk* or *mīrī*), and by determining the rights of the heirs under the two systems of law the *qāḍī* implied that the Land Registry official was to register the rights of the heirs in accordance with the classification of the property in the land register. In other words: the distribution of rights took place under the Ottoman Law of Succession in respect of *mīrī* property and under the Islamic law of succession in respect of *mulk* and movables.[196]

There is no basis for distributing *mulk* and movables under the *sharīᶜa* after the enactment of the Women's Equal Rights Law unless all the parties are 18 years of age or over and have voluntarily agreed before the *sharīᶜa* court to litigate under the law of their community. Yet, the author came across only a few cases in which the *qāḍī*s did so with express or implied reference to the Women's Equal Rights Law, and in all cases they deviated from its provisions in one way or another. Thus, in one case, Shaykh Mūsā al-Ṭabarī dismissed the application of the deceased's daughter for an amendment of the succession order and distribution of the estate under the Ottoman Law of Succession, holding that the application was contrary to the *sharīᶜa* and to section 7 of the Women's Equal Rights Law because all the adult heirs and the guardians of the minor heirs had agreed in writing before the court that the estate should be distributed under the *sharīᶜa* and the Ottoman Law of Succession[197]; it is doubtful whether this is a correct interpretation of the Women's Equal Rights Law, for where the heirs include minors it is from the outset impossible to distribute the estate under the *sharīᶜa*. As the procedure of making a succession order does not involve the presence of all the heirs,[198] the *qāḍī* was unable to ascertain their wishes as to the law to be applied to the estate. He distributed the estate under both systems of law, apparently in reliance on the request of the initiator of the order and the signatories to the *maḍbaṭa*,[199] at any rate not on the basis of the agreement of all the heirs, as required by the Israeli law.

The *qāḍī*s' deviation in this matter seems in part to be a *bona fide* practice carried over without a break from the Mandate period. At the same time, it is difficult to assume that they should so long have been unaware (until the enactment of the Succession Law in 1965) that the agreement of the parties was required for the application of religious law to *mulk* and movables. It seems that they felt strongly impelled to oppose the Knesset's intervention because of the substantive character of the legislation concerned.[200]

On the other hand, the impact of the Israeli Succession Law on the *sharīʿa* courts is clearly discernible although their interpretation of it was not always in accord with the Knesset's intention. Only Shaykh Amīn Qāsim Mudlij and, in recent years, Shaykh Ḥusnī al-Zuʿbī were careful to obtain the agreement of the heirs to the *sharīʿa* court's *jurisdiction*, as required by law.[201] Most of the *qāḍī*s, in so far as they attended to the matter of the agreement of the heirs, did so with reference to the applicability of religious law (instead of to the competence of the religious court).[202] They seem to have been unaware that their jurisdiction had been reduced from exclusive to concurrent. Some were careful to obtain the agreement of the heirs in writing, as required by law,[203] but others contented themselves with the initiator of the succession order or with only those of the heirs who requested that the estate be distributed under the *sharīʿa*.[204] The author was informed by the Ministry of Religious Affairs that the *qāḍī*s had been requested to obtain the written agreement of *all* the heirs to the *jurisdiction* of the *sharīʿa* court (and not to the application of religious law).[205]

The *qāḍī*s usually applied *sharʿī* law to *mulk* and movables, as they had done before approval of the Israeli Succession Law. Surprisingly enough, in one case, Shaykh Ḥusnī al-Zuʿbī distributed the whole estate under the Israeli Succession Law,[206] although the legislator had meant that law to apply in civil courts only. The *qāḍī*s were divided as to the law applicable to *mīrī*. As already stated, the Knesset empowered the religious court "to follow its religious law" after the parties had agreed to its jurisdiction, i.e., the religious court is authorized to distribute also *mīrī* property under religious law. Indeed, the *qāḍī*s are expected to do so, since the agreement of the parties to the jurisdiction of the religious court apparently implies the application of the religious law, although it is not obligatory.[207] But only Shaykh Ḥasan Amīn al-Ḥabash, Shaykh Tawfīq ʿAsaliyya and Shaykh Amīn Qāsim Mudlij applied religious law to all categories of property, without distinguishing between *mulk* and *mīrī*,[208] and the two latter did not do so regularly.

Shaykh Amīn Qāsim Mudlij noted in many cases that as far as the estate consisted of *mulk* and movables he distributed it under the *sharīʿa*; he passed over in silence the mode of distribution of *mīrī*.[209] Shaykh Ḥusnī al-Zuʿbī in many cases distributed the estate under *sharʿī* law and the Ottoman Law of Succession, as in the past, after obtaining the agreement of the parties under the new law.[210] In other cases, he and Shaykh Amīn Qāsim Mudlij and Shaykh Tawfīq ʿAsaliyya distributed the estate under *sharʿī* law and the Israeli Succession Law, that is to say, they applied the new law to *mīrī* property.[211] In fact, Shaykh Ḥusnī usually did so, and he explained to the author that in his opinion this was the meaning of Section 155(b) of the Succession Law.[212]

As stated, the Knesset imposed a restriction on the application of religious law to the whole estate, viz., that where the parties included a minor his succession rights should not be less than they were according to the Israeli Succession Law. Shaykh Amīn Qasīm Mudlij and Shaykh Tawfīq ʿAsaliyya were alive to this point, and in several cases in which they distributed the estate under *sharʿī* law they stressed that this mode of distribution was of advantage and benefit (*al-ḥaẓẓ waʾl-maṣlaḥa*) to the minors among the heirs.[213] The impression is sometimes gained that where there were minors among the heirs, the *qāḍī*s meant to satisfy the requirements of the law by obtaining the agreement of the heirs, including the guardians of the minors, to the application of religious law, as required by section 7 of the Women's Equal Rights Law, or to the jurisdiction of the religious court, instead of by being alive to the succession rights of the minors.[214] In one case, Shaykh Tawfīq ʿAsaliyya combined the agreement aspect with the succession rights aspect. The order stated that all the heirs except an absent daughter (viz., sons and another daughter) had asked for the estate to be distributed under *sharʿī* law, and in reliance on section 155 of the Israeli Succession Law he granted their request but awarded to the absent daughter a share equal to that of the sons, i.e., double that of her sister who had agreed to the *sharʿī* distribution.[215] In no case did the *qāḍī*s refer to the matter of maintenance out of the estate, which was introduced by the Israeli Succession Law.

The original Succession Bill of 1952 was more radical: exclusive jurisdiction in matters of succession was to be transferred to the district court, and religious law was to be superseded entirely by the provisions of the new law. The publication of the bill led to vehement opposition from the *qāḍī*s and the Muslim public in general. Protest meetings were held in mosques, telegrams and delegations were sent to State leaders with a view to preventing the enactment of the law or to toning down its provisions.[216] Under pressure from the Jewish religious parties, the sting was largely taken out of the bill: the religious courts were to retain concurrent jurisdiction, and within these limits the application of religious law was to be extended to all categories of property.[217] This may account for the careful—if sometimes incorrect—implementation of this law by the *qāḍī*s as against their disregard of the Women's Equal Rights Law in matters of succession.

Shaykh Ḥasan Amīn al-Ḥabash and Shaykh Tawfīq Maḥmūd ᶜAsaliyya took care that a woman's renunciation of succession rights was "without compulsion or constraint" and that a person renouncing declared before the court that he or she did so voluntarily,[218] but it is difficult to assess whether such declarations were meaningful or merely routine. Shaykh Ḥusnī al-Zuᶜbī insisted that the renunciation be in writing[219] and Shaykh Ṭāhir Ḥamād that it be under both *sharᶜī* and Ottoman law.[220] Shaykh Muḥammad Ḥubayshī, who for many years served as secretary of the *Sharīᶜa* Court of Acre, told the author that Shaykh Mūsā al-Ṭabarī would refuse to accept a woman's renunciation of succession rights, and if she insisted, would, after issuing the succession order, refer her to the Land Registry or the Land Settlement Officer[221]; the author found no instances of renunciation of succession rights in the Acre *sijill*s of Shaykh Mūsā's period of tenure. In one case, in which the daughters renounced their share in the succession in favor of the son and subsequently restricted their renunciation to some particular property of the estate, Shaykh Tawfīq ᶜAsaliyya allowed the retraction, declaring that the renunciation was in the nature of a gift and might be withdrawn so long as the property existed unchanged.[222]

As stated, the deceased's wife is not, according to the Ḥanafī school, entitled to enjoy the *radd*, the residue which remains of the estate when the Qurʾānic heirs have taken their shares and there are no other heirs. In the absence of heirs in the inner family, the residue passes to members of the outer family or, if there are none, to the *bayt al-māl* (public treasury).[223] The *qāḍī*s adopted different modes of action in this matter. Shaykh Ṭāhir Ḥamād and Shaykh Amīn Qāsim Mudlij awarded to the widow what was her maximum Qurʾānic share in the absence of children (one-quarter) and assigned the remainder to the public treasury for distribution to the Muslim poor.[224] On the other hand, in some cases, Shaykh Ṭāhir al-Ṭabarī and Shaykh Mūsā al-Ṭabarī decided, contrary to the Ḥanafī school, that the widow should take the whole estate.[225]

It seems that the *qāḍī*s were generally alive to the question of the agreement of the legal heirs to the contents of the will where the latter related to more than one-third of the estate or was in favor of a legal heir. Shaykh Ṭāhir Ḥamād and Shaykh Amīn Qasīm Mudlij were careful to obtain the agreement of the heirs before confirming the will.[226] Shaykh Tawfīq ᶜAsaliyya took evidence when it was alleged that there were no legal heirs.[227] The *qāḍī*s acted in accordance with the *sharᶜī* norm and there is no indication that they specifically were guided by the wish to prevent the disinheritance of women.

NOTES

1. Coulson, *Succession*, pp.3, 22, 29, 33. For a systematic discussion of the order of priority and shares of the heirs see *ibid.*, chs.2–7; Qadrī, arts.582 *seq.*; Fyzee, ch.13; Goitein and Ben-Shemesh, pp.142 *seq.*
2. See Coulson, *Succession*, pp.1–2, chs.13–14; Qadrī, arts.530 *seq.*; Anderson, *Islamic Law*, pp.72–3.
3. Silberg, pp.178–88, 207–10; *SB52*, Explanatory Note, p.52.
4. Ottoman Law of Succession, arts.1, 7; see Ben-Shemesh, pp.115–16, 166, 198–9; Goadby, p.121.
5. See Silberg, p.182; Goadby, p.122; Vitta, p.206. The Ordinance also permits the making of a will in civil form for *mulk* property and movables (but not for *mīrī* property). This innovation, however, does not affect Muslims (sec.20).
6. See Silberg, pp.417–19, 425–6; Zadok, pp.71–2; Weines, p.319; Goitein and Ben-Shemesh, p.246.
7. See Yadin, *Reflections*, pp.134–6; Succession Bill, 5718–1958, Explanatory Note, pp.59–61.
8. See the remarks of the Chairman of the Constitution, Legislation and Juridical Committee of the Knesset, *KP*, vol.42, p.964 col.2–p.965 col.1.
9. See Succession Bill, 5718–1958, Explanatory Note, p.234; Yadin, *Reflections*, p.137; Remarks of Minister of Justice in the Knesset, *KP*, vol.24, p.2106; *KP*, vol.32, p.195.
10. See remarks of the Chairman of the Constitution, Legislation and Judicial Committee of the Knesset, *KP*, vol.42, p.955 col.1.

11. *FRL*, art.152.
12. See Yadin, *Reflections*, p.136.
13. *Ibid.*, p.133.
14. Over 70% of the orders were issued on the initiative of men of different degrees of relationship to the deceased, but may indirectly serve the interests of women as well since the *qāḍī* in the order—either under religious or secular law—determines the rights of the heirs, including female heirs. Anyhow, only orders issued on the initiative of women were analysed.
15. Rosenfeld, *Peasants*, p.120.
16. See, e.g., *JFQ1*, p.68:no.109–f.68/52 (inheriting along with sons and daughters; order issued three months after husband's death), p.239:no.369–f.13/56 (along with husband's brothers; a few months after husband's death); *ṬbḤ2*, p.207:no.103 (along with sons and daughters, father and brothers; after a year).
17. See, e.g., *ṬbḤ1*, p.124:no.9/13 and p.125:no.10/14; *NzḤ19*, p.89:no.10/90 and p.142:no.5/35; *AcIr2*, p.76:no.19/51 and p.77:no.20/52. For a more extensive discussion see the chapter on "Guardianship," pp.265–6. Cf. Marx, *Bedouin*, p.185 (Marx found that Beduin women did not inherit but watched over the rights of their sons until they reached adulthood).
18. See, e.g., *JfQ1*, p.90:no.144–f.3/53 and p.93:no.148–f.15/53.
19. Rosenfeld, *Recent Changes*, p.29.
20. These may include her father. See, e.g., *NzḤ18*, p.94:no.29/188, p.102: no.41/194; *ṬbḤ4*, p.270:no.1–f.89/66.
21. See Rosenfeld, *Peasants*, pp.80, 144–9; cf. Cohen, p.124.
22. See, e.g., *ṬbḤ2*, p.24:no.46, p.79:no.46; *ṬbḤ3*, p.84:no.55 (in all these cases, the orders were issued 50–60 years after the death of the deceased).
23. Through marriage, a woman reaches the status of a legal personality, while Islamic law is not clear on this point as regards an unmarried woman. See Gibb, p.240; Coulson, *Succession*, p.247.
24. This was confirmed to the author by the *mukhtār* of Bayt Ṣafāfā, interviewee Muṣṭafā ᶜAlayān.
25. Rosenfeld, *Peasants*, p.29; Cohen, pp.77, 122. This was confirmed to the author by interviewee S. ᶜAmir, an expert on land affairs in the Jerusalem region.
26. Thus it was said in one case in the order that the daughter who initiated it "refers (*muntasiba*) to her husband's family." See *AcIr2*, p.98:f.40/51. In the Jaffa *sijill* of the Mandate period the author came across a case in which a woman initiating a succession order for her mother's estate was represented by her husband as a proxy (*wakīl*) for this purpose. See *JfḤ19*, p.82:no.376.
27. See, e.g., *ṬbḤ1*, p.163:no.4; *ṬbḤ2*, p.12:no.31; *NzḤ21*, p.74:no.1/62–

f.91/60; *NzḤ22*, p.59:no.2/50–f.78/63; *ṬbḤ4*, p.140:no.3; *JfQ1*, p.172:no. 283–f.15/55; *ṬbḤ4*, pp.152, 156:no.19; *AcIr2*, p.168:no.62–f.139/52; *AcIr6*, p.43:f.87/61; *AcIr7*, p.15:f.74/65.

28. See, e.g., *ṬbḤ2*, p.133:no.8 and p.134:no.9; *AcIr2*, p.146:no.41–f.105/52 and p.147:no.42–f.106/52.
29. See, e.g., *ṬbḤ1*, p.4:no.7/8.
30. See, e.g., *JfQ2*, p.509:no.470–f.58/61; *NzḤ14*, p.137:no.4/4.
31. See, e.g., *JfQ1*, p.129:no.218–f.50/53; *NzḤ20*, p.6:no.9/100.
32. See, e.g., *AcIr3*, p.25:no.23/55–f.89/55; *AcIr7*, p.34:f.141/64; *JfQ3*, p.164: no.265–f.11/65; *ṬbḤ2*, p.34:no.59.
33. See, e.g., *AcIr6*, p.26:no.33/62, p.57:f.135/63.
34. See, e.g., *JfQ2*, p.557:no.561–f.55/62; *NzḤ17*, p.49:no.54/178.
35. *AcIr4*, p.81:no.55–f.100/59; *NzḤ19*, p.103:no.6/106.
36. See, e.g., *NzḤ20*, p.114:no.1/37; *NzḤ21*, p.42:no.6/6–f.5/60.
37. See, e.g., *JfQ2*, p.457:no.469–f.18/61; *ṬbḤ4*, p.206:no.35.
38. See, e.g., *JfQ2*, p.512:no.477–f.106/61; *AcIr3*, p.114:no.34/57–f.64/57.
39. See, e.g., *JfQ2*, p.317:no.495–f.32/58.
40. Rosenfeld, *Peasants*, p.145; Cohen, p.122. Cf. Granqvist, vol.1, p.128.
41. See, e.g., *NzḤ19*, p.220:no.7/30 (the woman who left the estate died in 1950; her husband died in 1956, and the daughter initiated the issue of the order three months later); *AcIr2*, p.55:no.52/56–f.17/56; *ṬbḤ1*, p. 148:no. 5/25; *ṬbḤ4*, p.84:no.51 (in both cases, 14 years elapsed until the issue of the order on the daughter's initiative; meanwhile, several of the legal heirs died; shortly before the issue of the order, the initiating daughter's only brother died).
42. See, e.g., *JfQ4*, p.132:no.156–f.97/48 (under the Ottoman Law of Succession, the daughter took everything (*mīrī*); under *sharᶜī* law, the daughter took one-half (*mulk* and movables), and the deceased's germane brothers took the residue); *NzḤ20*, p.86:no.8/82 (a widow inherited along with two daughters, the mother, and germane brothers and sisters who did not inherit under Ottoman law); *AcIr6*, p.2:no.2/62–f.31/61 (three germane sisters and two consanguine sisters; the latter inherited only under the Ottoman Law of Succession).
43. See, e.g., *JfQ2*, p.305:no.472–f.13/58; *ṬbḤ1*, p.17:no.7/33; *NzḤ17*, p.49: no.54/178; *AcIr3*, p.221:no.55–f.66/59.
44. See, e.g., *JfQ3*, p.221:no.360–f.31/66; *ṬbḤ1*, p.35:no.17/63; *NzḤ21*, p.86:no.1/75–f.114/60. Cf. al-ᶜĀrif, p.126.
45. See, e.g., *ṬbḤ3*, p.109:no.18.
46. See, e.g., *ṬbḤ1*, p.56:no.2/95 (aunt); *ṬbḤ2*, p.34:no.59 (mother-in-law); *NzḤ20*, p.114:no.1/37 (sister).
47. See, e.g., *ṬbḤ2*, p.222:no.129.
48. See, e.g., *ṬbḤ1*, p.59:no.6/99; *NzḤ21*, p.122:no.7/43–f.71/61 (along with

two wives and mother-in-law); *AcIr2*, p.14:no.11/50 (along with second wife and her children and a daughter by a divorced wife).

49. See, e.g., *ṬbḤ2*, p.45:no.8, p.125:no.50 (in both cases, the initiating wife had only daughters, while the rival wife had a son or sons); *NzḤ21*, p.96: no.5/5–f.4/61 (along with sons and daughters by a deceased wife and with the deceased's mother); *AcIr1*, p.12:no.10 (along with a son by another wife).
50. See, e.g., *NzḤ17*, p.238:no.4/9; *NzḤ22*, p.27:no.1/11–f.23/63; *AcIr5*, p.133:f.189/58; *NzḤ24*, p.76:no.44/2–f.67/98; *NzḤ18*, p.38:no.22/107; *ṬbḤ2*, p.181:no.66.
51. See, e.g., *ṬbḤ1*, p.46:no.6/80; *NzḤ18*, p.19:no.25/178; *AcIr3*, p.175: f.182/57. For the problem of the distribution of the inheritance among consanguine brothers by polygamous marriages see Cohen, p.77.
52. See Rosenfeld, *Peasants*, pp.32 *seq.*
53. The son excludes not only the descendants who inherit through him, but also who inherit through other sons who predeceased the deceased.
54. See, e.g., *AcIr2*, p.12:f.9/50 (ʿArab al-Saʿdiyya); *AcIr3*, p.117:no.37/57–f.104/57 (ʿArab al-Sawāʿid); *AcIr7*, p.12:f.41/66 (ʿArab al-Maksūr, Ḥajīrāt), p.14:no.14/67–f.175/66 (ʿArab al-Kaʿbiyya); *NzḤ17*, p.278:no.25/55 (ʿArab al-Hayb, Ṭūbā); *NzḤ19*, p.65:no.8/67 (ʿArab al-Shiblī), p.198:no.6/6 (ʿArab al-Ṣubayḥ); *JfQ4*, p.90:no.90–f.32/68 (ʿAshīrat Abū Ruqayyiq).
55. See, e.g., *JfQ3*, p.189:no.309–f.63/65; *ṬbḤ4*, p.302:no.7–f.79/67; *NzḤ19*, p.165:no.1/56.
56. See, e.g., *ṬbḤ2*, p.45:no.8; *NzḤ21*, p.122:no.7/43–f.71/61; *AcIr7*, p.2: no.2/66–f.109/65 (in all these cases, the exogamous wife was alive at the time the order was issued).
57. See, e.g., *ṬbḤ3*, p.7:no.8; *NzḤ16*, p.66:no.12/12; *AcIr3*, p.184:no.21–f.4/58 (in all these cases, the endogamous wife was alive at the time the order was issued).
58. Cf. Cohen, pp.77, 122, 124; Rosenfeld, *Peasants*, pp.29, 102, 145. In cousin marriages, the husband succeeds the wife in two capacities: *qua* husband who takes the Qurʾānic share and *qua* agnatic heir (*ʿaṣaba*).
59. This practice was not regular. It was abandoned in the Little Triangle in late 1966.
60. See, e.g., *NzḤ24*, p.99:no.4/70–f.149/67, p.130:no.3/23–f.42/68, p.151: no.2/49–f.88/68; *ṬbḤ4*, p.176:no.3.
61. See, e.g., *JfQ1*, p.248:no.385–f.39/56 (the heirs applied for the issue of a succession order "that would clarify the portion of each of them according to the *sharʿī* distribution and according to the (secular) legal distribution" (*fī al-masʾalatayn al-sharʿiyya waʾl-qānūniyya*)).
62. See, e.g., *NzḤ18*, p.16:no.15/78; *NzḤ19*, p.103:no.6/106 (the widow inherited along with another widow and a daughter by a deceased wife;

according to Ottoman law, each of the two widows received one-eighth of the estate, while according to the *sharīʿa*, they would have received one-eighth together).

63. See Qadrī, art.638; Coulson, *Succession*, pp.31, 49–50.
64. *NzḤ18*, p.1:no.26/56, p.17:no.16/79.
65. See, e.g., *NzḤ19*, p.98:no.1/101 (the deceased left a daughter, a son and several sisters; the sisters inherited under *sharʿī* law, while under Ottoman law they took nothing and the estate was evenly divided between the son and the daughter).
66. See Coulson, *Succession*, pp.54–7. See, e.g., *NzḤ19*, p.35:no.2/32; *NzḤ20*, p.6:no.9/100.
67. Sources for this case: Advocate J. Meḥrez, who represented the woman in her application to the Land Registry; Advocate S. Darwish, who represented her in the *sharīʿa* court (his office file: P/24–3–appeal to *Sharīʿa* Court of Appeal against refusal of *Sharīʿa* Court of Acre to amend and/or revoke Succession Order No.68 of 1965); Dr. A. Link and D. Etun of the Ministry of Justice, Jerusalem.
68. Only after the enactment of the Israeli Succession Law were they directed to insist on consent to jurisdiction in the case of *sharīʿa* court orders, as they had even previously done in the case of orders of Rabbinical and Christian courts, which throughout the whole period had only had concurrent jurisdiction. In the absence of consent, they returned the orders to the court (*ibid.*).
69. See, e.g., *NzḤ18*, p. 117:no.13/211 (the mother, under the *sharīʿa*, took one-third of the estate along with a germane sister and paternal uncle of the deceased, while under Ottoman law the estate would have been evenly divided between her and the germane sister).
70. *NzḤ18*, p.117:no.13/211 (estate being compensation for the death of the deceased in a work accident), p.146:no.8/246 (salaries and compensation in consequence of death of the deceased in a road accident).
71. See, e.g., *NzḤ14*, p.68:no.1/10; *NzS26*, p.238:no.18; *JfḤ19*, p.89:no. 390.
72. *NzḤ24*, p.163:no.4/62–f.123/68, p.182:no.24/93–f.165/68, p.210:no.4/21–f.153/69, p.241:no.6/61–f.122/69, p.250:no.7/73–f.141/69, p.263:no.3/3–f.7/70; *AcIr7*, p.14:no.14/67–f.175/66 (the widow and all the heirs filed "an affidavit vesting power in the court to ascertain the share of each of them in the estate according to the *sharʿī* method"; all the heirs signed the declaration vesting this power), p.31:f.128/66; *AcIr8*, p.18:f.63/68.
73. See, e.g., *JfQ3*, p.346:no.488–f.142/66; *JfQ4*, p.70:no.66–f.4/68; *ṬbḤ4*, p.302:no.8–f.17/68.
74. *JfQ3*, p.344:no.486–f.18/67.
75. See, e.g., *JfQ4*, p.59:no.55–f.139/67; *JfQ5*, p.109:no.183–f.291/69; *ṬbḤ4*,

p.302: no.7–f.79/67, p.309: no.17–f.37/68; *AcIr7,* p.1: no.1/67–f.146/66; *AcIr8*, p.17: f.144/68.

76. In one case, granddaughters (and grandsons) were deprived of rights in the estate of their grandfather, a wealthy Jaffaite, because their guardian (an agnatic relative) had asked that the estate, which had previously been distributed according to both laws, be distributed according to *sharīᶜ* law only. As a result, the deceased's son, the granddaughters' uncle, took the whole estate. The graddaughters indeed certified in writing, on reaching puberty, that they agreed to distribution according to the *sharīᶜa*, but it is doubtful that they did so of their own free will. See *JfQ2*, p.302: no.467–f.64/57 and p.573: no.590–f.99/62.
77. This was attested by Muḥammad Nimr al-Hawwārī, Judge of the District Court of Nazareth, A. Shrem, Registrar of Lands, Nazareth District, B. Z. Cohen, Assistant Registrar of Lands, Netanya Region (who recalled no instance of a Muslim of the Little Triangle taking out a succession order in a district court), Shaykh Ḥusnī al-Zuᶜbī (who knew of several women applying to the district court in matters of succession) and S. Nawi.
78. *JfQ4*, p.188: no.244–f.66/69 (the file was transferred from the district court to the *sharīᶜa* court on the ground that until November 20, 1965, the power to issue succession orders was vested in the latter; this shows at least that application was made to the district court).
79. See Baer, p.39, and the sources mentioned there.
80. See, e.g., *JfQ3*, p.293: no.433–f.109/66, p.302: no.442–f.118/66.
81. This is what Shaykh Muḥammad Ḥubayshī maintained during an interview.
82. See, e.g., *JfQ3*, p.293: no.433–f.109/66; *NzḤ24*, p.71: no.4/39–f.76/67.
83. *JfQ4*, p.95: no.100–f.90/62, p.187: no.243–f.42/69.
84. *JfQ4*, p.4: no.4–f.87/67.
85. See, e.g., *JfQ2*, p.574: no.591–f.112/62; *JfQ3*, p.45: no.73–f.150/63, p.317: no.456–f.9/67; *NzḤ24*, p.199: no.1/7–f.69/18; *NzI4*, p.52: no.3/15–f.26/49.
86. *NzḤ24*, p.270: no.3/13–f.24/70 (renouncing widow was childless).
87. *ṬbḤ2*, p.168: no.51; *NzḤ14*, p.68: no.1/10; *NzI4*, p.84: no.2/41–f.106/50.
88. *JfQ4*, p.144: no.173–f.11/69.
89. *NzḤ24*, p.197: no.5/5–f.12/69.
90. See Marx, *Bedouin*, p.185.
91. The author found evidence of monetary compensation in the *sijill* of Jaffa of the Mandate period. See *JfḤ19*, p.149: no.507, p.137: no.480. Renunciation of a right in an estate in favor of a relative in return for economic assistance from him is practically maintenance out of the estate, such as is found in systems of succession—e.g., the Jewish—under which a woman does not inherit along with certain relatives.
92. *JfQ3*, p.292: no.432–f.114/66; *JfQ4*, p.95: no.100–f.90/62; and *NzḤ24*, p.71: no.4/39–f.76/67, respectively.

93. *JfQ4,* p.101:no.111–f.90/62 (the order was amended in accordance with their request).
94. *JfQ2*, p.443:no.436–f.30/60 and p.443:no.437–f.33/60; and *JfQ4*, p.70: no.66–f.4/68, respectively.
95. Two wills were made in villages, one among Negev Beduin (al-Huzayyil) and one among Galilee Beduin (ᶜArab al-Shiblī). See *JfQ2*, p.558:no.564–f.106/62 (Abū Ghūsh); *AcD6*, p.1:f.1/64 (Tarshīḥā); *JfQ2*, p.521:no.497–f.21/62; and *NzḤ24*, p.110:no.5/82–f.174/67, respectively.
96. Coulson, *Succession*, pp.215–16.
97. See, e.g., *JfQ2,* p.76:no.116–f.1/64, p.140:no.219–f.110/64, p.142:no.224–f.119/64.
98. *JfQ2*, p.601:no.646, and p.521:no.497–f.21/62, respectively (in the latter case, it is not indicated how, if at all, the uterine sister's consent to the will was obtained). In a further case, a man of the ᶜArab al-Shiblī tribe in Galilee willed his property to his wife and four sons, directing that they (also the wife?) should take equal shares. One of the sons was appointed executor. The man revoked all the wills that preceded this one. See *NzḤ24*, p.110:no.5/82–f.174/67.
99. *JfQ3*, p.8:no.14–f.97/63 (no indication of the testator's motives). See also *JfQ3*, p.16:no.24–f.55/63.
100. *JfQ2*, p.475:no.498–f.34/61 (the man willed all his property to his two sons and his daughter; his daughter was to have "her right (*istiḥqāquhā*) in the estate under the *shariᶜa*, as if he had died intestate"); *JfQ3*, p.111: no.174–f.58/64 (the head of the family made a will assuring the rights of all the legal heirs, viz., the widow, the daughters and the sons, under the *shariᶜa*; at the end of the will, it is expressly stated that it was made "for fear of denial and abandonment [of the rights of the heirs]"; he probably meant to protect the rights of the wife and daughters rather than of the sons).
101. *AcQ5*, p.44:f.80/63 (and in the event that he should have no offspring, he willed his property for the renovation of the mosques in Acre; this is structurally very similar to prescribing the order of beneficiaries of an endowment).
102. *JfQ2*, p.311:no.481–f.29/58, p.385:no.539–f.23/59.
103. *JfQ2*, p.312:no.483–f.28/58.
104. See Coulson, *Succession*, p.16.
105. In the *sijill*s of the courts of Jaffa and Nazareth of the Ottoman period, the author also found a will in favor of the widow and other female relatives; see *JfS43*, p.85:no.89 (will in favor of the widow despite the existence of legal heirs, viz., sons and daughters); *JfS88*, p.83:no.316; *NzS26*, p.166:no.56, p.205:no.49 (will in favor of testator's sister-in-law and her children).

106. *AcQ5*, p.45: f.82/63 (the order does not indicate if the blind woman was alive at the time the will was made).
107. *JfQ1*, p.252: no.392–f.47/56. For a further will by one of the sisters in favor of the same brother see *JfQ2*, p.474: no.497–f.49/61.
108. *JfQ2*, p.392: no.550–f.20/59.
109. *NzḤ15*, p.34: no.5/58. For further wills in favor of the son see *JfQ2*, p.506: no.566–f.101/61; *JfQ3*, p.59: no.48–f.142/63 and p.124: no.197–f.89/64 (in the latter case, the son applied for a decision that his mother's property was his by virtue of the will and of his being the sole heir).
110. *JfQ3*, p.62: no.96–f.202/63; and *JfQ2*, p.540: no.532–f.69/62, respectively.
111. *JfQ2*, p.601: no.646; *JfQ3*, p.19: no.29–f.29/63, p.20: no.31–f.109/63.
112. *JfQ2*, p.329: no.516–f.60/58, p.570: no.584–f.130/62, p.571, no.589–f.4/63 and p.591: no.627–f.49/63; *JfQ3*, p.194: no.321–f.99/65.
113. *JfQ2*, p.524: no.53–f.34/62.
114. *JfQ3*, p.76: no.116–f.1/64, p.90: no.139–f.5/65. See also *JfQ3*, p.96: no.151–f.38/64.
115. There is a resemblance here to a family endowment which entitles the daughter to enjoy the income of the *waqf* and to use the dedicated property so long as she is single, while her right terminates on her marriage. The resemblance lies in the principle that the woman may not transfer the family property to her husband, but that she has rights in it in her lifetime or until her marriage.
116. A noteworthy phenomenon is the occurrence of two wills made among Beduin in Galilee and the Negev in accordance with the *sharīʿa*. This is a clear sign of the Islamization that tribal society is undergoing. This process was at the time confined to tribes in an advanced stage of sedenterization (al-Huzayyil in the Negev and al-Shiblī in Galilee).
117. The author indeed came across a will made in relation to *mīrī* in 1964, but such a will was contrary to the law then in force. See, *JfQ3*, p.124: no.197–f.64/89. In another case the court, relying on the Israeli Succession Law, confirmed a will leaving the entire property—movables and immovables—to a stranger, but there is no certainty that it was made under the new law (it states that there were no legal heirs) and that the property (situated in Jaffa) included also *mīrī*. See *JfQ5*, p.96: no.162–f.279/69.
118. Nazareth District Judge Muḥammad Nimr al-Hawwārī and the Directors of the Land Registries at Nazareth and Netanya.
119. Which she had obtained "by civil purchase." See *JfQ1*, p.34: no.59–f.13/52.
120. According to another version, the gift comprised only part of the property and was made also in favor of the daughter. See *JfQ1*, p.200: no.324–f.20/55.
121. *JfQ1*, p.168: no.277–f.14/55 and p.169: no.279–f.20/55.

122. *JfQ1*, p.197:no.319–f.23/55, p.200:no.324–f.20/55 and p.205:no.328–f.20/55.
123. Since gifts are not within the jurisdiction of the *sharīʿa* courts, no clarification of the position can be expected from the *sijill*s.
124. Cf. Baer, pp.39–40.
125. Registration of a *waqf* with the court is not a condition of its validity. See Qadrī, *Waqf*, art.2.
126. See Baer, pp.142–3; Goitein and Ben-Shemesh, pp.154–7.
127. See Layish, *Waqf*, pp.41–72.
128. *JfQ1*, p.38:no.68–f.29/52. The son afterward resigned his position as *mutawallī* and claimed an appropriate remuneration for his services. *JfQ1*, p.69:no.110–f.51/52.
129. This may be the reason for the proportion fixed between the daughter's share in the proceeds and the share assigned for public purposes.
130. *JfQ1*, p.235:no.363–f.16/56.
131. *AcD6*, p.21:no.45/64. For other endowments established by women during the Mandate and perhaps even earlier see *JfQ3*, p.193:no.311–f.102/65; *AcQ4*, p.87:f.82/60.
132. *AcD7*, p.18:no.80/66; *AcD8*, p.23:no.23/68.
133. *JfQ5*, p.66:no.113–f.223/69.
134. See, e.g., *NzḤ24*, p.228:no.6/42–f.94/69; *AcI3*, p.7:no.9/55–f.26/55.
135. See, e.g., *JfQ1*, p.22:no.37–f.52/51; *JfQ2*, p.440:no.431–f.4/60, p.441:no.432–f.19/60, p.566:no.577–f.123/62; *JfQ3*, p.236:no.375–f.64/66.
136. The reference is to the succession of a wealthy real estate dealer of Jaffa. In a dispute between his two wives, with their respective sons, one of the sons was appointed administrator. See *JfQ3*, p.236:no.375–f.64/66. On a subsequent occasion, a stranger was appointed administrator of the same estate for fear that the son might nullify or curtail the rights of the other heirs. See *JfQ3*, p.185:no.304–58/65 and p.224:no.364–f.58/65.
137. *NzḤ14*, p.100:no.1/53 (widow); *JfQ5*, order of October 16, 1969 (unmarried daughter).
138. See, e.g., *JfQ2*, p.576:no.595–f.24/63.
139. See, e.g., *JfQ3*, p.31:no.52–f.148/63.
140. *JfQ2*, p.576:no.595–f.24/63; *JfQ3*, p.31:no.52–f.148/63.
141. *Ṭb11*, p.21:no.7–f.12/51 (the woman, who had been irrevocably divorced, contended that her husband had taken her back after three or four days and that she had even borne him a child, but she was not able to prove that he had legally remarried her); *AcD6*, p.37:f.32/64 (the legal wife opposed the confirmation of the marriage of the divorced wife); *Ap1*, p.14:no.14 (a woman's claim to a share in the inheritance was dismissed because she had been divorced in the deceased's lifetime and it had not been proven that he had remarried her).

142. *NzḤ17*, p.78:no.32/212; *NzḤ24*, p.12:no.8/58–f.93/66.
143. See, e.g., *JfQ2*, p.492:no.444–f.32/57; *ṬbḤ3*, p.34:no.46; *NzḤ17*, p.59: no.10/190; *AcIr2*, p.45:no.38.
144. Coulson, *Succession*, pp.54–7.
145. *NzḤ17*, p.128:no.28/278. He was correct, but their omission prejudiced rights they had under the Ottoman Law of Succession.
146. See, e.g., *NzḤ19*, p.163:no.2/54; *JfQ4*, p.167:no.207–f.8/69.
147. See, e.g., *ṬbḤ3*, p.34:no.46; *NzḤ17*, p.204:no.32/382.
148. See Coulson, *Succession*, p.245.
149. See, e.g., *JfQ2*, p.563:no.569–f.110/62 (the *maḍbaṭa* notes that the uncle was "the worthiest of persons" to act as guardian in the absence of the father).
150. See the chapter "Guardianship," pp.269–70.
151. *AcQ4*, p.82:f.60 (her application was dismissed). See also *NzḤ15*, p.38: no.10/63.
152. See Weines, pp.274–5; Ben-Shemesh, p.274.
153. In the *JrLR*, the transactions in blocks 29520–29525 in Abū Ghūsh village were examined; in Netanya, some of the transactions in block 7824 and in Ṭayyiba village; and in Nazareth, at random, transactions in recent years.
154. See, e.g., *JfQ1*, p.22:no.37–f.52/51; *ṬbḤ3*, p.118:no.31 (one year after the issue of the succession order, the widow of the deceased notified that the heirs had agreed to distribute the estate between them in accordance with the succession order); *NzḤ19*, p.163:no.2/54 (five years after the issue of the succession order, one of the heirs applied for its amendment, remarking on this occasion that "the order has not yet been made use of"), p.259:no.6/77. See also *JrLR*, f.2570/65 (registration 13 years after issue of the order), f.2161/64 (ten years), f.2109/64 (nine years).
155. What follows was recorded at an interview with P. Kviti.
156. See, e.g., *JrLR*, deed of sale no.1730/66.
157. This cannot be proved from the land registers because a woman bears her father's name even after her marriage while her son is named after her husband (his father). See, e.g., *JrLR*, deed of sale no.3049–3050/61.
158. This was communicated to the author by Dr. J. Tartakover, formerly Director of the Department of Land Registration and Land Settlement at the Ministry of Justice.
159. See, e.g., *JfQ2*, p.291:no.452–f.53/57 (the deceased had died 35 years before the succession order was issued on the initiative of a son; in the meantime, the widow, the two daughters, and one of the two sons had also died); *JfQ3*, p.356:no.498–f.36/67 (the deceased died in the early days of the Mandate, and the succession order was issued in 1967 on the initiative of a grandson; in the meantime, the widow and most of the children had died); *ṬbḤ4*, p.135:no.115 (the deceased died 50 years before the succes-

sion order was issued on the initiative of a son); *NzḤ19*, p.212:no.14/23 (the deceased died 70 years before the order was issued on the initiative of a grandson after the children and many of the grandchildren had died); *NzḤ23*, p.103:no.7/27–f.51/65 (the deceased died 46 years before the issue of the succession order; the number of shares according to *sharʿī* law was over 400 million, and according to Ottoman Law six million); *AcIr7*, p.26:f.57/67 (the deceased died 50 years before the order was issued on the initiative of his son-in-law; the widow and the daughter had died by then).

160. Rosenfeld, *Peasants*, pp.29–30, 96, 102, 120, 144–5, 148–9; Cohen, pp.77, 122, 124; Marx, *Bedouin*, p.185. Cf. Goadby, p.122; al-ʿArif, p.125; Baer, pp.35, 38–40.
161. See, e.g., *JfQ1*, p.27:no.45; *JfQ3*, p.35:no.57–f.107/63, p.35:no.60–f.15/52.
162. See, e.g., *JfQ2*, p.305:no.472–f.13/58; *NzḤ18*, p.55:no.17/129; *AcIr3*, p.81:no.2/57–f.27/56. Cf. al-ʿĀrif, p.126.
163. See, e.g., *JfQ1*, p.135:no.228–f.30/54; *NzI4*, p.74:no.5/24–f.63/50.
164. See, e.g., *NzḤ19*, p.266:no.7/85; *NzḤ17*, p.144:no.3/298; *AcIr5*, p.112:f.114/60; *AcIr3*, p.204:no.39/58–f.179/57.
165. See, e.g., *JfQ3*, p.3:no.5–f.64/63; *NzḤ19*, p.90:no.11/91.
166. See, e.g., *ṬbḤ1*, p.35:no.17/63; *ṬbḤ3*, p.43:no.1; *NzḤ18*, p.95:no.31/184; *NzḤ20*, p.162:no.105.
167. See, e.g., *JfQ2*, p.459:no.474–f.68/60; *ṬbḤ2*, p.47:no.11; *NzḤ20*, p.112:no.9/35; *AcIr3*, p.69:no.67/56–f.82/56.
168. See, e.g., *NzḤ17*, p.91:no.11/226; *AcIr4*, p.15:no.90–f.179/58.
169. See *AcIr4*, p.8:no.83–f.164/58; *AcIr7*, p.3:no.3/66–f.40/65; *ṬbḤ2*, p.34:no.59; *NzḤ19*, p.112:no.4/4.
170. See, e.g., *JfQ2*, p.578:no.599–f.114/62.
171. See, e.g., *JfQ2*, p.392:no.550–f.20/59, p.506:no.566–f.101/66, p.601:no.646; *NzḤ15*, p.25:no.32/47, p.26:no.33/48.
172. See the chapter "Guardianship," pp.265–6.
173. See, e.g., *NzḤ14*, p.116:no.9/77; *NzḤ17*, p.85:no.5/220; *NzḤ23*, p.173:no.5/32–f.44/66. See also *NzḤ19*, p.151:no.2/45.
174. See, e.g., *AcI2*, p.64:f.26/54; *ṬbI1*, p.49:no.10–f.24/53, p.194:no.15–f.25/61 and p.196:no.18–f.25/61; *JfQ3*, p.199:no.327–f.84/65.
175. See, e.g., *JfQ1*, p.275:no.424–f.29/57; *JfQ4*, p.102:no.114–f.70/68; *NzḤ14*, p.85:no.14/30; *NzḤ24*, p.29:no.7/77–f.134/66; *AcṬ3*, p.28:f.19/57.
176. See, e.g., *JfQ2*, p.426:no.413–f.59/79, p.434:no.421–f.27/59; *JfQ3*, p.163:no.264–f.13/65; *NzI4*, p.182:no.1/12–f.43/57.
177. See, e.g., *NzI4*, p.71:no.1/20–f.51/50; *NzḤ18*, p.29:no.11/96. Cf. Baer, pp.39–40, 64–6.

178. See, e.g., *JrLR*, fs.2161/64, 2153/66, 2819/67. This was also confirmed to the author by S. ᶜAmir.
179. For specimens of such agreements see *JrILA*, f.821/79.
180. For specimens of such powers of attorney see *JrLR*, fs.2109/64, 2153/66.
181. Such a transaction is popularly called *bayᶜ barrānī* (external sale). Interviewee Shrem estimated that tens of thousands of transactions were effected in the Northern District in this way, and Advocate Fārūq al-Zuᶜbī, of Nazareth, estimated that 90% of all transactions in immovable property in the Nazareth area were effected outside the Land Registry.
182. See the remarks of the Minister of Justice in the Knesset, *KP*, Fifth Knesset, third session, no.32, p.2128 col.2, p.2129 col.1. Cf. Weines, p.274; Ben-Shemesh, p.189.
183. There are many dozens of cases in the blocks examined by the author in Abū Ghūsh (land settlement completed in 1942) and Ṭayyiba (1937). See, e.g., *JrLR*, f.2161/64 (the widow owned one quarter of the property and all the children, sons and daughters alike, owned equal shares, in accordance with the Ottoman Law of Succession), f.2987/65 (as above), f.2153/66 (property registered in the name of two sisters in equal shares), f.1699/64 (property registered wholly in the name of a woman). For instances in the Little Triangle see *NtLR*, block 7824.
184. See, e.g., *JrLR*, f.2153/66 (when the sons wished to register their mother's estate in their name, it appeared that she had sold the property to several persons by means of an irrevocable power of attorney), f.1588/64 (a woman bought some tens of dunams of *mirī* land from her husband), f.394/58 (a woman sold some property wholly owned by her to two persons); *NtLR*, block 7824.
185. See, e.g., *JrILA*, f.79/821, f.119/821 (a woman sold a parcel of land registered wholly in her name to a resident of the village; after his death, his daughter initiated a succession order and applied to the Israel Lands Administration for compensation for property which had been vested in the Development Authority), f.137/821 (three brothers and a sister of the deceased received equal shares of the estate in accordance with the Ottoman Law of Succession and divided the land among them; an affidavit states expressly that the sister also received a parcel of land).
186. Recorded at an interview with Shaykh Ḥusnī al-Zuᶜbī.
187. Recorded at an interview with Advocate Fārūq al-Zuᶜbī, a son of the *qāḍī* of the *Sharīᶜa* Court of Nazareth and frequently present in that court.
188. Recorded at an interview with S. ᶜAmir. Cf. al-ᶜĀrif, p.125. The author indeed found instances in the *sijill*s of aged fathers dividing their property among their sons and even registering it in their names in the Land Registry and then claiming maintenance from them. See, e.g., *JfQ4*, p.173: no.216–

f.117/69; *ṬbI1*, p.53:no.3–f.4/54, p.256:no.9–f.12/64. See also *JfQ2*, p.316:no.493–f.40/58.

189. Recorded at an interview with Muṣṭafā ᶜAlayān.
190. Recorded during a symposium at Beyt ha-Gefen in Haifa, on May 26, 1971.
191. Rosenfeld's and Cohen's researches of Galilean and Little Triangle villages and Marx's research on the Negev Beduin certainly reflect social conditions in the localities concerned, but these are not representative of all types of settlement and social groups of Muslims in Israel.
192. That is to say, women who had married outside their own villages, took their shares in the estates of their fathers, which were situated in their original places of residence. See Granott, pp.166 *seq.*, 235, and the sources quoted there. Cf. al-ᶜĀrif, pp.125–6.
193. Z. Urieli, of the Israel Lands Administration, regarded land transactions as the principal motive in the initiation of succession orders.
194. See, e.g., *ṬbḤ1*, p.51:no.4/86; *JfQ1*, p.333:no.522–f.73/58; *NzḤ17*, p.277:no.24/54; *AcIr5*, p.104:f.141/60. See *AI*, vol.1 (1950), No.5, p.2; *AI*, vol.2 (1951), No.1, p.5.
195. See, e.g., *JfQ1*, p.9:no.16; *ṬbḤ1*, p.4:no.7/8; *NzḤ14*, p.98:no.6/49; *AcIr2*, p.19:no.16/50. For the distribution of the estate according to both systems of law during the Mandate see, e.g., *JfḤ19*, p.1:no.233; *NzḤ14*, p.3:no.56. Cf. Eilon, pp.42–3.
196. Hence the terminological distinction in the orders between "transmission by way of inheritance" (*irth*), which relates to immovable property in full ownership, movables and money, and "transfer" (*intiqāl*), which relates to immovable property of the *mīrī* category. See, e.g., *JfQ2*, p.573: no.590–f.99/62; *AcI1*, p.42:no.35; *AcIr3*, p.1:no.1/55–f.83/54; *NzḤ18*, p.146:no.8/246; *NzI4*, p.226:no.4/17–f.97/63.
197. *AcQ4*, p.82:f.60/40. See also *JfQ2*, p.302:no.467–f.64/57 and 573:no.590–f.99/62; *JfQ3*, p.232:no.371–f.29/65.
198. The author came across only one case in which all the heirs appeared in court for the receipt of a succession order. See *ṬbḤ1*, p.101:no.3/80.
199. See, e.g., *JfQ1*, p.234:no.385–f.39/65.
200. This assumption was confirmed to the author by S. Nawi, Director of the Muslim Division in the Ministry of Religious Affairs, and by interviewee Rāᵓiq Jarjūra, a Nazareth advocate who frequently appeared in *sharīᶜa* courts.
201. See, e.g., *AcIr7*, p.18:f.39/67, p.27:no.27/67–f.138/66; *NzḤ24*, p.163: no.4/62–f.123/68, p.250:no.7/73–f.141/69, p.263:no.3/3–f.7/70.
202. See, e.g., *ṬbḤ4*, p.297:no.2–f.83/67, p.309:no.17–f.37/68; *JfQ4*, p.4:no.4–f.87/67.
203. See, e.g., *AcIr8*, p.39:no.15–f.124/69; *JfQ4*, p.36:no.35–f.55/67; *ṬbḤ4*,

p.297:no.2–f.83/67, p.302, no.7–f.17/68, p.308:no.16–f.40/68; *NzḤ24*, p.58:no.1/23–f.42/67, p.67:no.7/34–f.63/67.

204. See, e.g., *JfQ3*, p.346:no.488–f.142/66; *JfQ5*, p.72:no.122–f.203/69.
205. Interview with S. Nawi.
206. *NzḤ24*, p.82:no.9/51–f.111/67.
207. Interview with Prof. U. Yadin.
208. See, e.g., *ṬbḤ4*, p.297:no.2–f.83/67, p.308:no.16–f.40/68; *JfQ3*, p.295:no. 414–f.85/66; *JfQ4*, p.171:f.24/69; *AcIr8*, p.34:no.10/69–f.56/69, p.52:no. 13–f.95/70.
209. See, e.g., *AcIr7*, p.14:no.14/67–f.175/66, p.26:f.119/66; *AcIr8*, p.38:no. 14–f.79/69.
210. See, e.g., *NzḤ24*, p.58:no.1/23–f.42/67, p.58:no.2/24–f.46/67, p.67:no.7/34–f.63/67. The issue of such a succession order was justified only if the deceased died before the "determining date," viz., November 10, 1965.
211. See, e.g., *NzḤ24*, p.197:no.5/5–f.12/69, p.199:no.1/7–f.18/69, p.270: no.3/13–f.24/70; *AcIr8*, p.32:no.8–f.47/49; *JfQ4*, p.87:no.86–f.136/67.
212. Interview with Shaykh Ḥusnī al-Zuʿbī.
213. See, e.g., *AcIr8*, p.29:no.6/69–f.14/69, p.33:no.9/69–f.137/68, p.37:no.13–f.68/69; *JfQ3*, p.369:no.510–f.77/67; *JfQ4*, p.59:no.55–f.139/67, p.90: no.90–f.32/68.
214. See, e.g., *NzḤ24*, p.71:no.4/39–f.76/67.
215. *JfQ4*, p.66:no.62–f.1/68 (the order does not say that the absent daughter was a minor).
216. Shaykh Mūsā al-Ṭabarī sent a cable to the Prime Minister "in the name of the people assembled in the al-Jazzār Mosque" (see the file of the Adviser on Arab Affairs in the Prime Minister's Office). See also *ha-Boqer* and *Zemanim* of October 21, 1953, and *The Jerusalem Post* of December 15, 1953.
217. See Yadin, *Civil Code*, pp.105-6.
218. See, e.g., *NzḤ14*, p.68:no.1/10; *JfQ3*, p.293:no.433–f.109/66, p.302: no.442–f.118/66.
219. See, e.g., *NzḤ24*, p.71:no.4/39–f.76/67.
220. See, e.g., *JfQ2*, p.443:no.437–f.33/60, p.574:no.591–f.112/62.
221. Interview with Shaykh Muḥammad Ḥubayshi. Shaykh Ḥusnī al-Zuʿbī, too, told the author that he was not prepared to recognize a woman's renunciation of her share of an inheritance if he had the impression that it was made under pressure.
222. *JfQ4*, p.95:no.100–f.90/62 and p.101:no.111–f.90/62.
223. See Coulson, *Succession*, p.50.
224. *JfQ2*, p.480:no.509–f.43/61, p.578:no.598–f.126/62; *JfQ3*, p.76:no.117–f.203/63, p.164:no.265–f.11/65. Shaykh Ṭāhir Ḥamād adopted the same

practice in the case of a husband who was the sole heir of his wife. See *JfQ2*, p.601 : no.645.

225. *NzḤ17*, p.278 : no.25/55; *NzḤ19*, p.22 : no.1/16; *NzḤ22*, p.9 : no.7/61–f.87/62; *AcIr4*, p.81 : no.55–f.100/59.

226. See, e.g., *JfQ2*, p.573 : no.503–f.34/62; *JfQ3*, p.16 : no.24–f.55/63; *AcD6*, p.1 : f.1/64. But there were exceptions. See, e.g., *JfQ2*, p.521 : no.497–f.31/62.

227. See, e.g., *JfQ3*, p.194 : no.321–f.99/65. For recent reforms with regard to wills in several Arab countries see Coulson, *Succession*, pp.255–7.

SUMMARY

In an organically developing society, law reflects the social conditions under which it grows and crystallizes.[1] In traditional Muslim society, an equilibrium exists between the social and the legal status of women because Muslim family law is adapted to the structure of the patrilineal and patriarchal family. The salient features of the extended family, viz., the supremacy of men, patrilineal relationships, patrilocal residence and endogamous customs, find exact legal expression in Muslim matrimonial law, with a few deviations induced by Muḥammad's legal norms, which were designed to protect women. The basic cause of women's inferiority is thus social custom, in part legitimized by the *sharīʿa*; women's low legal status is chiefly attributable to the factors shaping the Arab extended family. In order to maintain a dynamic balance between social and legal status, the family law should be capable of constant adaptation to changing social conditions. Late Ottoman legislation was the first modern attempt to maintain such a balance. The objects of the Ottoman Family Rights Law were limited and relatively moderate because the changes in the structure of the family and the status of women were only in their beginnings, and reforms in the status of women could be introduced within the existing legal system.[2] Any attempt to assign to women artificially, from above, a legal status not consonant with their social status disturbs the equilibrium between the two spheres, creates tensions and usually does not stand the test of reality, for social custom is stronger than law, even *sharʿī* law. Muḥammad's reforms, intended to improve the legal status of women, were circumvented or ridiculed because they did not reflect women's social status at that period. Thus, for example, the regulation that a woman inherits, which originated in urban society, does not fit a tribal society in which only male agnates (*ʿaṣabāt*) inherit.[3]

In Israel, the balance between the legal and the social status of Muslim women has been drastically upset because developments on the two planes, the social and the legal, have not come about through internal growth, but are mainly the result of direct contact with a Western society in all its aspects. Owing to the dual, religious-secular, legal system obtaining in Israel, that imbalance, too, has twofold dimensions: on the one hand, the social status of women today is generally better than their status under religious law, but on the other hand—and this is the crux of the problem—it is still far from catching up with their legal status under secular law. An anomaly has thus been created in that social conditions, which normally change slowly and over a long period, are required to adapt instantly to a legal framework shaped in accordance with the needs of a modern society and imposed on Muslim society from above.

Muslim women in Israel are at a transitional stage. On the one hand, there are the usual manifestations of female inferiority in traditional society: marriages of minor girls and polygamy; deprivation of the right to dower, succession and custody of the children; residence at the home of the husband's family; obedience to the husband, confinement to the house and restriction of freedom of movement and social contacts; unilateral divorce, and so forth. These phenomena are contrary not only to secular law but in part also to express provisions of the Qurʾān. The causes of the deprivation of women's rights are social inferiority, owing to which they are ignorant of their rights or incapable of exercising them, and social custom, which in day-to-day reality still takes precedence over religious precepts[4]; this custom is mainly operative in the domain of kinship and property relations within the extended family.

But beside these phenomena there are significant indications of a change in the status of women: the age of marriage of the bride has risen, marriages of minor girls have become considerably less frequent and polygamy has become rare; women are now paid the whole or part of the dower into their own hands; the dower is changing its function, and becoming a means to prevent divorce or to assure the economic position of divorced women, and there is even the emergent phenomenon of marriages without dower (which may be to the advantage of women); women strive for a dwelling separate from the residence of the husband's family and sometimes in their own home locality, availing themselves of the device of the stipulation inserted in the marriage contract;

they frequently leave the house against the will of the husband, work away from home, earn money and support themselves and their children; they renounce their right to maintenance and are not afraid of being declared rebellious; they exercise their right of succession and enjoy great freedom in disposing of property; they enjoy their *sharʿī* right to custody and their secular-legal right to guardianship of their children; most divorces are by mutual agreement of the parties; the practice is spreading of compensating the wife or paying her maintenance beyond the waiting-period (*ʿidda*) in return for her consent to the divorce; in many cases, the wife is the active party in the dissolution of the marriage, using various devices to obtain her freedom. The change cannot always be appraised in quantitative terms, but there can be no doubt that it is on a significant scale. Some of the phenomena are not new, but it seems that they were not so frequent and marked in the past as they are today. The change is more pronounced and comprehensive in towns than in villages and more in mixed than in Arab towns, and more in the villages of the Little Triangle than in those of other regions. Incipient changes are noticeable also in the status of Beduin women, especially in Galilee.

The intervention of the Knesset has undoubtedly made an important contribution to the improvement of the social status of women. Its impact is mainly due to the penal sanction attached to several enactments. Clear indications of a deterrent effect are applications to the court for permission to divorce one's wife without her consent and in a few cases for the marriage of a girl under 17 or for polygamy; the payment of compensation to a divorced woman in return for her consent to the divorce; and the conversion of traditional grounds for polygamy—as far as an inclination for this type of marriage still exists—into frequent grounds for divorce (especially in the Little Triangle villages). The fact that men resort to various devices in order to circumvent Israeli legislation is also significant in this connection. The impact of substantive legislation is especially noticeable in the matter of guardianship and of the agreement of the parties to the jurisdiction of the *sharīʿa* court under the Israeli Succession Law.

At the same time, it is doubtful that secular legislation is the main cause of the improvement in the position of women in matters of personal status, since there are numerous instances of circumvention of that legislation by various means. This is mainly true for marriages of minor girls, divorces against the wife's will and the application of the Ottoman Law of Succession to *mulk* and movables under the Women's Equal

Rights Law. Secular legislation is circumvented in those social strata which cannot live up to the norms prescribed by the Knesset, just as it is usual to circumvent the *sharʿī* norms; but whereas Muḥammad's reforms are supported by toothless ethical sanctions, the Knesset's reforms are bound up with legal and penal sanctions, which is why more sophisticated devices are required to circumvent them.[5]

Moreover, the Knesset, in its eagerness to impose on the Muslim public progressive norms, tailored to Israeli society, has sometimes harmed more than helped Muslim women. The ban on polygamy has caused an increase in the divorce rate and reduced the opportunities for levirate marriages (by which the dead man's brother marries his widow), which are the structural solution for widows wishing to remain united with their children at the house of the husband's family[6]; and the intervention of the welfare officer, who is guided by the principle of the best interest of the child, may impair the status of a woman as a natural guardian of her children when that principle is translated into traditional terms. The sporadic character of the secular legislation has led in many cases to a disturbance of delicate balances in the Muslim family. The accidental, unsystematic mixture of elements of two legal systems, religious and secular, based on completely different social norms, has created distortions and anomalies which have sometimes shaken the legal frame of that family. Thus, for example, the restriction of the husband's freedom of *ṭalāq* without his being given grounds for judicial dissolution or a good defense to the charge of divorce against the wife's will in special circumstances, such as when she is rebellious, has created a practically intolerable situation because the husband cannot divorce the wife without her consent whereas the wife has a long series of definite grounds for judicial dissolution without need of the husband's consent. The husband cannot protect himself against such a predicament by taking a second wife because polygamy is forbidden, too. As a result, the traditional equilibrium in the sphere of divorce is disturbed (as indeed the Knesset had intended it to be), but a new equilibrium has not been created, even on the basis of equality of the sexes.[7] Compensation to the wife for her consent to the divorce is one of the manifestations of this new situation.[8] The two prohibitions have also disturbed the traditional equilibrium between the mutual rights and obligations of the spouses, for *ṭalāq* and polygamy were means to enforce the wife's obedience, and in this case also a new balance, based on progressive social norms, has not taken the place of the old. In sum, the importance of the secular legislation lies mainly in increasing the wife's legal security by the creation of a mechanism enabling her to realize her rights through the threat of penal or other legal sanctions. The mere existence of such a mechanism, even if it is not frequently resorted to, may to a certain extent deter potential offenders.

It seems that the changes in the social position of women in matters of personal status are mainly attributable to economic, cultural, social and other factors: their joining the labor force, especially their penetration into occupations requiring education and specialized skills; the spread of education among girls; the social, vocational and cultural activities of State and public bodies among women; the development of the villages and the raising of the standard of living; the transition from the extended to the nuclear family; the absorption of modern concepts of the institution of marriage, and so on. In this connection, Israeli legislation is important as a medium for imparting the normative values of Israeli society to Muslim society. The impact of these factors is particularly noticeable in the mixed towns because of the direct contact with Israeli society.[9] The educational factor is operative in the comparatively young age-groups of women who have acquired their education in the State of Israel. This is clearly reflected in marriage contracts drawn up in recent years, viz., in dower practices and stipulations. On the other hand, this factor has so far not been noticeable in other matters of personal status, such as succession and divorce, which by the nature of things relate to older women. The exogamous type of marriage no doubt makes it easier for women to exercise their rights in various matrimonial matters because it leaves them free from pressures arising out of blood-relationship and family loyalty. It seems, on the other hand, that endogamy does not present very serious obstacles to women who are aware of their rights and not prepared to forgo them.

Muslim women do not tend to settle matrimonial matters before a civil court although their legal position is incomparably better there than before a *sharīʿa* court both as regards the substantive law and the rules of evidence and procedure. As stated, in 1965 the jurisdiction of *sharīʿa* courts in matters of succession was reduced from exclusive to concurrent. Women, and the Muslim public in general, prefer the more intimate atmosphere of the *sharīʿa* court (the proceedings of which are conducted in Arabic) and the *qāḍī*, who is close to them in his religious and social outlook and firmly rooted in the day-to-day life of his community, to an alien, impersonal civil court, which is identified with the government authority, and a judge remote from the Muslim environment.[10]

Thus, there exist in Israel, side by side, women deprived of their rights by both secular and religious law and women who enjoy their rights to a greater or lesser degree. This is, as stated, a transitional phase, and there can be no doubt that, as the factors of change become more powerful, the gap between women's social status and their legal status under secular law will narrow. Paradoxically, many of Muḥammad's reforms and ethical commands, as in the matter of polygamy and divorce and of women's right to dower and succession, are for the first time given significant effect at a time when the *sharīʿa* is in retreat and has lost much of its power in society and state, particularly in Israel. The reason for this is that the religious norms Muḥammad sought to impose on his believers were unsuitable for the patrilineal and patriarchal family and society and are more in keeping with the nuclear family and the modern concept of the social status of women.[11] Thus, for example, it is only within the framework of the nuclear family that the *sharʿī* principles, basic to modern Israeli legislation, of the separation of property and of women's capacity to own and dispose of property, can be realized.

The creation of a new equilibrium between the social and the legal status of women depends largely on the *qāḍī*s, who are competent to interpret both religious and secular law. As far as can be judged by declared attitudes, most *qāḍī*s acknowledge the need to adapt the law of personal status to the changes in the structure of the family and in the position of women, and some even challenge the inflexible *sharīʿa*. They are guided by humanitarian motives, the most typical manifestation of which is the doctrine of *maṣlaḥa*, the public interest, and by the principle that innovations are permissible to the extent that—as, for example, in the matter of compensation to a divorced woman for her consent to the divorce—they are not opposed by express prohibitions in the textual sources of religious law. Although the *qāḍī*s denounce arbitrary divorces and one of them even suggested negating their validity, they are not prepared to go far in this matter because the *ṭalāq* is rooted in the Qurʾān. Their attitude is generally liberal and favorable to the woman; it is marked by pragmatism. On the other hand, they find themselves in a conscientious conflict where religious and secular law clash.[12]

The most important and meaningful measure of the *qāḍī*s' attitude regarding the status of women is found in their judgments, which, indeed, sometimes reveal a gap between the declared positions of some of them and their day-to-day practice.[13] Ambivalence is the most characteristic trait of their approach to religious and secular law. They usually interpret religious law in strict adherence to the *taqlīd* ("imitation," the unquestioning acceptance of the Sunnite orthodox schools of law), regardless of the consequences for the woman involved. This formal approach is to her advantage where there is a question of realizing her *sharʿī* rights, such as dower, maintenance or the custody of the children, but to her detriment where there is a question of a man's rights, such as obedience, guardianship or *ṭalāq*, where she renounces any right (such as her share in an inheritance) or where she is to be deprived of a right on *sharʿī* grounds based on traditional norms (as by her disqualification from custody on account of her marriage to a stranger). By their formal approach, the *qāḍī*s assist in depriving women of their right to dower in exchange marriages; they make no normative distinction between types of divorce with their various legal effects; in matters of custody and guardianship, they are guided by religious-legal norms, which are not always consistent with the best interest of the child. Moreover, some *qāḍī*s adhere so staunchly to the Ḥanafī school as to deliberately refrain from applying provisions of the Ottoman Family Rights Law because they deviate from the teachings of that school, such as, for instance, provisions permitting dissolution on the grounds of a defect or illness of the husband, non-payment of maintenance to the wife of an absent husband or discord between the spouses. Some uphold the rigorous classification of irregular and void marriages, consciously or unconsciously disregarding reforms introduced by the Ottoman legislator.

But beside the aforesaid approach, there are many instances of decisions other than in accordance with the rigid *sharʿī* norm. The *qāḍī*s' most customary method of reaching a desirable solution without conflicting with religious law is by using their personal authority (sometimes through middlemen) in order to reconcile the parties and give the compromise arrived at the force of a judgment; this method does not involve the application of religious law. This practice is most noticeable in matters of maintenance, obedience and divorce, and it seems that the principal concern of the *qāḍī*s is the preservation of the marriage. The institutionalized organ of arbitration in reaching judicial decisions is the family council within the meaning of article 130 of the Family

Rights Law. But there are also express deviations from the teachings of the Ḥanafī school. Thus, some *qāḍī*s add to the grounds for judicial dissolution the non-payment of maintenance, injury, cruelty and the husband's imprisonment, which are recognized by schools other than the Ḥanafī (and provide legitimation for modern legislation in Arab countries), and most *qāḍī*s confirm stipulations inserted in the marriage contract even if they mean a change in the matrimonial rights or obligations of one of the parties, such as the establishment of the marital dwelling in the wife's home locality; in fact, it is through the active assistance of the *qāḍī*s that the stipulation in the marriage contract has become an efficient instrument for improving the status of women.

There are *qāḍī*s who award the *radd* to the widow or hold that the dissolution of the marriage of the wife of an absent husband is a revocable divorce, again in deviation from the teachings of the Ḥanafī school. The flexibility of the *qāḍī*s as regards the different schools of law has probably something to do with the fact that most Israeli Muslims belong to the Shāfiᶜī school (the Ḥanbalī school is also represented—in the Little Triangle villages); at any rate, there is evidence that *sharīᶜa* courts were already giving judgments in accordance with Shāfiᶜī teachings in the Mandate period.[14] By using the mechanism of the *talfīq* (selective combination of legal doctrines) in their decisions, the *qāḍī*s have scored impressive achievements, some not inferior, perhaps even superior, to those attained in Arab countries by means of secular legislation.

The sanctifying role of the *qāḍī*s is crucial in the process of Islamization of social custom, both traditional (among the Beduin) and modern (in the cities), which still continues in Muslim society. This is so, for instance, in the matter of token dower, marriages without dower, compensation to the divorced wife, and compensation to the ex-husband on the remarriage of his former wife. The process occurs through a compromise between the customary and the *sharᶜī* norms, and is aided by the mechanism of arbitration.[15] There is, of course, a close connection between custom and the social motivation underlying the principle of the *maṣlaḥa* (public interest).

Ambivalence is also conspicuous in the *qāḍī*s' attitude toward Israeli legislation. On the one hand, there are those who ignore the Knesset's intervention in matters such as age of marriage offenses, polygamy and divorce against the wife's will; most of them do not use the wide discretion given them by the Knesset as to permission for divorce against the wife's will and polygamous marriages (in so far as the court is resorted to in these matters), and consider themselves bound by the accepted *sharʿī* norms as to marriage and divorce; permission is granted almost automatically or the divorce, marriage of a girl under age or polygamous marriage is registered *ex post facto* without any reference to the question of criminality. The *qāḍī*s, contrary to the expectations of the Knesset, do not recognize the bride's being under the age of 17 as a ground for dissolution.[16] Some misinterpret and misapply substantive provisions, as in the matter of guardianship or succession. Lastly, there are those who, consciously or unconsciously, assist in circumventing secular legislation, as by using the mechanism of suspended repudiation for the purposes of divorce against the wife's will.

On the other hand, there are many indications that secular legislation has made an impact on the *qāḍī*s. Some rely on it explicitly in their decisions, adopting its principles even when these conflict with the *sharʿī* view, as in the matter of the recognition of a woman as a natural guardian of her children or the appointment of a guardian with reference to the best interest of the child. Some frequently have recourse to the welfare officer in this connection. Some display a keen awareness of the ban on divorce against the wife's will and the ban on polygamy, warn the husband against committing an offense and when it has been committed, although confirming the divorce or marriage *ex post facto*, call the wife's attention to her right to bring a criminal charge against the husband.

The *qāḍī*s' perplexity and vacillation between religious and secular law is sometimes expressed in simultaneous application of substantive elements of both legal systems, despite material contradictions between them. Thus, there are those who recognize the status of a woman as a natural guardian of her children by virtue of secular legislation and at the same time appoint the grandfather guardian over them on the ground that he is the natural guardian according to religious law. There are those who warn the husband against divorcing the wife against her will and at the same time recognize his *sharʿī* right to divorce her unilaterally. This ambivalent attitude has an ideological basis in the declared positions of the *qāḍī*s. They are not opposed to the Knesset's intervention in matters of personal status so long as no encroachment on the *sharīʿa* is involved. Some of them would even welcome further reforms of a procedural or penal nature, such as additional defenses to the charge of divorce against the wife's will or of polygamy in the case of a rebellious, sick or barren wife, with a view to creating a new equilibrium between the social and the legal status of women. There are even those who believe that a secular penal sanction can be used in matters of marriage and divorce to reinforce a *sharʿī* norm supported by ethical sanction lacking deterrent effect. But there are also *qāḍī*s who do not shrink from calling for secular legislation of an expressly substantive character—for example, in order to ensure the subsistence of a divorced woman—as a matter of *siyāsa* (policy), a governmental regulation designed to supplement the *sharīʿa*.[17]

In conclusion, it would seem that, considering the theoretically immutable character of religious law and the difficulty of imposing secular legislation on religious courts, the *qāḍī*s have, nonetheless, made an important contribution to the improvement of the position of women in matters of personal status.[18]

NOTES

1. See Smith, p.25.
2. See Anderson, *Islamic Law*, p.26.
3. See Goitein and Ben-Shemesh, pp.142–3; Fyzee, pp.380 *seq.*, 411, 416–17.
4. See Baer, p.34 *seq.*
5. Cf. Dirks, pp.146, 176 *seq.*; *MḤ.*, vol.21 (1971), p.459.
6. See Rosenfeld, *Peasants*, pp.40–2. Cf. Goitein and Ben-Shemesh, pp.136–7.
7. The ban on polygamy without radically tackling divorce might, in Anderson's opinion, harm women more than help them. See Anderson, *Patriarchal Family*, p. 231.
8. The husband's stipulation in the marriage contract that he shall be permitted to divorce the wife against her will or that their dwelling shall be in his home locality is likewise significant in this connection.
9. Cf. Woodsmall, p.86.
10. A Muslim District Judge has recently been appointed in Nazareth, but it is too early to assess the significance of this fact in relation to the matter under reference.
11. Cf. Coulson, *History*, pp.219–20; *idem*, *Conflicts*, pp.97–8; *idem*, *Succession*, pp.135–6.
12. For a more detailed discussion see Layish, *Qāḍīs*, pp.240–51, 255–72.
13. Cf. Anderson, *Africa*, pp.69, 321.

14. Shaykh Ṭāhir Ḥamād, *AI*, vol.4 (1956), No.1, p.8. Most of the *qāḍī*s, at a conference in 1966, adopted the position of the Shāfiʿī school concerning relationship by suckling as an impediment to marriage (*AI*, vol.10 (1966), Nos.1–2, p.83) and Shaykh Ḥusnī al-Zuʿbī relied on a collection of *fatwās* of a Shāfiʿī *muftī* in support of his attitude with regard to birth control (*AI*, vol. 9 (1964), Nos.3–4, p.11). Cf. Anderson, *Dissolution*, p.271; *idem*, *Africa*, pp.30, 55–6, 79, 110, 146, 280.
15. For a more detailed discussion see Layish, *Custom*, pp. 402–9. Cf. Anderson, *Africa*, pp.211–12, 218.
16. Cf. Coulson, *Conflicts*, pp.115–16; el-Naqeb, pp.202–3.
17. See Layish, *Qāḍīs*, pp.255–8; Schacht, p.54; Coulson, *Succession*, p.137. The *qāḍī*s' practice of relying on the welfare services of the State in judgments for maintenance contributes, indirectly and unintentionally, to the disruption of the balanced system of rights and obligations underlying the traditional family.
18. Cf. Tedeschi, p.229.

SOURCES AND BIBLIOGRAPHY

The definite articles al *in Arabic and* ha *in Hebrew have been disregarded in the alphabetical arrangement.*

1. ARCHIVAL MATERIAL, according to Types of Sources, with a key to Abbreviations Used in the Notes

a. Sijills of the Sharīᶜa Courts, according to Place, Type and Period

Sharīᶜa Court of Jaffa

JfQ1(–5)	*Sijill Qarārāt*, vols.1–5(1950–70)
JfS6a	*Sijill* (General), vol.6a(1824–26)
JfS7	*Sijill* (General), vol.7(1826–27)
JfS43	*Sijill* (General), vol.43(1876–79)
JfS88	*Sijill* (General), vol.88(1902–03)
JfḤ19	*Sijill Ḥujaj*, vol.19(1926)

Sharīᶜa Court of Ṭayyiba

ṬbḤ1(–4)	*Sijill Ḥujaj*, vols.1–4(1950–68)
ṬbI1	*Sijill Iᶜlāmāt*, vol.1(1950–64)

Sharīᶜa Court of Nazareth

NzḤ14(–24)	*Sijill Ḥujaj*, vols.14–24(1947–70)
NzI4	*Sijill Iᶜlāmāt*, vol.4(1947–68)
NzS5	*Sijill* (General), vol.5(1885–90)
NzS16	*Sijill* (General), vol.16(1897–1903)
NzS26	*Sijill* (General), vol.26(1913–18)

Sharīᶜa Court of Acre

AcI1(–3)	*Sijill Iᶜlāmāt*, vols.1–3(1948–58)
AcQ4(–5)	*Sijill Qarārāt*, vols.4–5(1959–63)
AcD6(–8)	*Sijill Daᶜāwā*, vols.6–8(1964–70)
AcṬ1(–4)	*Sijill Ṭalāq*, vols.1–4(1948–68)
AcIr1(–8)	*Sijill Irth waWiṣāya*, vols.1–8(1948–70)

Sharīʿa Court of Appeal

Ap1	*Sijill Qarārāt*, Appeals vol.1(1954–66)

b. Registers of Marriage Contracts, according to Place and Period

JfMC62(68)	Register of Marriage Contracts, Court of Jaffa, 1962 and 1968
ṬbMC62(68)	Register of Marriage Contracts, Court of Ṭayyiba, 1962 and 1968
NzMC62(68)	Register of Marriage Contracts, Court of Nazareth, 1962 and 1968
AcMC62(68)	Register of Marriage Contracts, Court of Acre, 1962 and 1968

c. Land Registry and Israel Lands Administration, Jerusalem

JrLR	Jerusalem Land Registry
NzLR	Nazareth Land Registry
NtLR	Netanya Land Registry
JrILA	Israel Lands Administration, Jerusalem

d. Letters from Qāḍīs to the Author

Answers to Legal and Social Questions Addressed to Them.

2. *AI* **MAJALLAT AL-AKHBĀR AL-ISLĀMIYYA,** vols.1–12(1950–71)

Bulletin of the Muslim Division, Ministry of Religious Affairs. Editor: J. Yehoshua, former Director of the Division. In the first year of its publication, the bulletin was called *Anbāʾ al-Dāʾira al-Islāmiyya waʾl-Darziyya*, in the second year *Nashrat al-Dāʾira al-Islāmiyya waʾl-Darziyya*, and until 1957 *Majallat al-Akhbār al-Islāmiyya waʾl-Darziyya*. In the initial years, it appeared in two versions, Arabic and Hebrew, afterward only in Arabic, with summaries in other languages.

3. INTERVIEWEES, in Alphabetical Order, with Dates of Interviews

ʿAbbāsī, Maḥmūd, writer and public figure. Remarks at a round table on "The Arabs in Israel," *Kol Yisraʾel* (Israel Radio), June 14, 1971.

Abū Ṭuʿma, Jamīl, former head of the Council of Bāqa al-Gharbiyya. June 2, 1970.

ʿAlayān, Muṣṭafā, *mukhtār* of Bayt Ṣafāfā. June 30, 1969.

ʿAmir, S., Jerusalem. Concerned for years past with real estate matters in the Jerusalem area. July 1, 1969.

Cohen, B. Z., Assistant Registrar of Lands, Netanya Region. July 18, 1969.

Darwish, S., advocate, Haifa. Frequently appears in *sharīʿa* courts. Several interviews.

Dasūqī, Yūsuf, Secretary of the *Sharīʿa* Court of Ṭayyiba. May 26, 1971.

Eton, D., Land Registration and Settlement Department, Ministry of Justice. July, 1969.

al-Ḥabash, Shaykh Ḥasan Amīn, *Qāḍī* of the *Sharīʿa* Court of Ṭayyiba. June 6, 1970, and May 26, 1971.

al-Hawwārī, Muḥammad Nimr. Judge of the District Court of Nazareth. Before being appointed to this post he frequently appeared in *sharīʿa* courts. May 27, 1971.

Horvitz, M., Legal Adviser to the Ministry of Social Welfare, Jerusalem. September 10, 1968.

al-Ḥubayshī, Shaykh Muḥammad, was recently appointed *Qāḍī* of the *Sharīʿa* Court of Acre, of which he had been secretary for many years previously. He was also Deputy Mayor of Acre. Several interviews in the course of the research, the last on May 9, 1971.

Jarjūra, Rāʾiq, advocate, Nazareth. July 3, 1969.

Kteylī, Eliyās, Judge of the Magistrates' Court of Nazareth. Remarks at a symposium at the Beʾeri Club in Jerusalem on July 19, 1965.

Kviti, P., Netanya. Concerned for decades past with real estate matters in the Little Triangle. July 18, 1969.

Link, Dr. A., Director of the Land Registration and Settlement Department, Ministry of Justice, Jerusalem. July, 1969.

Mudlij, Shaykh Amīn Qāsim, *Qāḍī* of the *Sharīʿa* Court of Acre. May 17, 1968.

Nadaf, H., former Registrar of Lands, Haifa District. July 4, 1969.

Nawi, S., Director of the Muslim Division, Ministry of Religious Affairs, Jerusalem. Was for many years Assistant Director of the *sharīʿa* courts. Numerous interviews.

Qaramān, Suʿād, Ibṭīn. Active in the cause of Arab women. Remarks at symposia on the status of women at Beit ha-Gefen, Haifa, on May 16, 1968, and May 26, 1971.

Rabi, Z., Head of the Demography Section, Central Bureau of Statistics, Jerusalem. May 25, 1971.

Rosenfeld, Prof. H., Hebrew University of Jerusalem and University of Haifa. November 2, 1968, and July 23, 1970.

Shrem, A., Registrar of Lands, Nazareth District. July 3, 1969.

Tartakover, Dr. J., former Director of the Land Registration and Settlement Department, Ministry of Justice. June, 1969.

Urieli, Z., Director of the Ownership and Registration Department, Israel Lands Administration, Jerusalem. July, 1967.

Yadin, Prof. U., Deputy Attorney-General, Ministry of Justice. June 24, 1974.

al-Zuʿbī, Fārūq, advocate, Nazareth. Frequently appears in the *Sharīʿa* Court of Nazareth. July 3, 1969.

al-Zuᶜbī, Shaykh Ḥusnī, *Qāḍī* of the *Sharīᶜa* Court of Nazareth. July 3, 1969, and April 27, 1970.

4. ISLAMIC LEGAL COLLECTIONS AND COMMENTARIES, in Alphabetical Order of the Abbreviations

al-Abayānī	Muḥammad Zayd al-Abayānī, *Sharḥ al-Aḥkām al-Sharᶜiyya fī al-Aḥwāl al-Shakhṣiyya*, 4th ed. (Cairo, 1924).
ENFRL	Explanatory Note to Ottoman Family Rights Law, based on the Arabic version kept at the Muslim Division of the Ministry of Religious Affairs.
FRL	Family Rights Law of 1917, according to the Arabic version prepared by Shaykh Ṭāhir Ḥamād and published by the Ministry of Religious Affairs in 1957. This version appears in Goitein and Ben-Shemesh, pp.289–311.
Ibn ᶜĀbidīn	Ibn ᶜĀbidīn, *Radd al-Muḥtār ᶜalā al-Durr al-Mukhtār*, Part Two (Cairo, 1294H.).
Mejelle	The *Mejelle* translated into Hebrew by G. Frumkin, 3rd ed. (Jerusalem, 1951–52 (5712)).
Qadrī	Muḥammad Qadrī Pasha, *Kitāb al-Aḥkām al-Sharᶜiyya fī al-Aḥwāl al-Shakhṣiyya ᶜalā Madhhab al-ʾImām Abī Ḥanīfa al-Nuᶜmān*, in the version contained in Rushdī al-Sarrāj, *Kitāb Majmūᶜat al-Qawānīn al-Sharᶜiyya* (Jaffa, 1944), pp.80–182.
Qadrī, *Waqf*	Muḥammad Qadrī Pasha, *al-ᶜAdl waʾl-Inṣāf fī al-Waqf*, in the version contained in Rushdī al-Sarrāj, *op. cit.*, pp.199–314.

5. OFFICIAL PUBLICATIONS, in Alphabetical Order of the Abbreviations

Bills	*Hatzaᶜot Ḥoq* (the section of the Israeli Official Gazette containing bills).
IFB	*Hatzaᶜat Ḥoq ha-Yaḥid weha-Mishpaḥa* (Individual and Family Bill), Ministry of Justice (Jerusalem, 1955).
KP	*Divrey ha-Knesset*, Proceedings of the Israeli Parliament (Knesset), Jerusalem.
SB52	*Hatzaᶜat Ḥoq ha-Yerusha* (Succession Bill), Ministry of Justice (Jerusalem, 1952).
SCH	*Sefer ha-Chukkim* (the section of the Israeli Official Gazette containing statutes).

6. STATISTICAL PUBLICATIONS, in Alphabetical Order of the Abbreviations

Census Publication No.17	*Moslems, Christians and Druzes in Israel*, Population and Housing Census 1961, Publication No.17, Central Bureau of Statistics (Jerusalem, 1964).
Census Publication No.26	*Marriage and Fertility*, Part I, Population and Housing Census 1961, Publication No.26, Central Bureau of Statistics (Jerusalem, 1965).
Census Publication No.32	*Marriage and Fertility*, Part II, Population and Housing Census 1961, Publication No.32, Central Bureau of Statistics (Jerusalem, 1966).
Criminal Stats., *1968*	*Criminal Statistics, 1968*, Special Publications, No.344, Central Bureau of Statistics (Jerusalem, 1971).
DCPI	*Demographic Characteristics of the Population in Israel* (1968), offprint from Supplement to *ha-Yarḥon ha-Sṭaṭisṭi le-Yisraʾel* (Monthly Statistical Bulletin of Israel), No.12, Central Bureau of Statistics (Jerusalem, 1969).
GMBCS, 1948	*General Monthly Bulletin of Current Statistics* (Jerusalem, March 1948).
Labour Force, 1963–1967	*Seqer Koaḥ Adam be-Qerev ha-Miʿuṭim 1963–1967* (Survey of the Labour Force of the Minorities, 1963–1967), internal, Central Bureau of Statistics (Jerusalem, 1968).
Marriages 1957–1958	*Nisuʾin shel Muslimim, Notzrim u-Druzim be-Yisraʾel* (Marriages of Muslims, Christians and Druzes in Israel) (1957–1958), offprint from *ha-Yarḥon ha-Sṭaṭisṭi le-Yisraʾel* (Monthly Statistical Bulletin of Israel), Part I, *Ḥevra* (Society), vol.11, No.1, Central Bureau of Statistics (Jerusalem, n.d.).
SAI	*Statistical Abstract of Israel*, Central Bureau of Statics (Jerusalem).
SAP, 1944–45	*Statistical Abstract of Palestine 1944–45*, 8th ed. (Jerusalem, 1946).
Society, 1960	*ha-Yarḥon ha-Sṭaṭisṭi le-Yisraʾel* (Monthly Statistical Bulletin of Israel) Part I, *Ḥevra* (Society), vol.11, Central Bureau of Statistics (Jerusalem, January 1960).
Vital Stats. 1965; 1966	*Vital Statistics 1965; 1966*, Special Series, No.268, Central Bureau of Statistics (Jerusalem, 1969).
Vital Stats. 1967; 1968	*Vital Statistics 1967; 1968*, Special Series, No.318, Central Bureau of Statistics (Jerusalem, 1970).

7. BOOKS, ARTICLES AND UNPUBLISHED DISSERTATIONS, in Alphabetical Order of the Abbreviations

ᶜAbduh and Riḍā — Muḥammad ᶜAbduh and Muḥammad Rashīd Riḍā, *Tafsīr al-Qurʾān al-Ḥakīm* (Cairo, 1346–54H. [1927–36], vol.4).

Abu Zahra — M. Abu Zahra, "Family Law," in M. Khadduri and H. J. Liebesny (eds.), *Law in the Middle East*, vol.1 (Washington, 1955), pp.132–78.

Amīn — Qāsim Amīn, *Taḥrir al-Marʾa* (2nd ed., Cairo, 1941).

Anderson, *Africa* — J. N. D. Anderson, *Islamic Law in Africa* (new impression, London, 1970).

Anderson, *Contract of Marriage* — J. N. D. Anderson, "Recent Developments in *Sharīᶜa* Law III. The Contract of Marriage," *MW*, vol.41 (1951), pp.113–26.

Anderson, *Dissolution* — J. N. D. Anderson, "Recent Developments in *Sharīᶜa* Law V. The Dissolution of Marriage," *MW*, vol.41 (1951), pp. 271–88.

Anderson, *Islamic Law* — J. N. D. Anderson, *Islamic Law in the Modern World* (London, 1959).

Anderson, *Jordan* — J. N. D. Anderson, "Recent Developments in *Sharīᶜa* Law VIII. The Jordanian Law of Family Rights, 1951," *MW*, vol.42 (1952), pp. 190–206.

Anderson, *Patriarchal Family* — J. N. D. Anderson, "The Eclipse of the Patriarchal Family in Contemporary Islamic Law," in his (ed.), *Family Law in Asia and Africa* (London, 1967), pp.221–34.

Anderson, *Syria* — J. N. D. Anderson, "The Syrian Law of Personal Status," *BSOAS*, vol.17(1955), pp.34–49.

Anderson, *Tunis* — J. N. D. Anderson, "The Tunisian Law of Personal Status," *ICLQ*, vol.7(1958), pp.262–79.

Arami — Arami, "Nisuʾey Kefel ᶜal-Yedey Muslimim" (Muslim Bigamy), *ha-Praklit*, vol.11(1954–55), pp.115–18.

al-ᶜĀrif — ᶜĀrif al-ᶜĀrif, *Kitāb al-Qaḍāʾ bayn al-Badw* (Jerusalem, 1933).

Baer — G. Baer, *Population and Society in the Arab East* (London, 1964).

Ben-Amram — E. Ben-Amram, "Ha-Ukhlusiyah ha-ᶜArvit be-Yisraʾel—Teʾur Demografi" (A Demographic Description of the Arab Population in Israel), *MḤ*, vol.15(1965), pp.2–24.

Ben-Porath — Y. Ben-Porath, *Koaḥ ha-ᶜAvodah ha-ᶜArvi be-Yisraʾel* (The Arab Labor Force in Israel) (Jerusalem, 1966).

Ben-Shemesh — A. Ben-Shemesh, *Ḥuqey ha-Qarqaʿot bi-Medinat Yisraʾel* (Land Laws in the State of Israel) (Tel Aviv, 1953).

Berger — M. Berger, *The Arab World Today* (New York, 1964).

Canaan — I. Canaan, "Unwritten Laws Affecting the Arab Woman of Palestine," *JPOS*, vol.11(1931), pp.172–203.

Chatila — K. Chatila, *Le mariage chez les musulmans en Syrie* (Paris, 1934).

Cohen — A. Cohen, *Arab Border-Villages in Israel. A Study of Continuity and Change in Social Organization* (Manchester, 1965).

Coulson, *Conflicts* — N. J. Coulson, *Conflicts and Tensions in Islamic Jurisprudence* (Chicago, 1969).

Coulson, *History* — N. J. Coulson, *A History of Islamic Law* (Edinburgh, 1964).

Coulson, *Succession* — N. J. Coulson, *Succession in the Muslim Family* (Cambridge, 1971).

Dirks — S. Dirks, *La famille musulmane turque, son évolution au 20e siècle* (La Haye, 1969).

Dykan — P. D. [Dykan], "Ha-Ḥoq ʿal Gil ha-Nisuʾin" (The Law Concerning the Age of Marriage), *ha-Praklit*, vol.7 (1950), pp.5–9.

Eilon — M. Eilon, *Ḥaqiqa datit be-Ḥuqey Medinat Yisraʾel uba-Shfiṭa shel Batey-Mishpaṭ u-Batey ha-Din ha-Rabaniyim* (Religious Legislation in the Laws of the State of Israel and in the Decisions of the Civil and Rabbinical Courts) (Tel Aviv, 1967–68).

Eisenman — R. H. Eisenman, *Islamic Law in Mandate Palestine and Modern Israel, A Study of Survival and Repeal of Ottoman Legislative Reform*, submitted for the degree of Doctor of Philosophy, Columbia University, 1970 (unpublished).

Fyzee — A. A. A. Fyzee, *Outlines of Muhammadan Law* (3rd ed., London, 1964).

Gibb — H. A. R. Gibb, "Women and the Law," *Actes du colloque sur la sociologie musulmane* (Bruxelles, 1961), pp.233–45.

Glasner — Y. Glasner, "Ḥoq ha-Bigamya" (The Bigamy Law), *ha-Praklit*, vol.16(1959–60), pp.274–80.

Goadby — F. M. Goadby, *International and Inter-Religious Private Law in Palestine* (Jerusalem, 1926).

Goitein and Ben-Shemesh — S. D. Goitein and A. Ben-Shemesh, *Ha-Mishpaṭ ha-Muslimi bi-Medinat Yisraʾel* (Muslim Law in Israel) (Jerusalem, 1957).

Granott — A. Granott, *The Land System in Palestine, History and Structure* (London, 1952).

Granqvist — H. Granqvist, *Marriage Conditions in a Palestinian Village*, Vol.1 (Helsingfors, 1931), Vol.2 (Helsingfors, 1935).

el-Hamamsy — L. S. el-Hamamsy, "The Changing Role of the Egyptian Woman," in A. Lutfiyya and Ch. W. Churchill (eds.), *Readings in Arab Middle Eastern Societies and Cultures* (The Hague, 1970), pp.592–601.

Hinchcliffe, *Divorce* — Doreen Hinchcliffe, "Divorce in Pakistan: Judicial Reform," *JICL*, vol.2(1968), pp.13–25.

Hinchcliffe, *Polygamy* — Doreen Hinchcliffe, "Polygamy in Traditional and Contemporary Islamic Law," *IMA*, vol.1(1970), no.3, pp.13–38.

Katsab — N. Katsab, *Duaḥ Peʿulot ha-Mador la-ʾIsha ha-ʿArvit be-Moʿetzet ha-Poʿalot le-1966* (Report on the Activities of the Arab Women's Section of the Working Women's Council for 1966). The Executive Committee of the General Labour Federation.

Kerr — M. H. Kerr, *Islamic Reform. The Political and Legal Theories of Muḥammad ʿAbduh and Rashīd Riḍā* (Berkeley and Los Angeles, 1966).

Kressel — G. M. Kressel, "Nisuʾey *Wlād ʿAmm* be-Jawārīsh—Aspektim shel ʿIyur u-Masoret" (Cousin Marriage among the Jawārīsh—Aspects of Urbanization and Tradition), *MḤ*, vol.20(1970), pp.20–51.

Layish, *Absentees* — A. Liskovski [Layish], "Ha-Nifqadim ha-Nokhehim be-Yisraʾel" (Resident Absentees in Israel), *MḤ*, vol.10(1960), pp.186–92.

Layish, *Changes* — A. Layish, "Temurot ba-Ḥevrah ha-ʿArvit be-Yisraʾel" (Changes in Arab Society in Israel), *Ha-Ḥevrah ha-ʿArvit be-Yisraʾel—Temurot u-Megamot* (Arab Society in Israel—Changes and Trends) (Jerusalem, n.d.), pp.1–8.

Layish, *Communal Organization* — A. Layish, *Ha-ʾIrgun ha-ʿAdati shel ha-Muslimim be-Yisraʾel* (The Communal Organization of Muslims in Israel), submitted for the degree of M.A., the Hebrew University of Jerusalem, 1962 (unpublished).

Layish, *Custom* — A. Layish, "*Sharīʿa* u-Minhag ba-Mishpaḥah ha-

	Muslimit be-Yisra'el" (*Sharīʿa* and Custom in the Muslim Family in Israel), *MḤ*, vol.23(1974), pp.377–409.
Layish, *Jurisdiction*	A. Layish, "Muslim Religious Jurisdiction in Israel," *AAS*, vol.1(1965), pp.49–79.
Layish, *Qāḍīs*	A. Layish, "*Qāḍīs* and *Sharīʿa* in Israel," *AAS*, vol.7(1971), pp.237–72.
Layish, *Waqf*	A. Layish, "The Muslim *Waqf* in Israel," *AAS*, vol.2(1966), pp.41–76.
Lecerf	J. Lecerf, "ʿĀʾila," *EI*, vol.1, p.306.
Levy	R. Levy, *The Social Structure of Islam* (reprint, Cambridge, 1962).
Linant de Bellefonds	Y. Linant de Bellefonds, *Traité de droit musulman comparé,* vol.2 (Paris and La Haye, 1965).
Marx, *Bedouin*	E. Marx, *Bedouin of the Negev* (Manchester, 1967).
Marx, *Marriage Patterns*	E. Marx, "Defusey Nisuʾin shel Bedwey ha-Negev" (Marriage Patterns of the Negev Beduin), *MḤ,* vol.13(1963), pp.395–409.
Marx, *Social Structure*	E. Marx, "Ha-Mivneh ha-Ḥevrati shel Bedwey ha-Negev" (The Social Structure of the Negev Beduin), *MḤ*, vol.8(1957), pp.1–18.
Meron	Y. Meron, "Ribuy Nashim la-Muslimim ve-Ḥuqatiyut Isuro" (Muslim Polygamy and the Constitutionality of Its Prohibition), *Mishpatim*, vol.3(1972), no.3, pp.515–39.
Muhsam, *Marriage Habits*	H. V. Muhsam, "Some Notes on Beduin Marriage Habits," in his *Beduin of the Negev* (Jerusalem, 1966), pp.59–76. (Reprint from: *Proceedings of the XIV International Congress of Sociology*, Rome, 1950, vol.4, pp.1–18).
Muhsam, *Polygamy*	H. V. Muhsam, "Fertility of Polygamous Marriages," in his *Beduin of the Negev* (Jerusalem, 1966), pp.87–100. (Reprint from: *Population Studies*, vol.10(1956), no.1, pp.3–16).
el-Naqeb	N. el-Naqeb, *Problems of Matrimonial Law in Contemporary Iraq*, A Dissertation Submitted to the University of London for the Degree of Master of Laws, July 1967 (unpublished).
NzDS	*Hitpateḥutah shel ha-ʿIr Natzeret veha-Derakhim le-Qidumah ha-Kalkali* (The Development of the Town of Nazareth and Methods of Its Economic Advancement) (Jerusalem, 1966).

Palmon	R. Palmon, Internal Memorandum on Dower in 1968. Demographic Section, Central Bureau of Statistics (Jerusalem, n.d.).
Robertson Smith	W. Robertson Smith, *Kinship and Marriage in Early Arabia* (reprint, Boston, n.d.).
Rosenfeld, *Change and Conservation*	H. Rosenfeld, "Tahalikhey Shinuy ve-Gormey Shimur ba-Mishpaḥa ha-ʿArvit ha-Kefarit be-Yisraʾel" (Processes of Change and Factors of Conservation in the Rural Arab Family in Israel), *MḤ*, vol.19(1969), pp.208–17.
Rosenfeld, *Peasants*	H. Rosenfeld, *Hem Hayu Falaḥim* (They Were Peasants) (Tel Aviv, 1964).
Rosenfeld, *Recent Changes*	H. Rosenfeld, "Tahalikhey Shinuy Meʾuḥarim be-Mivneh ha-Mishpaḥa ha-Murḥevet ba-Kefar ha-ʿArvi" (Recent Changes in the Structure of the Extended Family in Arab Villages), *Ha-Ḥevra ha-ʿArvit be-Yisraʾel—Temurot u-Megamot* (Arab Society in Israel—Changes and Trends) (Jerusalem, n.d.), pp.21–30.
Schacht	J. Schacht, *An Introduction to Islamic Law* (Oxford, 1964).
Schereschewsky	B. Schereschewsky, *Diney Mishpaḥa* (Family Law in Israel) (Jerusalem, 1958).
Shafik	D. Ragaï (Shafik), *La femme et le droit religieux de l'Egypte contemporaine* (Paris, 1940).
Shaki	A. Shaki, "Samkhut Beynleʾumit ve-Datit u-Vrerat ha-Din le-ʿInyan Ḥoq ha-Kashrut ha-Mishpaṭit veha-Apoṭropsut, 5722–1962" (International and Religious Jurisdiction and Conflict of Laws in Relation to the Capacity and Guardianship Law, 5722–1962), *ha-Praklit*, vol.20(1963), pp.259–66.
Shidlovsky	B. Shidlovsky, *Ha-Yishuvim ha-ʿArviyim veha-Druziyim be-Yisraʾel* (Arab and Druze Settlements in Israel) (Jerusalem, 1969).
Silberg	M. Silberg, *Ha-Maʿamad ha-ʾIshi be-Yisraʾel* (Personal Status in Israel), (3rd impression, Jerusalem, 1964).
Smith	M. G. Smith, "The Sociological Framework of Law," in H. Kuper and L. Kuper (eds.), *African Law: Adaption and Development* (Berkeley and Los Angeles, 1965), pp.24–48.
Stendel	O. Stendel, *Miʿuṭim* (Minorities) (Jerusalem, 1970).

Tedeschi — G. Tedeschi, "On the Problems of Marriage in the State of Israel," in his *Studies in Israel Private Law* (Jerusalem, 1966), pp.218–33.

Vitta — E. Vitta, *The Conflict of Laws in Matters of Personal Status in Palestine* (Tel Aviv, 1947).

Weines — Y. Weines, "Diney Qarqaʿot" (Land Law), in Z. Silbiger (ed.), *Sidrey Shilṭon u-Mishpaṭ be-Yisraʾel* (Law and Administration in Israel) (Jerusalem, 1954).

Woodsmall — R. F. Woodsmall, *Moslem Women Enter a New World* (London, 1936).

Yadin, *Civil Code* — U. Yadin, "The Law of Succession and Other Steps towards a Civil Code," in G. Tedeschi and U. Yadin (eds.), *Studies in Israel Legislative Problems. Scripta Hierosolymitana* (Jerusalem, 1966), pp.104–33.

Yadin, *Reflections* — U. Yadin, "Reflections on a New Law of Succession," *ILR*, vol.1(1966), no.1, pp.132–8.

Zadok — H. Zadok, "Ḥoq Shiwuy Zekhuyot ha-ʾIshah" (The Women's Equal Rights Law), *ha-Praklit*, vol.8(1951–52), pp.66–79.

8. **NEWSPAPERS AND PERIODICALS** (A = Arabic; H = Hebrew), in alphabetical order of the abbreviations

AAS — *Asian and African Studies*, Jerusalem.

AD — *Majallat al-Akhbār al-Darziyya*, Jerusalem (A).

AI — *Majallat al-Akhbār al-Islāmiyya*, Jerusalem (A).

ʿAl ha-Mishmar — Tel Aviv, daily (H).

al-Anbāʾ — Jerusalem, daily (A).

ha-Aretz — Tel Aviv, daily (H).

ha-Boqer — Tel Aviv, daily (H).

BSOAS — *Bulletin of the School of Oriental and African Studies*, London.

Davar — Tel Aviv, daily (H).

EI — *The Encyclopedia of Islam*, new ed. (Leiden and London, 1960 ff.).

Ḥerut — Tel Aviv, daily (H).

ICLQ — *The International and Comparative Law Quarterly*, London.

ILR — *Israel Law Review*, Jerusalem, quarterly.

IMA — *Islam and the Modern Age*, quarterly, New Delhi.

al-Ittiḥād — Haifa, half-weekly (A).

The Jerusalem Post — Jerusalem, daily.

JICL	*Journal of Islamic and Comparative Law*, Zaria (Nigeria).
JPOS	*Journal of the Palestine Oriental Society*, Jerusalem (ceased publication).
Lamerḥav	Tel Aviv, daily (H).
Maʿariv	Tel Aviv, daily (H).
MḤ	*ha-Mizraḥ he-Ḥadash*, Jerusalem, quarterly (H).
al-Mirṣād	Tel Aviv, weekly (A).
Mishpatim	Jerusalem, quarterly (H).
ha-Modiʿa	Tel Aviv, daily (H).
MW	*The Muslim World*, Hartford, Conn., quarterly.
PD	*Piskei Din*, Official Publication of Judgments of the Israel Supreme Court, Jerusalem (H).
PM	*Pesakim Meḥoziim*, Unofficial Publication of Judgments of the District Courts, Jerusalem (H).
ha-Praklit	Tel Aviv, quarterly (H).
ha-Tzofeh	Tel Aviv, daily (H).
al-Yawm	Tel Aviv, daily (A).
Yediʿon	*Yediʿon ha-Maḥlaqa haMuslimit veha-Druzit* (The Bulletin of the Muslim and Druze Division), Jerusalem (H).
Yediʿot Aḥaronoth	Tel Aviv, daily (H).
ha-Yom	Tel Aviv, daily (H).
Zemanim	Tel Aviv, daily (H).

GENERAL INDEX*

(Page numbers in italics indicate principal references)

* The Arabic definite article *al* has been disregarded in alphabetization.

GLOSSARY OF ARABIC TECHNICAL TERMS*

(Page numbers in italics indicate principal references)

ʿāda, custom 37, 182, see also custom
ʿadl, equality between wives in polygamous marriage 98
ʿafsh al-bayt, household effects 45, 95, 131
al-aḥkām al-khamsa, the five religious-legal qualifications under which any aspect of Muslim behavior is categorized 81–2
ʿalayya al-ḥarām, "forbidden on myself," a formula of suspended repudiation by which the husband swears that his wife will be considered divorced if she does not fulfill a certain condition 114, 138, 235
ʿaṣabāt, male agnate 3, 246, 252–3, 259, 270, 274, 279–87, 291–2, 294, 295, 299, 302–6, 315, 317, 327
ʿaṭāʾ, gift (marriage) 47
athāth, household effects 45, 95
ʿayn, substance 47

badīla, exchange wife in exchange marriage 100, see also marriage: exchange marriage
barrānī, "external" marriage, performed without the participation of the *maʾdhūn* 27, 75, 87–8
basma, fingermark 21, 127, 162, 267, 286
bāṭil, null and void 30, 172
bayʿ, sale
– *barrānī,* external sale, performed outside the Land Registry 323
– *jawwānī,* internal sale, performed at the Land Registry 88
bayt al-ʿidda, the residence of the divorced wife during the waiting-period 215
bayt al-māl, public treasury 287, 311
bayt al-shaʿr, a Beduin tent of woven goat hair 38
bayt al-ṭāʿa, "house of obedience," a legally enforceable judgment for obedience 101

ḍarar, damage, legal cruelty, prejudice 82, 132, 146, 165, 167, 200, 203–4, 207–8, 217, 252
ḍarūra, necessity 185
dhawū al-frāʾiḍ, Qurʾānic heirs 279
diya, blood-money 209

fāsid, irregular 14, 41, 80, 172
fatwā, religious-legal opinion of *muftī* 152, 176, 228, 337
fuqahāʾ, specialists in science of *sharīʿa* 202

gharāma, fine 31, 144, 159, 252
ghayr mumayyiz, undiscriminating minor 93

---

*The Arabic definite article *al* has been disregarded in alphabetization.

ḥaḍāna, custody of minor children 246, see also custody

ḥāḍina, custodian of minor children, see custody

ḥadīth, formal tradition deriving from the Prophet 56, 61–2, 126

ḥakam, arbitrator 120, 122, 154, 168–9, see also arbitration

ḥakūra, vegetable garden 45, 291

ḥaly, ornaments 45, 49, 93

ḥamūla, clan 28, 95, 148, 179, 286, 302

ḥarām, forbidden 82

ḥardāna, ill-tempered woman 117

hiba, gift, donation 49, 295–6, 306, 311, 319–20

ḥusn al-muʿāshara, kind treatment of wife 32, 91

ʿidda, waiting-period of woman after termination of marriage, usually three menstruations 36, 51, 72, 77, 132, *177–8*, 188, see also waiting-period

ījāb waqabūl, offer and acceptance 18

ijtihād, "effort," use of individual reasoning 194

ikhtilāf al-dīn, difference of religion 132, 172

ilāʾ, dissolution of marriage by oath of husband to abstain from marital intercourse for four months 174

imām, prayer leader 1, 56, 63, 68, 91, 191, 223

intiqāl, "transfer" of property of *miri* category by *sharīʿa* court 324, see succession

iqrār, admission 193

ʿirḍ, family or female honor 59, 128

irth, inheritance 324, see succession

ʿiṣma, "protection" of husband 77, 83, 90, 126, 129, 155, 213

istibdāl, exchange of *waqf* property for another property 297

istidāna, wife's borrowing money in name of her husband, which he is obliged to repay 92

ithbāt ḥāla madaniyya, confirmation of marital status 19

ithbāt al-zawāj or *zawjiyya* or *al-nikāḥ*, confirmation of marriage 18, 19, 21, 74, 293–4, 320, see also marriage: confirmation.

iʿtirāf, admission 193, 194

ʿiwaḍ, compensation 159

jihāz, equipment, clothing and household effects 40, 45–9, 93, 159

kafāʾa, principle requiring husband to be the equal of his wife (or her family) in various specified respects including lineage, financial standing and profession 31

kashf, inspection of dwelling 85, 117

khādima, maidservant 31, 99

khalwa, privacy of husband and wife 41, 46, 177

khaṭīb, preacher at Friday prayer in mosque 1

khiyār al-bulūgh, option of puberty 163–4, 171

khulʿ, divorce by agreement by which wife redeems herself from marriage for a consideration 159, 230–1, see also divorce; renunciation and compensation, compensation to ex-husband after woman's remarriage

khuṭba, betrothal 25

kiswa, clothing 91

liʿān, dissolution of marriage through process of mutual imprecation 164

maḍbaṭa, petition 17–18, 26, 267, 308, 321

maʾdhūn, abbr. of *maʾdhūn liʿuqūd al-ankiḥa al-sharʿiyya*, authorized *sharʿi* marriage notary 17–21, 24, 27, 32, 37, 44–5, 47, 52, 74–5, 77

mahjūra, woman whose husband has deserted her and disappeared 168, 204
mahr, dower
- al-*mithl*, fair dower 40
- *muʾajjal*, deferred dower, payable at termination of marriage 35–6 see also dower: deferred
- *muʿajjal*, prompt dower, payable immediately on marriage 41, see also dower: prompt
- *musammā*, specified dower 40

maḥram, a kinsman within the forbidden degrees 246, 250, 269, 271
al-majlis al-ʿāʾilī, family council 169–71, see also family council
masāfat al-qaṣr, distance measured by three days' journey on camelback 167, 202, 233
maṣāgh, jewelry 45, 48, 93
maskan sharʿi, legal dwelling 32, 91, *93–5*, 123
maṣlaḥa, the public interest 185, 267, 310
mīrī, land property owned by the State, right of possession of which is granted to the individual 280–2, 287, 288–90, 292, 295, 301, 305, 308–14, 319, 323
mubāraʾa or *ibrāʾ*, divorce by agreement with mutual waiving of any financial obligations 159, 230, see also divorce: renunciation
muftī, specialist in religious law who gives authoritative legal opinion 1, 337
mukhaddara, woman veiled or kept indoors 98
mukhbirūn, experts, representatives of the spouses and the court appointed by *qāḍī* to assess amount of maintenance 91, 105, 111, 177
mukhtār, functionary appointed by Government from among village notables 17, 20, 26, 91, 170, 288, 306, 313
mulk, property in which individual has full ownership 280, 282, 287–90, 292, 301, 308–12, 314
muʾnisa, female companion provided by husband to relieve his wife's boredom on nights when he is away from home 95
murshid, instructor 62
muṣālaḥa, reconciliation 120, 122, see also arbitration
mushāʿ, joint ownership 307
mutʿa, indemnity payable to woman in case of divorce before valid privacy 41, 64
mutawallī, *waqf* administrator 296–8, 320

nafaqa, maintenance 91, see also maintenance
nāshiza, rebellious wife 92, 101–4, 110, 128, 158, 177, 250, 329
naẓir, supervisor of guardian's activities 265, 275
niyya, intent 133, 173, 238
nuqūṭ, bridal gifts 112
nushūz, rebelliousness 101, 110, see also *nāshiza*

qāḍī, Muslim religious judge of *sharīʿa* court 1, see General Index: *qāḍī*s
qasm, apportionment of husband's time among his wives 72, 99, 117
qinṭār, measure mentioned in Qurʾān (IV:19) 62–4, 71
qurūʾ, menstrual periods of *ʿidda* 133

radd, residue of estate when Qurʾānic heirs have taken their shares and there are no other heirs 287, 293
raʾīs, middleman 7

ṣaḥīḥ, valid, legally effective 41
shighār, exchange marriage 21, see marriage: exchange marriage

shurūṭ, "terms" (of marriage) 20
siyāsa, policy 336

ṭāʿa, obedience 91, see obedience
ṭaʿām, food 91
tabādul al-zawjāt, exchange marriage 21, see marriage: exchange marriage
tābiʿūn, the followers of the Prophet 61
tablīgh, notice 201, 202, 205
tafrīq, dissolution of marriage 26, 82, 207, see also divorce
tafwīḍ al-ṭalāq, "delegated repudiation," delegation to wife of power to divorce herself 31, 135, 141–2, *153–6*, 190, see also divorce: by repudiation
taḥlīl, device of intermediate marriage enabling thrice-repudiated wife to be permitted to her original husband 132, 173–5
ṭalāq, dissolution of marriage without resort to legal proceedings 132, see divorce: by repudiation
– *bāʾin*, irrevocable divorce, becomes operative immediately with all legal effects attendant on dissolution of marriage 173, see also divorce: legal effects
– *al-bidʿa*, disapproved forms of divorce: triple repudiation pronounced in one declaration or single irrevocable repudiation 173, 177, 181, see also divorce: legal effects
– *muḍāf ilā al-mustaqbal*, divorce made effective from specified future date 133, 139
– *rajiʿi*, revocable divorce, becomes operative only after expiry of waiting-period 132, 173, see also divorce: legal effects
– *al-sunna*, approved forms of divorce: one single revocable divorce or three successive pronouncements during three consecutive periods of purity of woman 173, 177, 181, see also divorce: legal effects
talfīq, "patchwork," selective combination of various legal doctrines 3, 4, 184, 334
taʿlīq al-ṭalāq, suspended repudiation 133, 135, 137–40, see also divorce: by repudiation
taqlīd, "imitation," unquestioning acceptance of a Sunnite orthodox school of law 332
taṣarruf, possession rights in property 301
taʿwīḍ, compensation 214
tawliya, administration of endowment 297–8

ʿulamāʾ, religious scholars of Islam 1, 184, 194
umma, Muslim community 106, 182
ʿurf, custom 37, see custom

waʿd, "promise" (of marriage) 25
waqf, religious endowment 1, 2, *296–8*, 303–4, 318–20
ghayrṣaḥīḥ, endowed *mīri* 280
– *khayrī*, endowment for public purposes 1
– *ṣaḥīḥ*, endowed *mulk* 280
waqfiyya, deed of endowment 297
wāhib, donator 296
wāʿiẓ, preacher 62
wakīl, proxy 61, 150, 161–2, 313
waṣī, administrator of inheritances of minor heirs 268
– *mukthār*, guardian elected by legal guardian 263, 273, 276
wilāya, guardianship 246, see guardianship
wiṣāya, administration of inheritances of minor heirs 263
wusaṭāʾ, mediators 99, 120, see also arbitration

yamīn al-taʾdīb, oath of chastisement 138

zaʿlāna, ill-tempered woman 117

zāwiya, center of worship of dervishes 298

zifāf, wife moving in with husband after conclusion of marriage contract 93

ẓihār, archaic form of divorce by which husband swears that to him the wife is like "the back (*ẓahr*) of my mother" 174, 235

zinā, adultery 164, 169, see also women: chastity and female honor